by the R.t Hon.ble Robert L.t Lucas.
de LONDRES.

# THE
# ROYAL PALACES

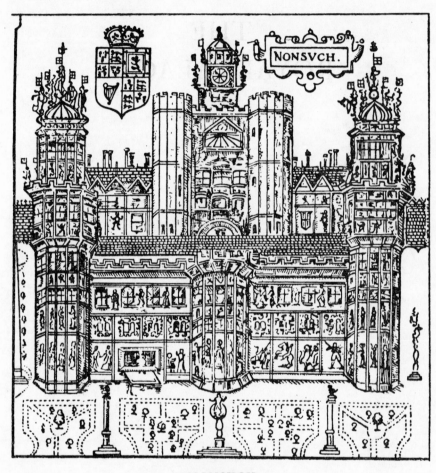

NONSUCH

Engraving from John Speed's
*Theatre of Great Britain,* 1611

# THE
# ROYAL
# PALACES

## PHILIP HOWARD

Gambit
Incorporated
Boston
1970

FOR

M.J.M.H., D.E.H.

M.M.H., R.D.H.H.

# CONTENTS

| | | | |
|---|---|---|---|
| I | INTRODUCTION: PALACES AND KINGS | *page* | 1 |
| II | THE FIRST ROYAL RESIDENCES | | 14 |
| III | THE TOWER OF LONDON | | 28 |
| IV | THE PALACE OF WESTMINSTER | | 41 |
| V | WINDSOR CASTLE | | 55 |
| VI | WOODSTOCK | | 79 |
| VII | RICHMOND AND GREENWICH | | 88 |
| VIII | WHITEHALL | | 104 |
| IX | HAMPTON COURT | | 129 |
| X | ST JAMES'S PALACE | | 144 |
| XI | HOLYROODHOUSE | | 164 |
| XII | NONSUCH | | 176 |
| XIII | KENSINGTON | | 191 |
| XIV | BUCKINGHAM PALACE | | 208 |
| XV | BRIGHTON PAVILION | | 221 |
| XVI | OSBORNE AND BALMORAL | | 237 |
| XVII | THE NEW PALACE | | 254 |
| | *Bibliography* | | 261 |
| | *Index* | | 269 |

# LIST OF ILLUSTRATIONS

NONSUCH                                                    *frontispiece*
The south front drawn by John Speed for his
*Theatre of Great Britain* in 1611

STONEHENGE                                              *facing page* 4

FISHBOURNE ROMAN PALACE                                            4

CAMELOT                                                            5
A fourteenth-century French miniature of the Round Table

CAMELOT                                                           20
A nineteenth-century version by Gustave Doré

CAERNARVON CASTLE                                                21

THE TOWER OF LONDON                                              36
A medieval manuscript showing the Duke of Orleans
imprisoned in the White Tower

THE TOWER OF LONDON                                              37
A plan of 1597

THE TOWER OF LONDON FROM THE AIR                                 37

THE PALACE OF WESTMINSTER                                        52
An etching by Hollar, 1647

WINDSOR                                                          53
A nineteenth-century engraving after Foster

WINDSOR CASTLE IN THE EARLY SEVENTEENTH
    CENTURY                                                      84

WINDSOR CASTLE                                                   84

GREENWICH PALACE                                                 85
A seventeenth-century view from the land side, after Hollar

GREENWICH PALACE FROM THE THAMES                                85

GREENWICH FROM THE AIR                              100

RICHMOND PALACE                                     101

WHITEHALL PALACE FROM THE THAMES                    116

WHITEHALL PALACE                                    117
The Holbein Gate and the Banqueting House, a seventeenth-
century engraving by Silvestre

WHITEHALL PALACE, THE INTERIOR OF THE
    BANQUETING HALL                                 132

HAMPTON COURT FROM ACROSS THE THAMES                133
An eighteenth-century print

HAMPTON COURT FROM THE PUBLIC GARDENS               133

HAMPTON COURT FROM THE AIR                          148

ST JAMES'S PALACE FROM PALL MALL                    149
An eighteenth-century engraving

ST JAMES'S PALACE IN THE EIGHTEENTH CENTURY         149
From the painting by Scott

ST JAMES'S PALACE                                   164

THE PALACE OF HOLYROODHOUSE FROM THE AIR            165

NONSUCH PALACE                                      180
A watercolour, 1568, by Hoefnagel

NONSUCH PALACE                                      180
The arrival of Queen Elizabeth, 1582, by Hoefnagel

RAM'S HEAD AND CHERUB'S HEAD, TWO RELICS
    FROM NONSUCH                                     181

KENSINGTON PALACE                                   196
The formal gardens as altered for Queen Anne

KENSINGTON PALACE, THE KING'S GALLERY               196

BUCKINGHAM PALACE                                   197
Nash's reconstruction, an engraving c. 1840

BUCKINGHAM PALACE FROM THE GARDENS                  197

THE ROYAL PAVILION, BRIGHTON, ILLUMINATED
    FOR SON ET LUMIÈRE                               228

THE ROYAL PAVILION, THE ROOF                        229

THE ROYAL PAVILION, THE BANQUETING ROOM             229

OSBORNE HOUSE 244

BALMORAL CASTLE 245

*Endpapers*

THE TOWER OF LONDON
Engraving by Kip after a painting by Knyff, 1708

# I

## INTRODUCTION:

## PALACES AND KINGS

'PALATIUM', the Palatine, was one of the seven hills of Rome. The first emperor, Augustus, had his house there, and the house came naturally to be called by the name of the hill. Tiberius, Nero, and subsequent artistic Caesars added their own lavish architectural contributions to the Palatine, until the whole hill was one huge royal residence, the first 'palace' in etymology. Since then the word has been devalued, until it can mean any large and impressive building, in which, for instance, a bishop lives. It is even possible to have, in the sardonic and slightly old-fashioned phrase, a gin palace; and, optimistically, a *palais de danse*. On this basis there are a great many palaces in Britain.

The word 'king' is not much more exact. It was brought to Britain by the Anglian and Saxon 'kins' or tribes, who invaded across the North Sea from the south-east from the fourth century onwards. Their leaders, or 'Cynings', were elected from a recognised royal 'cynn', or family, which traced its pedigree carefully back to Woden. When Wessex became dominant in the ninth and tenth centuries, the king of the West Saxons became the king of the Angelcynn, or English, and the petty tribal kings faded away. In any case, before the Saxons came, the native British tribes had autocratic leaders, even though they did not have the word 'king' to describe them.

So a British king can mean anything from the pirate chief of a small band of itinerant Saxon marauders, to a Tudor despot sitting absolute and precarious on the throne of a united England (as recommended by Hobbes in *The Leviathan*), to the rather less formidable constitutional sovereign under contract to a united kingdom. And his royal residence, the king's palace, can be anything from a modest mud and wattle hall, to a towering stronghold grim with machicolation and *meurtrières*, to a classic renaissance country mansion, to a mock-Baronial shooting lodge.

The palace develops as the king does; the concomitant masonry follows and grows with the institution. In the beginning, in tribal and Saxon England, both kings and palaces were naturally primitive. In the kingdoms of Wessex, Mercia, and Northumbria the *Curia Regis*, the king's court, was indistinguishable from the establishments of his great earls and magnates around the countryside. It was in the same category of place, where the same sort of activities went on, and the same sort of people were found. The main feature inside the stockade was a great hall in which the court could eat its communal meals, meet for council or justice, and sleep in rows on the floor. Even after the Conquest, the palace of a Norman or Plantagenet king was merely a bigger and grander version of the residence of one of his great barons. A major castle, whether of king or magnate, had its private army, its regiment of tame clerics, its household officers, its feudal councils with the chief tenants, and its regional law court. Administering the law locally was one of the principal and most profitable perquisites of a great landowner in his manorial court. Almost every offence extracted a fine, which explains the cynical medieval maxim: '*magnum est emolumentum iustitia*' – 'justice is a distinctly profitable occupation'.

The king's court in these early days was an astonishingly modest and informal place, in which high state business was jumbled up indiscriminately side by side with hearty sport and domestic routine; in which statesmen strode through dung and hens to council; and in which kings would ride their horses into hall, bow in hand, from hunting, and vault over the table to drink beside their chancellors. A revealing picture of the small scale of the royal household is given in the *Constitutio Domus Regis*, court regulations drawn up shortly after the death of Henry I. This laid down the wages and duties of everyone at court from the scullions and washerwomen to the great officers of state. Everybody is allotted a ration of bread, wine, and candles, which is adjusted depending on whether he boards at court, or goes home for his meals.

At the top of the hierarchy is the chancellor, the chief of the royal chaplains, who receives a wage of five shillings a day, and an allowance of one lord's simnel cake, two salted simnels, a measure of clear and a measure of ordinary wine, one thick wax candle, and forty bits of candle. Down at the bottom are the watchmen, who receive double rations, a penny-halfpenny a day for their men, four candles, two loaves, one dish, and a gallon of beer.

The steward (*dapifer*) is in charge of the hall (*aula*), and all affiliated offices, including the kitchen, pantry, and larder. He gets a wage of five shillings a day if he eats *extra domum*, and three shillings and sixpence if he risks his own catering and eats in. The chamberlain (*camerarius*) is in charge of the king's bedroom (*camera*). His staff include the bearer of the king's bed, the king's tailor, and the ewerer, or *aquarius*, whose function is to dry the king's clothes and prepare his bath. The treasurer looks after the money and jewels which are kept in a chest in the king's bedroom. The butler (*pincerna*) has a staff of cellarers, cupbearers, and fruiterers to organise the wine and the dessert. The constable is in charge of the out-door staff, especially the king's bodyguard of archers and the stables. In his department is the marshal, whose function is to maintain discipline at court. Under them are the motley regiment of keepers of hounds, keepers of the king's mews (where the royal hawks were penned), stag-hunters, wolf-hunters, and even the king's hunters of unfortunate cats (*catatores*), and everybody else connected with the incessant, indiscriminate royal sport.

Every department is equipped with its own carters and pack-horses; a provision which indicates the peripatetic nature of the early court, which was always on the move. From these domestic beginnings, from a box by the king's bed, from the chamber where he slept, and the wardrobe where he kept his clothes, the glorious edifice of the modern British civil service is directly descended.

Gradually, between the twelfth and fourteenth centuries, a change, not just of size but also of character, came over the royal court. As Parliament, the law, and the administration were centralised there, the place where the king lived became bigger and quite different from any other residence in Britain. Court culture, etiquette, and ceremonial developed. The court was the nucleus of government. So, the king's *familia*, his household, became the obvious ladder of promotion and training school for ambitious statesmen. Inside it men of talent and administrative ability rose to the top rapidly. Many of the great politicians of the State or the Church started their careers as royal chaplains at court.

The court also became the place where, for example, artists and authors had the best hope of making a living – three of the greatest scholars of the age, Giraldus Cambrensis, Walter Map, and Peter of Blois were all attached to the court of Henry II. Chaucer and Froissart both spent much of their writing lives at court. Ronsard, William Dunbar, and David Lindsay lived and found patronage at Holyrood under James IV and V. As well as being a major influence on literature, and on the formation of the English language, the court was a school of manners and of fashion. It became the residence of an ever-increasing circle of courtiers on the make, and of patrician women; consequently it also became the centre of an intricate tangle of court politics and intrigue. It was the source of patronage, and power, and money, and inevitably attracted the ambitious, the brilliant, and the fashionable.

These changes in social character were faithfully reflected in the masonry of the royal residence, which became strictly formalised. The hall ceased to be the hub of the court; the monarch, forced by the congestion around him to become more unapproachable, only ate there on red-letter days. The royal apartments, normally on the first floor, consisted of, at least, a Presence Chamber, where audiences were given, a Privy Chamber, or Withdrawing Room, where the king ate his meals, and his Bedchamber, which was used when he was not sleeping as a private conference room. A duplicate set of apartments for the queen often led out of the king's. And an elaborate protocol established who was allowed in where, and when.

After the absolute power of the monarch was finally and formally tamed by the revolution of 1688–1689, the functions of the court inevitably declined. And this decline had gradual architectural repercussions. The king's great council and the law courts still met in the royal palace of Westminster, but Westminster had ceased being a royal residence under Henry VIII. The vestigial and atavistic belief in the monarch as the sacred witch-doctor, or the incarnate spirit of the tribe, was dying; so there was no longer any need for great public halls where the monarch could be on show to his subjects, who could buy tickets in order to watch him eat his Sunday dinner, or could be cured of scrofula by laying on of hands.

The distinct court culture finally faded during Victoria's long withdrawal from public life. It gave a dying flicker under Edward VII. Then the Great War of 1914 extinguished the power and the private world of courts all over Europe. Today palaces are the private homes of the sovereign, with a few residual and amiable feudal eccentricities for the benefit of the tourist trade, and with large administrative offices for the mountain of public relations and morale-boosting work which is extracted from a harassed modern monarch.

The crown has only three official royal residences today: Buckingham Palace, Windsor Castle, and Holyroodhouse, which is sadly seldom visited. There are two private houses, Balmoral and Sandringham. And there are a considerable number of extinct palaces, like St James's, the

Stonehenge, built in three stages between 1800 B.C. and 1400 B.C., one of the oldest pieces of building and civil engineering in Britain, possibly built by a 'king' but not a residence

*Photo The Times*

Fishbourne Roman Palace. The finest of the mosaic floors, laid in the middle of the 2nd century A.D., showing in the centre a boy riding on a dolphin

*Photo The Times*

Camelot. A 14th century French miniature of the Round Table

Tower of London, and Kensington, which are still official royal palaces, but are no longer used by the monarch as residences. In no other century has the monarch been so ill-equipped with houses. Elizabeth I had fourteen major palaces in regular annual use, and many smaller residences where she could stay for an occasional night. And, compared with her medieval predecessors, Elizabeth was virtually homeless. If elastic terms of reference for kings and palaces are used, Britain is littered with hundreds if not thousands of buildings which can be described as royal residences. It is reasonable to ask why anybody ever needed so many.

The first and primitive reason is strategic: in days when communication and travel were slow, a royal castle with a royal castellan was essential in each region, to hold it for the king. This is why the Normans built chains of strongholds across England to keep the conquered country quiet. Subsequent kings paid ceaseless routine visits around their scattered castles to show the flag, to keep their stewards up to the mark, to collect rents and dispense justice, and to give the locals a chance, in the days before press and television, to have a look at the king. The early king was perpetually on the move from place to place around England and his continental dominions, seldom staying anywhere for more than a few days. It is easy to forget how short a time most early kings and queens spent in England anyway, let alone in any single one of their English residences. They thought of Normandy, and then Anjou, as their proper homeland.

The *Anglo-Saxon Chronicle* records: 'thrice he [William I] wore his crown every year, as often as he was in England; at Easter he wore it at Winchester; at Whitsuntide at Westminster; at Midwinter at Gloucester; and then there were with him all the rich men over all England, archbishops and suffragan bishops, abbots and earls, thegns and knights.' The detailed records, however, show that neither William nor his successors were particularly often in England to be able to keep to this theoretical routine.

Even such a notable 'English' king as Henry II had his heart and his priorities very firmly on the continent. This he demonstrated often; for instance, in his terrible words as he rode out of the burning fortress of Le Mans, pursued by his rebellious son Richard: 'The city I have loved best on earth, the city where I was born and bred, where my father lies buried, where is the body of Saint Julian, this, O God, to the increase of my shame, Thou hast reft from me. I will requite as best I can. I will assuredly rob Thee of the thing Thou prizest most in me, my soul.'

A less obvious reason for perpetual motion by early kings is provided by the food supply problem. Any medieval king who had stayed with his entourage for a year in one palace would have starved. Each district was self-supporting, and there were no arrangements for transporting produce to some vast metropolitan mart. The king, his great nobles, and his court had to keep moving, on continual progress from estate to estate, if they were not to go hungry. Tenants usually paid their rent in kind or in service. The entire court would descend like omnivorous vultures on a manor, devour the year's produce in a few days, and then travel on hungrily to pastures new, to eat up the next estate, which had been salting away its meat for a year for the royal invasion.

This ambulatory life was not particularly glamorous. Walter Map compared life at Henry II's court with hell:

It is true that from the former we escape by death, though not from the latter. Otherwise there is about as much difference between the two as between a horse-shoe and a mare's shoe.

And a fellow-victim of Map's, Peter of Blois, described the upheaval when the court moved camp:

We therefore, wandering for three or four miles through unknown forests, and oftentimes in the black darkness, esteemed ourselves fortunate if perchance we fell upon some vile and sordid hovel. Oftentimes the courtiers would fight bitterly and obstinately for mere huts, and contend with drawn sword for a lair which had been unworthy of contention among swine.

Of course, Henry II was a particularly restless king, perpetually flitting around his uneasy dominions across the Channel and in England, followed by his court of at least 200, from chamberlain to scullion, with his chancellor and clerks with their writing materials and all the parapher-nalia of government, with wagons carrying his chapel, his bed, kitchen utensils, plate, treasure, clothes, papers. Map says he moved in stages intolerable, like a common carrier: 'We wear out our garments, break our bodies and our beasts, and never find a moment for the cure of our sick souls.'

Court life may not have been much fun for the courtiers. It was even worse for the countryside on which they periodically descended. There are constant records of grievances about the passage of the licentious and undisciplined court, which often so petrified the permanent inhabitants of a district that they took to the woods until the royal caravan had moved on.

The court was still basically an itinerant circus in Tudor times. Jacob Rathgeb, a visiting German at Elizabeth's court noted:

When the Queen breaks up her Court with the intention of visiting another place, there commonly follow more than three hundred carts laden with bag and baggage.

Another witness put the number of carts at 400, with 2,400 horses. Yet another, Lupold von Wedel, described the Queen and her court arriving *en masse* at Westminster:

Riding ahead were her servants, then followed two of her guard, then came her equerries and behind these her chamberlains, of whom there were about twenty. Then came the Privy Councillors.

Then rode the Archbishop of Canterbury with fifty of his own followers. Then Burghley and Walsingham, in front of Elizabeth herself in a gold coach – 'The Queen, sitting all alone in her splendid coach, appeared like a Goddess such as painters are wont to depict'. Next came the Master of the Horse, Leicester, with more of the Privy Council. Then rode twenty-four maids of honour, finely mounted and in their best clothes, followed by another fifty of the Queen's guard. Finally came two empty coaches, as spares in case of accidents. The heavy baggage and many of the servants would have gone in an advance party to prepare the new palace.

Even as late as Victoria, the court moved residence in an immense cavalcade, with mountains of leather suitcases. When the Queen borrowed Cliveden for the summer of 1866, she arrived with an entourage of ninety-one, including three doctors, ten horses, twelve ponies, and eight carriages.

In 1969, while Queen Elizabeth II was at Balmoral for the summer holidays, about eighty London-based people (including police and Post Office officials) went north for all or some of the time. Most of them spent about half the time at Balmoral, and were then replaced. Motor cars, livestock, the inevitable corgis, dogs from Sandringham for the shooting, some of the horses also travelled to Scotland. It is still the case, as it always has been, that when the Queen is not in residence in one of her palaces no permanent indoor staff stays on there, except for a minimum skeleton corps for care and maintenance. Modern transport makes the court far more mobile and harder to count than ever before. And during the Queen's normal two months at Balmoral there is continual coming and going to and from London.

As well as the problem of catering for an army of courtiers in a country where the mechanics of food distribution were uncouth, another primitive

reason for never staying long in any one palace was the stern com-
pulsion of sanitation. After the court had been in residence anywhere for
any length of time, inevitably an unhealthy stink percolated through the
building from the lavatories. At Hampton Court there was 'a great house
of easement over the moat'. In a survey of Windsor Castle Christopher
Wren noted how the place where the jakes were emptied made the
atmosphere 'very noisome to their Majesties' Court'. Before the smell
became intolerable, the whole court moved on to a new residence; and the
gong-farmers moved in to clean out the jakes, and to scrape the glutinous
compost of rushes, straw, human and canine litter off the floors.

Besides all these, there were more frivolous reasons for having a sur-
plus of palaces. Kings built hunting-lodges, like Woodstock, just to be
near their favourite sport. The elaborate royal hunting-box at Clarendon
near Salisbury has been partly excavated. In Kinver forest in Stafford-
shire Richard I built a hunting-lodge which is described in the exchequer
accounts. Surrounded by a fortified enclosure, it stood sixteen perches in
length, sixteen feet high, and consisted of a hall with adjacent offices, a
kitchen, a chamber, a jail (for forest offenders), and a fish-pond.

St James's was built as a discreet retreat for a current royal mistress. A
great many residences were built as wistful and totally ineffectual bolt-
holes from the crowded life of court. Henry VIII even bought a manor at
Chelsea because he had grown to like the district when his old friend Sir
Thomas More had lived there, and when the King had strolled in a
Chelsea garden with his arm round his Lord Chancellor's shoulders. This
sentimental nostalgia was not in the least spoiled by the fact that since
those days the old friend's head had been removed from his shoulders by
the same King. Henry also acquired More's own estate in 1536 and gave
it to Katherine Parr. Some palaces (Nonsuch, and, to a certain extent, the
Royal Pavilion, Brighton) seem to have been built from nothing short of
an exuberant lust for architecture; extravagant building-mania was one
of the primordial functions and attributes of a king. There were so many
assorted reasons for royal palace-building; sheer architectural caprice
played such a large part; so many kings wanted to build a symbol and
place of their own that any attempt to distil a general pattern of the
growth of royal residences from the mass of evidence is as useless as most
attempts to extract tidy patterns from history.

It is however worth noticing the increasing importance to kings of
living within range of the Thames. For centuries the big river was the
quickest and safest road in the kingdom. Since the Vikings and even the

Romans it had also been strategically the most vulnerable point of England. A dagger stab into the heart of the country could be made up it, swiftly and without warning. The most successful invasions of England in fact arrived in London up the Roman road from Dover; in which case it was equally sensible for the invaded king to be within easy reach of the Thames, and so of London, and what was rapidly becoming his centre of power. Early medieval kings had distributed their castles broadly all round the country. York and Tynemouth held the north, and looked warily towards Scotland. Portchester and Dover were keys to the south coast, and jumping off points for adventures in France. But gradually, by the same centripetal process which concentrates industry and government into the overcrowded south-east corner of these islands today, palaces and castles congregated towards London. The monarch with an itch for a new palace increasingly selected a site

> Along the shoars of silver streaming Themmes:
> Whose rutty bank, the which his river hemmes,
> was paynted all with variable flowers. . . .

As well as being florally picturesque, a Thames-side residence was politically prudent.

Another interesting theme, which repeats itself regularly in the building of royal residences, is the pattern of escapism by the king, and pursuit by his court. A king builds a new palace as a private residence, in the vain and perhaps insincere hope of getting away from affairs of state. Hot on his heels comes the patter of pursuing feet of magnates, politicians, bishops, place-seekers, spectators, courtiers, whose essential function as well as their ambition entails that they must not be cut off from the source of power, the king. So William Rufus seems to have built Westminster Hall as a personal extravaganza, rather than an official administrative building. Before long the administrators and the court had taken over, and Westminster became the main official palace. Henry VIII left the administration at Westminster, and moved into Whitehall as his private residence. Within a few years Whitehall had become so congested with the inescapable acolytes and parasites of royalty that Henry built a lodge at St James's as a very private retreat for himself and Anne Boleyn. Even before Whitehall burned, the court had automatically moved into St James's and into the new royal residence at Kensington, which became the official palaces. George III bought Buckingham Palace as a private house where his domesticated Queen, Charlotte, could avoid the pomp and formality of St James's. The formality and pomp followed them briskly into Buckingham Palace.

Victoria bought Osborne as a holiday house where she and Albert could live private lives away from the official court at Buckingham Palace. She at once rebuilt Osborne as a more formal palace, and then complained that her private residence had lost its old character, and that the court had followed her from Buckingham Palace down to the Isle of Wight. A conclusion seems to be that, just as the court necessarily, almost by definition, follows the king wherever he goes, so any king by his nature feels the subconscious need to be surrounded by his court, even if he sometimes complains about it. A private royal residence is a contradiction in terms. Where a king goes, there also go his functions, his duties, and his courtiers.

Balmoral and Sandringham have been the most successful recent attempts to create private royal residences. But privacy is far easier now that the practical as opposed to the mythical power of the monarch has dwindled away to a thread. And in any case the pastoral peace of the long holidays at Sandringham and Balmoral is still disturbed by state business. The red and blue leather 'boxes' from the Ministries still arrive and depart as remorselessly and punctually as the state papers used to follow Henry II or Elizabeth I on their progresses around their palaces. The difference today is that the monarch can do nothing about them except read them – the residual constitutional function of the sovereign consists only in a right to be consulted, to encourage, and to warn.

Balmoral and Sandringham are also invaded by occasional emergency meetings of the Privy Council, or by deputations of recently reshuffled Ministers, urgently needing to kiss hands. Even in the second half of the twentieth century a royal residence is different in category and in the activities that go on inside it from any other building in the kingdom.

It is tempting to deduce a general theory about kings as palace-builders. This could run that the more unsuccessful a monarch is politically, the more successful he is as an architect. Almost the only worthwhile achievement of William Rufus's extravagant and turbulent reign was the construction of the original Westminster Hall. Both Richard II and Henry VI were total disasters in the rough arena of medieval power politics; both were eventually and unsurprisingly removed from the throne and discreetly exterminated. But their palaces, chapels, and colleges still stand magnificent when the political imbecility of the builders is long forgotten and forgiven. The greatest palace-builder of them all, Henry VIII, in spite of his bluff image as the 'patriot king' who saved us all from thraldom to Rome, was on most views a considerable failure. His megalomaniac foreign policy ended in ruins and confusion. His campaigns against France were as unsuccessful as they were unnecessary. The vast wealth he had inherited from his father and extorted from the Church was squandered so that he died almost bankrupt. His matrimonial experiments were notoriously unfortunate. Of all the things he put his hand to, almost the only unmitigated successes were his tennis and his architecture. His buildings at Eltham, Greenwich, Whitehall, St James's, Hampton Court, Nonsuch, Hatfield House, and his numerous other palaces are better advertisements and memorials than he deserves.

It would be a strenuous effort for the most charitable or the most perverse observer to argue that George IV was either a great or a successful king. But he was a triumphant palace-builder, second only to Henry VIII, and responsible for the present appearance of Windsor Castle, for Nash's complete reconstruction of Buckingham Palace, for the Corinthian elegance of Carlton House, and for the Oriental fantasy of the Royal Pavilion, Brighton.

On the other hand, the generally accepted 'good' or great kings seldom seem to build palaces. Henry II's life was too hectic and hurly-burly for him to have much time for civilian architecture, at least in England, with the important exception of the Round Tower and the first stone walls at Windsor. He is more famous for demolition than construction; when he came to the throne he ordered the destruction of several scores of the original Norman castles. Edward I's massive building operations around North Wales or at the Tower of London were military rather than domestic. Elizabeth I, pinched for money and therefore parsimonious, preferred to invite herself to stay in the palaces of her wealthy subjects rather than to build palaces of her own.

Unhappily this doctrine, that it takes a bad king to build a good palace, is as riddled with exceptions as most general historical theories. All generalisations are hazardous, even this one. Even the most dedicated Jacobite-Tory would need to admit that William of Orange was politically a successful statesman-king. But he found time, in the intervals of organising the Grand Alliance against the imperialism of Louis XIV, to build Kensington Palace, and to rebuild Hampton Court and Greenwich.

It is a fair question to ask what point there is, in the purposive, technological twentieth century, in devoting time to such anachronisms as royal palaces.

The palaces of Britain are in a sense frozen history. From the Middle Ages until the nineteenth century almost every state event, as well as most of the entertaining anecdotes of British history, either originated in, or had repercussions in, or had some connection with, the galleries and halls of some royal residence. The surviving palaces are history fossilised in brick and stone, and in many ways more real and intelligible than the chronicles. Thousands of tourists every year, who will never open a history-book again, visit Hampton Court, and Windsor Castle, and the Tower of London, to stand among the 'No Smoking' signs and the roped-off enclosures, and reverently to hear the footfalls of Henry VIII echo in their misty memories.

Several massive volumes could be, and indeed often have been, devoted to the history of a single major palace such as Windsor. Details of the building operations are recorded in minute detail in the account rolls. Official records lovingly chronicle the perpetual cycle of palace life – birth (with occasional changeling rumour), marriage, coronation, death – with full catalogues in strict order of precedence of who was present at each interesting occasion. These seemed the important events worth recording to the participants and inhabitants of the court at the time. However, in the retrospect of some centuries, one coronation is very like another; that is one of the essential points about coronations, which the College of Arms exists to maintain.

One can wish that there were fewer records of public occasions in palaces, and rather more private detail about personal life back-stage on a normal working day. One could wish, for that matter, that more accounts survived of what life was like for an ordinary citizen in his private house in the Middle Ages. But it is the palaces and the red-letter occasions that have mainly come down to us across the blind gulf of the centuries. The menus of hundred-course coronation banquets are preserved in gory detail; as well as the protocol for the official washing of the king's hands, or for serving him dinner as a public spectacle and ritual. What he ate and what he said behind the scene in his Privy Chamber has generally been forgotten – at least from the years before the sixteenth century, when sharp-eyed visitors and courtiers started keeping intimate journals. Nevertheless, from the official accounts of what kings did, and from the palaces they lived in, it is possible to approach as close as anybody with twentieth-century preconceptions and terms of reference can manage, to what life was like for kings and ordinary men in the vanished years.

A comprehensive list of every royal residence and every king's palace in Britain would be as long and hard reading as Domesday Book. There are about a dozen major state palaces, whose importance has extended over many centuries and many monarchs. These obviously have to be considered in any survey of royal residences. For the rest, the best that can be done is to take a brief selection from the minor, short-lived palaces, extending over as wide a range of period and type as possible, even though this means leaving out many important buildings of the Middle Ages like Odiham and Bamburgh castles, and some promising recent palaces, like Charles II's rural residence for the Newmarket races and informal jolli-fication, Audley End.

One of the tiresome consequences of this procedure of treating a wide range of royal residences is that so many kings overlap so many of them. A palace like Windsor has 900 years of continuous history, and was lived in by almost every king during that period. It is disconcerting to run across Henry VIII in one palace as a gross, senile, bloodthirsty tyrant, and then, four palaces later, to meet him as a handsome, athletic, seventeen-year-old 'new Apollo' absorbed in tennis and the tilt-yard, music and masque. It is tiresome, but unavoidable.

It is on the whole inadvisable to pursue the history of palaces too far into the twentieth century. For one thing, the regular flow of history through the palaces of Britain has dried up to a formal trickle, as the power of the monarch has declined. For another, it takes about a century for private life in a royal residence to stop being gossip, and to become history, as the diaries, memoirs, biographies, and letters are published. History can explore the most unconventional happenings back-stage at the court of Charles II, or even of Victoria. It cannot tread far into this century without falling into the sentimental or malicious pit, where lurk 'Crawfie', and corgis, and nameless creatures that are gossip columnists. Only time can turn an indiscreet spiller of beans like Pepys or the original Charles Greville into a respectable source.

# II

# THE FIRST ROYAL RESIDENCES

THE early inhabitants of Britain were considerable builders and civil engineers. So far, unfortunately, their work has only been recognised in their burials, their barrows, and their places of worship. What their palaces were like, nobody knows. Since they have vanished, it seems reasonable to guess that they were made of wood – wood only survives from prehistory in waterlogged deposits. In any case, timber was the natural and most convenient building material in an England hirsute with black primeval forest; just as Cyclopean walls of massive rock came naturally to palace builders on stone-strewn hilltops like Mycenae.

It also seems sensible to infer that, for example, the genius who, around 1500 B.C., organised the third phase of Stonehenge, the great Sarsen trilithons with their horizontal lintels, would have lived in a remarkable and magnificent dwelling. Whoever he was, the tribal leader from the Wessex burial culture who arranged for the huge stones to be dressed and transported from the area between Marlborough and New-bury, and then had them erected so precisely that the Sun God at the winter solstice sets symbolically through the gateway of the great trili-thon, to die and be born again, does not sound the sort of man to be content with a modest mud hut. Among the many fanatical and far-fetched fictions about Stonehenge, at least nobody has yet suggested that it was lived in.

Nor was it anything to do with the Druids, who only arrived in Britain during the early Iron Age invasions around the third century B.C. So it is possible to have the double delight of disagreeing with Dr Johnson twice in one opinion. He was taken to see a stone circle near Inverness, and, laying down the law in his usual Juggernaut way, observed 'to go and see one druidical temple is only to see that it is nothing, for there is neither art nor power in it; and seeing one is quite enough'. On the con-trary, to see the mighty and undruidical power and art of Stonehenge is to wish for more, to want to know what sort of houses these extraordinary builders made.

The same irritating enigma still surrounds Silbury Hill near Marlborough, the vast prehistoric artificial mound 130 feet high, covering five and a quarter acres at its base. To produce a similar enormous plum-pudding sand-castle, the largest ancient man-made mound in Europe, every man, woman, and child in Britain today would have to contribute a full bucket of soil. But in spite of assiduous excavations during 1968 and 1969 sponsored by the British Broadcasting Corporation the date and purpose of Silbury Hill remain obscure. Is it the biggest of all Bronze Age barrows containing, cunningly concealed, some immensely rich royal burial? According to John Aubrey, the Wiltshire antiquary, three centuries ago: 'No history gives us any account of this Hill. The tradition only is, that King Sil (or Zel, as the country folk pronounce) was buried here on horseback and that the hill was raised while a posset of milk was seething.'

Nothing is known of Sil, alias Zel, whose name was presumably invented to explain the name of the hill. In the eighteenth century he and his horse were supposed to lie buried under the hill, 'the size of life, and of solid gold'. Disappointingly, none of the many excavators have yet bumped into him, nor gazed upon the golden face of Zel. Another theory is that the hill was built as the site of a beacon in some distinctly extravagant prehistoric system of signalling. Welsh enthusiasts allege that Silbury Hill is a great Gorsedd, or 'supreme seat' where assemblies were held near a sacred mound. All that can safely be said in such a vortex of speculation is that the hill is probably somehow connected with the monuments of prehistoric Wessex religion and the cult of the dead that surround it; and that the man who erected it, or who was buried beneath it, must have had a palace worth visiting.

Nothing that can really be described as a royal residence has yet been unearthed from prehistory. Private houses there are. The little neolithic village at Skarabrae in the Orkneys is enchanting, but the chief charm of its one-roomed dwellings is that they are so unregal and domestic. The spaces for the beds and the fireplaces, the cupboards and little paths from one house to another bring the Stone Age to life, but do not suggest the home of anybody who could possibly be described as a king.

With the Romans history and palaces arrived in Britain. The first and greatest palace was discovered in 1960 by a workman digging a trench for a water-main at Fishbourne, just west of Chichester in Sussex. His mechanical digger scooped into a great mass of Roman tiles, mosaic, and masonry. Over the next eight years the excited archaeologists uncovered and pieced together the ground plan of a building which makes every other Roman villa in Britain of the period look like a doll's house, and is as big as the palaces of Nero or Domitian at Rome. It is just as well that neither of these particular Emperors visited Sussex to draw suspicious, green-eyed deductions about the occupier.

'Palace' is not too enthusiastic a word for a six-acre building which is without parallel outside the heart of the Roman world. It was built some time around A.D. 75 in the form of a hollow square with sides a hundred yards long. Inside the square was an enormous formal garden, laid out with paths and box hedges, and the Italian passion for horticultural symmetry and statuary. The English unofficial rose, and the unkempt, overflowing herbaceous border are evidently native inventions, not imported. In the east wing was an impressive entrance hall with ornamental fountain, and flanked by guest rooms. Across the garden, reached by a forty-foot wide avenue between a symmetrical twisting pattern of low box hedges, was the west wing with its audience chamber and other large state rooms.

The north wing contained private and luxurious suites of apartments arranged around two small colonnaded gardens; presumably for the use of important visitors. The south wing still lies under the modern road and some houses, but trial trenches confirm the hypothesis that this was the private wing of the palace, with a colonnade facing the south, and a garden running down to the beach. In these southern courts the owner of the palace himself gloried and drank deep his imported wine. The bath suite, so essential to Roman standards of living, and so strange and alarming to Britain, was in the south-east corner of the palace, and is actually larger than the public baths later erected at Roman Silchester.

Almost all the rooms in the palace had bright mosaic floors of an intricacy and geometric beauty not found anywhere else outside the Mediterranean; more than sixty of them have been uncovered so far. The most magnificent surviving floor shows Cupid riding on a dolphin, surrounded by horrendous sea monsters. This one was laid by second-generation owners of the palace in the middle of the second century A.D. The interior decoration was ornate and sumptuous. Some of the walls were inlaid with streaky, Gorgonzola marbles imported from as far away as Greece and Turkey. Mouldings of white and blue marble framed the doors and windows. Other rooms had brightly painted plaster or moulded stucco friezes. Indubitably a great many specialists, craftsmen, marble-workers, plasterers, painters, mosaic-makers must have been brought to Britain expressly to create this palace, regardless of expense.

Such a building would have raised eyebrows in Rome itself. Its impact on barbarian Britain at the end of the first century A.D. must have been stupendous. The tantalising question, of course, is, whose palace was it? The historians plausibly deduce that it must have belonged to *Rex Cogidubnus*, King of the Atrebates (in other words, of the tribes that lived in the area that later became Sussex, Hampshire, and Berkshire). He was the client-king who collaborated with the Roman immigrants, and gave them a firm base on the south coast from which the Second Legion under the future Emperor Vespasian could fan out and conquer the west. Tacitus (calling him *Cogidumnus*) awards him a slightly double-edged pat on the back for remaining consistently loyal to Rome 'down to our own times'. A famous but difficult inscription found at Chichester attributes to him the title of '*legatus Augusti*', a unique, unheard-of honour for a vassal-prince, giving him the equivalent rank of a Roman Senator. The main arguments for Fishbourne Palace having been built for Cogidubnus are negative. There are no other obvious candidates in the field. Chichester was his capital. For anybody else to have lived in the palace on his doorstep would have been a humiliating insult to the old Quisling, which Rome would never have allowed.

Fishbourne flourished in spectacular magnificence until about A.D. 100, when there are signs of a change of ownership. The building was divided into a series of flats, and the Roman architects, having found out about the British climate, installed central heating. Finally, around A.D. 270, while further alterations were taking place, including construction of new under-floor heating, almost the whole building went up in disastrous flames.

This may have been an accidental fire started by the workmen. Or the palace may have been burnt in a raid by the pirates who were busy in the Channel during the late third century. The charred debris, the brilliant mosaics, even the memory disappeared beneath the Sussex turf until 1960. They have now been disinterred and put on public exhibition, the earliest royal residence, the oldest stately home in Britain. Here can be seen coins stamped with the plump, benevolent face of Vespasian, the tweezers for plucking the eyebrows of elegant Ancient British girls, the tiles marked with the foot-prints of a long-dead dog. The palace and its garden, ashes under Chichester for so long, provoke sobering thoughts of mortality and of the vanity of interior decoration. But they also give a comforting feeling of continuity, that 2,000 years ago green-fingered English gardeners loved their roses and their Madonna lilies. At Fishbourne, better than anywhere else in Britain, a man can see not only the grandeur, but also the green-gardened veranda, that was Rome.

In the twilight of the centuries, after the last legions were withdrawn around A.D. 410, emerges that most famous and at the same time most nebulous of all British royal residences, many-towered, many-fabled Camelot. The basic trouble about both Camelot and King Arthur is that they have been so covered with intricate layers of romance, and superstition, and religious mysticism, and historical propaganda, and archaeological wishful thinking, and sheer dottiness that it is hard to know whether underneath the mountain of literature there really ever was a hard kernel of fact. Perhaps in the Dark Ages after the Romans left a Romanised British war leader fought off the encroaching tide of Teutonic tribes, propped up a collapsing civilisation for a time, and became a legend for his eventual conquerors. Perhaps he even revived the thunderous mailed cavalry of fourth-century Rome, the *cataphractarii* and *clibanarii*, to rout the unequestrian Saxons, and to rally the last surviving pocket of the Western Empire of Rome.

The sixth-century monk Gildas gives the earliest report of these victories over the Saxons, listing various British chieftains, but nobody called Arthur. 'Artorius' is first mentioned by name in writing by Nennius, a ninth-century Bangor monk, who tried to collate the oral traditions of England and Wales in his confused *History of Britain*.

He wrote that Arthur turned the Saxons back in the west at the Battle of Badon, '*Mons Badonicus*', around A.D. 500. But even as early as Nennius, Arthur has some distinctly romantic and implausible attributes which would make a wary man draw in his breath sharply. He has a suspicious passion for the number twelve – twelve great battles, just as he later acquired twelve Knights of the Round Table, just as across the Channel Charlemagne had twelve paladins. And 'at the 12th battle at the hill Badon, 960 fell by his hand alone, no one but the Lord giving him aid.'

Geoffrey of Monmouth really launched the Arthurian romance down its primrose path to gaudy musical epic and the oblong screen in his *History of the Kings of Britain*, finished about A.D. 1136. This was an attempt to construct a pseudo-historical epic origin, a pedigree, and a sense of vocation for the new Norman Kingdom of Britain, as Homer had done for Greece, and Virgil for Rome. Geoffrey probably had some access to Celtic tradition, to Welsh day-dreams of future triumph over the Saxons. But he was also an exceedingly inventive and unscrupulous forger, working in purple patches from the classics and the Bible wherever possible, as well as memories of the Crusades, and of the world-wide dominion of Charlemagne. His Arthur, not content with repelling the invading Saxons, also conquers Scotland, Norway, and France; and in a final effulgent explosion of anachronism defeats the legendary Roman Emperor 'Lucius' in Gaul.

Gibbon, who believed in the existence and exploits of Arthur, on this side idolatry, puts it characteristically: 'His [Arthur's] romance, transcribed in the Latin of Jeffrey of Monmouth, and afterwards translated into the fashionable idiom of the times, was enriched with the various, though incoherent, ornaments which were familiar to the experience, the learning, or the fancy of the twelfth century.'

From ingenious Geoffrey French poets, wandering *troubadours* of the south, and *trouvères* of the north, eagerly picked up the Arthurian legend, fitting into it their contemporary themes of courtly, soap opera love and star-crossed passion, and broadcasting it to the remotest corners of Europe, as far as Sicily and Prague. The Church became jealous of the popularity of the fable. So the monks at Glastonbury in A.D. 1190 arranged for a fraudulent but extremely profitable exhumation of Arthur's and Guinevere's remains. A huge hollow oak was found sixteen feet down under a lead cross, lettered 'HIC IACET SEPULTUS INCLITUS REX ARTURIUS IN INSULA AVALONIA' – 'Here lies buried the renowned King Arthur in the Isle of Avalon'. The log, embedded in the soil at a slight angle, contained the skeleton of a tall man with a damaged skull, and the smaller bones of a woman. According to one account, the woman's remains were shrouded in long golden hair, which fell to dust on exposure to the air. All these interesting objects were reburied, and later lost at the dissolution of the monasteries.

The Church also promoted, as a counteracting influence, a cycle of Arthuriana whose mystical theme was the religious allegory of the quest for the Holy Grail, the San Graal, which held the blood of the Cross, invisible to all eyes but those of the pure in heart. After some centuries of embellishment and improvement, during which the legend had absorbed Lancelot from Brittany, the older and more mysterious legend of the Enchanter Merlin, and the independent stories of Tristram and Gawaine, the definitive version was handed down by Sir Thomas Malory, who was probably a Warwickshire Knight who fought in the Wars of the Roses, and died in 1471. His *Morte Darthur* was taken, he said, from a 'Frensshe boke'. In it Camelot is a medieval court of chivalry, where knights in armour joust for the favour of fair, frail ladies. It bears no conceivable similarity to the rude, crude, crumbling world of the sixth century.

Malory, perhaps in a temporary aberration, says that Camelot was Winchester – 'the cite of Camelot, that ys in Englysh called Wynchester.' John Leland, Henry VIII's antiquary and a better topographer than Malory, which is not saying much, states: '. . . at South-Cadbyri [in Somerset] standith Camallate, sumtyme a famous toun or castelle. . . . The people can telle nothing thar but that they have hard say that Arture much resortid to Camalat.'

In 1966 archaeologists started digging into the huge hill fortress at South Cadbury in the quest for Camelot. They found sherds of wine jars imported from the eastern Mediterranean in the fifth-sixth century A.D.: an iron knife and other metalwork of characteristic sixth-century form; and post-holes more than a foot in diameter of substantial timber build-ings of the Arthurian period. From these admittedly fairly flimsy clues they deduced that Cadbury Castle was the stronghold around A.D. 500 of a military leader with a rich and cultured court, who had Roman standards of living, tastes, and foreign connections, who might have rallied the last of Romano-British society against the infiltrating Saxons. Perhaps even Arthur himself, but at least 'an Arthurian type of person had a residence here'.

With the predictability that is almost the first law of academic life, this deduction was at once ferociously attacked by other archaeologists for its ballyhoo. 'To say you have found a post-Roman occupation of an Iron Age hill fort is one thing. But to go on and imply that this is Camelot, and that Arthur lived there, is quite another.' However, ever since Schliemann in the nineteenth century followed Homer as his guide, and uncovered Troy and Mycenae, archaeologists ignore legend and tradi-tion at their peril. It is wild wishful-thinking, but it is not entirely incon-ceivable that some day, somewhere, something Arthurian may turn up – though probably nothing quite as dramatic as Excalibur, the Siege Peri-lous, or the Holy Grail itself. The idea of gazing upon the face of Aga-memnon must have seemed almost as fantastic in the days before Schliemann.

Camelot. A 19th century French version of a Gothic revival Camelot by Gustave Doré. In the foreground Tennyson's Elaine, the lily maid of Astolat, dead, makes her way to Sir Lancelot with a lily in her right hand and a letter in her left

Caernarvon Castle reflected in the River Seiont

The question is, where to look if not at South Cadbury. A few features of Camelot constantly recur in Arthurian literature. Near the castle there was a flat field large enough for tournaments. There was a forest into which questing knights vanished. And there was a river running by down which the lady of Astolat came floating. These details are distressingly vague, but at least they are more useful than other typical information about the court at Camelot, such as that Arthur would not go into dinner 'until he had heard or seen a great marvel'.

From these faint hints it is possible to make a case for Camelot being almost anywhere. The name itself does not appear until the twelfth century, when Chrétien de Troyes located Arthur's court at Camelot. Malory said Winchester. His first printer Caxton persisted doggedly that in Wales could be found 'the town of Camelot, the great stones and marvellous works of iron, lying under the ground, and royal vaults, which divers now living hath seen'. Leland said South Cadbury. Froissart insisted on Carlisle. The nineteenth-century French scholar Paulin Paris asserts nonchalantly in a footnote: '*Kamaloth, aujourd'hui Colchester*'. Caerleon-upon-Usk, the huge legionary fortress of the Romans, reoccupied after the legions left? Edinburgh? Camelford in Cornwall?

Shakespeare, for what it is worth, seems to have supported the Camelford theory. In *King Lear* he makes cantankerous Kent in disguise say to the Duke of Cornwall:

> Goose, if I had you upon Sarum plain,
> I'd drive ye cackling home to Camelot.

The Duke of Cornwall lived in his castle of Tintagel at Camelford. However, one eminent commentator on this passage claims that Camelot is here Queen's Camel in Somerset, because of the reference to the cackling goose – near Queen's Camel 'are many large moors where are bred great quantities of geese, so that many other places are from hence supplied with quills and feathers'. The Duke of Cornwall's reply in *Lear* is not exactly encouraging to either location.

> What, art thou mad, old fellow?

A Professor from Kansas has recently proposed the ingenious theory that London was the site of Camelot. He quotes the tradition that it took two days for Arthur's Court to reach Camelot from Winchester, and two days for Gawaine's body to reach Camelot from Dover. The two circles meet at London – 'in both cases it was a slow journey'. Moreover the name of the church at Camelot was St Stephen's, which is also the name of the chapel at Westminster built by King Stephen. And, of course, there is a major muddy stream down which the unhappy lady of Astolat can float most satisfactorily.

In this chaos of conjecture it is impossible to say exactly where if anywhere this early royal residence was. It is safer to accept the spirit of the *Black Book of Carmarthen*, written in the twelfth century or earlier, and one of the earliest references to Arthur in Welsh literature:

> *Bet y march, bet y guythur,*
> *bet y gugaun cletyfrut;*
> *anoeth bid bet y arthur.*

'March has a grave, Gwythur has a grave, Gwgawn of the bloody sword has a grave; but Arthur's grave is the puzzle of the world.' Camelot also is the puzzle of the world. Or as a more recent poet, Francis Brett Young, put the same sobering thought:

> Where do the vanes and towers of Camelot
> And tall Tintagil crumble? Where do those tragic
> Lovers and all their bright-eyed ladies rot?
> We cannot tell – for lost is Merlin's magic.

But wherever, if ever Camelot was, there is a pleasant irony in that, just as Charlemagne and Roland, the paladins and stars of the Matter of France and French romantic literature, were in fact not French; so Arthur, the hero and first fountain of English literature, was a devoted and successful enemy of the English.

Perhaps the

> gray king whose name, a ghost,
> Streams like a cloud, man-shaped, from mountain-peak
> And cleaves to cairn and cromlech . . .

was one hundred per cent legend and wistful-thinking of a conquered people. But even if it never existed, Camelot has been a potent symbol ever since, down to the Kennedy dynasty in the United States, and no doubt beyond. It has even influenced the solid masonry and mortar of other less insubstantial royal residences. Edward III began to build a circular banqueting hall at Windsor 200 feet in diameter to hold his own Round Table; a project which was promptly and jealously imitated by King Philip VI of France.

Winchester was not Camelot. But as soon as the West Saxons finally conquered Wessex early in the sixth century it became their capital; and presumably they must have had some sort of royal residence in it. When Egbert had himself crowned King of one realm, Angle-land, at a Witan at Winchester, the city became in a sense the capital of England, though it soon had a formidable rival in London. Any palace at Winchester must have been destroyed in the frequent, ferocious raids of the ninth century by those sea-wolves that lived on the pillage of the world, the Danes, with their gaudy shields and wolf-pack cry to Odin. In 860 for example a big Danish expedition landed at Southampton and 'destrued Winchester al out'. And soon after Alfred became King in 871 it was evacuated and comprehensively sacked again.

As soon as Alfred finally smashed Guthrum and his great jarls at the glorious battle of Ethandune, he returned to Winchester and rebuilt his palace. It was just east of the cathedral, at Wolvesey, on the river Itchen, surrounded by marshes. It does not seem to have been a very healthy place. Asser, the King's biographer, lay ill with fever in it for 'a year and a week'. And Alfred himself was harassed by a periodic illness, possibly malaria, for many years. His palace at Winchester was probably built largely of wood. All that remains of it today is some Anglo-Saxon 'herring-bone' masonry.

Alfred spent much of the rest of his life at Winchester, and his court there became a centre of culture and learning, a Mecca for scholars from all over Europe. He himself had a passion for books and scholarship. 'There is not one priest south of the Thames,' he complained, 'who can properly understand the Latin of his own church books, and very few in the whole of England.' At Winchester he translated himself, or sponsored others to translate, many Latin books into English. Here he codified the laws of the country in the *Codex Wintoniensis* or *Domboc*, which was kept at Winchester, and became known after his death as the *Laws of Alfred*. But his greatest literary achievement was to be found in the *Anglo-Saxon Chronicle*, the first history in their own language by any of the Teutonic races, which eventually covered the years from A.D. 1 to 1154. He had his chronicle, which is the beginning of history in English, chained up in the cathedral so that all who could might read 'of adventures and of laws, and of battles, of the land and kings who made laws'. When some marauding Danes broke his peace, the prisoners were executed, and their bodies hung over the walls of Wolvesey Palace facing the river, *pour décourager les autres*. When Alfred died, he was buried at Winchester.

Winchester continued to be the centre of Anglo-Saxon government after Alfred. And after the Norman Conquest, William built himself a new palace in the centre of the city, of which a few fragments remain. He kept up the Saxon tradition of 'wearing his crown' at Winchester at Easter. The records, the mint, the royal treasure, and Domesday Book, that most unpopular public survey produced in a year for a stark and iron-willed man in a hurry to reorganise his revenues, were stored at Winchester. According to one tradition the 'Hoard' was kept, rather uncouthly, in a box under the king's bed. The fact that Winchester, together with London, was omitted from Domesday is some indication of the city's peculiar importance. It always had a special attraction for Norman kings. Partly, it was on their regular route home to Normandy via Southampton or Chichester. Partly, it was within convenient range for those dedicated hunters to get at the deer in the New Forest, which William had created. In his first, and significant, act after his father's death, William Rufus 'rode to Winchester and opened the Treasure House'.

The Norman palace was destroyed in the violent anarchy of Stephen's reign, but a new one was built, and Parliament was still occasionally summoned to Winchester until the fifteenth century. The last entry about it in the *Anglo-Saxon Chronicle* says that when Henry Plantagenet came to the throne, he was received with 'great worship' in Winchester and London – a suggestive order of precedence and importance.

It was on the wall of his chamber in Winchester Palace that Henry had painted the famous and bitter allegorical picture of the tragedy of his life. Four eaglets were shown preying upon their parent eagle. One of them was perched on his neck, waiting for a chance to peck out his eyes. The King explained: 'The four eaglets are my four sons who cease not to persecute me even unto death. The youngest of them, whom I now embrace with so much affection, will sometime in the end insult me more grievously and more dangerously than any of the others.' The traditional and sombre dying words of the first great Plantagenet king, who was eventually torn down by his voracious young eaglets, were 'Shame, shame on a conquered king'.

Once Normandy was lost by John, Winchester lost its strategic position, and London inevitably took capital place. Kings still occasionally stayed in the castle. And Charles II even spent £20,000 beginning a new red-brick palace at Winchester, designed by Wren. But, by the inexorable centralisation of history, kings needed to live nearer to the centre of things, in London.

While the Saxons were building and rebuilding their royal palace at

Winchester, other palaces were proliferating profusely all over Britain. From now on there is an *embarras de richesses*, literally hundreds of structures which can be described as royal residences. For obscure example, at Rendlesham in Suffolk are the remains of a palace which probably belonged to Redwald, a seventh-century king of the East Angles – 'who was the first of all his nation that was baptised, and received Christianity; but afterwards seduced by his wife, he had in the self-same church, as saith Bede, one altar for Christ's religion and another for sacrifices unto devils'.

Or, for a much later but equally obscure example, Cubbie Roo's twelfth-century castle still stands magnificently with its grey stone walls on Wyre in the Orkneys. It was built by Kolbein Hruga, 'the burly', 'a mighty man from Norway', who was at least a local king in those days when the clover-scented, seaweed-fringed, green and treeless islands were pretty independent Norse territories. If places like his are to be counted as royal residences, the catalogue will be as interminable as a Viking saga.

But there is one more category of early palace which needs to be disposed of, before returning to the main-stream of royal residences. This is the very large collection of castles which were built primarily as military strongholds, but in which early soldier kings as well as their garrisons often lived. William the Conqueror was a prolific builder of this type of grim residence. Dozens of motte-and-bailey castles were hastily thrown up in the early years of the Norman Conquest at strategic points, to consolidate the military victory, and to impress and tyrannise the conquered population, some of whose homes were usually destroyed to make room for the castle. As a single example of this large category of fortress-residence, one of the latest, and unquestionably one of the most impressive, is Caernarvon Castle.

Edward I began to build it in 1283 as a symbol and a sentinel to guard his victories over Llywelyn, the last native Prince of Wales, and his brother David. Its site, at the mouth of the river Seiont, glowering out over the Menai straits to Anglesey, had already been a strategic military base for the oppressors of the Welsh for more than a thousand years. Imperial Rome had an outpost fortress and garrison at Segontium, just beside the present castle, to keep watch on Mona, that haven for dissidence and Druids. In their turn the Normans also built a castle here around 1090.

Edward incorporated the Norman earthwork mound in his castle. It was designed as a heavily symbolic as well as an impregnable building, with explicit references back to Roman imperial power, and to folk-memories in the *Mabinogion*, in order to proclaim to all comers that here was the seat of the new English imperial power, and of the new Princes of Wales. For instance, the greatest tower facing Anglesey, the Eagle Tower, was capped with three turrets each crowned with a large stone eagle, the standard of the Roman legions. The walls of the castle were consciously modelled on those of Constantinople; bands of different coloured sandstone were used to produce the 'great towers of many colours'. As in Constantine's imperial city, the towers were polygonal instead of the usual contemporary round shape.

Work on Caernarvon went on intermittently for fifty years. The accounts in the Public Record Office keep the score of the gradual progress. For instance, in 1304 Master Walter of Hereford is named as 'mason and master of all the works of construction', with a weekly wage of seven shillings. Under him were twenty-nine other masons, with wages ranging from 11½d to 4s. Stone-quarriers, stone-layers, smiths, carpenters, and labourers brought the week's labour force up to 160, with a wages bill of £12 12s 10¼d. By July of the next year there were 231 workmen on the building site, drawing wages of £16 15s 0¾d.

The castle was still unfinished when work on it was abandoned in 1330. So it was never used as the imperial residence and setting for medieval pageantry for which it was designed. Later legend alleged that Edward of Caernarvon, disastrous Edward II, was born in the castle in 1284. When Mrs Thrale visited the castle with Dr Johnson in 1774 she recorded: 'They shew one a little closet of perhaps some seven feet square, and tell one that Edward 2nd was born there; but a Lieutenant of a Man of War, who shewed us the curiosities of the place, remarked that they had no other room left entire, and therefore they called this the Prince of Wales's birth Chamber, for nothing could be more unlikely than that a Queen of England should lye in a chamber scarce capable of holding a bed.' The Lieutenant was only too right. In 1284 the castle was hardly started, and Queen Eleanor must have given birth to Edward of Caernarvon in a lodging on the building site.

Popular tradition also makes Caernarvon the place where Edward I pacified the defeated Welsh with the promise of 'a prince who was born in Wales, could speak no English, and whose life and conversation nobody could stain'; and then, distinctly disappointingly, presented them with his own infant son. In sober fact the promise was made at another of Edward's north Welsh castles, Rhuddlan. And the first English Prince of Wales was invested at Lincoln at the strapping and talkative age of seventeen. Not only did he not speak a single convoluted syllable of Welsh, but his everyday language was French, not English.

The magnificence of Caernarvon has always been recognised. A seventeenth-century visitor wrote: 'I have seen many gallant fabrics and fortifications, but for compactness and completeness of Caernarvon I never yet saw a parallel; and it is by Art and Nature so fitted and seated, that it stands impregnable.' Dr Johnson said that its stupendous magnitude and strength surpassed his ideas, and he did not think there had been such buildings.

By one of the ludicrous ironies of history the fortress-palace of the Princes of Wales was not used for the purpose for which it was built for 600 years, until the twentieth century. A medieval fortress is no longer needed or effective to hold down and overawe the dissident Welsh. Nor is it in any condition to be used as a residence. But since 1911 the great castle, ringed by the eagle walls of Snowdonia, has become the highly appropriate setting for that ceremony which still rather self-consciously whispers the last enchantments of the Middle Ages, the Investiture of Princes of Wales.

III

# THE TOWER OF LONDON

DARKNESS, decay, and decapitation hold illimitable dominion over the history of the Tower of London:

> Ye towers of Julius, London's lasting shame,
> With many a foul and midnight murther fed.

The gruesome catalogue of scaffolds draped in black, fatal steps, great firmness being shown by all concerned, gallows humour, the condemned man eating the original hearty breakfast, skull-like laughter, loyal hearts being landed at the Traitor's Gate ('more tragic pathos attaches to this black water-gate than to the Bridge of Sighs in Venice') obscures the other sides of the story of the Tower.

As well as being the great state prison into which many entered, but few came out except head first, the Tower has also been fortress, palace, home of the Royal Mint, the Royal Menagerie, the public records, arsenal for small arms, and briefly the Royal Observatory. It has always guarded the Crown Jewels. During the Middle Ages it was regularly used as a royal residence. Because of its reassuring impregnability, it tended to be most used as a palace by uneasy kings in turbulent periods. Until the seventeenth century the significant, symbolic custom survived of the monarch lodging in the Tower until his coronation, and riding from there in procession through the City to Westminster: the man who held the Tower held the master key to London and to the kingdom, and was therefore competent to be crowned.

In spite of the poets, and persistent folk-lore, Julius Caesar was not responsible for the ill-erected Tower. It has been improbably conjectured that he left behind the first semi-permanent bridge over the Thames at London, to remind the natives of the power of Rome after the eagles had gone home. But there is neither record nor probability of Caesar having built any permanent fortifications there. By A.D. 61 Londinium was not important enough to be given the title of colony, but according to Tacitus it was already famous for its concentration of trade and businessmen. Its walls were less adequate. The great rising of the Britons of the eastern districts under Boudicca had no trouble at all in sacking the town, and inflicting on the businessmen, in the terse and terrible Tacitean phrase, *'caedes, patibula, ignes, cruces'*. The archaeological evidence of a silver ingot, gold coins, a tombstone, and a ditch suggests that the Romans were in considerable residence on the site of the Tower from the end of the first century A.D. onwards. In painful memory of Boudicca they built a fort there, the *Arx Palatina*, to guard the eastern approaches to the city, and the vulnerable entrance to the Thames from the sea.

Only misty and extravagant myths of London's fortifications survive from the twilight ages after the legions left. For example, imaginative Geoffrey of Monmouth records that King Belinus built a prodigious tower and haven for ships at Billingsgate. Slightly more convincingly, the *Anglo-Saxon Chronicle* says that in 886 King Alfred recovered London from the Vikings, and built a strong 'burh' or citadel to protect it in future.

The firm, factual history of the Tower begins with William the Conqueror. William made a big issue of being crowned in Westminster Abbey, but his massive Tower was the true symbol of his reign, and of Norman supremacy in an occupied city that had submitted extremely reluctantly. 'Stark man he was, and great awe men had of him' was the verdict of his subjects. He began the fortifications at the Tower directly after his coronation at Christmas 1066. The central keep, the White Tower, was started in 1078.

The archaeologists are in dispute about whether William imported the concept of motte-and-bailey castles with him from Normandy, emblems of Norman aggression, and of a feudal regime imposed on a conquered country. Or whether he incorporated the defensive earthworks and design of late Saxon 'burhs' which he found already here. In either case he proceeded to peg down his new kingdom with indomitable castles. The Great Tower or Keep of London, called the White Tower, was the most crucial of his typical hall-keeps – square towers surrounded by a ditch and palisades. He built it in the south-east corner of the old Roman city wall. The building was in the charge of Gundulf, a monk of Bec in Normandy, who later became Bishop of Rochester. Work on it was still going on in 1097 under William Rufus. According to John Stow's *Survey of London*, in 1091 the White Tower was 'by tempest & wind sore shaken' so that there had to be extensive repairs.

The statistics of the '*Tour Blanche*' confirm the impression that its primary function was to be a secure fortress rather than a comfortable royal residence. It is 90 feet high from base to battlements, and its irregular sides measure 107 by 118 feet (in fact none of its four sides are of exactly the same length). Only the keep at Colchester is bigger. The Tower is crowned by four turrets, three of them square and one circular. The outside walls taper from a formidable 15 feet thick at the bottom to a solid 11 feet at the top. Originally, until Wren enlarged them, its only windows were narrow arrow-slits, grimly but appropriately called *meurtrières*. As usual in Norman castles, the entrance was on the first floor, inconspicuous on the south side, reached by an external staircase which disappeared long ago.

The interior is suitably stark, stern, and businesslike. The spiral staircase has a right-handed twist, so that any attacker coming up from below has the disadvantage of having to fight left-handed. There is a basement, a first or entrance floor, a second floor with the banqueting hall, sword room, and Chapel of St John (which extends up to the third storey), and a third floor with the Council Chamber, and state apartments, where presumably the king slept when he stayed in the Tower, with the Crown Jewels in a box under his bed, and his sword by his side.

The dank, dark dungeons in the basement, particularly the claustrophobic hell-hole called 'Little Ease' where there is not room to lie down, are adequately horrific. The ultimate horror that they are below the river level, which is published with relish in one famous account of the Tower, is in fact fable. The dungeons in the White Tower are more than ten feet above high-water mark.

The grim Tower was called White because it was built mainly of stone imported from the quarries of Caen; and from its earliest days there was an ironic custom of whitewashing it both inside and outside. William Fitz-Stephen, writing in Latin in the twelfth century, has a lurid story about the foundation of the Tower. London, he says, has at its east end 'a palace-tower, very big and very strong, whose walls rise from the deepest foundations; the mortar is tempered with the blood of beasts'. In spite of the superstitious and highly satisfactory symbolism of blood-mixed cement, a more convincing explanation of any sanguinary pinkness in the mortar would be the use of pulverised Roman red bricks and tiles in the mixture.

The first formal record of a king keeping his court in the Tower is of Stephen during his civil war over the succession, when the Tower was one of the key pieces on the chess-board. Richard I's Chancellor enlarged the moat, and began the process of converting the obsolete Norman keep into the professional crusader's idea of a proper fortress. The moat defensive to the Tower was filled with water from the Thames, until it was drained in the nineteenth century.

Under Richard and John, and their disgruntled barons, the Tower changed hands with bewildering frequency. It was held in pledge for the completion of Magna Carta in 1215 and 1216. The strongest fortress in the kingdom was the first target for rebellious factions, and the Tower's history is already so full of blood and battles, battering and besieging, that its domestic uses are blotted out. The Constable of the Tower, as well as being the dominant man in London, had a fixed salary and lucrative perquisites that went with his office. Passing ships paid him a toll; a wine-ship paid two flagons, a rush-boat a bundle of rushes. All swans below London Bridge were his, and also any cattle that fell into the Thames while crossing the bridge, and all assorted flotsam and jetsam floating past on the alternate tides. One of the grievances removed by Magna Carta was the habit of Constables of the Tower of putting 'kiddles' or weirs across the Thames (made of fishnets so fine that not even a minnow could slip through). The royal treasury gave the Constable an allowance for keeping prisoners, many of whom brought with them large retinues of servants.

The full conversion of William the Conqueror's hall-keep into a fortress ringed with a curtain wall and thirteen bastion towers was carried out by Henry III, a king who, because of his tempestuous relations with Simon de Montfort and his other magnates, had a more than academic interest in living behind impregnable walls.

During his refortification, the new tower over the Traitor's Gate collapsed on the night of St George's day in 1240. Exactly a year later, exactly the same disaster happened again. The chronicler Matthew Paris confidently explained this curious coincidence. A reliable witness actually saw the ghost of St Thomas Becket push over the tower, which the King was building to oppress and dominate the liberty-loving citizens of London.

As well as strengthening his stronghold, Henry III did much to improve living conditions and the interior decoration of the Tower. In 1241 he decorated the Chapel of St John in the White Tower with richly coloured stained glass, and whitewashed the royal apartments and the whole exterior. To the south-east, between the Tower and the Thames, he built palace rooms, a great hall, galleries and gardens, where the court could live more comfortably than in the gloomy Norman keep. His hall disappeared long ago, but parts of its foundation were uncovered during the Second World War, when fire destroyed a nineteenth-century building standing on its old site. A passage from the new palace probably led directly into the Chapel and the state rooms in the White Tower. The King's 'bedechamber and prevy closet' were in the Lanthorn Tower looking out over the private garden of the palace. This tower was almost completely destroyed by a fire in the eighteenth century.

Most of these residential buildings were pulled down by Cromwell. The only fragment that remains is part of the Wardrobe Tower, just at the south-east corner of the White Tower. This was used for storing the royal robes and armour, as well as the tapestries, hangings, and other essential upholstery for civilised medieval living. Underneath the Wardrobe Tower the archaeologists have unearthed the remains of a semi-circular bastion of the Roman wall.

There are frequent, if fleeting references in the chronicles of Henry's reign to his works and his magnificence in the Tower, to the paintings as well as the lavish coats of lime wash with which he decorated his rooms – in his bedroom he had an anthropomorphic painting of Winter, who was probably only too infuriatingly appropriate in the chilly damp which has always been one of the specialities of the Tower.

Henry III's other unexpected contribution to the Tower was his introduction of a menagerie for wild beasts, which survived there until the nineteenth century, when London's zoo was moved to Regent's Park. Stow read that in 1235 the Emperor Frederick sent his brother-in-law Henry a present of three leopards (speaking heraldically, lions passant gardant), to match his coat of arms. They and their keepers were lodged in what came to be called the Lion Tower, by the moat, where the modern entrance to the Tower stands with its refreshment rooms and public lavatories. They were shortly joined by a camel.

A few years later the Sheriffs of the City had to contribute to the safe-keeping in the Tower of a white bear from Norway. They 'provided four-pence daily, with a muzzle and iron chain, to keep him when *extra aquam*, and a stout cord to hold him when a-fishing in the Thames'. King Louis IX of France presented an elephant, the first seen in England since the Romans left. 'A strong and suitable house' was built for him, and there was much consultation about his menu, but the home-sick beast died within three years. It soon became the custom to name any new lion in the Tower after the current king. As late as James I it was a rude and dirty, but royal, after-dinner pastime to watch the superfluous beasts in the Tower tearing each other to death. It is unfortunately almost true that more is known about the life of the wild beasts in the Tower than of the early human inhabitants. This English sense of priorities is perfectly demonstrated by the statistics in the Liberate Rolls, lovingly noted by several authorities, that the keeper of the king's leopard in the Tower in the thirteenth century was paid three-halfpence a day for his own food, but 'sixpence a day for the sustenance of the leopard'. In 1341 the Tower contained one lion, one lioness, four young lions, and a leopard. There are no figures for human inhabitants.

Visiting England at the end of the sixteenth century the tutor to a young German nobleman, Paul Hentzner, blessedly conscientious about his journal, wrote:

On coming out of the Tower we were led to a small house close by, where are kept variety of creatures – viz. three lionesses, one lion of great size, called Edward VI, from his having been born in that reign; a tyger; a lynx; a wolf excessively old; this is a very scarce animal in England, so that their sheep and cattle stray about in great numbers, free from any dangers, though without anybody to keep them; there is besides, a porcupine, and an eagle. All these creatures are kept in a remote place, fitted up for the purpose with wooden lattices at the Queen's expense.

Edward I completed the fortification of the Tower as it stands today by encircling it with an outer wall and towers. The White Tower therefore became the nucleus of a series of concentric defences. With its inner bailey and outer bailey it covers twelve acres. Including the moat and wharf the area is eighteen acres.

Under the belligerent Edwards the Tower became increasingly used for the incarceration of state prisoners. The campaigns in Wales and Scotland filled the dark towers with chiefs and knights waiting to be ransomed. Edward III used it to lock up not only David Bruce, the King of Scotland, but also John, King of France, his son Philip, and an imposing selection of French nobility after the battle of Poitiers.

At first the French King was lodged fairly hospitably in the Savoy Palace. But when Edward returned to campaign in France, Froissart notes:

To be more sure of them the French King was set in the Tower of London, and his young son with him, and much of his pleasure and sport restrained, for he was then straitlier kept than he was before.

The records show that Edward was sensitive about keeping the Tower in good repair, as a secure base behind his back while he was away at the big wars. He had a minute survey made of the fortress, and ordered repairs, 'on account of certain news which had lately come to his ears, and which sat heavy at his heart; the gates, walls, and bulwarks shall be kept with all diligence, lest they be surprised by his enemies'. He ordered that the gates of the Tower should be closed 'from the setting till the rising of the sun.' A few years later, arriving back from France unexpectedly by night, he found the Tower inadequately defended. The Constable and some of his officers were imprisoned, and replaced by the Black Prince, who was ordered to live in the Tower and keep it with strict discipline.

Inevitably the Tower was much in use in the disturbed and violent reign of the Black Prince's son, Richard II. There are records of the fashionable young King keeping his court there with his customary luxury, and also of the great fortress in its more usual role as a safe ship surrounded by a raging sea of violence.

Raphael Holinshed described the elegance of the coronation in considerable detail. On coronation eve in the Tower the King created a number of Knights of the Bath, who attended him while he took a ceremonial bath, kept vigil over their arms in the Chapel in the White Tower all night, and then escorted their sovereign to Westminster. Richard made the king's traditional exit from the Tower wearing white, 'as beautiful as an archangel'.

The noise of trumpets and other instruments was marvellous. The city was adorned in all sorts most rich. The water conduits ran with wine for the space of three hours together. In the upper end of Cheape was a certain castle made with four towers, out of the which castle, on two sides of it, there ran forth wine abundantly. In the towers were placed four beautiful virgins, of stature and age like to the king, apparelled in white vestures, in every tower one, who blew in the king's face, at his approaching near to them, leaves of gold; and as he approached also, they threw on him and his horse florins of gold counterfeit . . . and so with great triumphing of citizens, and joy of the lords and noblemen, he was conveyed into his palace at Westminster, where he rested for the night.

The accounts show Richard spending money on decoration of his residence in the Tower. In 1398 he spent £200 on ornament, and ordered 105 square feet of stained glass, painted with fleurs-de-lis and bordered with the royal arms. Recent discoveries in the Byward Tower turned up some typical fragments of court ornament in his reign – floor tiles painted with leopards and Richard's heraldic white hart, wall paintings in gold and vermilion, popinjays and fleurs-de-lis.

Jean Froissart, the Flemish poet at the English court, described a magnificent feast and tournament, in which sixty ladies on fair palfreys came riding out of the Tower, each leading a knight ready for the joust by a chain of silver. After the hearty heroics, at night 'there was goodly dancing in the queen's lodging, in the presence of the king and his uncles, and other barons of England, and ladies and demoiselles, continuing till it was day, which was time for every person to draw to their lodgings'.

However the gold and popinjays of Richard's cultured court in the Tower are obscured by the usual dark and violent happenings. The King and his demoralised nobles took refuge in the obvious place from the wildfire of the Peasant Revolt. According to Froissart, they 'sat still with awful eye' in the Tower, listening to the roar of the mob surging around its walls. From the Tower the sixteen-year-old King left for his famous conference with the rebels at Mile End, where he promised to free them and their lands for ever, and that they 'be never named nor held for serfs'.

Probably while Richard was actually out at this confrontation, a band of 700 peasants under Wat Tyler himself broke into the Tower, to hunt for 'traitors' hiding there. The drawbridge was down, and the portcullis up, which encourages the deduction that the King allowed the mob in. The peasants shook the knights of the garrison by their beards, and promised that from now on they were going to be their equals and good comrades. The King's bed was broken up, in case some enemy of the people was skulking in it. Some of the crowd burst into Richard's mother's room, who judiciously fainted when one of them tried to kiss her: many of the rebels 'went into the Kynge's Privie Chamber, and plaied the wantons, in sitting, lying and sporting them on the King's bed. And that which is more saucily, invited the King's mother to kisse with them'.

In St John's Chapel in the White Tower they caught the Archbishop of Canterbury, Simon Sudbury, whom they rightly suspected of being a hard-liner hawk, who had encouraged the King not to give in to the peasants. They dragged him from the altar to Tower Hill, and there chopped off his head. The Treasurer, the chief administrator of the hated poll-tax, and a Franciscan friar were also winkled out of the Tower and briskly decapitated.

Richard was brought back to the Tower as a prisoner after the revolution of Henry Bolingbroke of Hereford and Lancaster. The details of his last months as King are obscure. Froissart gives an account of his abdication:

The Duke of Lancaster, accompanied with lords, dukes, prelates, earls, barons, and knights, and with the notablest men in London, and of other good towns, rode to the

Tower, and there alighted. Then King Richard was brought into the hall, apparelled like a king, in his robes of estate, his sceptre in his hand, and his crown on his head. Then he stood up alone, not holden nor stayed by any man, and said, aloud, 'I have been King of England, Duke of Aquitaine, and lord of Ireland above twenty-two years, which signory, royalty, sceptre, crown, and heritage I clearly resign here to my cousin, Henry of Lancaster; and I desire him here in this open presence, in entering on the same possession, to take this sceptre'; and so delivered it to the duke, who took it. Then King Richard took his crown from his head with both his hands, and set it before him, and said, 'Fair Cousin, Henry, Duke of Lancaster, I give and deliver you this crown, wherewith I was crowned King of England, and therewith all the right thereto depending'.

Another curious account, in the *Annales Ricardi*, has Richard being visited in the White Tower by lawyers, representatives of the Estates, and certain lords. 'With a smiling face' ('*vultus hillaris*'), he abdicated, and signed a document asking that Henry should succeed him, and sent Henry his signet ring. Perhaps it was a cynical smile of defeat. But one interpretation is that Richard was smiling because he thought he was resigning the rule of the kingdom (*regimen*), not the actual kingship itself (*regnum*) to Henry. An unsuccessful *coup d'état* that winter by Richard's faction made his permanent removal politically advisable. So he died most carefully upon his hour in prison at Pontefract Castle, probably having been starved or suffocated. The official government version was that he starved himself to death.

The Lancastrian kings kept the ancient ritual of spending a few nights in the Tower before their coronations, but no records apart from this exist of their having kept court there for any length of time. Even Edward IV observed the custom before his hasty coronation. In the Tower he made thirty-two of his victorious supporters, including his two brothers, Knights of the Bath, 'who, being arrayed in blue gowns with hoods and tokens of white silk upon their shoulders, rode before him to Westminster'.

All through the Wars of the Roses the Tower was the setting for big events, most of them sombre. Henry VI spent a great deal of time in the Tower, part of it as monarch in residence in his palace, much more of it as prisoner in the strongest fortress in the kingdom. Edward IV and the Yorkists imprisoned Henry in the White Tower for five years (while his son was alive, there was nothing to be gained by killing him). He was taken there in considerable humiliation, for propaganda purposes; his gilt spurs were struck off, his legs tied to the stirrups of his horse, and he was displayed in front of the Tower. Once safely inside he was treated comparatively kindly. He was allowed some visitors, the company of his pet

The Tower of London. A medieval manuscript in the British Museum shows the Duke of Orleans in three different poses imprisoned in the White Tower

*Photo Mansell Collection*

The Tower of London. A plan made in 1597.

The Tower of London

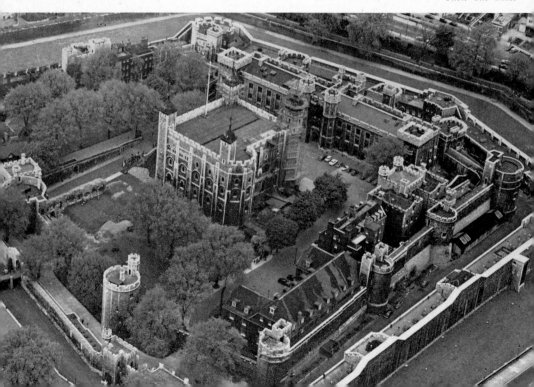

bird and dog, an allowance of five marks a week, and an occasional cask of wine. The Queen, Elizabeth Woodville, also spent much time in the safe royal lodgings in the Tower during these dangerous years, while her husband was away participating in the death-struggle of the feudal world.

In 1471 that devious diplomat Warwick the King-Maker organised a brief restoration for Henry VI. The bishops who went to break the glad news to him in the Tower found him 'not so worshipfully arrayed nor so cleanly kept as should seem such a prince.' Henry himself behaved 'as mute as a crowned calf'. He was led from the Tower 'apparelled in a long gown of blue velvet through the streets of London to the cathedral church of St Paul: the people on the right hand and on the left rejoicing and cry-ing "God save the King"'. Which the people, understandably indifferent whether Yorkist or Lancastrian was King, could be persuaded to do for almost anybody.

Within a very few months Henry was back again in the Tower as a prisoner, after the battles of Barnet and Tewkesbury had destroyed Lancastrian hopes, and killed his son. There was no longer any point in keeping him alive, and he therefore died mysteriously in the Tower. The official story was that he had faded away 'of pure displeasure and melan-choly' on hearing of his son's death and his wife's capture. But it was noticed by others with sinister emphasis that when he lay in state, only his face was uncovered; 'and in his lying he bled upon the pavement there'.

The Tower now entered its most melodramatic cycle of foul and mid-night murders. Edward IV's brother George, false, fleeting, perjured Duke of Clarence, was attainted of high treason, and died suddenly and con-veniently in the Tower. The awful discovery that kings can be made and unmade by violence is extremely likely to encourage more violence. The story that Clarence was drowned in a butt of Malmsey (the famous wine of the crusaders from Monemvasia in the south-east of the Peloponnese) was given by Robert Fabyan, a Londoner, and enthusiastically repeated by contemporary French chroniclers. One of them added the ingenious embroidery that Clarence was given the option of how he was to die, and chose the Malmsey. Other versions have him poisoned in a glass of, or suffocated by fumes from, the wine. By the time of Holinshed the most sensational version had passed into history: 'finallie the duke was cast into the Tower, and therewith adjudged for a traitor, and privily drowned in a butt of malmesie.' However it was done, there has never been much argument that Clarence was murdered secretly in the Tower.

The next and most notorious resident victims in the Tower were
Edward IV's sons and heirs, Edward V and the Duke of York. Their
murder, possibly in August 1483, is one of the best-known stories of life
and death in the dark tower of London, mainly thanks to Shakespeare. The
facts, not surprisingly, are dim and elusive. All the authorities from whom
Shakespeare drew wrote under Henry VII, and are partial witnesses, having a great interest in making propaganda for the new regime, and in
painting Richard III as a crouch-backed monster of whom the country was
well rid. The first account was given by Polydore Vergil, Henry Tudor's
official journalist. The life of Richard III, attributed unconvincingly to
Sir Thomas More, gives the most authoritative version, and that is not
saying much:

. . . the princes were in charge of Will Slaughter called 'Black Will', who was set
to serve them and see them sure. Sir James Tyrrel devised that they should be
murdered in their beds; to the execution whereof he appointed Miles Forest, one of
the four who kept them, a fellow flesh-bred in murder before time. To him he joined
his horse-keeper, John Dighton, a big, broad, square, strong knave. . . . They came
into the chamber, and suddenly wrapped them up amongst the clothes, keeping
down by force the feather bed and pillows hard upon their mouths, that within
awhile they smothered and stifled them, and their breaths failing, they gave up to
God their innocent souls into the joys of heaven, leaving to their tormentors their
bodies dead in bed. . . . Tyrrel ordered the murderers to bury them at the stair
foot, metely deep in the ground, under a great heap of stones.

Later chroniclers, Fabyan and Hall, Holinshed and Stow, and so to
Shakespeare, followed the authorised Tudor version, with minor embel-
lishments. Some have found this ghoulish blood and blunder and Tudor
propaganda as implausible as the beasts' blood mixed with the mortar of
the Tower. However, compelling circumstantial evidence was uncovered
by workmen in the reign of Charles II. While repairing the stairs in the
White Tower they dug up two small skeletons, which were reburied at
Westminster Abbey. Modern examination of the remains indicates that
the bones are those of two boys aged ten and twelve. And a bloodstain on
the jaw-bone of the elder has been interpreted as evidence of death by
suffocation.

The other famous set-piece in the Tower, when Richard III comes
cheerfully into the council chamber in the White Tower, sends the Bishop
of Ely out to get him strawberries from his garden, and then suddenly bares
his withered arm, and demands to have the head off Lord Hastings before
dinner, suffers from similar combined defects of Tudor propaganda and
Shakespeare's genius. The chief authority for the melodrama is the Thomas

More life of Richard III, much of which was in fact probably compiled by the strawberry-growing Bishop of Ely, John Morton, himself. And Morton was an eye-witness, but a prejudiced one, with an interest in justifying the new dynasty from Wales.

By the end of the Middle Ages the Tower was obsolete as a residence. The Tudors constructed a new generation of unfortified manor-house palaces to replace the old, moated fortress-palaces. Henry VIII built a wall round the outside of the moat of the Tower, with embrasures for cannon. He lived in temporary lodgings in the Tower for a time early in his reign after the fire at Westminster Palace; but the use of the Tower as a residence was very rapidly overshadowed by its darker functions with dungeon, rack, and block.

Its amenities as a place to live, never great, were not improved by the grisly and interminable list of executions. Two of Henry's queens had their heads removed on Tower Green. The chroniclers continually record, with lugubrious relish, the executioner 'performing his office with a single blow', or, for a change, with three strokes in honour of the Trinity.

Elizabeth, having been imprisoned and in hazard of her head in the Tower, seems to have developed an understandable lack of enthusiasm for living there voluntarily. Writing in her reign John Stow does not think of the Tower as a place where kings and queens live. It is

the citadel to defend and command the city, a royal palace for assemblies and treaties, a state prison for dangerous offenders, the only place for coining money, an armoury of warlike provisions, the treasury of the Crown jewels, and the storehouse of the Records of the Royal Courts of Justice at Westminster.

When Paul Hentzner made his tour of the Tower in 1598 it was an armoury, a prison, and a museum:

Upon entering the Tower we were obliged to quit our swords at the gate and deliver them to the guard. When we were introduced, we were shown above a hundred pieces of arras belonging to the Crown, made of gold, silver, and silk; several saddles covered with velvet of different colours; an immense quantity of bed furniture, such as canopies and the like, some of them most richly ornamented with pearl; some royal dresses, so extremely magnificent as to raise one's admiration at the sums they must have cost.

Later Hentzner observed:

It is to be noted, that when any of the nobility are sent hither on the charge of high crimes punishable with death, such as treason, etc., they seldom or never recover their liberty.

And this is the impression of the Tower that has lingered on in the popular memory, obliterating its earlier use as a royal residence. James I was the last king to keep his court briefly in the Tower, causing much consternation because of the leaking roofs and general dilapidation of the apartments.

The last traditional coronation procession from the Tower was made by Charles II in 1661. Pepys watched:

Up early and made myself as fine as I could, and put on my velvet coat, the first day that I put it on, though made half a year ago. . . . It is impossible to relate the glory of the day, expressed in the clothes of them that rid, and their horses and horse-clothes . . . Glorious was the show with gold and silver, that we were not able to look at it, our eyes at last being so much overcome with it.

The procession tooks five hours to pass.

James II abandoned the atavistic tradition of keeping pre-coronation court at the Tower, and of the procession through the City to Westminster, 'because of the great expense as well to the government as the city'. Under William and Mary the last surviving domestic apartments in the ancient palace apart from the White Tower were pulled down. Since when the Tower has never been used as a royal home. It is still a royal 'liberty', which means it is outside the jurisdiction of the Lord Mayor, and the Bishop of London. A Constable still holds the old key to the kingdom for the Crown; today he is always a Field Marshal.

# IV

# THE PALACE OF WESTMINSTER

WESTMINSTER is still technically a royal palace, though no king of England has lived in it for more than 400 years. But when Henry VIII moved out to more up-to-date lodgings, he left behind him in the old palace some of his royal functions, which lingered on there for centuries after their official connection with the monarch had withered away to a formal thread – the law courts, the embryo civil service, the exchequer, and the most ancient and important of all royal prerogatives, which stretches back into the oblivion of the black ages, the function of meeting with the Witenagemot, the national assembly of the *witan*, the 'wise men' of the land. This assembly still meets there above the foundations of buildings that have been there for at least 900 years. It came to be called a great parley, or 'Parliament', in the thirteenth century.

In the dim days before London Bridge was built, Westminster, called Thorn-ea or Bramble Island, was important as the first ford across the Thames, which was a marshy mile wide at high tide at this point, and full of salmon instead of sewage. At low tide a man could wade across, guided by rows of stakes. Archaeology has shown that the Romans had a settlement at this strategic cross-roads. But which king first built a palace at Westminster is one of those questions, like what song the Sirens sang, puzzling, though not beyond all conjecture.

Kingston was the crowning place for Anglo-Saxon kings, and Winchester was their main palace. However, in those days the concept of a palace was primitive and informal. There was a royal church at Westminster from the beginning of the seventh century. Legend alleges that the Danish immigrant Canute built the first palace at Westminster for his itinerant court and his horde of house-carles. Westminster is one of the traditional scenes for the one story that everybody knows about Cnut, King: his argument with sycophantic courtiers about the rising tide. Southampton is another candidate for the honour.

With Edward the Confessor we leave the marshy ground of legend for fairly firm facts. He built a residence at Westminster while he was rebuilding the monastery and its church. The chroniclers agree that he spent his last days here, saw his remarkable visions, and died in the room which was afterwards called the Painted Chamber, because of the frescoes on the walls of the wars of the bellicose Maccabees, and scenes from the life of Edward himself. This huge, historic room stood until Victoria's reign. Edward spent a tenth of his substance 'in gold, silver, cattle and all other possessions' on his buildings at Westminster. But it is impossible to recreate in the imagination more than misty fragments of his palace. It was, we are told, 'an incomparable structure furnished with a breastwork and bastion'. He seems to have introduced the revolutionary idea of having a separate bedroom to sleep in.

We know the titles of some of Edward's officials who lived in the palace – the Marshal; the Stallere (*Comes stabuli*, or Constable); the Bower-Thane (Chamberlain); the Dish-Thane (*Seneschal*); the Hordere (*Treasurer*); Carver, Cup-Bearer, Wardrobe-Thane, Harper, Headsman, and so on. There seems to have been a fairly regular council and crown-wearing ceremony at Westminster over Whitsun, but courts and kings were so naturally peripatetic in the Middle Ages that for centuries Westminster was not so much a regular royal residence, more one of several official addresses.

William the Conqueror had himself crowned at Westminster, escorted by steely ranks of mailed knights, to demonstrate his legitimacy, at least to the throne. William according to the chronicler 'so stark and fierce that none dared resist his will', seems to have been too busy building motte-and-bailey castles around the country in order to hold fast his conquest to have time for doing much to Westminster. But a picture of Westminster Palace is embroidered in the Bayeux tapestry. And the *Anglo-Saxon Chronicle* describes his solemn court and crown-wearing there at Whitsun. In practice the Conqueror's reign was so disrupted by rebellion, crisis, and travels to his continental dominions that this schedule was more honoured in the breach than the observance. But the old crown-wearing assembly which he sometimes observed at Westminster went back in its origins beyond the oldest annals of the English race to the days of the sacrificial king, and to the remoter speculations of anthropology. The crown-wearing gathering in Westminster Palace still survives today, as the state opening of Parliament, which must make it the oldest continuous assembly in the world.

The Conqueror's son, red-faced William Rufus, built a great hall in the old palace, the foundation and shell of the majestic Westminster Hall which still broods there, nowadays used almost exclusively for lyings-in-state. His hall was 239 feet 6 inches long, 67 feet 6 inches wide, with a gallery round the inside 20 feet above the ground. Two rows of pillars down the middle divided the hall into three aisles, and supported the roof. There was a hole in the ceiling to let out the smoke from the huge open hearth. A chronicler reports that one of Rufus's attendants said, with some courage, that the new hall was much larger than was needed. 'To which the King replied that it was not half large enough.' Matthew Paris, writing almost a century and a half later, gives the King the famous line: 'It is a mere bedchamber compared with what I had intended to build.' The phrase fits the imperious image of a man who said 'Kings never drown', when they tried to stop him crossing the Channel in a storm. The building was paid for partly from the revenue of vacant bishoprics, and partly from taxes so heavy that the *Anglo-Saxon Chronicle*, not exactly unbiased in the matter, says that 'many men perished from want'. In 1099 the King 'at Whitsuntide held his court for the first time in his new hall, at Westminster'. But the great hall was never a place of council. From the beginning its function was for public pageantry, proclamation, and coronation feast.

William was shot with a Norman arrow while hunting in the New Forest. In those days the succession was a distinctly nervous time, and his younger brother Henry hurried hastily sixty-five miles in two days to be crowned at Westminster, and tactfully if unconvincingly issued a charter promising to 'abolish all the evil practices with which the realm of England was unjustly oppressed'. Henry seems to have started the gradual division of the king's judicial powers between the courts of Exchequer, Common Pleas, and the King's Bench. Over the years the law stopped perambulating around with the king, and became anchored at Westminster, until the lawyers emigrated to the Strand in 1882.

The accounts of Henry I's household at Westminster go into considerable and curious detail. For instance the King's ewerer is allowed 1d a day for drying the King's clothes after a journey; and 4d on the rare occasions when he took a bath, apart from his ceremonial baths at the crown-wearings at Christmas, Easter, and Whitsun.

After Henry's death in Normandy came the anarchy. In order to win support among the magnates, the rival claimants Stephen and Matilda created earls as lavishly as a modern Prime Minster packing the House of

Lords with Life Peers. In 1136 Stephen held a full council at Westminster, 'and never was there held council in England more splendid in number and greatness [of those present, and] in gold, silver, jewels, clothes and all sorts of wealth.'

Tradition says that Stephen found time in the turbulence to build St Stephen's Chapel in Westminster Palace to his patron Saint. In the crypt of this Chapel, which was built by Edward I, Members of Parliament still christen their infants.

Chaos was ended by the accession of Matilda's son Henry Plantagenet, that formidable, ambitious, energetic king, whose court was a bedlam of panic peregrination and unseasonable *chevauchées* on the spur of the moment. 'He never sits down,' wrote Walter Map; 'he is always on his legs from morning till night.' And 'it pleased his humour to vex his stewards with the pandemonium and uncertainty of his plans'. He was crowned at Westminster in the presence of 'an innumerable multitude of people', to relieved cries of 'Vivat Rex' from the Normans, and 'Waes Hael' from the Saxon burghers. But the palace had been so stripped by Stephen's followers that it was uninhabitable, and the Plantagenets had to take up residence in Bermondsey opposite the Tower. Thomas Becket was ordered to have the dilapidated palace of Westminster restored as the official royal residence in London. Becket's ancient biographer, William Fitz-Stephen, says that the great work, undertaken in a hurry, was completed between Easter and Whitsun with such a babel of activity on the site that men could not hear each other speak. In any case, after it was repaired, Henry still preferred to hold his councils at the royal hunting-lodges, Clarendon, Woodstock, or Geddington, rather than in the traditional centres. He seldom stayed more than a few days in one place, and during the whole of his long reign he was only in Westminster Palace on seventeen occasions.

A man called Alnoth was Henry's '*ingeniator*', or clerk of the works at Westminster. The accounts show that in 1163 he was given 10s to have the palace cleaned, and another 10s for rushes for the floor. Four years later he was given the large sum of £190 for what must have been extensive repairs, and in the next year £64 for work on the 'new hall', and 'the Queen's chamber'. Alnoth's salary was £7 10s a year.

At a council at Westminster in 1163 Henry had his first public clash with his old favourite friend Becket over the acrimonious contemporary issue of the trials of persons in holy orders accused of serious crimes, the 'criminous clerks'. The quarrel boiled up next year to Henry's ominous question: 'Has the island grown too narrow to contain us both?' The echoing halls of Westminster Palace were perpetually disturbed in this century by the power struggle on the intricate feudal chess-board, the never-ending feuds of the Plantagenet house, the ravenous-falcon nego- tiations over the carving-up of Eleanor of Aquitaine's huge dowry; by thunder and lightning of excommunication, anathema, and Antipope at Cologne; above all by the jockeying for the succession. In an ingenious attempt to establish his dynasty over his shaky, centrifugal dominions, Henry had his heir crowned at Westminster during his own life-time.

The ceremony itself was a slightly suspect, second-rate affair, since it took place without the blessings of either the Pope or the Archbishop of Canterbury, Becket, who was in exile. To make up for this, the feastings in Westminster Palace afterwards were unusually extravagant. Curt- mantle himself brought in the boar's head, 'with trumpets before it according to the manner', and served his son on bended knee. The Archbishop of York made an obsequious joke: 'Not every prince can be served at table by a king.' To which Prince Henry, showing the cold arrogance of his family, replied: 'Certainly it can be no condescension for the son of a count to serve the son of a king.' Perhaps it was meant to be a joke. But a chronicler, writing within a hundred years of the feast, comments: 'Thus the young man of an evil and perverse nature was puffed up in pride by his father's unseemly doing.' The Prince eventually died in arms against his father.

Richard Lion Heart spent little time in his palace of Westminster. But then he spent only six months of his reign of ten years in England, and went on record that he would sell London itself to raise money for his crusade, if he could find a purchaser. At least his coronation feast at Westminster seems to have been brilliant, according to Ambrose, a French eye-witness: 'Little time was gone by ere he had himself crowned at London. There did I see great gifts given, and I saw such abundance of meats set forth that none might keep tally thereof; nor ever in my life have I seen a court served in nobler fashion. And I saw vessels of great price in that hall so fair, and tables saw I so close pressed together that they could in no wise be numbered.'

We catch brief glimpses of the next king, John, at Westminster Palace. De rigueur by now, he was crowned in the Abbey, and feasted in the great hall. The records show that he kept the Christmas of 1212 in Westminster Palace, and had a ceremonial bath at a cost of 6d. They also show that he had a new lavatory built in the palace, and gave 'the old tin lavatory' to the Abbot of Waltham Holy Cross. But so much of John Lackland's life was spent in travelling to try to deal with civil war, rebellion, foreign invasion, and the loss of his overseas possessions, that he had little time to devote to such domestic details or to Westminster.

By contrast his son Henry III, who succeeded at the age of nine, was a great Westminster-resident, and spent, for those days, much of his reign of fifty-six years in, and much money on, his favourite palace. By 1261 he had lavished the enormous sum of £29,345 19s 8d on his works at Westminster, which included rebuilding most of the Abbey church. The Rolls are full of detail of payments for work in the palace. For example, in 1244 nearly £2,000 was paid to the clerk of the works for building 'a new chamber near to our hall . . . and our conduit and other works there'. From the conduit, which was set up to supply the kitchens and lavatory with Thames water, a pipe 'of the size of a goose quill' was to be run off to the clerk's private apartments. In the next year a great porch was built in the palace 'so that the King can descend in it from his horse with befitting dignity and go under it'.

Much interior decoration was also done. The King's great bedroom (that is, the Painted Chamber) was painted 'a good green colour in the manner of a curtain', and was also decorated with its heroic frescoes on the walls. Over the door was inscribed the motto, in ancient French: '*Ke ne dune ke ne tine ne pret ke desire*'. Which apparently means in modern English: 'the man who doesn't give what he has doesn't get what he wants'. In the 'wardrobe where the King was accustomed to wash his face was painted a picture representing the King who was rescued by his dog from the seditious barons who plotted against him'.

Under Henry the palace sprawled out into a congested, animated small town with four chapels and the biggest kitchens in Europe. Henry's wedding feast in Westminster Hall was described by Matthew Paris, who was there. The citizens of London supplied the wine. The citizens of Winchester were in charge of the kitchens and the table linen. The hall was congested with waiters, jesters, hordes of *histriones* or players, and great officials of the court, whose duties were to pour water over the royal hands, or to remove (and keep) the dirty dishes. Paris, unfortunately, is afflicted with a sudden spasm of aposiopesis, and says he is unable adequately to describe 'the dainties of the table and the abundance of divers liquors . . . the quantities of game and varieties of fish'. After the party there were 'royal solemnities and goodly jousting' lasting eight days in Tothill Fields beside the palace.

Historically the two immense events at Westminster Palace of Henry III's reign were the beginning of the formal connection between Parliament and Westminster, and the crystallisation of the idea that the law courts should have a permanent base there. Councils and courts were held in other places afterwards. But government was becoming more centralised. The king was becoming more stationary. And from now on Westminster Palace is increasingly the official centre for Parliament and justice. Henry's attempts to wriggle out of his oath to keep the terms of the Great Charter; his imaginative methods of raising money in order to finance his unsuccessful expeditions to recover his lost inheritance across the Channel; his upstart, arrogant foreign favourites imported mostly from Poitou, eventually drove his wolfish magnates into open revolt. When Simon de Montfort in 1264 sent out writs summoning the pre-lates, barons, and 'communitas' to Parliament in Westminster Hall in January 1265, he was starting a formal link between Westminster and Parliament which looks like lasting for ever. De Montfort was inspired not so much by a thirst for democracy and freedom of speech, as by his own feudal and autocratic ambitions and fears.

In the same way, during Henry's reign the *Curia Domini Regis*, or court of the King's Bench, and the other wandering courts came to rest in Westminster Hall, which from now on was crowded with lawyers, litigants, students, sightseers, gossip, stalls selling the latest political pamphlets and the oldest food, booths offering for sale everything from hats to sweets, and men of straw, who showed their willingness to act as a witness for either side for a consideration by wearing a piece of straw in their boots.

King Alexander of Scotland came to the coronation feast of the new king, Edward I, in Westminster Hall. He brought with him a hundred knights who shattered their national reputation for financial canniness because, 'as soon as they had dismounted, they turned their steeds loose for anyone to catch and keep that thought proper'. In order not to lose face, the English knights followed suit, and the palace was filled with stampeding horses, and scrummaging prospective horse-owners. For the coronation 'the aqueduct in Chepe poured forth white wine and red like rain-water, for those who would to drink as they pleased'. The menu at the feast promised 440 oxen and cows, 430 sheep, 450 pigs, 16 fat boars, 278 flitches of bacon, and 22,460 'capons and other poultry'.

The major state events at Westminster during Edward's reign were the

trial of William Wallace for treason in Westminster Hall; and the development of the rhythm and rights of Parliament at Westminster. Wallace,
with a mocking wreath of laurel on his head, was described by John
Fordun, a man whose father may have seen him at his trial. 'He was of a
tall, almost gigantic stature, broad-shouldered, large-boned with long
muscular arms, yet thin in the shanks, and unencumbered by much flesh
or fat round the reins.' His defence, unassailable under feudal law, was
that he owed no allegiance to Edward to be betrayed, and therefore could
not betray it or be a traitor. Nevertheless, for nearly another four centuries a treason trial was just another phrase for judicial murder of the
inconvenient, and Wallace was dragged to the customary, revolting death
introduced into England by the Normans.

In the last years of Edward I the palace fell into considerable decay
because of economic difficulties. But Edward II at once started a programme of repair and rebuilding. He built a 'White chamber . . . the
chamber which is for the private bed of the king', and the huge old bedroom, the 'Painted Chamber', was from now on used entirely for meetings
of the magnates, and other public business. A traveller during this reign
wrote: 'Near the abbey stands that celebrated palace of the Kings of
England . . . on whose walls all the warlike scenes of the Bible are painted
with marvellous skill.'

Edward III performed the most significant act of his reign, the declaration of his interminable and futile war with France, at Westminster.
Froissart says that war was declared

. . . at the Palace of Westminster; and the Great Hall was all full of prelates, nobles
and counsellors from the cities and good towns of England. And there all men were
set down on stools, that each might see the king more at his ease. And the said king
was seated like a pontiff, in cloth of Rouen, with a crown on his head, and a royal
sceptre in his hand. And two degrees lower sat prelate, earl, and baron; and yet
below them were more than six hundred knights.

When the wars gave him time, Edward was a great builder-king, and
under his patronage the English Gothic style grew to glory. In the
accounts of his rebuilding at Westminster 'the house called Hell' underneath the Exchequer building first impinges on history. It was, unsurprisingly, a prison. And so was the building with the almost equally
uninviting name of Purgatory'. Edward's chief contributions to the palace
were the great bell 'Edward of Westminster', weighing 9,261 lb, on its
clock-tower, the decoration of St Stephen's Chapel, and new public rooms
like the 'Chambre des Étoiles', the Star Chamber. Did the 'star' come

from the stellar ornamentation on the ceiling, or from the 'starrs' or bonds which since the Conquest Jewish traders had been required to deposit at Westminster?

In 1377 another boy came to the throne, who once again made immense improvements and alterations to Westminster Palace. Edward III's ten-year-old grandson Richard II had a reign that was a political disaster, troubled with the Peasant revolt, and perpetual quarrels with his uncles, and ending in deposition and ugly death. But culturally it was brilliant. The young king with the dark yellow hair was an aesthete, interested in beauty, books, exotic cooking, and especially in clothes. Under him English court culture moved into a new dimension of elegance, elaborate ceremonial, civilian urbanity, bright colours, a blossoming of the arts, and astonishing head-dresses. Courtiers 'wore their estates on their backs'.

The new cultural *ambiance* of court showed in the architecture as well as in everything else. For example, the accounts reveal that Richard installed two large bronze taps at Westminster, 'for the King's bath to bring hot and cold water into the bath'. He commissioned thirteen stone statues of the kings from Edward the Confessor onwards to decorate the palace, as well two larger statues of the Confessor and himself. He installed marble pillars. He built a bell-tower and a new Great Gateway. Geoffrey Chaucer was his clerk of the works for two years while Richard was enlarging and modernising the Palace of Westminster.

But Richard's lasting memorial and contribution to the palace was the rebuilding of William Rufus's Great Hall into the form in which it still stands today. In 1393 orders were given 'to repair the Great Hall within the Palace of Westminster, to take masons, carpenters and other work-men, and set them to the said repairs; and also to take such stone as should be necessary for the work; and to sell to the king's use the old materials of the hall together with a certain old bridge over the Thames . . .'

The two aged men who collaborated on the great building were the most famous stone-mason in London, Henry Yevele; and the master carpenter Hugh Herland, who with his new hammer-beams, struts, and braces could vault the soaring sixty-eight feet of the hall in a single swoop without the old supporting pillars.

Yevele buttressed the walls to support the monstrous downthrust of the roof, raised them two feet, and covered them with new stone. The string course was decorated with the King's badge, the sad, symbolic white hart with a chain round its neck. The oak beams for the roof were brought from Sussex and from Kingston-on-Thames, and were twenty-three feet long and two and a quarter feet wide. Huge angels were carved at the end of the hammer-beams. In niches of the walls stood the statues of the kings. The roof outside was covered with lead, and it took fifty pounds of tin to solder the drain pipes. The heavy cost of rebuilding was paid for by a special tax on foreign immigrants who had come to live in England. In all Richard spent £12,304 on his works at Westminster during his last years.

The Great Hall was virtually finished in 1399. Ironically its first use was for the extraordinary meeting of Parliament on September 30 to depose Richard. 'The duke of Lancaster and the other dukes and lords spiritual and temporal and the people of the realm in great numbers' assembled there 'in the place duly prepared for holding parliament'. The throne 'solemnly adorned with cloth of gold' was vacant. A schedule of thirty-three charges of misgovernment was read out, laying much emphasis throughout on Richard's perjury. Henry IV claimed the vacant throne 'by right of descent vindicated by conquest'. And 'the estates, with the whole people, unanimously agreed that the duke should rule over them'.

Something of what Westminster Palace was like to live in emerges from Chaucer's court poem, the 'Book of the Duchesse'. It gives a description of a courtier's perfect billet in a royal palace:

> and sooth to seyn my chambre was
> Full well depeynted and with glas
> were all the windows well y glased.
> . . . . . . . .
> and alle the walles with colour fyne
> were peynted bothe text and glose
> of al the Romaunce of the Rose.

The bed sounds equally gorgeous

> I will yive him a fether bed
> Rayed with golde and right wel cled
> In fyn blak satin doutremere
> and many a pilow.

It has been calculated that 20,000 people lived in Westminster Palace in Richard's court, and had 'bouche of court', or board and lodging, pay and arms. They ranged from the *Dapifer Angliae*, Lord High Steward, Constable, Marshal, and Chamberlain, to the regiments of coopers, artillers, bowyers and fletchers, brewers and blacksmiths, armourers and pavilioners, and the 4,000 archers Richard kept always with him.

A contemporary rhyming chronicler, John Hardyng, wrote of Westminster Palace, in his customary agonising verse:

> Truly I herd Robert Ireliffe say,
>   Clerk of the Green Cloth, that to the household
> Came every daye, for moost partie alwaye,
>   Ten thousand folke by his messe is told,
>   That followed the hous, aye, as thei would;
> And in the kechin three hundred servitours,
> And in eche office many occupiours.
> And ladies faire, with their gentilwomen,
>   Chamberers also and lavenders . . .

These statistics evidently do not include wives and children, who also lived in the congested little royal city.

It is possible, very roughly, to visualise what Westminster Palace looked like in the fourteenth century. It was entirely surrounded by a wall, and most of the many buildings inside it lay between Westminster Hall and the river. The King's private apartments, the Great Palace, the Privy Palace, and the Prince's Palace were two-storey buildings of stone looking out on the Thames, and the immense flocks of stately-sailing swans. Their feathers were picked once a year to upholster the palace furniture. Paul Hentzner, visiting London two centuries later, was particularly impressed by the sight: the river 'abounds in swans, swimming in flocks; the sight of them and their noise is vastly agreeable to the fleets that meet them in their course'.

There was a water gate called the King's Stairs leading from the river into the palace, and a postern at the Queen's Stairs. An underground passage led from the palace to Westminster Abbey. The outer bailey or courtyard with its clock tower stood where New Palace Yard stands today, and was used for parades, tournaments, and large exercises involving horses. The inner bailey surrounded by the palace buildings was where Old Palace Yard is today. Huddled everywhere were jumbled tenements of lath-and-plaster where courtiers lodged. The most famous buildings of which any reliable record survives lay in a cluster just south and upstream of Westminster Hall – St Stephen's Chapel, the White Hall, which was later used as the House of Lords, and the Painted Chamber.

For the next century Westminster Palace was the building in the background of the stormy and sinister politics of England as the Wars of the Roses and the Middle Ages dragged to an end. But there was no time between the wars and rebellions, the making and unmaking of kings, to do any major building at the palace. Westminster crops up in the chronicles, for Parliaments, state trials, and always for coronation feasts, whose glutinous menus are now recorded in lip-licking detail – bitterns and peacocks, fritters and young eagles, quinces in confit, and sticky 'subtleties' *ad nauseam.*

Then, early in Henry VIII's reign, that persistent old enemy of palaces, fire, burnt down most of the living quarters at Westminster. Henry, who was in any case impatient with medieval standards of comfort and plumbing, moved his residence out of Westminster into other modern accommodation, more suitable to his inflated idea of his own importance. 'Since which time,' wrote a chronicler later in the century, 'it hath not been re-edified; only the Great Hall with the offices near adjoining are kept in good repair, and it serveth, as before it did, for feasts at coronations, arraignments of great persons, and keeping of the courts of justice. But the princes have been lodged in other places, as at Whitehall and St James's.'

By Elizabeth's time even the memory of the Gothic grandeur of the old palace was fading from men's minds. The antiquary John Norden records that Westminster was once the chief residence of the king, 'though now brought to the ground, and green grass grows where it stood . . . The place which now carrieth the name of the Old Palace showeth itself to have been in times past full of buildings'. He found 'apparent tokens in a wall yet standing, that there were many vaults, cellars, and such like offices, in that place which is now a plain field', and near by, 'certain towers which seem to have been parcel of that Palace'. As he stood among the overgrown mounds of rubble, the melancholy tag from Juvenal, 'there is nothing but shall come to ruin, be it now never so glorious in the earth', came gratifyingly into his mind.

The kings had departed. But the considerable remains of old Westminster continued to be used for state trials, for the more humdrum business of the daily law, and for Parliament. King Charles I was tried and condemned to death in Westminster Hall by his sixty-eight judges, or regicides, depending on a man's ideological bias. The judges waited nervously in the Painted Chamber for the King to arrive by river. When they heard he was coming, Cromwell ran to the window: 'He turned as white as the wall. Returning to the board . . . he said thus: "My masters, he is come, he is come, and now we are doing that great work that the whole nation will be full of."' After the sentence the commissioners signed the death warrant, again in the Painted Chamber, with Cromwell guiding the pens of the more timid, and splashing their faces

The Palace of Westminster from the Thames. An etching by Wenceslaus Hollar, 1647

*Photo Mansell Collection*

A 19th century view of Windsor, engraved after a painting by Birket Foster

with ink in grim horseplay after the tension. 'I tell you,' he boasted, 'we will cut off his head with the crown upon it.'

The one specifically domestic royal event which continued to be staged at Westminster for some centuries was the omnivorous orgy of the coronation feast, which still traditionally took place in Westminster Hall. At Charles II's coronation Pepys characteristically slipped away early from the service in the Abbey to be sure of a good place in the Hall, and managed to obtain from one of the tables four rabbits and a pullet. He ate these with his friends, while taking 'a great deal of pleasure to go up and down, and look upon the ladies'. He ended the great day of bonfires and jubilant boozing, as usual a-bed: 'but my head began to turn, and I to vomitt, and if ever I was foxed, it was now'.

The last coronation feast held in Westminster Hall was that of George IV, who made sure that the final faint residential connection of the kings with Westminster ended with a bang rather than a whimper. Preparations lasted for months, and the total cost of the coronation was £243,390 6s 2d. The menu included 160 tureens of soup (80 of turtle, 40 of rice, 40 of vermicelli); 160 dishes of fish (80 of turbot, 40 of trout, 40 of salmon); 160 hot joints (80 of venison, 40 of roast beef with three barons, 40 of mutton and veal); 160 dishes of vegetables (potatoes, peas, and cauliflowers); 480 sauce boats (240 of lobster, 120 of butter, 120 of mint); 80 dishes of braised ham; 80 savoury pies; 80 dishes of daubed geese (two on each dish); 80 dishes of savoury cakes; 80 pieces of braised beef; 80 dishes of braised capons; 1,190 side dishes; 320 dishes of mounted pastry; 320 dishes of small pastry; 400 dishes of jellies and creams, 160 dishes of shell-fish (80 of lobster and 80 of crayfish); 160 dishes of cold roast fowl; 80 dishes of cold house lamb.

The heat from the huge chandeliers hanging overhead was infernal, and wax cascaded in Niagaras over all the magnificent hired robes. The ladies, as usual, were confined in the galleries, and only allowed to watch the men eating. They were soon famished, and one peer was seen tying up a chicken in his handkerchief and throwing it up to his son. After the official banquet, there was a mass onslaught on the remains by the ravenous spectators: 'Sweetmeats, pastry and confectionery of all sorts vanished with the rapidity of lightning; the distinctions of sex, and almost the common rules of politeness, seemed to have been forgotten.'

In 1834 furious fire destroyed the Painted Chamber and all the other remains of the Palace of Westminster, except for the Great Hall and the crypt of St Stephen's. The fire started because the Exchequer decided to dispose of its vast accumulation of old wooden tallies: the pegs on which civil servants had notched their accounts from time immemorial until, astonishingly, as late as 1826. Official secrecy would not let the stocks be given away as firewood. So they were shovelled into a stove in the House of Lords, once the White Hall, the private bedroom of medieval kings. The stove became so hot that it set fire to the panelling. The panelling set fire to the House of Lords. The House of Lords set fire to St Stephen's Chapel and the Painted Chamber. And all of the old palace, with its memories and some of its masonry going back 800 years, went up in smoke. Except for the Great Hall, which still stands today, empty, impressive, and silent, but for the mating tick of the death-watch beetle, and the persistent technology of the Ministry of Public Building and Works, trying to smoke out the elusive little *Xestobium rufovillosum*.

# V

# WINDSOR CASTLE

IN the year after the Restoration, enthusiastic Samuel Pepys paid a visit to Windsor Castle. That night he wrote categorically in his diary: 'It is the most romantique castle that is in the world.' This is still the conventional view of the thousands of tourists who descend upon Windsor each summer to inspect one of the oldest homes of kings in the world still in occupation, or to watch the torrent of stately plumes and pageantry and ancient, reptilian public faces oozing down the old grey hill of the Castle to the Garter Service. The Castle lies 'couched like the swan upon her nest in the silvery Thames below', and is described in many other similarly ecstatic similes.

There is considerable truth in the conventional picture. It *is* a romantic place. The heath stone from Bagshot with which it is built is silicate and crystalline, and is therefore washed as clean as new by every shower of rain. So the Castle does not show its age. It glistens like a fairy-tale palace, or, by a stretch of the imagination, a silvery swan.

Windsor Castle and its romantic 900 years of history have attracted numerous, voluminous, learned, and favourably-disposed writers. As a change and an antidote to the full justice that has been done to the sunny side of Windsor, this chapter will concentrate on the less well-known sombre patches of its history. It will be a disenchanted, worm's-eye-view of Windsor by people who did not share Pepys's enthusiasm about its romance.

For instance, solemn, precocious, pathetic Edward VI said of Windsor when he was twelve: 'Methinks I am in prison. Here be no galleries, nor no gardens to walk in.' George III's Queen Charlotte was lukewarm in every sense about her new home at Windsor. Four November days after she moved in she wrote to a friend: 'We are now returned to our new habitation in the castle. Not to shock you . . . with my opinion on this subject I will briefly tell you that I have changed from a very comfortable and warm habitation to the coldest house, rooms and passages that ever existed'.

Romantic palace, or draughty prison, one general tendency of Windsor is unique. It developed in precisely the opposite direction to the normal pattern of a royal palace. Most major palaces start life as comparatively private residences of a king, and gradually become congested with officials, ministers, courtiers, ceremonial, and business. The over-crowded monarch then moves out into a new, fine and private place. And this is soon saturated in turn by the inevitable and essential parasites of royalty. Windsor, on the contrary, began as one of the great fortresses of Britain, a master-key of the kingdom, commanding the most important main road in the country, the Thames. It was the stage for councils and state ceremonials, for summit politics and international feasts. Down the centuries, as the country has become less violent and fortresses less crucial, Windsor has imperceptibly turned into the chief country retreat and relatively private residence of kings.

William the Conqueror built the first fortress at Windsor, three miles upstream from the hunting-lodge of Saxon kings at Old Windsor. It was the largest link in a chain of strongholds he threw around London to dominate his capital, and subdue his new kingdom. He built it on top of a steep chalk cliff, by the usual Norman method of digging a circular moat, and heaping a fifty-foot 'mount' in the middle, like a sand-castle. On top of the mound perched the *donjon*, or keep. On either side of the mound were two baileys, or courtyards. And, surrounding the whole thirteen-acre motte-and-bailey complex on the cliff-top, was a massive stockade.

William's castle was entirely built of wood. This was partly because the Normans were in a tearing hurry to get their grip on a hostile countryside; they threw up eighty-five similar castles around the country in twenty years. As the chronicle complains: the Normans 'wrought castles widely throughout the nation, and oppressed poor folk'. They had no masons, but any amount of timber; Windsor was in the middle of a vast, ancient royal forest of oak and beech. And in any case the fresh-piled mound had not settled down solid enough to carry the weight of stone walls.

The earliest mention of Windsor Castle is in the Domesday survey of 1086; the records show that William rented the site from its owner for twelve shillings a year.

Some idea of the importance of Windsor for the Normans as a state palace is given, for instance, in the *Anglo-Saxon Chronicle* under the year

1126: 'This year King Henry [I] held his court at Windsor, and David, king of Scots, was there, and all the chief men, both clerics and laymen, that were in England. And there he caused archbishops and bishops and abbots and earls and all the thegns that were there to swear to give England and Normandy after his death into the hand of his daughter Athelic [alias Maud, or Matilda].' This Christmas court at Windsor was enlivened by an acrimonious and physical squabble between the Archbishops of Canterbury and York about who was to put the crown on the king's head, one of many such violent ecclesiastical clashes of the period.

Maud's son, Henry II, the first Plantagenet, replaced the wooden stockades of his great-grandfather with stone walls and towers. Great blocks of stone were brought ten miles from Bagshot for the half-mile of tall masonry he built at Windsor. And from now on the account Rolls begin to show in detail and medieval Latin money spent on buildings at Windsor. One of the earliest and grimly evocative entries is for 1184, when Henry came home from one of his long visits to Normandy, and kept Christmas at Windsor. The accounts record that 8s 9d was spent '*in Emendatione Gaiole*' – for mending the jail, which was evidently an early and much-used building in the romantic palace. To look on the bright side, 37s 7d was spent 'on the work of the King's larder'.

Henry began to build the most characteristic feature of Windsor, the Round Tower, on top of the mound, which had now hardened into a foundation firm enough to hold the mass of masonry. Some idea of the high living at Henry's glamorous court at Windsor is given in a letter by Peter of Blois, one of the great scholars of Europe, who was in residence there. The court's constant peregrinations, he says, condemn the scholar with his love of sedentary life to a continual purgatory. He finds himself served with the scrambled, rough-and-ready meals of the traveller:

bread hastily made, without leaven, from the dregs of the ale-tub; leaden bread, bread of tares, bread unbaken. The wine is turned sour or mouldy; thick, greasy, stale, flat and smacking of pitch [from the cask]. I have sometimes seen even great lords served with wine so muddy that a man must needs close his eyes, and clench his teeth, wry-mouthed and shuddering, and filtering the stuff rather than drinking. The ale which men drink in that place is horrid to the taste and abominable to the sight. There, also, such is the concourse of people that sick and whole beasts are sold at random, with fishes even four days old; yet shall not all this corruption and stench abate one penny of the price; for the servants reck not whether an unhappy guest fall sick and die, so that their lords' tables be served with a multitude of dishes; thus we who sit at meat must needs fill our bellies with carrion, and become graves (as it were) for sundry corpses.

And then, just when the wretched retinue hopes to have dinner and go to sleep, the King suddenly takes it into his head to move on to a new palace.

Then may ye see men rush forth like madmen, sumpter-mules jostling sumpter-mules and chariots clashing against chariots in frantic confusion, a very Pandemonium made visible. . . . The abyss seems to have been opened, and hell to vomit forth his legions.

Nor does Henry's private life at Windsor seem to have been particularly attractive. In his livid Angevin rages he used to hurl himself on the floor and grind the rushes with his teeth.

This curious habit was inherited by his son John, who gave a memorable performance of it to work off the frustration of being made to sign Magna Carta. Under John Windsor was again much in demand as a grim prison. The King quarrelled with a former favourite William de Braose, who ran away overseas. John seized his wife and son, and locked them up in a tower at Windsor with only a piece of raw bacon and a sheaf of wheat as rations. After eleven days the tower was opened, and both prisoners were discovered distinctly dead. Lady de Braose was 'sitting upright between her son's legs, with her head leaning back on his breast, whilst he was also in a sitting position, with his face turned towards the ground. Maud de Braose, in her last pangs of hunger, had gnawed the cheeks of her son, then probably dead, and after this effort she appeared to have fallen into the position in which she was found'.

As well as hideous cannibalism, Windsor was the scene of pretty nauseous gluttony under John, who, according to one authority, 'loved the castle above all others'. For his Christmas court there in 1213 the sheriffs of the neighbouring counties were ordered to send to Windsor 3,000 capons, 15,000 herrings, 1,000 salted eels, 400 pigs, 100 pounds of fresh almonds, 6,000 gallons of wine, and four casks of best wine for the King's private swilling.

In this reign Windsor also became one of the very few British royal palaces ever to see any serious and messy fighting. After signing the Magna Carta in 1215, in a foaming frenzy of humiliation at the 'five and twenty over-kings' he had been given, John tried to get the Pope to release him from his oath. The dogged barons rebelled again, and brought in French allies. With a great army they laid siege to Windsor which was defended only by the Constable, Engelard de Cygony, 'a man very skilful in the art of war', assisted by sixty knights, and their attendant arrow-fodder. The barons 'brought engines of war close up to the castle, and fiercely attacked the defences'. A *petraria* hurled huge stones at the walls. The defenders made sorties at night by secret passages which led into the castle ditch, and twice cut through the beam of the boulder-bowling *petraria*. The lower bailey of Windsor was still partly protected by nothing more solid than earthworks and timber palisades. But the castle laughed to scorn a siege of three months, in which several of its buildings were reduced to rubble.

Eventually the frustrated barons gave up the siege, burned their battering machinery, and hurried off to chase John, who was ravaging their lands in East Anglia. And almost immediately, and suitably, he died, according to variant sources, 'from a surfeit of peaches and cider'; from a gluttonous debauch with lampreys; or, alternatively, less picturesquely, more probably, from appendicitis. The Round Tower seems to have received a considerable hammering during the siege. A writ of 1223 orders £20 from the treaury 'for smending the houses which are on the mount (*in mota*) of our castle of Windsor'.

John's son Henry III was a great building king, and did much at Windsor. The crusaders had brought back from the Middle East the revolutionary new concept that a D-shaped tower was more effective than the old-fashioned square ones, because it gave a better field of fire. Henry built D-shaped towers, and completed the circuit of stone walls around the castle. He also brought into the gaunt old stronghold something of comfort, and court-life, and culture for the first time, as well as his favourite green paint. The submerged social cost of these glorious improvements is hinted at, for instance, in a modest payment made in 1242 to 'our honest men of Windsor for the damage which they have sustained owing to the pulling down of their houses, on account of the ditch which we have caused to be made'.

A chronicler describes Windsor in Henry's reign as 'that very flourishing castle, than which, at that time, there was not another more splendid within the bounds of Europe'. The unromantic side of the coin is shown in the accounts – 'For 46 great nails for the step of the jail, and the step of the lodging over the gate of the tower: 6d; to mending a lock for the trapdoor of the jail: 1d.' Edward I gave feasts and tournaments at the castle whose lavish luxury was famous all over Europe; and he ordered seven new carpets for his bedroom at Windsor. On the underdog side of the picture, the Rolls are full of entries like that for 1297, when two women were paid one penny for the heavy work of carrying water for the workmen mending a tower in Windsor. A watchman at Windsor received 2d a day, and a chaplain 1d.

Edward III was born at Windsor, and brought many of its greatest glories to the castle. In January 1344 he had the absurdly romantic idea of founding a Round Table, a brotherhood of knights dedicated to chivalry and Arthurian idealism, and all the other imaginary and heroic old virtues, which were already obsolescent in the technological thunder of gunpowder on fourteeth-century battlefields. There was a tremendous feast at Windsor, according to one gratified guest, Adam de Murimuth, 'abounding in the most delicious drink until everybody was satisfied'. Afterwards, 'among the lords and ladies dances were not lacking, embraces and kisses alternately commingling'. There were then jousts for three days, in which the King and nineteen knights held the lists against all comers. Edward himself won three of the six prizes. A tactful spectator explained that this was 'not on account of the Royal favour, but by reason of the great labour which he sustained, and from the luck which he had'.

After that the King, with great pomp, 'took a corporeal oath that he would begin a Round Table in the same manner and condition as the Lord Arthur, formerly King of England, appointed it'. Then the kettle-drums and trumpets brayed all together. And the guests hurried to another orgy, 'which feast was complete with richness of fare, variety of dishes, and overflowing abundance of drinks: the delight was unutterable, the comfort inestimable, the enjoyment without murmuring, the hilarity without care'.

Work was started on a huge circular banqueting hall to house the Round Table, but the project was dropped in the following year because of the resumption of the French war, culminating in Crécy. But Edward, who was drunk with the glamour of heraldry and of gentle knights pricking on the plain, carried on with his dream by founding 'The Most Noble and amiable Company of St George, named the Garter', in 1348. The famous story of its origin suggests that fourteenth-century dances were as hazardous and informal as they are today. The most popular version is that Joan, the Fair Maid of Kent, whom Jean Froissart who was at court considered '*la plus belle dame de tout la roiaulme d'Engleterre, et la plus amoureuse*', dropped her blue garter while dancing with or near the King. Courtiers sniggered. Innuendoes flew through the air. And Edward, who was seized with 'a sparcle of fyne love that endured longe' for Joan, came to her rescue.

He picked up her garter and tied it round his own leg, uttering the almost immortal words, '*Honi soit qui mal y pense*' – Edward was the first English king since the Conquest to speak a little English, but he did not use it in ordinary conversation. The King went on, 'You make but small account of this garter, but within a few months I will cause the best of you all to reverence the like'. And he founded his order of knighthood whose members wore surcoats, mantles, and hoods, heavily embroidered with garters.

Later historians, horrified that so distinguished an order should be based on something as frivolous as a piece of female underwear, have suggested that the story is a myth, and that the garter is nothing to do with women's legs, just a vague symbol for unity and solidarity. In fact medieval chivalry was solidly based in sex rather than in chaste Tennysonian romance. The ladies not only gave away the prizes after a tournament, but sometimes acted as the prizes themselves. Other European orders of chivalry have as their badges articles of feminine clothing more intimate than a garter.

A highly ingenious and unromantic theory about the Garter, advanced by Dr Margaret Murray, is that it was a sign that the Fair Maid of Kent not only shook a lively leg in the dance, but also that she was head of a coven of witches. 'The confusion of the Countess was not from the shock to her modesty – it took more than a dropped garter to shock a lady of the fourteenth century – but the possession of that garter proved that she was not only a member of the Old Religion, but that she held the highest place in it.' Edward, by picking it up, showed that he was a devotee of the old religion of witches and devil-worshippers. This explanation sends a *frisson* of realism through the saccharine romance of Froissart. Unfortunately it depends entirely on French fifteenth-century evidence. And to have had sorcerous significance the garter should have been red.

The duties and privileges of a Knight of the Garter, his annual procession and pomp and gluttonous feasting, have been written about at length by many. It was not all gold and glittering romance, however. Some of his duties were stark and horrid. For example, at the annual service in April, 'After the Gospel is read, these two Relicks are to be brought, to wit, the Heart of St George by a Deacon, and his Fingers by a Sub-deacon, decently wrapped up in Knapkins and Coverings, which shall be reverently kissed by the Sovereign, and then by the Companions as the Order requires'.

The College of St George had an immense collection of holy bones and bits, which were a highly profitable tourist attraction. As well as the pieces of St George, it included a thorn of Christ's crown, some of his mother's milk, a piece of the Holy Cross, and enough ribs, skulls, and teeth of assorted saints to populate the Valley of Dry Bones. When St George's Chapel was repaired in the nineteenth century, there was great excitement when a hoard of bones was discovered hidden in holes in the fabric. Disappointingly, analysis reported that these were the bones of deer, picked up in the park by jackdaws, and discarded in the Chapel roof.

There was a daily mass in St George's Chapel for the Order of the Garter. To excuse the Knights themselves from the regular chore of church parade, the King established maintenance for an equal number of 'Poor Knights . . . decayed officers of gentle birth . . . impotent of themselves or inclining to poverty'. They earned their keep by attending the daily mass, as substitutes to pray for the souls of the Knights of the Garter.

Concurrent with his chivalrous charades, Edward did a lot of building at Windsor, under the supervision of William of Wykeham, the founder of Winchester and New College. Holinshed in his chronicles records that 'the King took in hand to repair that place, the rather indeed because he was born there, and therefore he took great pleasure to bestow cost in beautifying it with such buildings as may appear even unto this day'.

A worm's-eye-view of the sweat behind this beautifying emerges in the Rolls. For instance, under the year 1365 one Henry le Smythe is shown to have split no less than 156,200 heath stones at the quarries at Collingley near Bagshot. Whole woods were cut down as 600 oaks were worked into the building. In 1367 80 horses, 10 carts, and 20 men laboriously transported a reredos of alabaster from Nottingham to Windsor. And William of Wykeham got into trouble with his King by carving on the wall of a tower 'Hoc fecit Wykeham'. He escaped from his embarrassment by translating it to mean not the boast that Wykeham made the castle, but that the castle made Wykeham's name famous – which may have been inelegant Latin, but was good diplomacy.

Under Richard II Geoffrey Chaucer was clerk of the works at Windsor, and given the contract to restore 'our collegiate chapel of St George within our Castle of Windsor, which is threatened with ruin and on the point of falling to the ground, unless it be quickly repaired'. His salary was 2s a day. What a job like this actually meant in human terms in this period is hinted at dimly in the terms of Chaucer's commission, which gives him powers to 'impress' workmen of all sorts, to seize materials of every kind, and to force people to 'provide carriages for the same': and, automatically, to imprison 'refractory persons' in the castle jail, which was known for centuries by the black euphemism of the 'Colehouse'.

At Windsor Richard said good-bye to his pathetic, eleven-year-old second wife Isabel of France, before leaving on his fatal visit to Ireland. The little girl cried bitterly, and begged him not to leave her. She was partly pacified with sweets. The King lifted her in his arms and kissed her at least ten times, saying, 'Adieu, Madame, until we meet again.' The chronicler observes grimly: 'Great pity was it, for never saw they each other more.'

During the fifteenth century Windsor continued to be the main stage for pageantry, state visits, and the Garter ceremonies and banquets, with their bilious menus of 'soteltes' of marzipan and symbolism. Gentle Henry VI's chief contribution to the castle, and to England generally, was to found 'The King's College of Our Lady of Eton beside Windsor'. The bricks for the school were baked at a near-by hamlet on the Bath road called, forbiddingly, 'le slough'. Henry used to tell his scholars not to come to court at Windsor 'lest the young lambs should come to relish the corrupt deeds and habits of his courtiers'; and to admonish them in Latin words which are still invoked upon all King's scholars at Eton, to be 'good boys, gentle and teachable, and servants of the Lord'. A vivid idea of the uncouth court at Windsor in these days and of Henry's character emerges in the story that 'at Christmas time a certain great lord brought before him a Dance or show of young ladies with bared bosoms who were to dance in that guise before the King . . . who very angrily averted his eyes, turned his back upon them, and went out of his chamber, saying "Fy, fy, for shame"'.

Edward IV, who usurped Henry's throne, decided to pull down the decaying Chapel of St George at Windsor, and 'replace it by another and altogether more glorious building'. Partly his motive was to eclipse the glory of his predecessor's Chapel at Eton across the river, which for a time he considered razing in order to use its furniture at St George's. Partly it has always been the recurrent ambition of kings to build a splendid burial place where they can be the first to lie, to subsist in bones, and be Pyramidally extant. Whatever Edward's motives, this is the Chapel that stands at Windsor today, one of the world's great glories of the Gothic perpendicular style.

Henry VIII's chief architectural contribution to Windsor was to rebuild the entrance to the Lower Ward, where the gatehouse is still named after him. His reign at Windsor was predictably glamorous with the glitter of

Garter and other gaudy state ceremonial. The darker side of the story is notable because it contains the first full account of that rare and curious event, the degradation of a Knight of the Garter – an awful but ludicrous heraldic football scrummage. This unpleasant distinction happened in June 1521 to Edward, Duke of Buckingham, who was not among those present, having had his head cut off a month previously for alleged treason. From the choir of St George's, in front of the other Knights and a large congregation, Garter King of Arms solemnly proclaimed his offence and the formula for degradation.

Then Somerset Herald, who was waiting up in the roof with an axe for the cue words '. . . be expelled and put from among the Arms', violently cut down into the choir the crest, banner, and sword of the unfortunate Buckingham. And the other Knights 'spurned with their feete' these degraded objects through the Chapel, out of the Castle gate, and into the ditch, which was Windsor's open sewer in those days.

Under Henry the eating and swilling at Windsor were as exuberant as ever, probably more so, since the handsome young King with auburn hair was incredibly hearty about all his pleasures: 'He exercised himself daily in shooting, singing, dancing, wrestling, casting of the bar, playing at the recorders, flute, virginals; in setting of songs and making of ballads'. Even on paper some of his surviving menus at Windsor make the appetite sicken and die. For one dinner for thirty people he served 800 eggs, 90 dishes of butter, 80 loaves of chestnut bread, 300 wafers of marzipan, enough wine, ale, and beer for everybody to drink 20 pints each, six apples, seven pears, ten oranges per guest, plus the usual interminable, indigestible catalogue of main courses of beef, veal, lamb, capons, plovers, woodcock, partridges, herons, snipe, leverets, larks' tongues, *ad lib., ad nauseam.*

Not surprisingly in the circumstances, as he grew older Henry became monstrously fat. His successive suits of armour show that his waistline increased by seventeen inches in five years. 'He had a body and a half, very abdominous and unwieldy with fat. It was death to him to be dieted, so great his appetite, and death to him not to be dieted, so great his corpulency.' For adipose, and perhaps for lecherous, reasons, Henry's bed at Windsor was an impressive eleven feet square. And ropes and pulleys were installed to haul his huge, bad-tempered carcase up the stairs he was too fat to climb on his own.

The seamy side of all this feasting, what conditions were actually like in the Windsor kitchens and below stairs, is suggested in new court statutes of the period, the Eltham Ordinances. These found it necessary to forbid scullions in the royal kitchen to go about 'naked or in garments of such vilenesse as they now doe, and have been accustomed to do, nor lie in the nights and dayes in the kitchens or ground by the fire-side'. Waiters were warned not to wipe their greasy fingers on the tapestries. and not to put dishes down 'upon the King's bed for fear of hurting the King's rich counterpoints that lie thereon'.

Underneath the romance, life for the lower classes at Windsor tended to be as unromantic, nasty, brutish, and short as ever. In 1536, for example, a local butcher and a priest were hanged for speaking sympathetically of the Roman Catholics in the north, in their abortive rising known as the Pilgrimage of Grace. The accounts show an entry for 2d for nails for 'a new pair of gallows set up at the bridge and before the Castle gate', and 1s for the jailers who watched the prisoners for two nights. A few years later the three Windsor martyrs were burned at the stake outside the castle wall for the sin of extreme Protestantism. One of them, Testwood, was in the choir of St George's, and had earned the particular dislike of the Dean and canons by making mock of their relics and shrines which were so profitable for the tourist trade. Another, a priest called Pearson, covered his head with straw when the flames started: he 'pulling the straw unto him, layd a good deale thereof upon the top of his head, saying "This is God's hat; now am I dressed like a true soldier of Christ"'.

Under Elizabeth the first detailed topographical descriptions of the Castle began to be made. Paul Hentzner recorded that the English kings must have been attracted to Windsor by its 'deliciousness', and that the Castle was 'a town of proper extent, inexpugnable to any human force'.

Hentzner was equally enthusiastic about the view, 'a valley extended every way, and chequered with arable lands and pasture, cloathed up and down with the groves, and watered with that gentlest of rivers, the Thames'. He was inordinately impressed with the Queen's immense bed, 'covered with curious hangings of embroidery work', and the beds of her parents and grandparents 'all of them eleven feet square, covered with quilts shining with gold and silver'.

John Stow made a description of the Castle, which was more useful than his ingenious etymologies for the name. He suggested that it was called Windsor either because there was a ferry there with a rope and pulley, where passengers used to shout across to the far side: 'Wind us over.' Or, because of the height and the weather, it was called Windsor 'because ye *wynd* is *sore* and ye ayre very subtile and percynge there'.

Elizabeth built a stone terrace along the edge of the cliff on the north of the Castle; a gallery with windows along both sides where she could walk in vile weather when the wind was sore; and a new garden 'full of meanders and labyrinths' below the north terrace; as well as other minor towers, works, and restorations. She was fond of the Castle, but found it very cold in winter, which 'may be holpen with good fyres'.

Windsor seems to have been in a state of considerable dilapidation and discomfort. The accounts repeatedly refer to items like the roof of the Castle 'where the rain beateth in', and the need to 'keep out the choughes and piggins that doe much hurt to the Castle'. The room where the Maids of Honour slept was 'ruynous and coulde', unheated, with a leaking roof and no ceiling. The girls also complained that the partition was so low that the servants peered lewdly over the top at them.

Elizabeth, like her father, had a neurotic horror of illness, decay, and death. One of her darker constructions at Windsor was the gallows outside the gates for hanging without argument anybody who came from London in time of plague, bringing the threat of infection near the Queen. Anybody in Windsor town who received any goods from London during 'the Sickness' had his house summarily burned.

Shakespeare is said to have written *The Merry Wives of Windsor* at Elizabeth's request. She is supposed to have been so keen to see valiant Jack Falstaff in love, that she ordered the play to be finished in a fortnight. It reads like a rushed job. Traditionally the first performance took place in the Castle.

The chief attraction of Windsor for the uncouth, ungainly, ungracious, unstraight first Stuart King, with his morbid passion for hunting, was the great deer forest which stretched for miles in all directions. This passion impinged upon the mute, inglorious inhabitants of Windsor town, because James revived the old Plantagenet forest laws and restrictions. For many years the ordinary people had collected firewood, and poached rabbits and hares, and occasionally something bigger, in the park. James put a stop to it. Two brothers called Richbell who were caught riding in the Great Park at night 'with staves and greyhounds' were imprisoned in the Colehouse; and they were just two among many. One day the Vicar of Windsor, the Mayor, and four aldermen approached James while he was hunting, and presented a petition on behalf of the Vicar, who claimed that he did not have enough to live on. Instead of listening to the petition, the King launched into a bitter tirade in his Scottish accent about the trespassers in his park:

Am I any ill naighbor to you? Doe I doe you any hurte? Doth my coming be any hinderance to you? Why then do you vex me by permitting and suffering your poore to cutte downe and carey awaye my woodes out of my parkes and grounds?

He told the Mayor to punish all trespassers by whipping them. James even tried to revive the archaic ceremony of Forest Courts at which all his foresters at Windsor were expected to kneel before him and present him with their horses and axes, which they did not receive back until they had paid a fine of 6s 8d.

Norden made his survey of Windsor in the reign of James I, and gave the circuit of the forest as $77\frac{1}{2}$ miles, though formerly it had been 120 miles. It had 13 'rides' in it, each under the charge of a keeper, and contained 3,000 head of deer.

During the Civil War Windsor had a second modest taste of fighting, a second abortive siege. After the battle of Edgehill in 1642 Colonel John Venn with his dragoons took possession of the castle in the name of Parliament. Charles I's nephew, Prince Rupert, pounded it with his artillery for seven hours, to no major effect, but with unrecorded tragedy for the pawns of history. A Commonwealth leaflet reported with jubilation: 'As for the town, that is mightily battered and ruined, and the inhabitants very much damnified. All which stood well-affected to the Parliament went into the Castle and are safe.' Royalist papers riposted with heavy sarcasm about Colonel Venn intending to winter at his Castle of Windsor, using the Chapel as a stable, breaking the stained glass, and perpetrating 'many other outrages of that barbarous nature'.

Throughout the war the Castle remained the headquarters of the Parliamentary army, and was used for unromantic work for which it was thoroughly suitable, as a grim prison for captured Royalists. Penned for years up twisting turret staircases, or in the old Norman chalk dungeons, they laboriously carved their names and coats of arms, which can still be seen on the walls.

At a three-day prayer-meeting in the Castle the Parliamentary generals decided that it was their duty 'to call Charles Stuart, that man of blood, to an account for the blood he had shed, and mischief he had done'. Charles himself was brought to Windsor on his way to trial, and while he was there, 'came the order that he was no longer to be treated with the ceremonial of kingship'. He passed his days of imprisonment pacing up and down the terrace, and reading sermons and Shakespeare, a choice of books which, curiously, made Milton carp and cavil. On the fly-leaf of his second folio of Shakespeare's plays Charles wrote: *'Dum spiro spero'* – 'while there's life, there's hope'.

After his execution, Parliament allowed him to be 'buried at Windsor in a decent manner, provided that the whole expense should not exceed five hundred pounds'. The last act of the tragedy took place in a snow-storm, which gave superstitious Royalists something to gossip about. Charles, 'the White King', had worn a white velvet suit at his coronation, and this was supposed to be an unlucky and unconventional colour, as well as the colour of innocence. At his unceremonious funeral the snow floated thickly down. 'By the time the corpse had reached the west end of the Chapel, the black pall was white.'

After the Restoration Pepys came to Windsor and found it most romantic. And the new Constable of the Castle, Lord Mordaunt, found it so romantic that he was seized with a furious and dishonourable lust for the daughter of William Tayleur, his clerk and surveyor of the Castle. When the girl refused his proposition he 'swore by a most dreadful oath and Imprecation, He would persecute her, and her Family to all Eternity'. He imprisoned her father. He evicted her pregnant mother from their lodgings. He 'frightened a young child of the said Mr Tayleur out of his wits; whereof it soon after died'. Not before time, Charles II revoked Lord Mordaunt's patent, and appointed Prince Rupert Constable instead.

Soon afterwards John Evelyn visited the Castle and judged it 'exceed-ingly ragged and ruinous'; the old rooms 'melancholy and of ancient magnificence'. He noted that Prince Rupert had begun 'to trim up the keep, or high round tower', and was decorating the walls of the huge steep stairs ascending to it with clusters of pikes and muskets, and festoons of assorted martial equipment. 'From the hall we went into his bed-chamber, and ample rooms hung with tapestry, curious and effeminate pictures, so extremely different from the other.'

During his exile in France and Holland, Charles II had acquired a taste for the baroque style, which was sweeping lushly across Europe. So he rebuilt the royal apartments at Windsor in the new idiom. The architect was Hugh May, a friend of Pepys and Evelyn. Antonio Verrio painted allegorical figures over the ceilings and walls, including one of Charles in the improbable company of Temperance, Prudence, and Fortitude. Grinling Gibbons carved fish, fruit, game and green-grocery on every available wooden surface. Evelyn thought his work 'stupendous and beyond all description incomparable . . . without controversy, the greatest master both for invention and rareness of work, that the world ever had in any age'. (Evelyn in fact started slightly biased, because Gibbons had been first discovered and recommended by him.) The accounts of the period are encrusted with large sums for 'Sundry Extraordinary Painted Gilded and Carved Workes performed in his Ma'tie's New-buildings at Windsor by severall Forraigne Artists', or 'For Gilding the severall Painted Figures, Flutes, Apples, Ballisters, Pannells, and Trophyes in the Ceiling of the Queene's Gallery . . .' Charles's other major contribution to Windsor was to lay out the Long Walk lined with elms stretching straight for three miles into the Great Park 'which King Charles made for his going out in the divertion of shooteing'.

The Garter feasts were as glutinously gluttonous as before the Civil War. Prim Evelyn was horrified by the way, after the gorging, 'the banqueting stuff was flung about the room profusely' to the spectators. He stayed 'no longer than this sport, for fear of disorder. The cheer was extraordinary, each Knight having forty dishes to his mess, piled up five or six high'. The flamboyant three-day Garter festival was finally abandoned in 1674. Apart from this annual orgy, 'Ther was little resort' to Charles at Windsor, according to Sir John Reresby, one of his visitors; 'and he passed his day in fishing or walking in the parks which indeed he naturally loved more than to be in a crowd or in business.'

James II, in his blinkered bigotry to return England to its old faith, added to his provocations by celebrating mass publicly at Windsor, and by receiving the Papal Nuncio in state there. He arrived with thirty-six coaches, each drawn by six horses, and escorted by long lines of running footmen. The Duke of Somerset, a lord of the bedchamber, refused to participate in the ceremony, and was promptly dismissed from all his posts.

After the Glorious Revolution had in due course removed James from all his posts and palaces, aloof William never felt at home in the magnificence of Windsor, though a female visitor in 1698 called it 'the finest pallace the King has'. There is a touching story of a woman in Windsor towards the end of his reign peering into his coach, and saying, in a tactlessly loud voice: 'Is *that* the King? Why my husband is a handsomer man than he.' William 'stooped towards her and said, very seriously, "Good woman, don't speak so loud; consider I'm a widower"'.

Queen Anne liked a country life, and spent much time and most summers at Windsor both before and after her accession. Like most of her family, she was a great huntswoman, 'a mighty hunter, like Nimrod', according to Dean Swift. When she grew too fat to ride, after nearly twenty variously disastrous pregnancies, she rode to hounds in a one-seated 'calash' with huge wheels, which Swift described as 'a chaise with one horse, which she drives herself, and drives furiously, like Jehu'. There were those who speculated that her passion for hunting was partly an excuse to escape from the nagging and bullying bossiness of her over-powering former bosom friend, the Duchess of Marlborough. As she grew older, and fatter, and goutier the Queen had to be carried up and down stairs in her gout chair, and eventually hauled up and down through trap-doors as Henry VIII had been.

Anne spent much of her time at Windsor in a private house which she bought, just outside the rubbish gate of the Castle, a 'little retreate out of the Palace'. Miss Celia Fiennes, an energetic female visitor there described the homely furnishings in loving and tedious detail. She was impressed with 'a little place with a seate of Easement of Marble with sluces of water to wash all down'. This technologically marvellous plumbing was not yet available in the main castle. Christopher Wren, Comptroller of the works at the Castle, threw some light on this subterranean and unromantic subject, when he made a survey of the Castle for William III, with the object of converting it 'as far as might be practicable, into a regular edifice'. Nothing came of the plan. But the Wren report contained the dis-illusioning and malodorous passage: 'There is a small piece of void ground in the Castle Ditch at Windsor, formerly a garden, but at present a Common Nuisance, abused by the laying of Carrion and making Dung-hills and emptying Jakes's upon it, which makes it very noisome to their Majesties' Court and all persons passing yt way.'

The first two Georges disliked Windsor, and grudged the money needed to keep it in repair. For sixty years it was deserted as a royal home, and parts of it were gradually occupied as 'grace and favour residences' by squatters, with genuine or imaginary claims on the royal favour.

School-children used the place as a playground. Charles Knight, the son of a local book-seller, remembered:

The deserted courts of the Upper Quadrangle often re-echoed on the moonlit winter evenings with our whoo-whoop. The rooks and a few antique dowagers,who had each their domiciles in some lone turret of that spacious square, were the only personages who were disturbed by our revelry. In the magnificent playground of the Terrace, away we went along the narrow wall, and even the awful height of the north side could not abate the rash courage of *follow my leader*.

George III did not want to live at Kensington or Hampton Court which still echoed in his memory with the blood-curdling quarrels between his parents and grandparents. He decided to use Windsor as his country retreat; but instead of turning the dowagers out of his decaying Castle, he took over Queen Anne's 'small neat house on the Castle hill', rebuilt it as a barrack-like building to house his large and increasing family, and re-named it Queen's Lodge. Here the King lived his contented, unglamorous life as a royal farmer. Charles Knight wrote in his memoirs:

The park was a glory for cricket and kite-flying. The King would stand alone to see the boys at cricket. He was a quiet, good-humoured gentleman in a long blue coat; and many a time had he bidden us good morning when we were hunting for mush-rooms in the early dew and he was returning from his dairy to his eight o'clock breakfast. Everyone knew that most respectable and amiable of country squires, and His Majesty knew everyone.

Life was less fun for the staff. Fanny Burney (Mme d'Arblay) left an animated and gruelling description of her life there as Assistant Keeper to the Wardrobe to Queen Charlotte. It was not in fact a job for which Fanny was particularly suited, being unpunctual, untidy, no good with her hands, temperamental, and a well-known romantic novelist of the period. She was in the charge of a Teutonic dragon called Madame Schwellenberg who had come over with the Queen from Germany. Schwellenberg kept tame toads which she fed on flies, was constantly irritated by Fanny's incompetence, and forced her to play piquet, which she loathed, for two hours every evening. The unvarying daily routine of getting the Queen up, and putting her to bed again, Fanny found excruciatingly boring. In a letter to her sister she described the rigid formality of court:

If you find a cough tickling your throat you must arrest it from making any sound; if you find yourself choking with forbearance, you must choke – but not cough. In the second place, you must not sneeze. If you have a vehement cold, you must take no notice of it; if your nose-membranes feel a great irritation, you must hold your breath; if a sneeze still insists upon making its way, you must oppose it, by keeping your teeth grinding together; if the violence of the repulse break some blood-vessel, you must break the blood-vessel – but not sneeze.

Life was bounded by etiquette and uninteresting routine, monotony, embroidery, snuff, stiff conversation, and camouflaged yawns. It was also abominably cold. When she first arrived, one of the equerries, Colonel Goldsworthy, warned Miss Burney that she would certainly die of cold:

Running along in these cold passages, bless us. I believe in my heart there's wind enough in these passages to carry a man o' war. . . . One thing, however, pray let me caution you about – don't go to early prayers in November; if you do, that will completely kill you . . . all the poor attendants . . . drop off, one after another, like so many snuffs of candles: till at last, dwindle, dwindle, dwindle – not a soul goes to the Chapel but the King, the parson, and myself; and there we three freeze it out together.

Queen's Lodge was not a very satisfactory royal residence. It was something of a goldfish bowl. Every window looked in on it. Opposite was the town jail. And whenever the King rode past, the prisoners crowded to the bars, and shouted out: 'God bless Your Majesty. We wish Your Majesty would let us out.' So, at the turn of the century, James Wyatt, the new, young Surveyor-General, began to restore Windsor Castle for the King in the pseudo-romantic style of the Gothic revival, with elaborate arched windows, and a gloomy grand staircase to the state apartments. Like all George's architectural enterprises it was a substantial failure. And when the Queen moved in in 1804 she complained bitterly about the cold after Queen's Lodge, which she, if nobody else, loved and found comfortable.

By now George was lapsing gradually into total insanity and blindness. Some of the first alarming symptoms appeared while George was taking the Queen for a drive in the Great Park. According to a page, Philip Withers, who claimed to have been with them, the King jumped out of the carriage, shook hands with the branch of an oak tree, and engaged it in a long cordial conversation on the hypothesis that it was the King of Prussia. Charlotte told the page to go gently and fetch the King.

What I heard it would be unpardonable to divulge. I cannot, however, withold a remark that must fill every loyal bosom with pleasure; His Majesty, though under a momentary dereliction of reason, evinced the most cordial attachment to freedom and the Protestant faith. I approached with reverence.
'May it please your Majesty . . .'
'Don't you see I am engaged?' answered the King. I bowed and withdrew.
'Go again,' said the Queen. I went.
'May I presume to inform your Majesty that . . .'
'What is the matter?' said the King, in great surprise.
'Her Majesty is in the carriage, and I am commanded to intimate her desire of your Majesty's company.'
'Good lack-a-day,' said the King, 'that is true. Run on and inform her Majesty I am hastening to her.'

Partly his madness took the form of incessant, rambling, nervous talk, till the foam ran out of his mouth. He once talked solidly for sixteen hours non-stop. He also had a recurrent and distressing delusion that he was no longer married to the Queen, who had become so fat that somebody said, unkindly, that she looked as if she were having all her fifteen children simultaneously.

For the last ten years of his life George lingered on at Windsor, totally insane and withdrawn from the world, in his Gothic asylum on the north of the Castle. Sometimes he played a little Handel on the harpsichord. Sometimes he would recognise the tramp of soldiers on the terrace, and pull back his curtain. The soldiers would give an 'Eyes Right', and the old, blind King with the long white beard would raise his hand in salute. With a certain method in his madness, occasionally he decided to wear mourning 'in memory of George III, for he was a good man'. In 1820 he became the first king to die at Windsor.

The new King had already experienced something of the chilling anti-romance of Windsor. He had spent the first few days of his catastrophic honeymoon there. As Prince of Wales George had broken the Royal Marriage Act by secretly marrying the Roman Catholic Mrs Fitzherbert. Nine years later, urged on by the need for an heir and the even more pressing need for a larger allowance to pay his stupendous debts, he married Princess Caroline of Brunswick.

After the wedding, they drove to Windsor. It was not a success. Almost certainly after the first night of marriage they never again shared the same bed. According to a diary supposed to have been kept by Caroline, George was so drunk 'the night he married, that, when he came into her room, he was obliged to leave it again; and he remained away all night and did not return again till the morning; he then obliged her to remain in bed with him and that is the only time they were together as husband and wife'. She told her friends that the Prince forced her to smoke a pipe, and that her only companions were Lady Jersey, the Prince's elegant mistress, and his drunken friends 'sleeping and snoring in boots on the sofa'. This picture of Prinny's sophisticated circle does not quite ring true, and may be distorted by the malice of the ferocious feud which started almost as soon as they met.

Inevitably George IV, who was an exuberant if extravagant builder-king, decided to restore Windsor to a state fitting the dignity of the crown. He chose as his architect Jeffry Wyatt, the nephew of the Wyatt employed by George III, 'a busy-bustling, vain little man'. Wyatt asked the King's permission to change his name to Wyattville, to avoid confusion with other members of his family in the same line of business. George is said to have replied gaily: 'Veal or mutton, call yourself what you like.' The day after the change was announced, a newspaper wrote:

Let George, whose restlessness leaves nothing quiet,
Change if He must the good old name of Wyatt;
But let us hope that their united skill
Will not make Windsor Castle *Wyatt Ville.*

For the alterations Parliament initially voted £300,000; as with most of George's building operations, the price gradually escalated until it exceeded a million pounds. Wyattville created the comfortable modern palace as it is today. His work has been sneered at. And some of his more bogus ideas were eminently laughable – the Hollywood machicolations at the top of the towers through which, presumably, George was meant to pour boiling oil on his critics; the portcullis-grooves which he inserted in gates that had never seen a portcullis. But many have agreed that 'an essentially Gothic structure demands Gothic treatment', and that in spite of minor pretentious pomposities, Wyattville did his job solidly and well.

Victoria remembered her alarming but kind 'Uncle King' at Windsor: having to kiss him was 'too disgusting because his face was covered in grease paint'; saying to her: 'Give me your little paw'; giving her a ride in his phaeton with a jaunty cry of 'Pop her in'. George died in his Gothic castle, clutching his page's hand, with the typical and touching words: 'My boy, this is death. They have deceived me'.

Under William IV the memorable unfortunate event at Windsor was the most excruciatingly embarrassing of all the awful meals that have been eaten there down the centuries. At his birthday dinner there in 1836 the bluff old Admiral King publicly insulted his sister-in-law, the Duchess of Kent, in front of a hundred guests in one of those characteristically tactless speeches for which he had a preposterous talent. There was simmering bad blood anyway between the King and the custodians of Victoria, his heir presumptive. The bitterness was brought to the boil by the King's discovery on a snooping visit to Kensington Palace that Victoria's mother had taken over a set of seventeen unused state apartments which he had forbidden her to occupy. When the party assembled at Windsor for his birthday, he pointedly went up to Victoria, took both her hands, and said how pleased he was to see *her*, and how sorry he was not to see her more often. Then, turning in the direction of the Duchess, he said in a loud and furious voice that somebody had taken possession of his apartments at Kensington contrary to his commands, and that 'he neither understood nor would endure conduct so disrespectful to him'.

The next day after his birthday health had been drunk at the end of dinner, William launched thunderously into what Charles Greville described with malicious relish in his little red book as an 'awful philippic', and an 'extraordinary and *foudroyante* tirade'. Pointing his finger at his petrified niece, he said he intended to live another nine months until she came of age at eighteen, in order that the royal authority would pass to 'that young lady', and not to a regency 'in the hands of a person now near me, who is surrounded by evil advisers, and who is herself incompetent to act with propriety in the station in which she would be placed. I have no hesitation in saying that I have been insulted – grossly and continually – by that person, but I am determined to endure no longer a course of behaviour so disrespectful to me.'

Among her other sins, the Duchess had kept Victoria away from his court. In future he would insist that she appeared there always. And he said a great deal more with a loud voice and an excited manner. It is true however that the long verbatim extracts from his thunderbolt after-dinner oratory are based upon the recollections of one of his illegitimate sons a month after the event.

Victoria burst into tears. Queen Adelaide looked 'in deep distress'. The rest of the guests 'were aghast'. The Duchess of Kent ordered her carriage at once, but was persuaded to stay on for another day for the sake of appearances. She got her own back by keeping everyone waiting for dinner the next day. 'That woman is a nuisance,' growled the King loudly enough to be reported.

When Victoria became Queen, Windsor still had its sensationally awful moments. For one thing there were the nocturnal activities of Lord Palmerston, the Foreign Secretary, whose picaresque anti-Establishment policies in Europe so horrified Prince Albert, and consequently the Queen. How could Victoria take as her most confidential adviser, Albert asked the Prime Minister melodramatically, a man 'who as her Secretary of State and while a guest under her roof at Windsor Castle had commited a brutal attack upon one of her ladies? Had at night by stealth introduced himself into her apartment, barricaded afterwards the door, and would have consummated his fiendish scheme by violence, had not the miraculous efforts of his victim and such assistance attracted by her screams saved her?' What had in fact happened was that Palmerston, in search of other quarry with whom he was accustomed to pass the night, had blundered by accident into the bedroom of Mrs Brand, one of the Queen's ladies.

Apart from 'Pam', guests were always getting lost at Windsor, wandering unhappily in circles looking for their beds or for the way downstairs.

The French Foreign Minister, Monsieur Guizot, 'spent nearly an hour wandering about the corridors to try and identify his bedroom'. Eventually he opened a door, 'and came upon the Queen having her hair brushed by a maid'. One visitor gave up in despair and went to sleep on a sofa in one of the state galleries, where a housemaid found him, and supposing he was a drunk burglar, fetched a policeman.

Conversation and etiquette at meals were as stiff as a starched shirt. Greville is always grumbling on about being 'excessively disgusted with the dullness of the court'. He says that he usually refused invitations to dinner because he was so bored. Victoria's side of the story, told years later, was that she never invited him because of his shouting across the table and talking everyone down. But there is a wealth of confirmatory evidence for the tedium of life for visitors at Windsor, and for the frequent moans from Greville in the mood of '. . . it was fatiguing, but it served to occupy the evening, which is always the great difficulty in Royal society'. A rich young Vanderbilt girl who was presented at Windsor towards the end of the Queen's reign wrote that dinner was a 'most depressing function. Conversation was carried on in whispers, for the Queen's stern personality imposed restraint'. A maid-of-honour wrote home: 'The dullness of our evenings is a thing impossible to describe.'

As well as the strain of whispering banalities, there was the additional hazard of having one's plate whisked away before one had finished. The Queen gobbled her food, and the servants had 'a menial trick of depriving us of our plates as soon as she had finished'. Lord Hartington, one of Victoria's bolder guests, in the middle of a conversation with the Queen, saw his plate of delicious half-eaten mutton and peas receding into the distance. 'He stopped in the middle of a sentence in time to arrest the scarlet-clad marauder: "Here, bring that back."'

In later years there was the ultimate ordeal for thoroughly intimidated guests of being made to dance reels under the eagle eye of the Queen, and the aggressive direction of her favourite Highlander, John Brown. Lord Ribblesdale, a lord-in-waiting, described a tartan evening at Windsor:

. . . even with proficiency this dance requires constant attention, if not actual presence of mind, to be in the right place at the right moment – anyhow, more than I possessed in the mazy labyrinth. I was suddenly impelled almost into the Queen's lap with a push in the back and 'Where are you coming to?' It was Mr John Brown exercising his legitimate office as M.C. After a good many Caledonians, Mr Brown came to ask the Queen, 'Now what's Your Majesty for?' Mindful of her English subjects, the Queen suggested a country dance. This did not find favour. 'A country dance,' he repeated, turning angrily on his heels.

Smoking was not permitted anywhere in the Castle. Desperate Cabinet Ministers used to sit nervously in their bedrooms, hunched over the fireplace, puffing cigar smoke surreptitiously up the chimney. Even when he came of age, the Prince of Wales was not allowed to smoke in his own apartments.

Windsor was not one of Victoria's favourite palaces. At the beginning of her reign she wrote: 'Windsor always appears very melancholy to me, and there are so many sad associations with it.' Her early years there were made miserable by many of the scenes in the scandal of Lady Flora Hastings, her mother's lady-in-waiting whose stomach swelled up so suspiciously. Victoria wrote uncharitably in her journal: 'We have no doubt that she is – to use plain words – *with child*.' The man assumed to be responsible, 'the horrid cause of all this is the Monster & demon Incarnate', whose name she could not bring herself to write, Sir John Conroy, her mother's scheming confidential secretary. This was followed by the crisis of the Bedchamber plot, when Peel tried to persuade Victoria to replace some of her Whig ladies with Tories – '. . . I said I could *not* give up *any* of my Ladies, and never had imagined such a thing.' Prince Albert, who had a pastoral passion for the country generally as well as for slaughtering wild animals, converted Victoria to a love of the rural life; so that eventually she could write that coming to the Castle from London was like being 'freed from some dungeon'.

The most traumatic event of Victoria's reign at Windsor was Albert's death there in 1861. His typhoid was probably caused by that old, unromantic underworld of the Castle, the drains. In a report the Lord Chamberlain wrote: '. . . nothing has been done to improve the drains in connexion with the various water closets, sinks, etc., within the Castle. The noxious effluvia which escapes from the old drains and the numerous cesspools still remaining; is frequently so exceedingly offensive as to render many parts of the Castle almost uninhabitable.'

For more than ten years Victoria could not bring herself to describe 'this dreadful day' in her disciplined daily journal. Eventually she did: 'Two or three long but perfectly gentle breaths were drawn, the hand clasping mine, & (oh! it turns me sick to write it) *all all* was over . . . I stood up, kissing his dear heavenly forehead & called out in a bitter agonising cry: "Oh! my dear Darling." & then dropped on my knees in mute, distracted despair, unable to utter a word or shed a tear.'

For the rest of her reign Windsor became a shrine. Each evening a servant still put a jug of hot water in Albert's dressing-room and laid fresh clothes out on his bed. The glass from which he had taken his last dose of medicine stood by his bedside for the next forty years. To be in Windsor on the anniversary of his death became a sacred obligation. And the Widow at Windsor, shut away in her self-indulgent agony of mourning, became a subject for poems as well as for public discontent.

The most romantic (if that is the right adjective) event at Windsor in the twentieth century was Edward VIII's decision that he could not carry out his duties as King without the help and support of the woman he loved, Mrs Wallis Simpson, the American who had been married twice before. Most of the scenes of the Abdication drama were played at 'The Fort', Fort Belvedere, the castellated conglomeration on the edge of Windsor park which Edward had made into his private retreat while he was Prince of Wales. It became a battle headquarters, with telephones ringing continuously, and dispatch riders bringing state papers from London. Lurking photographers and predatory reporters crouched in the laurels. The King paced up and down his terrace in the fog, 'peering in the direction of London, I could almost feel the vibrations of the Fleet Street presses'. Here Winston Churchill, trying to organise the King's party, told him: 'Sir, it is a time for reflection. You must allow time for the battalions to march'; and advised him to retire to Windsor Castle, close the gates, and refuse to see anyone.

In fact he did not take the advice, but went to Windsor Castle instead to make his Abdication broadcast – 'The great quadrangle was dark and deserted as we entered . . . I mounted the Gothic staircase to my old rooms in the Augusta Tower, where I found Sir John Reith, Director of the British Broadcasting Corporation. . . . In a deep voice Sir John announced into the microphone: "This is Windsor Castle. His Royal Highness, Prince Edward."'

And the ex-King delivered his famous apologia, polished by Churchill, beginning: 'At long last I am able to say a few words of my own.' The main message of his few words was: 'I have found it impossible to carry the heavy burden of responsibility and to discharge my duties as King as I would wish to do without the help and support of the woman I love.'

One way and another, most things had happened at Windsor down the centuries, but never before an Abdication. It was a suitably extraordinary contribution to add to the curiously bitter-sweet, eccentric, and occasionally romantique history of Windsor.

# VI

# WOODSTOCK

THE truth about the ancient royal manor of Woodstock, near Oxford, is camouflaged beneath so many barnacle-accretions of ballad, chronicle, romance, folk-lore, and political propaganda that it is difficult to discriminate between fact and fiction among these old, unhappy, far-off things. But it is still possible to extract some hard fact from the candy-floss of fantasy; solid flotsam from the great ship-wreck of time, *tamquam tabula naufragii*.

The chief surviving character in the history of Woodstock Palace is 'Fair Rosamond', Henry II's mistress, the face that launched a thousand romances, England's home-grown answer to Helen of Troy. From the large and persistent chorus of Rosamond-poets, Thomas Campion put it as succinctly as most:

> Hellen, I grant, might pleasing be;
> And Ros'mond was as sweet as she.

She was of course also the cause of the shrubbery of legend that has overgrown Woodstock.

A sixteenth-century ballad gives the legend (which has a foundation of fact) in its authorised version:

> When as King Henry rulde this land,
> The second of that name,
> Besides the Queene, he dearly lovde
> A faire and comely dame.
>
> Most peerlesse was her beautye founde,
> Her favour, and her face;
> A sweeter creature in this worlde
> Could never prince embrace.
>
> Her crisped locks like threads of golde
> Appeared to each man's sight;

Her sparkling eyes, like Orient pearles,
Did cast a heavenlye light.

The blood within her crystal cheekes
Did such a colour drive,
As though the lillye and the rose
For mastership did strive.

Yea Rosamonde, fair Rosamonde,
Her name was called so,
To whom our queene, dame Ellinor,
Was known a deadlye foe.

The king therefore, for her defence
Against the furious queene,
At Woodstocke builded such a bower,
The like was never scene.

Most curiously that bower was built
Of stone and timber strong,
An hundred and fifty doors
Did to this bower belong.

And they so cunninglye contriv'd,
With turnings round about,
That none but with a clue of thread,
Could enter in or out.

And so on, to the grand opera ending of the triangular love affair.

However, long before the 'Flower of the World' arrived on the scene, trailing clouds of balladeers behind her, Woodstock had been a favourite royal residence. In Old English the name means 'woody place': it was at the centre of five great forests at the time of the arrival of the Normans. There is a dim tradition that there was a Saxon manor on the site. Henry I built himself a hunting lodge at Woodstock, and surrounded it with a great deer park, encircled with a stone wall seven miles long. A chronicler alleges that he destroyed several villages to provide stone for his wall: an improbable story, since Domesday records that only fourteen agricultural tenants lived in the whole district, and anyway Oxfordshire was full of stone. The allegation is more likely to reflect ancient resentment about the unprecedented enclosure.

Henry, who had the royal passion for rare animals as well as for hunting, started to collect a menagerie behind his stone wall. William of Malmesbury reports:

He was extremely fond of the wonders of distant countries, begging with great delight from foreign Kings lions, leopards, lynxes, or camels, animals which England does not produce. He had a park called Woodstock, in which he used to foster favourites of this kind. He had placed there also a creature called a porcupine, sent to him by William of Montpelier.

The records show Henry making constant visits to Woodstock all through the second half of his reign.

His grandson, Henry II, used Woodstock not only as a favourite hunting-lodge, but also as a popular place for holding councils. It was, for instance, at a council at Woodstock in July 1163 that the King had a violent clash with Thomas Becket, who had suddenly become so scrupulous-sedulous for the church, having been made Archbishop as the King's man. The King proposed an innovation that payments formerly made by the counties to the Sheriffs to reward them for their official services, should in future be accounted for at the exchequer, and added to the royal revenues. Becket led the opposition to the plan, successfully. 'By God's eyes,' said Henry, in one of his notorious Angevin rages ('black and bitter bile', said to be inherited from a Satanic ancestor, the demon Countess of Foulques the Black), 'they shall be given as revenue, and they shall be entered in the King's accounts. You have no right to contradict. Nobody would oppress *your* men against *your* will.'

Becket: 'My Lord King, by the reverence of the eyes by which you have sworn, not a penny shall be paid from my land or from where the church has rights.'

A few years after this council, Rosamond Clifford, daughter of Walter de Clifford, a Norman knight with an estate on the Welsh border, arrived at Woodstock. Writing at the end of the century Giraldus Cambrensis records that after 1173

the King, who had for some time been a secret adulterer, now flaunted his paramour openly and shamelessly, not the Rose of the World (*Rosa Mundi*) as some vain and frivolous people called her, but rather the Rose of Unchastity (*Rosa Immundi*).

By the next century it was common knowledge among ordinary people on a Clifford estate that Rosamond had been Henry's mistress.

The traditional story, briefly, is that Henry built Rosamond a secret bower 'of wonder craft wonderliche i-made by Daedalus werke' inside a labyrinth at Woodstock, to hide her away from the jealousy of his formidable Queen, Eleanor. While Henry was away from England, Eleanor threaded the maze. She followed a clue of silk which had fallen from a marvellous needlework casket which Henry had given to Rosamond. Once inside, the female Minotaur offered Rosamond the choice between drinking a bowl of poison, or being stabbed with a dagger. In most versions Rosamond chooses the poison. In his rage Henry parted from Eleanor, and locked her up for fifteen years. On Rosamond's tomb at the near-by nunnery at Godstow was inscribed the coarse, punning couplet, according to some implausible sources composed by Henry himself:

> Hic iacet in tumba Rosa mundi, non rosa munda;
> Non redolet, sed olet, quae redolere solet.
> Here lies the Rose of the world, not a clean rose;
> She no longer smells rosy, so hold your nose.

This story itself has a very ancient, fish-like, and derivative smell. Parts of it are suspicious echoes of folk-lore from other times and places – Ariadne, and Snow White's step-mother, and frequent German folk-tales of wives catching their husbands sleeping in the woods with a 'Wildfrau' by following threads. The few facts and dates show that much of it is impossible. The Queen cannot possibly have killed Rosamond, who died in pious retirement at Godstow nunnery in 1177. From 1173 onwards Eleanor was closely imprisoned in Salisbury or Winchester, for encouraging her children to conspire and revolt against the King. In any case, Henry's whoring was notorious, persistent, and omnivorous, and was not a matter to drive a tough twelfth-century lady to a *crime passionnel*.

From the evidence Henry must have had a considerable affair with Rosamond between 1166 and 1177. The most probable reconstruction of what really happened is that in the autumn of 1166 Eleanor came back to England, leaving Henry on the continent trying to cement together his fissile, centrifugal empire. She travelled through Oxfordshire, and on the day after Christmas in the castle of Oxford she gave birth to her youngest son, and called him John. 'It may be that in the course of her autumn journeyings, and perhaps alerted by informers, she closed in on Woodstock without harbingers and found her rival lodged in that most intimate, domestic, and beloved of all the Plantagenet residences in England.'

Whatever happened at this confrontation, Rosamond was not killed. It was the public flaunting of the mistress in the favourite royal palace which was so offensive about the Clifford affair, not the philandering, which was part of the accepted rough and tumble of medieval life. In any case Rosamond was not the cause of the breach between the Queen and the King. Eleanor was far more jealous, and with far more reason, of Alais

Capet, the French King's daughter, who was affianced to her favourite son, Richard. But it was dynastic rather than sexual jealousy. Henry toyed with the idea of marrying Alais himself, and breeding new heirs to disinherit Eleanor's ravenous-eaglet sons. For whatever reason, Eleanor retired to her own opulent provinces of Poitou and Aquitaine, the south-west quarter of France beneath the Loire, and set up Richard as her heir. It was for this incredible dereliction of female feudal duty, this blow at Henry's dreams of empire, that he locked up the Queen.

Henry was often at Woodstock in 1176 and 1177, and perhaps Rosamond kept him company there. Rosamond died at Godstow and the nuns buried her in their choir, with much pomp and the help of a rich royal alms.

Roger of Hoveden, writing his chronicles at the end of the sixteenth century, records that in 1191 or 1192 Bishop Hugh of Lincoln on his pastoral rounds was shocked to find Rosamond's tomb in the middle of the choir of the nunnery, honoured, covered with a rich pall, many-candled, decorated like a shrine. He took this to imply a distinctly dubious moral about the wages of sin, and ordered that Rosamond's body be exhumed and buried outside the church, in case virtuous women should be led astray by her example. Her remains were later restored, and rested undisturbed until the dissolution of the nunnery in the sixteenth century:

Rosamunde's tumbe at Godestow Nunnery was taken up a late; it is a stone with this inscription TUMBA ROSAMUNDAE. Her bones were closid in lede, and within that closid in lether; when it was openi'd there was a very swete smell came out of it.

The smell is a curious echo of a recurrent theme in the story.

It is possible to analyse how the later layers of legend attached themselves to this basis of fact.

The malodorous punning epitaph and the poison bowl seem to have been muddled into the story in confusion with the much older, popular medieval tale of Rosamunda, Queen of the Lombards, who died of poison in the sixth century A.D. There are grounds for believing that medieval monument-makers used the coarse couplet as an epitaph for any Rosamond. It is not inconceivable that there was a maze at Woodstock; labyrinths, 'Daedals', or 'Troy-towns' were popular amenities in the grounds of medieval houses. Monasteries used them as exercise and penance parades for the monks. Or the maze at Woodstock could be a faint folk-memory of the astonishment and mystery caused by Henry I's great stone wall with the extraordinary beasts behind it.

A fourteenth-century French *Chronicle of London* first introduces the *motif* of jealousy, revenge, and murder into the story. (The French chroniclers regularly made furious propaganda against Eleanor, who had been married to the pious French King Louis VII before taking herself, and, more important, her rich dower of Poitou and Aquitaine, off to rufous Henry Plantagenet of England.)

The French lay on the horrors with a lurid ladle, too gruesome for all but iron stomachs. Eleanor (whom they confuse with Eleanor of Provence, Henry III's Queen) catches Rosamond in her bower. She strips her clothes off, and roasts her naked for a while between two fires. Then she bleeds her to death in a bath, while at the same time placing two horrible toads on the breasts of the *'gentile damoisele'*. The toads promptly *'seiserent let mameles et commenserent à leiter'*. As the blood oozes, and the toads suck, the demon Queen cackles with grisly laughter. But she is a creature of pantomime; any resemblance to the real Eleanor of Aquitaine is pure accident.

Later chroniclers seized eagerly on to the theme, though diluting the Grand Guignol for English audiences:

The Queen went to her by a clewe of thread or silk, and dealt with her in such manner that she lived not long after. Of the manner of her death speaketh not mine author.

Mixed in with this turbulent spate of romance, tantalising fragments of fact still emerged to show that somewhere beneath it all there is a germ of truth. For instance, a letter in Edward III's reign orders repairs to be made at Woodstock, and 'the house beyond the gate in the new wall' to be built again, and that same chamber called Rosamond's chamber to be restored as before.

Woodstock continued to be a popular royal residence for the rest of the Middle Ages. But life in the palace was quieter, and the humdrum routine of royal hunting expeditions tends to be obscured by the prolific growth of the Fair Rosamond industry. Henry III was almost murdered in his bed at Woodstock by a disgruntled madman with a naked knife, 'but by God's providence he was with the Queen'. The Black Prince was born at the palace. Gradually as government became more complicated and centralised in London, Woodstock grew too remote.

By 1554 the old royal hunting palace was so dilapidated that its only suitable use was as a prison where Queen Mary could confine her perilous half-sister, whom she suspected of complicity in or at least foreknowledge

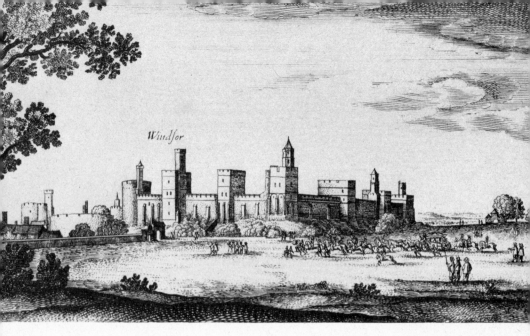

Windsor Castle in the early 17th century

Windsor Castle

A 17th century view of old Greenwich Palace from the land side, after Wenceslaus Hollar

Engraving of old Greenwich Palace or Placentia from the Thames by J. Basine

of Wyatt's anti-Catholic, anti-Spanish, incompetent insurrection. As a prison, it was a good ruin. Elizabeth was lodged in the newest and least decayed part of the old palace, the gatehouse. But her warder, Sir Henry Bedingfield, was extremely uneasy, grumbling that 'in the hoole house there was butte three doores onelye that were able to be locked and barred, to the grette disquiet and troble of mynde off the persons commanded to attende upon hir grace in so large an house and unacqueynted contraye'.

He also wrote to the Council (having had his rather irritating spelling adjusted):

The nights are long and cold and many of them wet, whereby the poor soldiers shall not be able to continue their watch about this house standing upon the hill.

Elizabeth was equally disgruntled, though her description of her condition as 'in worse case than the worst prisoner in Newgate' was a gross and self-pitying exaggeration. She was allotted four rooms 'hung with the Queen's stuff', and allowed to walk in the gardens. Raphael Holinshed in his *Chronicles* writes that one day she heard 'a certain milkmaid singing pleasantly' in the garden, and wished that she was a milkmaid herself, saying that the milkmaid's 'case was better and life more merrier than was hers'.

The German traveller Thomas Platter heard the same tradition at Woodstock in 1599, that 'she often declared that nothing would give her more happiness than to be a milkmaid like those whom she saw out in the field, so miserable and perilous was her captive plight'.

She spent an unhappy year at Woodstock, bombarding the Queen and the Privy Council with regular complaints, requests, protestations of innocence. She summed up her situation herself with more truth than poetry by cutting 'very legibly' on a window-pane with a diamond:

> 'Much suspected, of me
> nothing proved can be'
> Quoth Elizabeth, Prisoner.

While she was confined at Woodstock, Elizabeth had some 'secret consultations with a cunning clerk of Oxford, John Dee', whose astrological predictions that she would certainly come to the throne may have been reassuring; but in the circumstances were tactless, provocative, and to Mary's distrustful eyes would have seemed tinged with treason. After she did become Queen, Elizabeth revisited Woodstock occasionally on a progress, but it was in no case to become a regular residence.

The archaic discomforts of Woodstock were described with vivid disgust by Sir Robert Cecil, when James I dragged his Principal Secretary and his court there on a visit in 1603:

The King, regardless of the comfort of his courtiers, had it roughly fitted up for himself, while the household were obliged to lodge even in tents. . . . The place is unwholesome, all the house standing upon springs. It is unsavoury, for there is no savour but of cows and pigs. It is uneaseful, for only the King and Queen, with the Privy Chamber Ladies and some three or four of the Scottish Council are lodged in the house.

During the Civil War the palace was besieged and badly battered, but the Commonwealth commissioners concluded that the ruins were 'fitter to stand than to be demolished'. After another fifty years of mild decay, the ancient manor of Woodstock and its surrounding 2,330 acres of deer park were made over to the Duke of Marlborough by Queen Anne, in gratitude and memorial of his victory at Blenheim. An Act of Parliament was passed to regularise the grant, and the Queen selected Sir John Vanbrugh to build a palace for the Marlboroughs at Woodstock at her own expense.

Vanbrugh was the prodigious architect of the age, of whom a contemporary wrote the apt epitaph:

> Under this stone, Reader, survey,
> Dead Sir John Vanbrugh's house of clay.
> Lie heavy on him, Earth, for he
> Laid many heavy loads on thee.

His initial survey of the old manor described it as 'altogether ruinous and the site thereof of little value at present'. But while he built the monumental and ponderous pile of Blenheim across the valley, he also repaired the old palace and hoped to preserve it as a picturesque piece of landscape. He wrote a memorandum to Sarah, Duchess of Marlborough, urging the preservation of 'the small remains of ancient Woodstock Manor', which from the north window of Blenheim would appear 'one of the most agreeable objects that the best landscape painters can invent'. However the temperamental Duchess was in her favourite natural state of recurrent feud with her architect, over money, his plans, and his bills which were paid late and grudgingly. She had a sudden hideous suspicion that Vanbrugh wanted to restore the old palace in order to live in it himself as her nearest neighbour.

The Marlboroughs decided that the ruins were 'not in themselves a very agreeable sight'. While he was staying in unfinished Blenheim,

Godolphin, the Lord Treasurer, tartly compared the old palace of Woodstock on its mound to a man 'with a great wen upon his cheek'. It was doomed. In 1723 the last remains of the old manor were pulled down. Nothing remains but a great heap of legend and record, inextricably convoluted by that compulsive catalyst of romance, Rosamond Clifford.

# VII

# RICHMOND AND GREENWICH

ONE of the annoying things about royal residences is that they have a distinct geographical and chronological imbalance. In particular they have more than their fair share of the Thames and the Tudors flowing through them. The excess of Tudors is caused partly by both Henry VII and VIII being great builder-kings; partly, detailed eye-witness records of the sort of things that went on in palaces first survive in some quantity from their period.

And palaces proliferate around the banks of the Thames partly because for centuries it was the quickest and most comfortable main road in the kingdom; and partly because in those days the Thames really was comparatively sweet and softly-running (except for the rapids under London Bridge); an asset for a building to look out upon, instead of a great, grey-green, greasy smell. A less artistic reason was that it was an extremely convenient method of disposing of the sewage from a big house. Even by the sixteenth century it was death to drink Thames water. The latest government report shows that in the 1960s the Richmond sewage works alone was disgorging 2,900,000 gallons of processed sewage and brewery waste a day into the silvery Thames.

Two of the greatest Tudor palaces were at opposite ends of the tidal flow of the Thames, smiling, as the poets said, upon the silver flood, which may even have been silver in those days. Greenwich was their nautical residence, guarding the approaches to London by water and by the Roman road from Dover. Upstream, Richmond stood in green and wooded solitude undreamed of in the concrete conurbations of the twentieth century.

There was a palace at Richmond long before the Tudors. Only in those days it was called Sheen, otherwise spelled Shene, Shine, or Scenes, in the first fine careless rapture of early spelling. However it is spelled, it is an Old English word meaning a beauty spot. The earliest records from

Sheen show Edward I receiving a Scottish diplomatic mission there.

Sheen was always a great palace for dying in. It was the scene for the macabre death-bed of Edward III, 'in solitude and gloom', reported with lugubrious relish by the chronicles. The old man, worn out with a life of blood and battles, the loss of his French conquests, and the recent death of his son, the Black Prince, was deserted at the end by everyone except his mistress, Alice Perrers. Parliament described her as 'a most abandoned woman who was too familiar with the King'. During his last illness

that shameless harlot, Alice Perrers, continually spoke to him of those pleasures to which he was most attached, neither caring for the welfare of his soul herself, nor permitting others to do so. She continued to assure him that he would recover, until noting his voice fail, his eyes grow dim, and the natural warmth leave his body, the infamous jade took the rings from his fingers and departed.

Another chronicler added:

by her example other of his attendants, seizing what they could come by, shifted away, leaving his chamber empty.

Luckily a poor priest wandered in, found the room deserted and the King still breathing, and sent him on his way in peace.

Sheen was a favourite residence of Edward's grandson and successor, Richard II. Chaucer could confidently dedicate 'The Legend of Good Women':

> and whan this book is maad yive hit the Quene
> on my behalfe at Eltham or at Shene.

Richard built a private royal lodging opposite the old palace on an island in the Thames called La Neyt. And into it he put many of the civilised and luxurious innovations for which his reign was famous. There was a '*cuva ad Balneam*', a bath with big bronze taps for hot and cold water. Two thousand painted tiles were ordered to cover the walls and floors of 'the chamber assigned to the King's Bath'. Richard also built several more 'Great Houses' for his courtiers on to the palace on the mainland, and introduced into them the startling novelty of individual instead of communal lavatories, and of personal fireplaces for individual small rooms. At this period Geoffrey Chaucer was Clerk of the King's Works, in charge of the structure and furniture of Sheen.

As well as his revolutionary architectural activities, Richard invented or imported new fashions of dress, including the handkerchief. The wardrobe accounts describe this innovation in astonished blow-by-blow detail: '*Parvis peciis factus ad liberandum domino regi ad portandum in manu suo pro naso suo tergendo et mundando.*' Which, being translated with some difficulty from the medieval Latin, means: 'Made of small pieces for the Lord King to carry in his hand for wiping and cleaning his nose'. This fashion did not become generally popular for another century.

His Queen, Anne of Bohemia, sister of Wenceslaus, is said to have introduced the pin, and the side-saddle into England. She died in the royal annexe on La Neyt at Sheen in 1394. And the next year Richard ordered his Clerk of the Works, no longer Chaucer, to pull down to the ground not only La Neyt, but also all the palace of Sheen. The chroniclers say that he did this because of his intolerable grief:

> The King took her death so heavily, that besides cursing the place where she died, he did also for anger throwe down the buildings, unto which the former kings, being wearied of the Citie, were wont for pleasure to resort.

Some materialists have found this explanation too romantic to be plausible.

Henry V cleared the rubble and rebuilt at Sheen 'a delightful mansion, of curious and costly workmanship, and befitting the character and condition of a King'. This was the fifteenth century, so the palace still looked like a fortress, and was surrounded by a moat. Again it became a popular country home for kings, convenient for the court sports of hunting and jousting.

When Henry VII rose from an ambitious Welsh exile, tracing his pedigree wistfully back to Cadwallader, he made Sheen one of his most frequent homes. There is an account of a disastrous royal tournament he held there early in his reign, when one of the unfortunate competitors had a faulty helmet,

> and so he was stricken in the mouth, that his tongue was borne unto the hinder part of the head, and so he died incontinently.

In 1497 while the court was at Sheen a violent fire burnt down most of the old palace. According to Francis Bacon, in Latin,

> a great part of the building was consumed, with much costly household stuff, including hangings, beds, apparel, plate and many jewels.

The King himself only escaped from a collapsing gallery by the skin of his night-shirt. Henry at once rebuilt on the foundations of the medieval stronghold a red-brick Tudor Palace, which was conspicuous for its bristling forest of towers, copper cupolas, and plump onion-domes. He renamed the new palace Richmond, because he was the Earl of Richmond in Yorkshire, before he grabbed the long-usurped royalty from the dead temples of Richard III at Bosworth.

An ancient survey, in the hyperbolic prose of descriptions by estate agents in all centuries, called Richmond:

This erthely and secunde Paradise of our reign of England, and as I credeablie suppose of all the great part and circuyte of the worlde.

Rather more useful is a detailed but curiously muddled contemporary description of Richmond made while Henry was entertaining some visiting Spaniards there. Around the palace there was 'a mighty brick wall of great length and curious fashion'. Set in every angle and corner of this wall, and also in between them, were a great number of towers of different heights and shapes. The gates were double timber, heart of oak, 'stikkyd full of nailys right thikke, and crossyd wt barres of iron'. Inside, the main quadrangle was surrounded by galleries 'wt many wyndowes full lightsume and commodious', with doors leading to the sets of rooms. In the inner courtyard were the hall and chapel, and in the middle a huge ornamental fountain –

in the upper part there are lions and red dragons and other goodly beasts, and in the midst certain branches of red roses, out of which flowers and roses is evermore running and course of clear and most purest water unto the cistern beneath.

From the cistern water was piped to the rooms.

Between the windows of the hall were pictures of the more ferocious warrior kings of England, 'in their harness and robes of gold'. They included Henry himself. The chapel was hung with arras, cloth of gold, and the altars were covered with relics, jewels, and rich plate. On the walls hung pictures of the more saintly kings of England. They did not include Henry.

The King's privy closet was rich with silk and carpets and cushions. Its ceiling was painted in azure checks, with a pattern of a gold rose and a portcullis between the squares. The other 'goodly apartments, passages and galleries' all had stone floors, glass windows, and ceilings painted with gold. There were 'pleasant dauncyng chambers'. Beside the great hall were pantries, butteries, flesh and fish larders, poultry house and scalding house, and, 'right politickly conveyed and wisely', the 'House of Office'.

The famous gardens prowled with lions and dragons sculptured in yew, and other legendary pieces of topiary and 'strange fruit'. At the bottom of the garden were grounds and galleries for playing and watching tennis, archery, bowling, chess, dice, cards, and all the other games which Henry energetically enjoyed. He also established a library at Richmond, and the accounts show many payments for books. Looking back from the garden the visitor saw the unmistakable and fantastic outline of Richmond's many turrents and pinnacles. And on top of each of them was 'a vane of the King's arms painted and gilt with rich gold and azure'. The golden weather-vanes sang in the wind so sweet that this contemporary visitor wrote: 'As well as the pleasant sight of them, as the hearing in a windy day was right marvellous to know and understand.'

There was another fire at Richmond in 1506, but the damage was repaired within the year. Three years later the first Tudor King died of consumption in his many-turreted, golden weather-vaned palace.

His son Henry used Richmond often early in his reign for tilts and tourneys, for sporting week-ends and for escaping from town generally. His first son by Katherine of Aragon, called Henry also, was born there to great rejoicings, to a splendid baptism, but to a life of only one month. But gradually Henry's egotistical eyes turned ominously upstream to where Thomas Wolsey had rashly built himself a palace at Hampton Court with five courtyards and more magnificence than Richmond. The King made Wolsey give him Hampton Court, and in exchange for a brief period allowed the Cardinal to use Richmond. The snobbish local residents around Richmond apparently complained about the arrangement: 'So a butcher's dog doth lie in the Manor of Richmond.'

After Wolsey was disgraced and dead, Richmond was made over as a convenient billet for Anne of Cleves, whom Henry had married in haste as his fourth wife when he thought he might need an alliance with the German Protestants. He repented in haste too, dissolving the marriage in six months. When the commissioners arrived at Richmond to tell Anne about the divorce, she fainted in terror, and in the memory of the customary bleak future of Henry's ex-wives. She took off her wedding ring in a great hurry, and sent it back to the King with the message that from now on she would look on him as a brother. She promised to show no 'womanliness' towards her 'precious adopted brother'.

As a reward for being sensible, Anne was put out to pasture in the pleasant palace of Richmond. Her most famous and endearing remark while she was there was when she told a friend from the continent: 'There is no place like this England for feeding right well.' Richmond gardens were still celebrated for their rare fruit and animals. The accounts are full of payments for the carriage of grapes and apples, peaches and pears, filberts and damsons, rose-water, salad-herbs and flowers up river to the King at Hampton Court.

Henry's daughter Mary spent part of her honeymoon with Philip II of Spain at Richmond. Pedro Enriquez, a Spanish courtier who came with him, described the chaotic cooking arrangements at the palace:

Each officer has a cook to look after his food in the Queen's Kitchens. There are eighteen kitchens, and there is such a hurly-burly in them that each one is a veritable hell. So that notwithstanding the greatness of these palaces – and the smallest of the four we have been in has more rooms and better than the Alcazar of Madrid – the crowds in them are so great as to be hardly contained. . . . The ordinary consumption of the Palace every day is from eighty to a hundred sheep, with a dozen fat oxen and a dozen and a half of calves, besides vast quantities of game, poultry, venison, wild boar and rabbits, whilst in beer they drink more in summer than the river would hold at Valladolid.

Elizabeth used Richmond as one of her favourite country houses, especially in winter, and towards the end of her life; she called it 'a warm winter box to shelter her old age'. Here the Queen entertained a number of her hopeful suitors, including the Duke of Alençon, the Frog-Prince of the middle-aged Ophelia, in the coy vacillation of her mating ritual. At Richmond Sir John Harington, her witty godson, built her the first lavatory in an English palace that flushed with water, a project which started life as an intricate joke. The invention seems to have been a thundering success. At least, Harington headed one verse of his epigrams introducing his book *The Metamorphosis of Ajax* (a pun on 'A Jakes'): 'To the Ladies of the Queen's Privy-chamber, at the making of their perfumed privy at Richmond.'

Edmund Bohun described Elizabeth's life at Richmond in middle age:

Six or seven galliards of a morning, besides musics and singings were her ordinary exercise. . . . First in the morning she spent some time at her devotions, then she betook herself to the despatch of her civil affairs, reading letters, ordering answers, considering what should be brought before the council, and consulting with her ministers.

Later,

when she had thus wearied herself she would walk in a shady garden or pleasant gallery, without any other attendants than a few learned men; then she took coach and passed, in the sight of her people, to the neighbouring groves and fields, and sometimes would hunt or hawk; there was scarce a day but she employed some part of it in reading and study; she slept little, seldom drank wine, was sparing in her diet, and a religious observor of the fasts.

At Richmond in 1599 Thomas Platter saw her emerge from the Presence Chamber followed by her swarm of retinue:

As she looked down from a window in the Gallery on her people in the courtyard, they all knelt and she spoke to them in English, 'God bless my people', and they all cried in unison, 'God save the Queen', and they remained kneeling until she made them a sign with her hand to rise, which they did with the greatest possible reverence.

Platter and his friends played on the tennis court, and were invited to lunch in hall. 'But as we were afraid we should be kept too long,' he wrote nonchalantly, '. . . we made our excuses and took our lunch in the village at an inn.'

Four years later the Venetian ambassador to England, Giovanni Scaramelli, presented his credentials to the seventy-year-old Queen at Richmond. He reported back to the Doge how the extraordinary old woman in a red wig with a crown on top of it blazed with jewels even under her stomacher. She was 'covered with golden jewelled girdles and single gems'; across her forehead was a fringe of 'pearls like pears'. Elizabeth welcomed him in perfect Italian, and teased him because Venice only sent an ambassador to her now that it wanted a favour.

A fortnight later the Queen caught cold, and started one of the most famous and harrowing of all of Richmond's macabre death-bed dramas. For days she would not go to bed, would allow no doctors near her, but sat in a heap of cushions day and night, listless, but underneath fighting death with tremendous tenacity. According to Harington, of all women his godmother would not go gentle into that good night – 'She became gloomy and suspicious, and walks much in her privy chamber, and stamps with her feet at ill-news, and thrusts her rusty sword at times into the arras in great rage. The dangers are over, yet she always keeps a sword by her table.'

Her cousin's son, Sir Robert Carey, came down from the Borders to visit her:

She took me by the hand and wrung it hard, and said, 'No, Robin, I am not well', and then discoursed with me of her indisposition, and that her heart had been sad and heavy for ten or twelve days; and in her discourse she fetched in so few as forty or fifty great sighs. In all my life I have never heard her fetch a sigh before but when the Queen of Scots was beheaded.

She created panic and dismay among her Maids of Honour by suddenly asking for a looking-glass; her true reflection had tactfully been kept as far as possible from her for twenty years. When she saw the wrinkled old face peering back at her out of the mirror, she bitterly cursed her circle of courtiers for the grotesque flatteries she had squeezed out of them for so long. The atmosphere at court was Gothic with doom and hysterical nightmare. One of her ladies found a playing card, the Queen of Hearts, nailed to the bottom of a chair; nobody dared remove it, 'remembering that the like thing was reported to be of use to others for witchcraft'. Some said that the deep melancholy of her last days was caused by regret for Essex, by a mysterious ring she was supposed to have given him which could have saved his life, by delirious delusions and then disillusions that he was still alive.

Lord Macaulay's verdict seems less romantic, but more likely:

She knew that she was surrounded by men who were impatient for that new world which was to begin at her death, who had never been attached to her by affection, and who were now but very slightly attached to her by interest. Prostration and flattery could not conceal from her the cruel truth, that those whom she had trusted and promoted had never loved her, and were fast ceasing to fear her. Unable to avenge herself, and too proud to complain, she suffered sorrow and resentment to prey on her heart.

At last Cecil said boldly: 'Your Majesty, to content the people you must go to bed.'

'Little man, little man,' Elizabeth is said to have replied, 'If your father had lived, ye durst not have said so much, but ye know I must die, and that makes ye so presumptuous.' Another version gives her the line: 'The word "must" is not used to princes.'

Eventually she was carried to bed. On March 22 the Council gathered anxiously round her bedside. The Lord High Admiral, Howard, 'put her in mind of her speech concerning the succession', and stirred her to life. She replied: 'I told you my seat hath been the seat of kings, and I will have no rascal to succeed me; and who should succeed me but a King?'

The Council, 'not understanding this dark speech, and looking one on the other, Mr Secretary boldly asked her what she meant'. After a lifetime of shying away from the crucial question, 'Who, quoth she, but our cousin of Scotland?' And then, wearily, 'I pray you trouble me no more'.

When they came back the next afternoon, she could no longer speak. Cecil asked: 'We beseech your Majesty, if you remain in your former resolution and that you would have the King of Scots to succeed you in your kingdom, show some sign to us.' Elizabeth pulled herself up, raised her arms slowly over her head, and formed a crown with her fingers. John Whitgift, the old Archbishop of Canterbury, whom she used to call her 'little black husband', stayed kneeling by her bed to pray. When he tried to rise and finish, she motioned to him to continue.

In the dark hours of early morning of March 24 there was a change. The anxious Councillors, whose appointments all lapsed on the death of a monarch, bent over the bed, and 'perceived, yet once again, that the inexplicable spirit had eluded them. But it was for the last time: a haggard husk was all that was left of Queen Elizabeth'.

With the last of the Tudors the great days and the glory deserted Richmond. The new King's eldest son, Henry, lived there and swam in the river. When the 'sweating sickness' raged in London, Charles I moved his court there. During the Civil War like other royal palaces Richmond was sold for a puny pittance to raise money to pay the Roundhead regiments. Gradually during the seventeenth century it fell into decay and ruin, and its masonry was sold or stolen for new buildings; until the old Tudor, turreted palace of singing weather-vanes vanished almost without trace.

From Richmond it cost 14s to be rowed in the Queen's barge down the Thames through London to the other great Tudor palace at Greenwich. The twenty-one oarsmen were paid 8d each, and there was a bonus of 1s 4d 'for a barge beneath the bridge', in other words for the hazardous negotiation of the rapids under London Bridge.

The Crown had owned the strategic strip of land between wild Blackheath and the great loop in the Thames at Greenwich, the double water and land gateway to London, since long before the Norman invasion. For five centuries the manor of Greenwich was given to the Abbey of St Peter at Ghent. Henry V suppressed the alien priories in England. When he died of camp fever at the age of thirty-five, leaving the crown to his infant son, his youngest brother Humphrey, Duke of Gloucester, became Regent, and obtained the freehold of Greenwich. And here he built the first palace on the site, which he named 'Bella Court'. It was, naturally in this century, embattled, with towers at the corners and a moat. There was another fortress on top of the hill as a watch tower overlooking the Dover road.

'The Good Duke' Humphrey, who in fact seems to have been enthusiastically dissolute, was the cultured member of his family. He patronised Italian scholars of the new classical Renaissance. One of the features of Bella Court was its library, the first great library in England outside a monastery or a university, filled with Plato, Aristotle, Virgil, Dante, Petrarch, Boccaccio. When he died he left his books to his old university, Oxford, where they became the beginning of the Bodleian collection, though it took a good many years for the unmonastic, unmedieval spirit of the Italian Renaissance and Duke Humphrey to follow his volumes into Oxford. A few of his books still survive in the Bodleian, and are still called 'Duke Humphrey's library'. Humphrey's beautiful palace at Greenwich was a symptom and symbol of the pride and vaulting ambition which led to his arrest for high treason, followed immediately by his highly convenient and suspicious death in prison.

Three weeks later mild Henry VI's domineering French wife, Margaret of Anjou, moved into Bella Court, and changed its name to 'Placentia' or 'Pleasaunce'. The accounts show that she spent great sums on its interior decoration, covering the floors with terra-cotta tiles bearing her monogram, and filling the windows with glass, a luxury hardly known in England. She covered the pillars and arcades with sculptured daisies, her punning heraldic flower, built a 'vestry' to keep the crown jewels in, and a 'bridge' or pier which gave access to the river at all states of the tide.

The weakness of Henry VI and the central government brought on the power struggle called the Wars of the Roses, during which Placentia was one of the prize pieces of plunder, which passed backwards and forwards with tedious regularity to the winning side.

Stability and its great nautical days came to Greenwich under Henry Tudor, the founder not only of a rather necessary period of absolutism, but also, more than anyone else since Alfred, of the British navy. He modernised the palace by refacing it with red brick, and it became one of his most regular residences. From here his Queen, Elizabeth of York, left for her coronation in a water carnival, which became one of the peculiar specialities of life at Greenwich:

The mayor, sheriffs, aldermen, and many out of every craft, attended her in barges, adorned with banners and streamers of silk. The bachelors' barge outshone the rest, and contained a great red dragon [the emblem of the house of Tudor], which spouted flames of fire at the Thames; there were also many other 'gentilmanly pajants well & curiously devised'. The Queen was accompanied from Greenwich with the music of trumpets, clarions, and other minstrelsy, and at the Tower wharf the King welcomed her.

It is worth noting how even the coronation of a Queen had to go through the ancient symbolic form of starting at the Tower.

In addition to its aquatic activities, Greenwich was a regular resort for hunting in the park, and for indoor jollities at Christmas and the other set celebrations in the calendar. The Privy Purse accounts echo down the centuries faint, expensive sounds of the high life at Greenwich under

Henry VII – 'To the young damoysell that daunceth, £30'; 'To a litelle mayden that daunceth, £12.'

Henry VIII was born and brought up at Greenwich, and it was the stage for many of the important events of the first half of his life, including two of his marriages. 'He loved the place, where, within easy water distance of London, he could hawk and hunt; and where, from the windows and leaden roof of the palace, he could watch the large vessels of London bringing in silk and gold and spices, or carrying out wool and metal. Here, too, he could visit his ships of war anchored close to the palace.' His hereditary love of ships encouraged him to build two new naval dockyards on either side of his palace at Woolwich and Deptford. From Greenwich he would ride out in his gilded barge, dressed in cloth of gold, blowing upon his golden whistle 'as loudly as upon a trumpet' to show the world that he was head of the navy. From Greenwich he went in sumptuous water ceremonial to Woolwich to christen the greatest ship ever built till then, England's first battleship. After an enormous banquet on board, Henry splashed some wine on the deck from a silver-gilt goblet, and named the ship *Henry Grâce à Dieu*.

Jousting, Henry's other great passion, encouraged him to build Armouries and a Tilt-Yard behind the river front of the palace at Greenwich. Here his imported German craftsmen created the famous 'Greenwich' suits of mail, 'as deftly jointed as a lobster's shell, diapered and damascened with sweet devices and richly inlaid with gold'. The clanking, snorting, rather bogus blood and thunder in the Tilt-Yard became famous throughout Europe.

The history of the first twenty years of Henry's reign at Greenwich is largely a list of state visits and seasonal junketings, of embassies, of complicated diplomatic negotiations over European alliances, of the great Lutheran controversy. An example of the style of festivities that took place at Greenwich is given in the chronicles for the Christmas of 1513, when the King served food 'to all-comers of any honest behaviour'. On New Year's eve a pantomime castle, with gates, towers, dungeons and artillery, was towed into the hall. Its name was written on it, 'Le Fortresse Dangerus', and inside it sat six girls, as it were pantomime Principal Boys, dressed in russet satin positively covered with leaves of gold. Enter, predictably, the King and five friends clothed in cloth of gold, who assaulted the castle. 'The ladies seeing them so lusty and courageous were content to solace them, and to yield the castle, and so they came down and danced a long space. The ladies led the knights into the castle and then the castle suddenly vanished.' New Year charades, bringing home the May, masked balls at Epiphany, revelries at Twelfth Night were part of the revolving pattern of Greenwich life.

The palace was the scene for most episodes of Henry's romantic tragedy with Anne Boleyn, the dark girl with long black hair, a flat chest, and a wen on her throat, who was part reluctant royal concubine, and part symbol of the Reformation party. They met at Greenwich in 1522 when Anne came there after six years in Paris at Francis I's court. Her elder sister had probably already been the King's mistress. The dry accounts record her arrival at Greenwich and installation as Lady Marquess of Pembroke in rooms near the King, without comment. Wolsey and Campeggio came often to Greenwich during the devious procrastination of the King's divorce proceedings against Katherine of Aragon. A brave friar called Peto preached before Henry at Greenwich, warning him that he was putting his crown in danger by trying to dispose of his wife in order to marry Boleyn. The next Sunday at Greenwich a royal chaplain was put up in the pulpit to contradict Peto. Another friar at once replied, and in front of Henry denied his claim that all the universities of Europe were in favour of the divorce. Henry, infuriated at opposition, had both friars arrested. And the royal preachers poured forth a barrage of official propaganda through their pulpits, which were the mass media of the sixteenth century, to the effect that Henry's marriage with Katherine was null because she was his brother's widow.

Anne's eventual coronation procession up the Thames from Greenwich to the Tower was another amphibious extravaganza, with barges and bands, and floating dragons 'moving backwards and forwards, and casting wild-fire, while round it stood men also casting wild-fire and making hideous noises'. In the palace in 1533 she gave birth to Elizabeth: 'The Queen was delivered of a fair lady, for whose good deliverance *Te Deum* was sung incontinently.' Henry was less incontinently pleased. The Spanish ambassador wrote that the birth of a daughter was 'of great disappointment to the King, and a shame and confusion to the astrologers, wizards and witches, all of whom had foretold the arrival of a lusty son'. The document, made out beforehand, to announce the birth made the devoutly to be wished assumption that a Prince was to be born, and had to be altered by the insertion of an 's'.

At Greenwich also was staged the decline and death of the great romance, after Anne's miscarriage had extinguished Henry's dynastic hopes for a son. The legend has Anne signalling to one of her alleged lovers by dropping her handkerchief to him at a May Day tournament at Greenwich – a curious Desdemona motif. Henry is supposed to have left at once for London in a black temper. Anne was certainly indicted for incest with her brother and adultery with four other young men before the Council at Greenwich, and left for Traitor's Gate and the imported headsman's sword in a black, terrifying river procession.

Anne of Cleves came to Greenwich for her brief *mariage de politique* with Henry. Her wedding ring was engraved with the understandably pessimistic thought: 'God send me wel to kepe.' That night Henry told the terrified Thomas Cromwell, who had organised the match, that he would not be husband to that Dutch cow, or, alternatively, Flanders mare.

Under Henry the palace consisted of a complex of three quadrangles along the river front, reading from east to west, the 'Fountain', 'Cellar', and 'Tennis' courts. The main entrance was from the river, through a massive gatehouse tower overlooking Queen Margaret's 'Bridge', and leading into the central courtyard. Henry made extensive additions to Placentia, in addition to his Armouries and Tilt-Yard which ran back at right angles to the river. He made the gardens the finest in Europe, he built a Banqueting Hall, and in the account books for work at Greenwich Holbein's name appears for the first time. His wages were four shillings a day, and there are entries for 'senaper, lake and vermilion . . . spent by Mr Hans and his company upon the roof'.

Elizabeth came to Greenwich in the first year of her reign, and the London militia laid on a civic field day in the park to welcome her:

Guns were discharged on one another, the morris pikes encountered together with great alarm; each ran to their weapons again, and then they fell together as fast as they could in imitation of close fight.

Elizabeth watched the heroics from the gatehouse which straddled the Deptford–Woolwich road at the bottom of the garden. This muddy walled road which ran through the middle of the little gatehouse was the scene for the famous and possibly true incident of Sir Walter Raleigh, and his calculating manoeuvres with his cloak. The young Raleigh came hurrying with dispatches that the Spanish invasion of Ireland had been crushed, and caught up with the Queen standing before a 'plashy place' at the rear entrance to the palace, away from the river. In a flattering flash he spread his cloak over the mud, and knelt as the Queen walked over it. It seems to have worked, because soon afterwards he was knighted and appointed Captain of the Guard. The feeble pun ran that his muddied

Greenwich. William and Mary's proposed palace facing on to the Thames, with the Queen's House behind it

*Photo The Times*

Engraving of Richmond Palace from the Thames

*Photo Mansell Collection*

cloak had gained him many a good suit. Raleigh is said to have scratched on one of the windows of Greenwich with a diamond: 'Fain would I climb, but that I fear to fall.' The Queen, who enjoyed showing off her wit and learning, added flirtatiously underneath: 'If thy heart fail thee, climb not at all.'

There is more solid authority for the account of Elizabeth's revival of the obsolete distribution of the Royal Maundy at Greenwich on Maundy Thursday 1573. The Queen was thirty-nine, so thirty-nine pauper women were arranged in rows on benches in the hall. The yeomen of the laundry marched in, and washed and kissed the feet of the old ladies. Then the sub-almoner and the almoner repeated the ritual religious operation. Finally, when their feet were very clean indeed, the Queen came in with thirty-nine ladies each carrying a basin of warm water full of rose petals, and a clean towel. Elizabeth knelt down beside each of the old ladies in turn, washed, dried, and crossed their feet, and kissed their big toes. Then she went down the ranks again handing out to each presents of half a salmon, half a ling, six red herrings, two white loaves, a ration of claret, a white purse containing 39d, and a red leather purse holding 20s.

Foreign visitors were continually impressed by the magnificence of Greenwich and the Queen, and committed their impressions to paper. For instance the Austrian ambassador wrote back to the Archduke Charles, who was for a long time the official and impecunious Catholic candidate for Elizabeth's hand, and all that went with it:

I have seen several very fine summer residences that belong to Queen Elizabeth, in two of which (Greenwich being one) I have been myself, and, I may say that there are none in the world so richly garnished with costly furniture of silk, adorned with gold, pearls and precious stones. Then she has some twenty other houses, all of which might justly be called royal summer residences. Hence she is well worth the trouble.

At Christmas 1585 Lupold, or Leopold, von Wedel, from Pomerania had an audience with the Queen at, as he wrote it, 'Grunewitz', and watched the elaborate and rare spectacle of Elizabeth dining in public. Forty large silver dishes were brought in with much hierarchical kneeling, bowing and scraping, and served to the Queen. Around her stood the great men of England: 'Lord Hower'; 'My lord Lester the Master of the Horse. He is said to have had a love-affair with the Queen for a long time. Now he has a wife'; Lord Hertford, 'who, they say, of all Englishmen has the most right to the Throne'; and Hatton, 'who is said to have been her lover after Lester'. The gossipy von Wedel reported: 'All of them had white staffs in their hands and were handsome old gentlemen.' Every time the Queen spoke to one of them he had to kneel down until she told him to get up again. After more processions and triple bowings with the second course, which consisted of only twenty-four dishes, the Queen washed her hands. This simple operation involved three Earls holding a large silver basin, and two of the old gentlemen holding a towel, all advancing simultaneously towards Elizabeth on their knees. After dinner there was a dance, a pavanne and a galliard, while Elizabeth sat on the floor on a cushion:

During the dancing she chatted and jested most amiably with the young men, and pointing with her finger at the face of one Master or Captain Rall [Raleigh?], told him that there was posset on it. She also offered to wipe it off with her handkerchief, but he anticipating her removed it himself.

Paul Hentzner visited Greenwich in 1598, and saw the Queen coming out of chapel, and watched the pompous and ceremonial chimpanzees' tea-party of setting the Queen's table, which was laid on for tourists:

She was very majestic, her face oblong, fair, but wrinkled, her eyes small and black, but still pleasant, her nose a little hooked, her lips narrow, and her teeth black; (a defect the English seem subject to, from their too great use of sugar). She wore two pearls in her ears, with very rich drops; she also wore false hair, and that red; upon her head was a small crown, made, it is said, of some of the gold of the celebrated Lunebourgh table. Her bosom was uncovered, as all the English ladies have it, till they marry, adorned with a necklace of costly jewels; her hands were small and her fingers taper, her stature of middle height, and her manner of speaking mild and obliging . . . she spoke graciously to foreign ministers in English, French and Italian, for, in addition to her understanding Greek and Latin . . . she was mistress of Spanish, Scotch, and Dutch. Everyone spoke to her kneeling.

The eagle-eyed Hentzner noted the whole elaborate table-laying procedure: after general genuflections, the ladies 'rubbed the plates with bread and salt, with as much awe as if the Queen had been present': and another lady with a tasting-knife 'gave to each of the guard a mouthful to eat of the particular dish he had brought, for fear of any poison'. Finally, after all the fuss, the dishes were carried through to the Privy Chamber, where Elizabeth dined alone in peace, away from sight-seers.

The new King, James I, lived less at Greenwich than the Tudors, and eventually settled the palace on his Queen, Anne of Denmark. Inigo Jones was commissioned to replace the old gatehouse over the Deptford–Woolwich road at the back of the palace with a separate little palace. This was called the 'Queen's House', or the 'House of Delight', straddling the muddy road like Raleigh's dubious cloak. Anne died before it was finished, but Charles I ordered Inigo Jones to finish it for his Queen, Henrietta

Maria. The Queen's House was the archetype of the comfortable new Renaissance home, built around a black and white marble entrance hall and a grand staircase, instead of around open courtyards and galleries. Today it houses the National Maritime Museum. Charles used it to house his magnificent collection of paintings by Titian, Raphael, Rubens, and Van Dyck.

During the Civil Wars the gaudy old Tudor palace fell into irreparable and deliberate decay. The paintings were sold, and the buildings used as a jail for Dutch prisoners-of-war. After the wars Charles II decided that Placentia would have to go, and be replaced by a great Renaissance building, to be called the King's House, in order to balance Inigo Jones's Queen's House. It was to form three sides of a square, with the river as the fourth. John Webb, nephew by marriage of Inigo Jones, was appointed architect of the new palace. In 1664 Samuel Pepys wrote: 'At Greenwich, I observed the foundation laying of a very great house for the King, which will cost a great deal of money.' Money was short, progress was slow. In later years Pepys, after one of his routine visits to the dockyards, wrote: 'I go to Greenwich by water, and landed at the King's House, which goes on slow, but is very pretty.' By the time Charles died, only the west wing had been finished, at a cost of £36,000.

After the Revolution William and Mary inherited the unfinished building at Greenwich, but they had their own palaces to build. After the battle of La Hogue, when the French fleet was destroyed under the eyes of her deposed and exiled father James, Mary decided that the King's House at Greenwich should be completed as a hospital for disabled sailors, in the same way that Louis XIV had founded Les Invalides in Paris. Sir Christopher Wren drew up the plans, and would not accept a fee. After Mary died, William completed Greenwich Hospital as a memorial to his wife. In Macaulay's rolling periods:

. . . soon an edifice, surpassing that asylum which the magnificent Lewis had provided for his soldiers, rose on the margin of the Thames. . . . Few of those who now gaze on the noblest of European hospitals are aware that it is a memorial of the virtues of the good Queen Mary, of the love and sorrow of William, and of the great victory of La Hogue.

By 1869 naval pensioners were no longer anxious to live in a large, monastic hospital; and the Royal Naval College was appropriately transferred into the old palace, which from its medieval days has been intimately connected with men-of-war and dockyards, the salt slap of the sea and the scream of the vagrant gulls.

# VIII

# WHITEHALL

WHITEHALL today is the name of a wide, slab-faced street flanked by offices full of filing cabinets and official secrets. It is also a convenient shorthand symbol for referring to the civil service and the government, or, alternatively, to misgovernment and muddle. It is easy to forget that Whitehall started life as by far the largest royal palace in Europe; and that for 150 of the most tumultuous years of British history the man in Whitehall really did know best, since he was that most divinely conscious of his own omniscience of all creatures, a Tudor or a Stuart sovereign. In those days, when the glory still grew all up and down Whitehall, all twenty-three acres between Horse Guards and the palace of Westminster, and between a broader Thames and St James's Park, were royal palace; or, to be more precise, a rambling royal village of jumbled gates and galleries, quadrangles and gardens. In plain area it made Buckingham Palace ($2\frac{1}{2}$ acres), Hampton Court (6 acres), Versailles (7 acres), the Vatican ($13\frac{1}{2}$ acres), look puny, inconsiderable buildings. Today, except for the great Banqueting House, a few fragments of red brick tennis court, vaulted Tudor wine cellar, and river terrace, it is all gone, ashes under Thames. Lyons tea-rooms and civil servants keep the courts where Henry VIII and Charles II gloried and drank deep.

The Palace of Whitehall began its existence in the Middle Ages at York Place, the London residence of Archbishops of York, referred to modestly as 'our houses in the street of Westminster', and 'the inn of the Archbishop of York without the Bars of Westminster'. The modesty disappeared when Thomas Wolsey became Archbishop of York, and proceeded to compensate for his proletarian origins by the magnificence of his living standards, the multitude of his retainers, and the pomp of his palaces. Even his cooks were dressed in velvet and satin, and wore chains of gold around their necks. Wolsey at once enlarged York Place, and went on 'most sumptuously and gloriously to repair and furnish the same'. Here he entertained his master to feasts, masques, and mummeries; for instance, in 1518 he gave 'a most sumptuous supper, the like of which was never given by Cleopatra or Caligula'.

Wolsey's usher, secretary, and biographer, George Cavendish, who was enthusiastically present at many of these parties, gives a famous report of an elaborate masque at York Place which was gate-crashed by the King in fancy dress. Henry was masked, and wearing a typically Tudor idea of the costume worn by a simple shepherd – mainly fine cloth of gold and crimson satin. Shakespeare used this scene, not entirely implausibly, for the first meeting between Anne Boleyn and Henry.

The Cardinal was sitting at his solitary table of state, surrounded by his mountainous banquet and his glittering guests. Henry and his party rowed surreptitiously down to the water-gate, and announced their arrival with a thunderous blast of cannon. Everybody peered out of the windows into the Thames, pretending to be flabbergasted by the sudden shot. The King and his young companions about town were announced in French as foreign ambassadors who just happened to be passing, heard the fun, had been told about the number of 'excellent fair dames' at the Cardinal's triumphant banquet, and hoped they might be invited to join in. There was some gaming for a cup full of gold pieces. Then the Cardinal, playing what sounds like a carefully rehearsed part, said that he had a lurking suspicion that among his unexpected guests there was some noble man who had more right than he had to sit in the place of honour at the top table. The masked visitors admitted, with histrionic reluctance, that they did include a person of such importance, and invited Wolsey to pick him out. The Cardinal peered archly at them each in turn, and said: 'Me seemeth the gentleman with the black beard should be even he.' Of course it wasn't.

The King, hearing and perceiving the Cardinal so deceived in his estimation and choice, could not forbear laughing, but plucked down his visor . . . and dashed out with such a pleasant countenance and cheer, that all noble estates there assembled, seeing the King to be there amongst them, rejoiced very much.

Henry's hearty guffaws and the sycophantic laughter of the guests echo vividly down the centuries.

After his many summers in a sea of glory and gilt plate and cloth of gold, 'the proudest prelate that ever breathed' fell with a crash like Lucifer. This was partly because of Wolsey's failure to persuade the Pope to agree to Henry's divorce of poor, withered Katherine of Aragon. But, quite apart from the divorce campaign, the centrifugal, nationalist pressures for the break with Rome, necessarily involving the fall of Rome's Cardinal, were there anyway. Partly Wolsey's aggressive and pretentious foreign policy had collapsed in chaos and insolvency. But also Henry was quite simply jealous of Wolsey's lavish magnificence, which was intolerable in a subject. His own palace of Westminster, severely damaged by fire in 1512, gently decaying, was put in the shade by the opulence of York Place next door. In October 1529 the disgraced Cardinal offered Henry all his worldly goods, pathetically and vainly asking him to 'call to his most gracious remembrance that there is both heaven and hell'. Ten days later Henry moved into York Place. An inventory of all the massive plate and furniture was waiting for him.

The palace, of course, belonged to the Church, and not to Wolsey personally. But this was a trivial obstacle to Henry's sublime egotism, and remarkably elastic conscience. The name York Place was an embarrassing reminder. So it was promptly changed to 'Whitehall'. Shakespeare notes the change in *Henry VIII*, when one of the various gentlemen sight-seeing at Anne Boleyn's coronation, says:

> Sir,
> You must no more call it York Place; that's past:
> For since the Cardinal fell, that title's lost;
> 'Tis now the King's and called Whitehall.

Why he called it Whitehall is one of those puzzling questions almost beyond all conjecture. There have been some remarkably unconvincing guesses. One theory is that Henry constructed some new, Renaissance building in the palace out of white stone instead of traditional Tudor brick and timber. No trace of any such building is found in contemporary plans and accounts. Another explanation is based on the fact that several medieval buildings had a festival hall used for special occasions which was called the White Hall. One of the important buildings in old Westminster Palace, for example, was the White Hall. Therefore Henry meant to show by analogy that his new palace was the White Hall, or Festival Hall, of the whole kingdom.

The King at once embarked on a major building programme. He confiscated the great Privy Gallery from Wolsey's country palace at Esher, and re-erected it at Whitehall, connected to the Stone Gallery; 'the taking away thereof before my lord's face was to him a corrosive, which was invented by his enemies only to torment him', wrote Cavendish sadly. The galleries were always a particular feature of Whitehall. The Count of Belgrade, a visitor in 1531, described them:

Long porticoes or halls, without chambers, with windows on each side looking on gardens or rivers, the ceilings being marvellously wrought in stone and gold, and the wainscot of carved wood representing a thousand beautiful figures; and round about there are chambers and very large halls, all hung with tapestries.

Henry also acquired a large stretch of open land on the west or park side of the public thoroughfare between Charing Cross and Westminster, the road which is now called Whitehall. And here he constructed a selection of sporting and pleasure buildings: a Cockpit; a Tilt-Yard, in which he could break lances with his lords in the 'great justes', with the lethal aspects of the sport reduced by the safety-barrier or 'tilt' between the charging competitors; tennis courts in which the sportsman King, passionate to win, such a reluctant loser, could flog the ball; a bowling alley; 'a ball-house where they play at featherballs' – a diary notes 'the play at shuttlecocke is become soe muche in request at Court, that the making shuttlecockes is almost growne a trade in London'.

The new 'Cockpit' side of Whitehall was linked to the old palace by two tall gateways across the public road – the Holbein Gate, just opposite the southern end of the present Banqueting House, and the King Street Gate, down towards Westminster. For two and a half centuries the Holbein Gate, with its battlemented octagonal turrets, its chess-board pattern of two-toned bricks, its virtually obligatory busts of Roman emperors, was one of the landmarks of London. In spite of the tradition, Holbein did not design this gate, but he may have had lodgings over it while he was busy on the interior decoration of Whitehall for Henry, at a salary of 200 florins a year. Henry himself seems to have had his 'secrete studie' in the upper storey over the Holbein Gate.

Whitehall was a constantly changing and convoluted warren of chambers, galleries, courts, lodgings, the 'secreate Jewelhouse', and, just to vary the spelling, the 'Olde Juelhouse', 'secrete guarderobes', presence chambers and chapels, the Pebble Court (because of its paving), which was originally called the Preaching Court (because of its interminable sermons), and the Whalebone Court, from its 'monstrous gate of whalebone'. An unimpressed Italian visitor in the next century described it as 'nothing more than an assemblage of several houses, badly built at different times and for different purposes'.

Holbein painted ceilings, and decorated the wall of the Privy Chamber with an ornate royal group of Henry, his parents, and his wife of the moment, Jane Seymour –

The King as he stood there, majestic in his splendour, was so lifelike that the spectator felt abashed, annihilated in his presence.

We get a key-hole glimpse of the interior of Tudor Whitehall from the German traveller in Elizabeth's reign, Paul Hentzner, who was most impressed with the library, 'well stored with Greek, Latin, Italian, and French books'. There was also a little French work upon parchment, in Elizabeth's own hand, and addressed to her father. 'All these books are bound in velvet of different colours, though chiefly red, with clasps of gold and silver; some of pearls and precious stones set in their bindings.' He goes on to describe the paintings, and

two little silver cabinets of exquisite work in which the Queen keeps her paper; a chest, ornamented with pearls, containing the Queen's jewellery; various musical instruments; and a piece of clockwork, an Aethiop riding upon a rhinoceros with four attendants who make their obeisance when it strikes the hour.

Even Henry did not dare close the public rights of way through his palace, by road from Charing Cross to Westminster, and by river to Whitehall Stairs. But he was alarmed by the possibility of catching something unpleasant from the frequent hearses which besieged his gates on their way to burial at Westminster. So he gave orders that corpses from Charing village should not pass through Whitehall, but should be interred in their own parish of St-Martin-in-the-Fields.

Many of the ceremonial and historic events of Henry's reign happened in Whitehall. Here the swarthy and flat-chested Marquess of Pembroke, alias Anne Boleyn, had a lodging while she was refusing the post of royal mistress, and holding out for 'Quene or nott'. Henry, probably not a lascivious Bluebeard, perhaps even 'sexually cool, if not timid', but desperate for a legitimate male heir, hurriedly married the by now heavily pregnant Marquess in a turret of Whitehall – 'The Pope is agreeable,' he snarled at the worried chaplain. The day after Anne's head had been removed by the expert swordsman, snobbishly sent for from St Omer at a cost of £23 6s 8d, privately and by special license Henry married gentle Jane Seymour, 'in the Queen's closet at York Place'. 'She is,' an ambassador wrote home, 'of middle stature, and no great beauty; so fair that one would call her rather pale than otherwise.'

At Whitehall in January 1547 was that tremendous and macabre final scene, with the great, gross, burnt-out ogre dying, almost certainly not of syphilis, but of varicose ulcers or perhaps osteomyelitis. It was treason to prophesy the King's death, and the doctors hung back in fright, 'like unarmed men in the presence of a wounded and dying beast of prey'. Eventually Sir Anthony Denny screwed his courage to the sticking-point to tell Henry to prepare himself for death. Cranmer was sent for. By now Henry was almost speechless and unconscious. But he summoned up enough strength to squeeze the Archbishop's hand as a sign that he put his trust in Christ.

Elizabeth's stinginess and her difficulty in raising money made her less of a builder than her father who had died nearly bankrupt, less hospitable than a scrounger of hospitality, less entertaining than entertained. But Whitehall still had its brilliant moments. Tournaments were held in the Tilt-Yard at least twice a year in her honour, on her birthday, and on the anniversary of her accession. The tournament had by now long lost any relevance as a training-ground for contemporary war, and had become a bastard feudal pageant, in which the elements of fighting, feasting, music, dancing, graphic display, poetry, and speech were mixed together into an improbable but spectacular amalgam.

Prospective competitors had to ride up to the viewing gallery, ask permission to take part, and give Elizabeth a present. Crowds of attendants were fancy-dressed 'like savages or like Irishmen, with their hair hanging down to the girdle, and like women; others had horse manes on their heads'. The Earl of Leicester, Elizabeth's great and good friend, and her Master of Horse, galloped gallantly around looking magnificent. The Queen presented the winners with beautifully painted paper shields (they were expected to hand them straight back to her, to add to her collection in the Shield Gallery overlooking the Thames).

More sanguinary sports than the obsolete antics of chivalry were staged in the Tilt-Yard, which stood where Horse Guards stands today. Contemporary letters have several entries like: 'Tomorrow she [the Queen] hath commanded the bears, the bull, and the ape to be baited in the Tilt-Yard.' Henry Machyn's diary of October 1561 records:

. . . was at Whyt-hall grett baytyng of the bull and bere for the in-bassadurs of Franse . . . the wyche the Quee's grace was there, and her counsell and mony nobull men.

One of the significant differences about the organic society of the sixteenth century was that the audience for a play by Shakespeare came from all classes of society, and was the same sort of audience that the next day watched and enjoyed an ape being torn to pieces by greyhounds, or the reeking mutilation and execution of a traitor. In the fragmented societies of the twentieth century, the people who watch a groaning and grunting wrestling match one night are unlikely to turn out for a play by Shakespeare or a concert of chamber music the next.

In Elizabeth's Tilt-Yard the bull was normally tethered by the head by a long rope, and assaulted by one highly trained dog at a time. Thomas Platter, the German tourist at Elizabeth's court, describes a fight in which a massive white bull tossed dog after dog; attendant seconds caught the dogs on sticks to break their fall, so that they would not be killed, but could be nursed back for another bout. A bear was normally attacked by several dogs at once, and was handicapped by having his teeth filed down so that his only weapon was a buffet with his great paws. In the Cockpit next door specially bred and trained fighting-cocks, 'heeled' with three-inch spurs, hackle and wings and tail 'cut out' so as to offer a smaller target, butchered each other to make a Tudor holiday.

A precious number of eye-witness descriptions of scenes in Whitehall during Elizabeth's reign survive, from which it is possible to build up an incomplete jig-saw of what life was like in the labyrinthine palace. Most of the scenes were, unfortunately but inevitably, important state occasions; and so the picture has more glitter and glamour than would have been normal in regular, week-day Whitehall. For instance, in 1559 Elizabeth, aged twenty-six, gave a banquet in the Stone Gallery for the visiting Duke of Montmorency. The gallery

was all hung with gold and silver brocade, and divided into three apartments in the centre of which was the table prepared for her Majesty, and at a short distance from it another for the ambassadors. There was also a table fifty-four paces in length for the other lords, gentlemen and ladies. The whole gallery was closed in with wreaths of flowers and leaves of most beautiful designs, which gave a very sweet odour and were marvellous to behold, having been prepared in less than two evenings, so as to keep them fresh.

The Venetian ambassador was enthusiastic about 'the large and excellent joints', but grumbled that 'the delicacies and cleanliness customary in Italy were wanting'. There was such a squash because of the inordinate farthingales of the ladies that some of the party had to eat their dinner sitting on the rushes on the floor.

After the banquet the court came out into the gallery above the Tilt-Yard, and watched a thirteen-a-side joust by torchlight, 'the Guard in their rich coats holding an infinite number of torches'. It was all 'a sight exceeding glorious . . . as can hardly be seen the like in any Christian Court'.

In 1581 Elizabeth built herself a temporary and extraordinary Banqueting House in Whitehall for a temporary and ludicrous-pathetic occasion: the visit of the Duke of Alençon to propose marriage. Alençon was brother of the King of France, twenty years younger than the middle-ageing Queen, and a fairly irresponsible adventurer, with a puny figure, a bulbous, smallpox-pitted nose, and a wispy beard. Elizabeth, who used her ambiguous matrimonial intentions as a never-ending, stop-go political weapon, seems to have been genuinely taken with the little Frenchman. At least, she flirted with the idea of marriage to him for ten years. She always gave pet names to her close friends. And she nick-named Alençon's go-between in his courting, a certain de Simier, her 'Monkey'. She allowed Simier to steal her nightcap, handkerchief, and a garter as intimate trophies for his master. John Stubbs, who wrote a vitriolic attack on the rumoured French marriage, had his right hand chopped off to teach it a lesson. On the scaffold he made a pun: 'Pray for me, now my calamity is at hand.' After the axe had fallen, he took off his hat with his left hand, cried 'God Save the Queen', and fainted.

When Alençon himself arrived in 1581, after a horribly sea-sick crossing, Elizabeth added him to her menagerie of pet beasts, giving him the nickname of her 'Frog'. While walking in a gallery at Whitehall, in the presence of the French ambassador and others, Elizabeth kissed Alençon, drew a ring from her finger, and announced she would marry him. It is said she cried all that night. Perhaps Elizabeth recognised that her ugly little suitor was the last hope of marriage and children, which in her heart she knew she could never have, politically could never afford to have. Perhaps she was just playing politics, and exploiting him, as she steered her intricate two-faced way between threatening Scylla-France, and Charybdis-Spain.

Anyway, for the wooing of her Frog, she built, as a contemporary account puts it, rather xenophobically; 'the greate banketyng house at Whythall at the Intertaymt of mounsere by Queen Elizabeth'.

It seems to have been more like a flamboyant marquee at the Chelsea Flower Show than anything else. It was 'a long square 332 foot in measure about', supported by thirty 'great masts' 40 feet high. The walls were made of canvas, painted on the outside to look like stone. The inside, lit by 292 panes of glass, had the canvas gaudily painted with the sun and sun-beams, clouds and stars. From its ceiling hung festoons of exotic greengrocery:

baies, Rue and all manner of strang flowers . . . and strang fruits, as pomegarnetts, orrengs, pompions [pumpkins], Cowcombers, grapes, carretts, Peaes, and other such like, spanged with gould and most richly hanged.

It took twenty-four days to build, the cost precisely £1,744 19s 2d; 375 men were employed in erecting this canvas cornucopia, and according to the records two of them 'had mischances; one broke his leg, and so did the other'.

This was intended to be a temporary Banqueting House, but in fact it survived, patched, strengthened, redecorated, and 'with much propping' for a quarter of a century. Then in 1606 James I had the 'old, rotten, sleight builded' house pulled down, and replaced it with another Banqueting House, 'strongly builded with brick and stone'. He boasted to the Venetian ambassador that what his predecessors had left him in wood he had converted into stone.

During Elizabeth's marriage negotiations with Alençon in 1581 she staged an elaborate and Freudian tournament in the Tilt-Yard to impress the French. The gallery where the elderly Queen was sitting was called, 'and not without reason', the 'Fortress of Perfect Beauty'. It was attacked by an army led by courtiers dressed up as Desire and his four foster children ('men sore wearied and half overcome'), who summoned the fortress to surrender by reciting:

> Desire's great force no forces can withold,
> Then to Desire's desire, O yield, O yield,

and much other feeble verse. A concealed orchestra played 'verie doleful musicke'. Two cannons fired salvoes of scented powder and toilet water. There were assaults on the fortress with 'pretty scaling-ladders'. Footmen bombarded the walls with flowers, and 'all sort devices as might seem fit shot for Desire'. In extravagant uniforms the defenders of 'Beauty' entered the lists, and a regular tournament took place. It lasted for two days, and ended with the challengers surrendering to Elizabeth, and apologising for their 'degeneracy and unworthyness in making Violence accompany Desire'. To modern eyes these artificial happenings have faint symbolic and psychological similarities to the actual Alençon wooing.

In her old age the Queen, with her wrinkled face, beady eyes, hooked nose, and black teeth used to travel to Whitehall after dark because her wrinkles did not show up so badly by torch-light. An unsentimental contemporary Godfrey Goodman, Bishop of Gloucester, who composed memoirs of the court of James I, wrote:

In her early journey at her coming, you must understand that she did desire to be seen and magnified, but in her old age she had not only great wrinkles, but she had a goggle throat with a great gullet hanging out, as her grandfather, Henry VII, is painted withal.

A visitor to Whitehall described Elizabeth, who was nearly seventy, so loaded with jewels that he was 'amazed how she could carry them'. When Elizabeth died, James's wife, Anne of Denmark, found nearly 3,000 dresses in her wardrobe at Whitehall, as well as heaps of pearl and unvalued jewels.

The new Queen used these costumes for one of the most characteristic occasions at Whitehall under the new regime, the masque. This glorified, upper-crust charade originated in the mummings of the Middle Ages. Henry VIII, in his peacock passion for display, had given the art form a new stimulus from Italy. The masque reached its heyday under the early Stuarts, with Ben Jonson writing scripts for the courtly actors, and young Inigo Jones, the clothworker's son, contriving spectacular stage effects, costumes, scenery, and 'machinery'. In the true tradition of show business the two men became bitter rivals, jealous of their own departments, and feline about the other man's.

The main object of the masque was to give stage-struck Queen Anne and her ladies a chance to indulge their passion for dressing up, in a coy, classical setting, full of nymphs, gods, and shepherds posturing in Arcadia and satin. On one evening after a succession of lightning changes the Queen appeared as a goddess, then a nymph, then a Turkish Sultana, and finally, painted black, as an Indian princess. On Twelfth Night 1605 the first and most famous of these orgies of amateur dramatics, the Queen's 'Masque of Blacknesse', was performed in Elizabeth's old canvas Banqueting House. A member of the audience recorded:

There was a great engine at the lower end of the room which had motion, and in it were the images of sea-horses, with other terrible fishes, which were ridden by Moors. The indecorum was that there was all fish and no water. At the farther end was a great shell, in the form of a shallop, wherein were four seats.

In the shell sat the Queen with eleven court beauties, with their hands and faces blackened, representing 'the Black Daughters of the Niger'. The contemporary reporter notes primly: 'Their appearance was rich, but too light and courtezan-like for such great ones.'

The show cost £3,000.

The King was said to encourage his wife and her ladies to dress up in their glittering jewels, provocative dresses, and heavy scents, because he liked watching women 'being immodest'. Over the next years the royal accounts are full of surrealist entries which give an idea of what masques were all about: Four satyrs, £13 4s; two sea-gods at £5 a head; four 'gitarre men' at 18s each; two 'boyes in the cloudes', 7s each; four 'heavenly sprits', £2 12s; four 'Aryell sprits', £2 8s; a 'hero of the Sea', £8 3s 2d; 'Europe', £5 10s 8d; the 'Emperour of America', £7 5s 4d. Habits for 'two Afrycan Kinges' and three 'Afrycan slaves' set the production back £16. One masque used 500 yards of material, including gold and musk 'for to goe round ye breeches'. The bills are encrusted with such mysteriously evocative items as 'Bigge gold puple roses for ye Body; small gold purld roses for ye body and scollops, for ye sleeves and for ye capp'.

One carping Puritan critic of these Whitehall farces claimed that they were used 'only as incentives for debauchery, therefore the courtiers invited the citizens' wives to those shows'. At a masque staged in 1606 for the visit of the King of Denmark, the ladies of court were seen 'to abandon all sobriety and roll about in intoxication'. Sir John Harington, a member of the audience wrote:

. . . a great feast was held, and, after dinner, the representation of Solomon his Temple and the coming of the Queen of Sheba was made . . . His Majesty [of Denmark] then got up and would dance with . . . Sheba; but he fell down . . . Now did appear . . . Hope, Faith, and Charity: Hope did assay to speak, but wine rendered her endeavours so feeble that she withdrew . . . Faith was . . . not joyned with good works, and left the court in a staggering condition: Charity came to the King's feet, and . . . then returned to Hope and Faith, who were both sick and spewing in the lower hall.

James was not particularly pleased with his new stone Banqueting House built in 1606, because 'when he came into it he could scarce see by reason of certain pillars which are set up before the windows'. In 1619 two workmen were sweeping up the débris of the Christmas masques, and set fire to some oily cloths with their candles. The fire caught hold of the roof, and the two men, 'not able to quench, and fearing to be known that they did it, shut the doors, parting away without speaking thereof, till at last, perceived by others, when too late and irrecoverable'. The building was burned to the ground, and the rest of the palace was only saved from holocaust by pulling down the adjoining buildings with hooks. Important state papers stored in the basement of the Banqueting House went up in flames.

James ordered Inigo Jones, now his Surveyor-General, to design him a new Banqueting House. The result was the building that still stands today, a little lost and under-used, half-way down the modern Whitehall, the last and most glorious relic of the old palace. The new building was a perfect double cube, 110 feet long and 55 feet in breadth and height, faced with Portland stone, and a complete classical contrast to the Tudor brick and timber of the rest of the palace. At the entrance to Whitehall this Palladian masterpiece was a manifesto in the new Renaissance style sponsored by the new dynasty from Scotland.

The work took nearly three years, and cost over £15,600 – this included £712 19s 2d for building a new pier at Portland for loading the tons of stone from the enlarged quarries. There were delays in the building, partly because of the slowness in getting the stone from Portland, and partly because of labour troubles on the building site. There was no strike, but the masons were perpetually running away to jobs which were better, or more regularly, paid. Their wages were from 1s to 2s 6d a day. Inigo Jones's fee was 8s 4d a day, with an allowance of £46 a year in lieu of a house. One of the main and startling new features of the interior was the vast ceiling divided into a 'Frett made of Great Cornishes [cornices] inriched with carvings': a Venetian, instead of a fussy Tudor, ceiling. The largest of the nine great panels was 28 feet by 20, the smallest 25 feet by 10. At the south end of the hall was the 'Great Neech', the timber alcove fretted with golden paint, where the King sat on his throne on state occasions. Part of the basement of the Banqueting House was an exclusive night-club: 'a Rocke or Grotto where the King did regale himself privately' with his peculiarly intimate friends, Carr and Villiers, and other pretty young men.

Boozy Ben Jonson, of whom a friend said that drink 'is one of the elements in which he liveth', wrote a dedication to the King's new grotto in the cellar:

> Since, Bacchus, thou art father
> Of wines, to thee the rather
> We dedicate this cellar,
> Where thou art now made dweller . . .

and so on.

Opinion of the Banqueting House has always been enthusiastic. A

French architect visiting England later in the century said it was 'the most finished of the modern buildings on this side the Alps'. A Scot called Colin Campbell wrote: 'Here our excellent architect has introduced strength with politeness, ornament with simplicity, beauty with majesty; it is without doubt or dispute the finest room in the world.' And a contemporary described it as 'too handsome for the rest of the palace'.

In 1629 the great Flemish artist Peter Paul Rubens visited England, not as a painter but as a diplomat. His mission, which was reasonably successful, was to improve relations between Britain and Spain. *En passant*, Charles I commissioned him to fill the great ceiling panels of the Banqueting House with suitable paintings. Rubens made preliminary sketches, and discussed with Charles the subject, which was to be the benefits and blessings conferred upon the united kingdoms of England and Scotland by the wise rule of James I. Rubens went home to Antwerp, and over the next five years with his assistants produced the vast canvases showing with much pomp and scarlet the apotheosis of the wisest fool in Christendom, surrounded by improbable allegorical virtues which never exactly surrounded him in his life-time, by propaganda about the divine right of kings, and by Bacchanalian processions of cheerful, chubby cherubs, naked and nine feet high. For his labours Rubens received £3,000, two gold chains, a knighthood, and assorted minor gifts.

There was a danger that smoke from the torches used in masques would damage the paintings on the ceiling, so Charles built a wooden masque-house behind the Banqueting House. As the preface to the programme for the first masque performed in the new building put it:

There being now past three years of Intermission that the King and Queenes Majesties have not made Masques with Showes and Intermedii, by reason the roome where formerly they were presented, having the seeling since richly adorn'd with peeces of painting of great value, figuring the acts of King James of happy memory, and other enrichments: lest this might suffer by the smoke of many lights, his Majestie Commanded the Surveyor of his workes, that a new temporary roome of Timber, both for strength and capacitie of spectators, should be suddenly built for that use: which being performed in two months, the Scenes from this Masque were ordered.

The masques had left the Banqueting House, but the banqueting was still very much there. Charles provided eighty-six tables a day at Whitehall for the host of hangers-on hovering on the fringes of royal hospitality. Every day the King's table had twenty-eight courses, the Queen's twenty-four, and so on in descending order of gluttony. The list of

Engraving of the Thames front of Whitehall Palace

Whitehall Palace. The Holbein Gate with the Banqueting House on the left, by Israel Silvestre, the 17th century French engraver

provisions used in the kitchens of Whitehall in one year of Charles's reign give some idea of the scale of the eating and swilling: 1,500 oxen, 7,000 sheep, 1,200 calves, 300 porkers, 400 'young beefs', 6,800 lambs, 300 flitches of bacon, and 26 boars. For oddly assorted poultry they disposed of 1,680 geese, 3,000 capons, 5,640 hens, 9,000 pullets, 17,640 chickens. For bread, 364,000 bushels of wheat. They ate proportionate amounts of fish, game, venison, fruit, and spice. They drank 600 tuns of wine, and 1,700 tuns of beer.

And, of course, the court only spent part of the year in Whitehall.

Towards the end of Charles's reign his Surveyor, John Webb, submitted plans for rebuilding Whitehall as a single, grandiose palace in the Palladian style, 1,050 feet by 928, 'until his Majesty's unfortunate calamity caused him to desist'.

In January 1642 Charles left Whitehall to raise troops in the north. He only returned to it seven years later to die by the axe. During the Civil War a pamphlet describes the melancholy desolation of Whitehall. The palace lay 'in a dumb silence . . . as if it were the decayed buildings of ruined Troy'. Anybody could walk into the hall,

for surely there are no strong smells out of the Kitching to delight your Nostrells withall – nor the greasie scullions to bee seene over Head and Eares in a Kettle full of Kidnies, nor anything else to stoppe your progresse into the House. You may walke into the Presence Chamber with your Hat, Spurres, and sword on. And if you will presume to be so unmannerly, you may sit downe in the Chaire of State.

All the great rooms were deserted and stripped. Vanished were the lascivious crowds who had hung around the gates 'to ravish themselves with the sight of ladies' handsome legs and insteps as they took coach'. There was decay and looting. The palace was purged of 'all Papists, women with husbands serving against Parliament, their children and all other ill-affected persons or those of scandalous conversation'.

A gun battery was placed at the Holbein Gate to sweep the approach from Charing Cross if the Royalists attacked. Troops were billeted in the palace. And the Long Parliament passed resolutions for destroying 'Superstitiouse and idolatrose' pictures at Whitehall. In the fanatic spasm of Puritanism great stained glass windows were enthusiastically smashed, and carpenters were employed to scrape pictures by Holbein off the walls, and to replace them with decent plain paint. The ceiling of the Banqueting House, with its distinctly unparliamentary images, escaped because of its altitude.

In the bitter January of 1649 Whitehall was the stage for one of the climaxes of British history. On January 27 in Westminster Hall the president of the unconstitutional court, an obscure lawyer called John Bradshawe, after a vast rambling speech turgid with the scriptures, the classics, and medieval lawyers, condemned 'the said Charles Stuart' to be put to death 'by severing of his head from his Body'. So that he might not hear the hammering of the workmen building the scaffold outside his Banqueting House, Charles was removed to St James's. Here he said good-bye to his two youngest children, Princess Elizabeth, aged thirteen, and Henry, Duke of Gloucester, aged nine.

His daughter records:

He wished me not to grieve or torment myself for him, for that would be a glorious death he should die, it being for the laws and liberties of this land, and for maintaining the true Protestant religion. Taking his son on his knee, he said: 'Sweetheart, now they will cut off thy father's head; mark, child, what I say: they will cut off my head and perhaps make thee a king. But mark what I say. You must not be a king so long as your brothers Charles and James do live; for they will cut off your brothers' heads when they can catch them, and cut off thy head too at the last, and therefore I charge you do not be made a king by them.'

The little boy replied: 'I will be torn in pieces first.' Charles shared his trinkets, mostly broken Georges and Garter stars, between them. 'Most sorrowful was this parting, the young Princess shedding tears and crying lamentably, so as moved others to pity, that formerly were hard-hearted.'

Tuesday, January 30 dawned grey and very cold. Blocks of ice jammed the arches of old London Bridge. Charles got up between five and six o'clock, and put on an extra shirt, in case the cold made him tremble, 'which some observers', he said, 'will imagine proceeds from fear. I would have no such imputation. I fear not death. Death is not terrible to me. I bless my God I am prepared'. He put a clean handkerchief and an orange stuck full of cloves in the pocket of his doublet.

At ten it was time to go. The King, with his old friend Bishop Juxon of London and two Roundhead attendants, surrounded by an escort of halberdiers, walked across the park to Whitehall at his usual brisk pace. The route was lined with foot-soldiers. Drums throbbed and rolled remorselessly the whole way. Charles was taken into his private apartments in Whitehall for the last time. He refused lunch because he did not want to eat anything after Communion; but the Bishop persuaded him to eat a slice of bread and drink a glass of wine, 'in case some fitt of fainting might take him upon the scaffold'. He refused to let some pushing Puritan clergy, who had so often prayed against him during his life, come in to pray over him as he waited for his death.

At one o'clock he was summoned, and led through the galleries past crowds gathered 'to behold the saddest sight England ever saw'. He stepped out of the staircase window of the Banqueting House, which had been enlarged for the occasion, on to the scaffold, where two prudently anonymous, masked and fantastically disguised headsmen were waiting. The normal waist-high execution block at which the victim kneeled could not be found, so it had been replaced with a low, quartering-block on which the bodies of traitors were dismembered. Staples had been hammered into the sides of it, to which Charles could be tied if he struggled. He was going to have to lie flat on his face for his execution. A double regiment of horse stood several ranks deep around the scaffold to prevent demonstrations. The breast-high railing of the scaffold was draped in black cloth, so that all the dense crowds in the street would see would be the bright flash of the axe at the top of its swing. It was Whitehall's terrible second 'Masque of Blacknesse'. The roofs of all the neighbouring buildings were packed with spectators. One of them, Archbishop Usher, fainted when he saw the King step on to the scaffold. But one spectator watched Charles come out of the Banqueting House window 'with the same unconcernedness and motion, that he usually had, when he entered into it on a Masque-night'; and another reported that he 'strode the floor of death with a cheerful countenance'.

It was impossible to speak loud enough to make his voice heard by the crowd, so Charles made a short, formal dying speech to those on the scaffold, who included shorthand reporters. It set out his unbending political philosophy, and ended with the words: '. . . and therefore I tell you (and I pray God it be not laid to your charge) that I am the martyr of the people.' He told those who came forward to feel the axe: 'Do not spoil the axe; it would hurt more.'

Then he tucked his long hair under a white satin night-cap. Turning to Bishop Juxon, he said:

'I have a good cause and a gracious God on my side.'

Juxon: 'There is but one stage more. This stage is turbulent and troublesome: – it is a short one. . . . You haste to a crown of glory.'

Charles: 'I go from a corruptible to an incorruptible Crown, where no disturbance can be.'

Juxon: 'You are exchanged from a temporal to an eternal Crown, a good exchange.'

He took off his cloak, said the last word, 'Remember', to Juxon, and lay down with his head on the block. An eye-witness on the scaffold says the King was very 'majestick and steddy', and that when he laid his neck on the block, 'he perceived his eye as quick and lively, as ever he had seen it'. The executioner touched him to tuck some hair into the cap, and Charles, thinking it was the axe, told him sharply to wait for his signal. For a few minutes he lay there praying. Then he stretched out his arms, and the great axe fell. The second mysterious executioner held up the severed head, and shouted, 'Behold the head of a traitor.' A deep groan of horror rose from the crowd. One of them prayed that he might never hear such a sound on earth again. Then clattering troops of horse moved in, to drive the public towards Westminster and Charing Cross. Struggling crowds paid to dip their handkerchiefs in the King's blood, and to buy pieces of his hair as magical or grisly souvenirs.

Judgements of Whitehall's most famous scene have varied ever since, from the emotional Royalist's 'that horrible sentence upon the most innocent person in the world, the execution of that sentence by the most execrable murder that was ever committed since that of our blessed saviour'; to the Roundhead tract's view that Charles 'lived an enemy to the commonwealth, and died a martyr to prerogative'. But few have argued with the verdict of the bland, republican-inclined trimmer Marvell about Charles's dignity and courage on his death-day:

> He nothing common did or mean
> Upon that memorable scene:
> But with his keener eye
> The axe's edge did try.

Nothing in his life became him like the leaving it.

At first Cromwell lived in lodgings at the Cockpit, but when the Captain-General was declared Lord Protector, he moved himself across the road into the main palace of Whitehall. His wife Elizabeth was unenthusiastic about the move; and his mother 'very much mistrusted the issue of affairs, and would be often afraid, when she heard the noise of a musquet, that her son was shot, being exceedingly dissatisfied unless she might see him once a day at least'. The state apartments were used for strait-laced ceremonial to receive ambassadors or deputations from the House of Commons. The ambassadors from the States General of Holland were entertained in a Whitehall hung with royal tapestries and Cromwell's life-guards. After dinner they were joined by the Lady Protectress and other ladies, and enjoyed 'music, and voices and a psalm'.

A cookery book, published in 1664, and evidently written by a discarded and disgruntled master cook with chips on his shoulders, gives an intimate description of life in Whitehall under Elizabeth Cromwell:

She employed a surveyor to make her some little labyrinths and trap-stairs, by which she might, at all times, unseen, pass to and fro, and come unawares upon her servants, and keep them vigilant in their places and honest in the discharge thereof. Several repairs were likewise made in her own apartments, and many small partitions up and down, as well above stairs as in the cellars and kitchens, her highness-ship not yet being accustomed to that roomy and august dwelling, and perhaps afraid of the vastness and silentness thereof. She could never endure any whispering, or be alone by herself in any of the chambers. Much ado she had, at first, to raise her mind and deportment to this sovereign grandeur, and very difficult it was for her to lay aside those impertinent meannesses of her private fortune.

A snobbish Roundhead woman wrote that grandeur sat as ill on Elizabeth Cromwell as scarlet on an ape.

Cromwell saved the remains of the royal furniture from being dispersed. In 1656 John Evelyn ventured into Whitehall, 'where of many years I had not been, and found it very glorious and well-furnished, as far as I could safely go, and was glad to find they had not much defaced that rare piece of Henry VII etc., done on the walls of the King's privy chamber'.

From Whitehall the Lord Protector married his daughter Frances to Robert Rich 'with all imaginable pomp and lustre', and some scandal as well. There were '48 violins and 50 trumpets, and much mirth with frolics, besides mixt dancing (thing heretofore accounted profane), till 5 of the clock'. 'Insolent fools,' grumbled Lucy Hutchinson about the Cromwell ladies. Cromwell allowed himself £100,000 a year to spend on his household. In addition to his scarlet-coated life guards, and his servants, he had fifty gentlemen in personal attendance on him, in uniforms of black and grey with silver trimmings. He kept a good table, and his guests could eat the first pineapples imported to England.

On September 3, 1658, his lucky day, the anniversary of Dunbar and Worcester and the arrival before Drogheda, Cromwell died in his bed at Whitehall, after murmuring in his fever: 'It is a fearful thing to fall into the hands of the living God.' Offered a sleeping draught, he waved it aside, and said: 'It is not my design to drink of sleep, but my design is to make what haste I can to be gone.' He asked a chaplain if it was possible to fall from grace. When told it was not possible, he cried: 'Then I am safe, for I know that I was once in grace.' The sick-room was full of the rumour of the greatest storm England had known for a century. It tore out swathes of trees in St James's Park, swamped ships in the Thames, and ripped roofs off houses and steeples off churches. Cavaliers said it was the Devil coming to collect the regicide's soul. A breathless messenger brought the news to Charles II in Holland that it had 'pleased God out of his infinite goodness to do that which He would not allow any man the honour of doing'. The great Protector was buried with royal pomp; 'but,' wrote Evelyn, 'it was the joyfullest funeral I ever saw, for there were none that cried but dogs, which the soldiers hooted away with a barbarous noise, drinking, and taking tobacco in the streets as they went.'

The Rump Parliament ordered the sale of Whitehall, but before it could be done, General George Monk and his army had marched into London and lodged in the palace. People sang again the old ballad of 1643 :

> Though for a time we see Whitehall
> With cobwebs hanging on the wall
> Instead of gold and silver brave,
> Which formerly 'twas wont to have
> With rich perfumes,
> In every room,
> Delightful to that Princely train
> Which again you shall see
> When the time it shall be
> When the King enjoys his own again.

Charles II arrived to scenes of universal rapture which made that sardonic monarch remark that he was foolish not to have come home before, since every man in England was protesting that he had always longed for his return.

Restoration Whitehall was the most brilliant court in British history, the home of the King, his Ministers, courtiers, chaplains, mistresses (known behind their backs as 'the cattle'), and the gilded army that glittered round the throne. To pacify his panic-stricken Parliament Charles even allowed Titus Oates, whose venomous perjuries he saw through, apartments in Whitehall during the mass hysteria of the Popish Plot. The centre of intrigue and scandal, of cabal and the secret, black and grand design with France, life in Whitehall was described in unforgettable detail by Evelyn and Pepys. The hub of the Stuart government, as well as the focus of political intrigue and fashionable gaiety, was the Stone Gallery, which ran through the middle of Whitehall, open to all comers, and always packed with sight-seers, picture-gazers, place-seekers, rumour-mongers. 'It runs through the galleries,' was the traditional introduction to a piece of gossip, equivalent to the modern cliché, 'usually well-informed sources close to the corridors of power'. Charles could never bear to say no to anybody. So, to avoid ambitious or impecunious petitioners, he used to walk very fast through the galleries, and with his spaniels in the park, scattering corn to his ducks, and the inexpensive salutation 'God bless you, God bless you' in all directions.

A fragment of the merry informality and confusion of Whitehall is preserved in this contemporary letter:

There were lately several bullets, to the number of forty, shot into the King's gallery and garden; the Politicks judged there was treason intended . . . but at last it is found to be an ordinary fellow that keeps tame pigeons, which it seems his neighbour's cats are very lickorish of; he, to be revenged, watches to kill all cats with his stone-bag, and some of his shots have reached into Whitehall.

The King was a great tennis player, and had a 'steele-yard' installed in Henry VIII's old court on which to weigh himself before and after each match. He was highly gratified to have lost four and a half pounds, when Pepys weighed him after one match. He built a Pall Mall court behind Whitehall for that curious, golf-like pastime; according to Edmund Waller:

> No sooner has he touched the flying ball
> But 'tis already more than half the Mall,
> And such a fury from his arm has got
> As from a smoking culverin 'twere shot.
> May that ill fate my enemies befall
> To stand before his anger or his ball.

Restoration Whitehall is an inexhaustible source for the bedspring and chamber-pot school of history, with endless, famous scenes of bedroom farce featuring the virago Castlemaine, Frances Stewart, whose legs were the talk of Europe, and who was used as the model for Britannia on the coinage, pretty, witty Nell, and that 'known enemy to Virginity and Chastity, the Monarch of Great Britain'. Louise de Kérouaille, called Carwell by the insular English, and promoted Duchess of Portsmouth by Charles, had her lodgings rebuilt three times during her reign, in wildly extravagant profusion of Gobelin and gold, with ten times the 'richness and glory' of the Queen's rooms, and much furniture and painting which properly belonged to the Queen. The satirical Earl of Rochester, John Wilmot, wrote:

> Restless he rolls about from Whore to Whore,
> A Merry Monarch, scandalous and poor.

The epitome of the court was the great ball on the last night of 1662, when in the glitter of diamonds and tall candles, Charles led a single partner in the Coranto while everybody else stood, and then called out for the first country dance, which he said was 'Cuckolds all awry. The old dance of England'.

Queen Catherine eventually got over her jealousy of the seraglio of concubines, who sat in the royal box, and travelled in the royal coach with her. Visiting Charles one morning she noticed a female slipper beside the bed, and quickly left the room laughing, in case 'the pretty little fool' hiding behind the curtains should catch cold. The complicated nocturnal manoeuvres up the back stairs and through locked doors were organised by Charles's trusted servant, William Chiffinch, who held all his keys. The harem inevitably and hilariously quarrelled among themselves. Nell Gwynn, coming back to Whitehall during the frenzied anti-Papist agitation about the succession, was mistaken for one of the Catholic mistresses and mobbed by the crowd. She stuck her head out of the window and cried: 'Be silent, good people. I am the *Protestant* whore.'

The relaxed sexual atmosphere of Whitehall, after the stern rigours of the Commonwealth, was not confined to the royalties. Pepys, so honest at recording his unconsciously ludicrous moments, walking through the palace,

had a pleasant rencontre with a lady in mourning, that, by the little light I had, seemed handsome. I passing by her, I did observe she looked back again and again upon me, I suffering her to go before and it being now duske.

He followed her,

and took occasion, in the new passage now built, where the walke is to be to take her by the hand, to lead her through, which she willingly accepted, and I led her to the Great Gate, and there left her, she telling me, of her own accord, that she was going as far as Charing Cross; but my boy was at the Gate, and so je durst not go con her, which vexed me, and my mind (God forgive me) did run après her . . . that night, though I have reason to thank God, and so I do now, that I was not tempted to go further.

The Banqueting House was the setting for the ancient ceremony of Touching for the King's Evil, in which the King miraculously cured scrofula or struma by stroking the tuberculous ulcers and swellings on the neck with his hands. This faith in the supernatural and therapeutic virtues of the royal hand originated in the mists of the Dark Ages, and was obviously connected with the doctrine of divine right, and the sacred priest-king. As early as the Bible, and in Roman times, the royal touch was supposed to cure scrofula. Clovis, the sixth-century King of the Franks, and Philip I of France (1060–1108) are both reported to have cured by touch. In England the practice was performed by Edward the Confessor, and possibly by predecessors of his.

Royalist propaganda alleges that Cromwell tried to perform the miracle, and, but of course, naturally failed. Charles, in the course of his reign, touched nearly 100,000 persons. In one year the crowd struggling to get near him was so violent that half a dozen of the sick were trampled to death. Pepys called it 'a simple office and an ugly one', but it gained its greatest popularity under Charles.

Evelyn described its first performance after the Restoration, in July 1660:

His Majesty sitting under his State in the Banqueting House, the Chirurgeons cause the sick to be brought or led up to the throne who, kneeling, the King strokes their faces or cheekes with both hands at once: at which instant a Chaplaine in his formalities says, 'He put his hands upon them and he healed them'. This is said to every one in particular.

After he had touched the day's quota of strumous patients, Charles hung round the neck of each of them a white ribbon strung with an 'angel', a small gold coin engraved with the figure of an angel, sometimes called a touchpiece. The service ended with prayers and a blessing. Then the Lord Chamberlain and the Comptroller of the Household brought in a basin, jug and towel for the King to wash his hands. It was the business of the royal surgeons to examine applicants, to let in those who came for the cure, and shut out those who came for the gold. Honest, sensible William III refused to touch, and referred patients to his exiled predecessor James II, who continued to touch in exile, as did his Pretender son and grandsons. On a single occasion William was pestered into laying his hands on a scrofula-sufferer. 'God give you better health,' he said, 'and more sense.'

Queen Anne revived the practice, but it died with her. One of the last persons touched by her was Samuel Johnson, aged three, who later had 'a confused, but somehow a sort of solemn recollection of a lady in diamonds and a long black hood'.

Animals fared better than the strumous in a seventeenth-century court. The prevalence and status of dogs in Whitehall under Charles II is shown by orders in the accounts for 'cushions for ye Doggs', and for a wire screen with a walnut frame 'for his Majesties new Bedchamber, to preserve the Bed from being spoyled by the Doggs'. Unfortunately the Queen's bed was not similarly protected, and one day a tame fox followed Charles into her bedroom, jumped on the bed, and brought on a miscarriage. Pet birds were everywhere, even in the Queen's bedroom, in brass cages hanging from pulleys.

Charles died in Whitehall in one of the great death-bed scenes of English history or fiction. On the Sunday before his death the pious Evelyn visited the palace. 'I can never forget,' he wrote,

the inexpressible luxury and profaneness, gaming and all dissoluteness, and as it were total forgetfulness of God (it being Sunday evening) which . . . I was witness of, the King sitting and toying with his concubines, Portsmouth, Cleveland and Mazarin, a French boy singing love-songs in that glorious gallery, whilst about twenty of the great courtiers and other dissolute persons were at basset round a large table, a bank of at least two thousand in gold before them . . . Six days after all was in dust.

The next morning while he was being shaved Charles collapsed in a hideous, foaming fit. For the next few days with great stoicism and in great pain he put up with the purgatives, burning plasters, blisters, bleedings, and the other loathsome prescriptions of seventeenth-century medicine. But he refused to take Communion from the hands of the Bishops of the Church of England. Sometimes he said there was no hurry, sometimes that he was too weak. His brother James, the Duke of York, was too busy posting guards, obtaining signatures, and securing the succession to realise what was up. But the Duchess of Portsmouth got a message through to him that Charles wanted to die reconciled to the Roman Catholic Church, but could not tell anyone, because his sick room was permanently full of Protestant clergymen. Catholic James bent and whispered in his dying brother's ear. Charles replied: 'Yes, yes with all my heart.' The room was cleared, even of the doctors. A Benedictine monk, John Huddleston (who had saved the King's life after the battle of Worcester, and was therefore a privileged person though a Catholic in Whitehall), disguised in a cloak and a flowing wig, was smuggled up the back stairs by Chiffinch, and received Charles into the Roman Catholic Church.

Charles said good-bye to his mistresses and illegitimate children, and, according to one slightly suspect source, told James: 'Do not let poor Nelly starve.' The Queen fainted, and sent word that she was too upset to resume her post by the bedside, but begged his forgiveness. 'Alas, poor woman,' he replied; 'She ask my pardon? I beg hers with all my heart: take her back that answer.' And with a last flicker of the old urbanity, the wittiest British King died: 'I have been a most unconscionable time a-dying; but I hope you will excuse it.'

Whitehall was the location for most of the major and depressing events of the three-year reign of James II, that impenetrably obstinate man, who held the 'strange notion' that no regard was 'to be had to the pleasing of the people', and who was invincibly convinced that anybody who opposed him was a traitor. Sir Christopher Wren built him a 'Popish' chapel in Whitehall. At Whitehall James had his famous confrontations with the 'Seven Bishops', when his stubborn bigotry had driven even high Anglicans from the doctrine of passive obedience. On top of the Banqueting House James put up the large wrought-iron weather-vane which is still there, to show whether a Popish west wind was blowing, or a Protestant east wind, bringing his successors, his daughter Mary and his son-in-law William of Orange from Holland. And from Whitehall on a dark and stormy night Mary of Modena and her unfortunate infant son, wrapped in rumours of warming-pan, escaped across the Thames; followed shortly by James, who threw the Great Seal in the river as he left, in the childish hope of causing as much chaos as possible for the new regime.

William and Mary were offered the crown jointly at the last great national ceremony to be held in the Banqueting House.

The Lords and Commons of England . . . went in a body with their Speakers and Maces to Whitehall to pray the Prince and Princess of Orange to accept the Crown. Their Highnesses received them in the Banqueting House (under a Canopy of State), being at the upper (Westminster) end of the Room, and the Yeomen of the Guard ranged on both sides: the Lords and Commons entered at the lower end . . . their Highnesses were Graciouslie pleased to signifie their . . . consent to accept the Crown. . . . Whereupon there were shouts of joy both in the Banqueting House and in all the Courts of Whitehall. Then the Lords and Commons came down to Whitehall Gate, where . . . York Herald did . . . proclaim the Prince and Princess of Orange King and Queen of England, France and Ireland, with all the Dominions and territories thereto belonging.

Mary shocked even staunch Protestants by her behaviour when she arrived in Whitehall, 'laughing and jolly, as to a wedding, so as to seem quite transported'. Evelyn and everyone else felt she should have put on a sober face, out of respect for her father whom she had displaced, however pleased she was underneath the mask. Instead, 'she ran about it, looking into every closet and conveniency, and turning up the quilts upon the bed, as people do when they come to an inn'. Macaulay has a devilish, devious and implausible theory that she behaved this way under instructions from William, who wanted her to make herself unpopular so that she would not be made Queen on her own, without him as partner.

Mary may have been pleased with Whitehall, but William could not live there. His asthma could not stand the fog, the damp, the coal-smoke, and the fumes of the riverside palace. Evelyn compared London's 'poysoned air' to Lake Avernus, which was said to suffocate birds unwise enough to fly over it. Visitors to Whitehall were shocked to hear the King gasping for breath and coughing till the tears ran down his cheeks. So Kensington was built as his principal London residence.

Whitehall remained an essential trip for tourists. A guide-book for French visitors to London written in 1693 advises:

*Prennez un Hackney-Coach & vous en allez en droiture a 'Whitehall', vous y verrez le statue de Jacques Second. . . . Entrant dans le Jardin, n'oubliez pas d'ajuster votre montre au quandran Solaire qui y est, car c'est la plus belle pièce que vous puisses jamais voir en ce genre.*

The great, rambling palace, with its timber buildings and wooden galleries, had always had a fatal facility for conflagration. After one of the many fires, regulations were made in 1662 that for every chimney in the palace there should be a leather bucket filled with water. A fine of 10s was levied for any chimney that caught fire. A strict rule was made that nobody was to clear a chimney by firing a gun up it.

The palace nearly burned down in 1691. Then on January 4, 1698 a careless Dutchwoman lit a big charcoal fire in an upper room near the river to dry some linen. The fire caught the clothes, spread to the hangings, and burst irresistibly over the rest of the palace, blazing for seventeen hours, destroying all Whitehall except for the Banqueting House and the Holbein and Whitehall Gates. 'Whitehall burnt: nothing but walls and ruins left,' wrote an unhappy Evelyn, with Tacitean terseness. Another Londoner recorded:

It is a dismal sight to behold such a glorious, famous, and much renowned palace reduced to a heap of rubbish and ashes, which the day before might justly contend with any palace in the world for riches, nobility, honour, and grandeur.

William visited the smoking débris the next day, and vowed he would rebuild an even finer Whitehall. But he never did. The need for an unlimited palace to hold the court and the council and the sight-seeing general public had died at the Glorious Revolution, along with the idea of an unlimited monarchy.

# IX

# HAMPTON COURT

For he who has the affairs of his Prince in his hand, ought to lay aside all thoughts of himself, and regard nothing but what is for the profit of his master.

THE 'butcher's cur' from Ipswich, who became one of the choice and master politicians of his age, did not pay enough attention to this item of advice in Machiavelli's cool contemporary handbook of statecraft, though he did to most of the others. Of course, in the sixteenth century personal ostentation and magnificent palaces were weapons of diplomatic one-upmanship, in the same way that ludicrously ornate military uniforms were ploys of psychological warfare on the battlefield. Hampton Court, though it was, in fact, neither the favourite nor the most splendid of Thomas Wolsey's almost neurotically profuse building operations, became the red brick symbol for his pride, vain pomp and glory, and terrible fall. It was too royal for a subject. As John Skelton wrote, sarcastically:

> Why come ye not to Courte?
> To whyche Courte?
> To the Kynges Courte;
> Or to Hampton Courte.

In 1514, aged about forty, rising to the crest of his career, having just been made Archbishop of York, 'the most Rev. Father in God, Thomas Wolsey' leased the site of Hampton Court from the Knight Hospitallers of St John at an annual rent of £50. Apart from the convenience of the quick river-road to London, one of its main attractions for a hypochondriac was that all the experts agreed that it was a place of 'extraordinary salubrity'. The country house he built there was a palace. Its vast quadrangle, its thousand richly furnished rooms, including apartments for 280 guests, its arras and cloth of gold were described with bated and incredulous breath by contemporaries. Sebastian Giustiniani, the Venetian ambassador, wrote: 'One has to traverse eight rooms before one reaches his audience chamber, and they are all hung with tapestry, which is changed every week.' These famous tapestries illustrated all the most dramatic scenes in the Bible, classical mythology, Hannibal and Hercules, the Romance of the Rose, and such long-forgotten and alarming favourites as 'The Duke of Bry and the gyante Orrible'.

The most lavish of the many state functions at Hampton Court under the great Cardinal occurred in 1527, when at his own expense he entertained the French ambassador and his retinue of 400 over to sign a treaty. George Cavendish, who wrote Wolsey's biography, was involved in many of the arrangements, and gives an enthusiastic description of the party. The interminable banquet was interlarded with elaborate 'subtleties' – a model of St Paul's Cathedral, figures of knights fighting and courtiers dancing made out of sugar, 'as well counterfeited as if the painter should should have painted it'. Then 'went the cups merrily about, so that many of the Frenchmen were fain to be led up to their beds'. Even when they had staggered to bed, as if they had not eaten and swilled enough already, 'every chamber had a basin and a ewer of silver, some gilt, some parcel gilt . . . and one pot at the least with wine and beer . . . and a fine manchet and a chet-loaf of bread'.

By now Wolsey had become uneasily aware that his luxury at Hampton Court was attracting envious eyes, particularly the sinister and materialistic eyes of the King. He tried to stave off the danger by the subterfuge of 'giving' the palace to Henry. Letters to the King were addressed from 'your Grace's Manor of Hampton Court'. To everybody else it was still firmly the Cardinal's manor. The Flemish ambassador wrote home that Wolsey had given 'Hanten Court' to Henry: 'It seems to me that this is as good as if he had said, "I give you a little pig of your own breeding at your own great cost."' Whatever nervous semantic equivocation there was about the ownership of the palace, Wolsey continued to live there until his disgrace, dismissal and attainder in 1529, when he gave Hampton Court to Henry again, properly this time.

The King moved in with acquisitive and indecent haste, and began a programme of enlarging and altering the building. He built a Great Hall, a new gallery, new kitchens, squillery, sellery, spicery, scalding house, feather house, and all the other extraordinary modern conveniences. Henry was so impatient for his new possession that the accounts show the purchase of tallow candles, 'spent by the workmen in the night times upon the paving of the Hall, for the hasty expedition of the same at 18d the dozen'. The builders were also paid overtime for 'working in their own times and drinking times'. The King's new chief minister, Sir Thomas Cromwell, was so distressed by the extravagance of Henry's furious building craze that he wrote:

What a great charge it is to the King to continue his buildings in so many places at once. How proud and false the workmen be; and if the King would spare for one year how profitable it would be to him.

One of the priorities was to remove Wolsey's reproachful arms and motto, 'Dominus mihi adjutor', from the walls, and plaster them over with the King's arms, and with his initials coyly interlaced with those of his new 'awne darling', Anne Boleyn. Long before his divorce, men were building 'Anne Bouillayne's lodgynges at Hamptone Courte'. Equally indispensable additions for the relentlessly athletic King were the Tilt-Yard, bowling alleys, archery butts, and 'close tennys play'. That invaluable reporter Giustiniani wrote: 'He is most fond of tennis at which game it is the prettiest thing in the world to see him play, his fair skin glowing through a shirt of the finest texture.'

The paint was hardly dry on Boleyn's badges and initials when the workmen had to be called in again to alter them to 'J's for Jane Seymour. At Hampton Court the new Queen gave birth to that literal matter of life and death, a Tudor prince, Edward, and there she died shortly afterwards of puerperal septicaemia.

The next Queen but one, Katherine Howard, had a considerable and terrifying connection with Hampton Court. After she had been married to Henry for just over a year, during Mass at Hampton Court Cranmer slipped a note into the King's hand giving him the lethal details of the Queen's premarital sex life. In the palace the Archbishop conducted his harrowing, hysterical cross-examination of Katherine:

. . . as for carnall knowledge, I confess as I did before, that divers times he hath lyen with me, sometime in his doublet and hose, and two or three times naked: but not so naked that he had nothing upon him; for he had alwayes at the least his doublet, and as I do think, his hose also: but I mean naked, when his hose was put down.

During the petrified interview she let drop the finally fatal name of Thomas Culpeper, who had been her lover after her marriage. When Henry was shown the proofs,

his heart was so pierced with pensiveness, that long it was before his majesty could speak and utter the sorrow of his heart unto us, and finally with plenty of tears (which was strange in his courage) opened the same.

The King, after bitterly complaining about 'his ill-luck in meeting with such ill-conditioned wives', rode away from Hampton Court with no company but musicians.

Katherine, seeing the shadow of the axe, provided the palace with one of its ample stock of ghost stories. There is a horrid legend that she ran shrieking in panic to try to get to Henry while he was hearing Mass in the chapel, but was stopped by the guards and carried back to her room. Unperturbed, Henry went on hearing Mass through the screams in the background. Katherine's ghost is alleged to run screaming down the haunted gallery at Hampton Court, 'and on her face a ghastly look of despair', for all eternity. In fact, the legend appears to be based on a foundation of painted smoke, for Henry, with his typical horror of domestic confrontation, seems to have rushed away from the palace with his musicians before Katherine was told of the charges that had been brought against her.

In spite of his shuddering and mutual ill-luck with his wives, in spite of his farcically frequent honeymoons at Hampton Court, Henry came back there for his sixth and final attempt at matrimony, with domesticated Katherine Parr, who had the good luck and good management to outlive the formidable old ogre.

His daughter Mary spent her honeymoon with Philip of Spain at the palace; one of the rare moments of happiness, say the romantics, in her bleak and bitter life. A member of their court wrote: 'Their majesties are the happiest married couple in the world, and are more in love with each other than I can write here.' A young Spaniard was less starry-eyed, saying that Mary was 'not at all beautiful, small . . . of white complexion, and fair, and has no eyebrows'. Her voice was 'rough and loud, almost like a man's so that when she speaks she is always heard a long way off'. Her eyes were 'greyish and pale and so short-sighted that to read she must hold the page close to her face'.

Hampton Court was the setting for the pathetic and poignant episode of her false pregnancy. The thirty-eight-year-old Queen had always had irregular and agonising menstrual periods, and when in 1554 she started to swell significantly, it was joyfully diagnosed that she was about to produce that dangerous, rare, and longed-for creature, a Tudor heir. Jubilant bonfires and banquets were prepared. Letters announcing the birth were written, with the sex of the child and the date left blank, and signed by the King and Queen. Hampton Court was equipped with a regal establishment of nurses, midwives, rockers, and 'a cradle veri sump-

Whitehall Palace today. The Banqueting Hall interior and ceiling

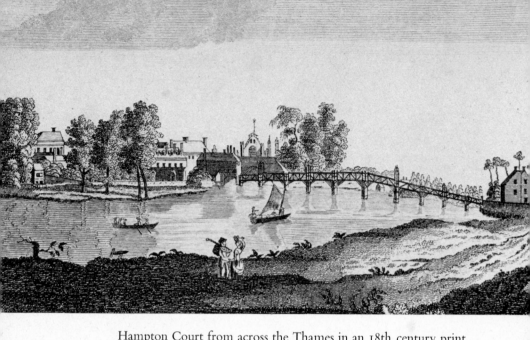

Hampton Court from across the Thames in an 18th century print

Hampton Court from the public gardens

tuouslie and gorgeouslie trimmed'. The cradle was inscribed in English and Latin:

> The child which thou to Mary, O Lord of Might, has sen[t],
> To England's joy, in health preserve, keep and defend.

But the sterile months dragged by with no sign of a baby. The doctors bumbled bombastically that after 'the full moon and its occultation', the Queen would give birth. Moons waxed and moons waned, but the Queen never did. So desperate was she for an heir that she showed all the symptoms of pregnancy, from morning sickness to the 'swelling of the paps and emission of milk'. Philip told the Venetian ambassador that she felt 'certain pains which indicate the announcement of childbirth'. The protracted pregnancy became a joke. The Polish ambassador, whose English was not fluent, misunderstood the gossip, and formally congratulated Philip on the birth of an heir, 'to the laughter and amusement of many personages who were there'.

In fact, tragically, Mary had ovarian dropsy, but clung desperately to her delusions of pregnancy. When at last even she had to admit the truth to herself, Philip, who was eleven years younger than she was, and was said to find her unattractive and lacking 'all sensibility of the flesh', made off home for Spain at high speed.

No great constitutional scenes happened at Hampton Court under Elizabeth, but it was the stage for some of her most characteristic informal appearances in history. Here for instance was played the notorious tennis match in which the scandal about her enigmatic relationship with Robert Dudley, Earl of Leicester, blazed up in public. Dudley was playing against the Duke of Norfolk, the leader of the conservative feudal potentates, who viewed with furious suspicion the rise to favour of Elizabeth's handsome, parvenu Master of Horse, whose house was founded upon corruption and treason. Dudley was described by a rival and more eligible suitor of the Queen as 'The King that is to be'. Sweating from the tennis, Dudley helped himself to the Queen's napkin and casually wiped his face. Norfolk, crying that he was too saucy, threatened to hit him with his racket. 'Here upon rose a great troble and the quene offendid sore with the duke.'

Whether Elizabeth and Dudley were lovers is one of those questions on which torrents of words have been expended without producing any competent conclusion. The state papers are full of second-hand gossip, of the Spanish ambassador reporting that his French colleague 'swore to me . . . that he had been assured by a person who was in a position to know that Lord Robert had slept with the Queen on New Year's night'. The only horse's mouth evidence on this intimate subject was given at Hampton Court, when Elizabeth thought she was dying of smallpox. The council, in justifiable panic about the succession, gathered round her bed. Recovering consciousness, the Queen swore to them 'that though she loved, and always had loved, Lord Robert, as God was her witness, nothing improper had ever passed between them'. And she begged that he might be made Protector if she died.

At Hampton Court Elizabeth had her diplomatic fencing matches with Sir James Melville, the young courtier who was sent to her as go-between by Mary, Queen of Scots. As well as talking politics and prevarication, insecure Elizabeth was extremely curious to hear all about the appearance and talents of the rival Queen who claimed her throne. Which of them had the prettier hair, and which was the fairer? Smooth Melville took pleasure in reporting his reply. Elizabeth was 'the fairest Queen in England, and mine the fairest Queen in Scotland'.

Who was the taller?

Well, actually, Mary, answered Melville.

Then, said Elizabeth smugly, 'she is too high; for I myself am neither too high nor too low'.

Did Mary play on the virginal well?

Melville: 'Reasonably for a Queen.'

So it was arranged for the Scottish courtier to listen by accident to the superiority of Elizabeth's performance.

He was taken quietly to a room where the Queen was tinkling away with her back to the door.

I stood a pretty space, hearing her play excellently well; but she left off immediately, so soon as she turned her about and saw me. She appeared to be surprised to see me, and came forward, seeming to strike me with her hand; alleging that she used not to play before men, but when she was solitary, to shun melancholy.

Finally, after two days of strenuous galliards,

she inquired to me, whether she or my Queen danced best? I answered, the Queen danced not so high, and disposedly as she did.

Elizabeth was always a vehement dancer. When she was nearly seventy somebody watched her through a window of Hampton Court, 'dancing the Spanish Panic to a whistle and a tabor [small drum], none other being with her but my Lady Warwick'.

In spite of many flirtatious and complimentary conversations, Melville could not pin Elizabeth down on the real purpose of his mission: the acknowledgement of Mary as her successor. 'She was not so old,' she told him, characteristically, 'that they need continually keep her death before her eyes by talking about the succession.'

Several tourist's accounts of Hampton Court from Elizabeth's reign survive. Lupold von Wedel came to 'Hampenkort' on a Sunday in 1585, and saw Elizabeth march in magnificent procession to chapel:

Then followed the Queen in black, because she is in mourning for the Prince of Orange and the Duke d'Alençon. On either side of her crisp hair hung a great pearl the size of a hazel-nut. The common people who formed 2 rows on either side her path, fell upon their knees. The Queen's demeanour, however, was gracious and gentle and so was her speech, and from rich and poor she took petitions in a modest manner. . . . It being late in the day there was no sermon, but only singing and prayers. Afterwards the Queen returned to her apartments. When the people fell on their knees, she said 'I thank you with all my heart'.

On his tour of England some years later, Paul Hentzner was vastly impressed with Hampton Court, which he described in detail:

. . . In short, all the walls of the palace shine with gold and silver. Here is also a certain cabinet called Paradise where besides that everything glitters so with silver, gold, and jewels, as to dazzle one's eyes, there is a musical instrument made all of glass except the strings.

And Thomas Platter reported that the walls of Hampton Court were 'hung with extremely costly tapestries worked in gold and silver and silk, so lifelike that one might take the people and plants for real'.

One of the famous features of Elizabeth's regular visits to Hampton Court for Christmas were the dramatic entertainments performed in the Great Hall. The *Accounts of the Revels of the Court* give curious details of the properties, lighting, casts, and scenery of these performances. Dressers were in charge of 'airing, repairing, amending, brushing, sponging, rubbing, wiping, sweeping, cleaning, putting in order, folding, laying-up and safe bestowal of the garments, vestures, apparel, disguising, properties, and furniture . . . which else would be mouldy, musty, moth-eaten, and rotten'. There is speculation that *The Historie of Error showen at Hampton Court on New Year's Day at night, enacted by the children of Powles'* was the foundation of Shakespeare's *Comedy of Errors*.

Elizabeth's last visit to Hampton Court in 1599 was typical of her intimate, private-life relationship with the palace, as well as of her horror of old age. When the time came to leave, the day being passing foul, she would (as was her custom) go on horseback, although she is scarce able to sit upright, and my Lord Hunsdon said, 'It was not meet for one of her majesty's years to ride in such a storm'. She answered in great anger, 'My years! Maids, to your horses quickly'; and so rode all the way, not vouchsafing any gracious countenance to him for two days.

Under pedantic James I the palace was used for the great Hampton Court conference in 1604 to try to reach a compromise between the irreconcilable Anglican bishops and the Puritan divines. The King displayed much theological and scriptural erudition, but does not seem to have been a very impartial chairman. He told the Puritans, who asked that their clergy might be allowed to meet for prophesyings, 'If you aim at a Scottish presbytery it agreeth as well with monarchy as God and the devil'. James wrote to a friend in Scotland: 'I have peppered thaime soundlie.' A neutral observer summed up:

The King talked much Latin, and disputed with Dr Reynolds [a Puritan]; but he rather used upbraidings than arguments; and told them they wanted to strip Christ again, and bid them *away with their snivelling*. Moreover he wished those who would take away the surplice *might want linen for their own breech*! The bishop seemed much pleased and said his Majesty spoke by the power of inspiration. I wist not what they mean: but the spirit was rather foul-mouthed.

The only positive achievement of the conference, but a magnificent one, was the decision to make a new translation of the Bible. After seven years' work by a body of about fifty scholars, the stately Authorised Version emerged.

Charles I's early visits to Hampton Court were chiefly remarkable for his noisy quarrels with his fifteen-year-old wife, Henrietta Maria, over her large, unpopular, French, and Roman Catholic household. The King's bosom comrade, the Duke of Buckingham, added fuel to the fracas by reminding the Queen, in a palace where the reminder was unnecessary, that 'queens of England had been beheaded before now'. Eventually the schism became so deep and notorious that the French sent over the Marquis de Bassompierre as a conciliator and marriage guidance counsellor. His success was limited. He persuaded the Queen to cut down her French retinue, and to scrape along with only one bishop, ten priests, and a confessor. But he himself wrote: 'I have received condescension from the Spaniards and civility even from the Swiss, but English arrogance I have never overcome.'

Charles was brought back to Hampton Court as a prisoner of the Roundheads during the Civil War, 'rather as a guarded and attended prince than as a conquered and purchased captive'. Cromwell visited him there several times for the intricate negotiations by which he hoped to restore Charles as a constitutional monarch with limited powers. John Evelyn visited him too: 'I came to Hampton Court, where I had the honour to kiss his majesty's hand, he being in the power of those execrable villains, who not long after murdered him.' The trouble was that Charles believed he had a divine right to bluff and lie to traitors, in order to regain his throne. It was impossible to do serious business with him. Underground he was working away like an indiscreet mole, putting himself up for auction to Parliament, to the Scots, to factions in the army simultaneously, always having at the back of his mind the ultimate bolt-hole to France and Henrietta Maria. While negotiating with Cromwell, he is supposed to have written to the Queen that 'he should know in time how to deal with the rogues, who instead of a silken garter should be fitted with a hempen cord'.

After two months of captivity and infuriating duplicity at Hampton Court, having withdrawn his parole, Charles escaped from the palace on a stormy night, and rode down the country to Carisbrooke Castle on the Isle of Wight. It was widely believed at the time that Cromwell connived at the escape, and indeed pushed Charles into it with a letter warning that he was in danger of being murdered. In a letter which he left behind for his jailer at Hampton Court, Charles explained:

I assure you it was not the letter you shewed me to-day (the hazard of assassination) that made me take this resolution, nor any advertisement of that kinde. But I confess that I am loath to be made a close prisoner, under pretence of securing my life. I had almost forgot to ask you to send the black grew bitch to the Duke of Richmond.

After Charles's head had fallen, Parliament voted to sell Hampton Court and all its priceless contents. That doctrinaire ideologue, Sir Harry Vane junior, proposed it should be pulled down as 'it was amongst those things that prove Temptations to Ambitious Men, and exceedingly tend to sharpen their Appetite to ascend the Throne'. But although many of the treasures were sold at bargain prices – Elizabeth's virginal fetched £10 – the palace was kept, 'for the public use of the Commonwealth'.

When Cromwell became Lord Protector he made it his country house where he was free to relax with his family, away from the threat of assassination. The Royalist propagandist James Heath in his *Flagellum*, writing with bias and embroidery, said:

His custom was now to divert himself frequently at *Hampton-Court* (which he had saved from Sale, with other Houses of the Kings, for his own greatnesse), whither he went and came in post, with his Guards behind and before, as not yet secure of his Life from the justice of some avenging hand; Here he used to hunt, and at the fall of a Deer, where he would be sure to be present, embrue his hands in the blood of it, and therewith asperse and sprinkle his Attendants. . . . His own Diet was very spare, and not so curious, except in publique Treatments, which were constantly given every Monday in the week to all the Officers of the Army not below a Captain, where he dined with them, and shewed a hundred Antick Tricks, as throwing of cushions, and putting live Coals into their Pockets and Boots. . . . He had twenty other freaks in his head, for sometimes before he had half dined, he would give order for a Drum to beat, and call in his Foot Guards, like a Kennel of Hounds, to snatch off the meat from his Table, and tear it in pieces.

At Hampton Court Cromwell caught what contemporary doctors described as a bastard tertian ague which was to kill him. George Fox visited him with a petition from the Quakers, and wrote: 'Before I came to him as he rode at the head of his life-guards, I saw and felt a waft of death go forth against him; and when I came to him he looked like a dead man.'

Charles II brought his Portuguese bride, Catherine of Braganza, to honeymoon at Hampton Court, and London flocked down to give her an extremely searching inspection, and to gossip how she would 'put Madame Castlemaine's nose out of joynt'. There was the customary British hostility about the nasty foreign appearance and clothes of her ladies: 'six frights . . . and a duenna, another monster.'

Evelyn peered at her having supper privately in her bed-chamber. 'Hampton Court,' he wrote,

is as noble and uniform a pile, and as capacious as any Gothic architecture can have made it. There is incomparable furniture in it, especially hangings designed by Raphael, very rich with gold; . . . of the tapestries, I believe the world can show nothing nobler of the kind than the stories of Abraham and Tobit. The gallery of horns is very particular for the vast beams of stags, elks, antelopes, &c. The Queen's bed was an embroidery of silver on crimson velvet, and cost 8000L, being a present made by the States of Holland when his Majesty returned. . . . The great looking-glass and toilet, of beaten and massive gold, was given by the Queen-Mother. The Queen brought over with her from Portugal such Indian cabinets as had never been seen here.

A French visitor at the same time was less overwhelmed with enthusiasm.

We likewise went to see *Hampton-Court*, where the court is at present, and which is the *Fountainbleau* of *England*. We had the honour of seeing their majesties there: The young queen is low, and of a brown complexion; and, by her face, 'tis easy to discover that she has a great deal of goodness and sweetness in her nature. . . . As for *Hampton-Court*, 'tis a magnificent pile of building; but, upon my word, comes not up either to our *St Germain's*, or *Fountainbleau*, no more than *Whitehall* is to be put in the same scale with the *Louvre*, or *St James's* house with *Luxemburgh* palace.

During the honeymoon Barbara Villiers, Countess of Castlemaine, produced a son christened Charles after the King, his father, who stood sponsor. With her highly developed talent for creating scenes, Castlemaine asked the King to prove his love for her by making her Lady of the Queen's Bedchamber. The Queen angrily crossed her name off the list. And the atmosphere at Hampton Court became strained and sulky. Charles tried to break the deadlock by bringing Castlemaine into the Queen's presence chamber suddenly, without warning, and introducing her. Catherine promptly fainted, and was carried out with her nose bleeding, having won that particular round. The Lord Chancellor, Clarendon, was given the unenviable job of persuading Catherine to be complaisant. Evenings at Hampton Court were spent wrestling with the Queen's conscience. With an aspersion at the morals of her brothers, Clarendon asked whether she imagined that a future Queen of Portugal would find that particular court so full of chaste affection. Eventually Catherine broke, and agreed to co-operate in her husband's unconventional idea of matrimony. Before the honeymoon was over Castlemaine had been given apartments at Hampton Court. Charles's chief contribution to the palace was to the gardens. His head gardener, called Rose, laid out the patterns of yew trees, the avenues of limes, and the great canal.

William and Mary made Hampton Court one of their principal residences, and massively rebuilt it, to make it suitable for contemporary state purposes. After hunting, William's favourite amusements were architecture and gardening. Sir Christopher Wren pulled down more than half of the informal, inconvenient, rambling, turreted Tudor palace, and replaced it with the formal symmetry of the Renaissance in red brick and Portland stone. Grinling Gibbons carved the woodwork. Verrio painted gaudy creatures from the classics sprawling over every available ceiling.

In every corner of the mansion appeared a profusion of geegaws, not yet familiar to English eyes. Mary had acquired at the Hague a taste for the porcelain of China, and amused herself by forming at Hampton a vast collection of hideous images, and of vases on which houses, trees, bridges, and mandarins were depicted in outrageous defiance of all the laws of perspective.

The Queen gardened in the formal French style, and planted orange trees in honour of William. When the King was away in Ireland or Holland, letters from Mary constantly complained about the delays in the rebuilding caused by the 'want of money and Portland stone'.

Because William and Mary were joint sovereigns, Wren had to build duplicate sets of state apartments around the Fountain Court. Protocol insisted that there had to be a King's staircase as well as Queen's staircase, and so on. Opinions have been furiously divided ever since about the great rebuilding. There have been wails of anguish about the barbarian destruction of Tudor Hampton Court. Daniel Defoe speaks for the defence:

When *Hampton Court* will find such another favourable Juncture as in King *William's* Time, when the remainder of her Ashes shall be swept away, and her compleat Fabric, as designed by King *William*, shall be finish'd, I cannot tell; but if ever that shall be, I know of no Palace in *Europe, Versailles* excepted, which can come up to her, either for Beauty or Magnificence, or for Extent of Building, and the Ornaments attending it.

Macaulay fence-sits about the reconstruction: '. . . not designed with the purest taste, but stately, spacious, and commodious.'

Hungry to find fault, the Tories complained bitterly about the expense of the works at Hampton. And almost everybody complained that the King spent far too much time there. Bishop Burnet, dedicated Whig, wrote:

The King, a very few days after he was set on the throne, went out to Hampton Court, and from that palace came into town only on council days: so that the face of a court and the rendezvous, usual in the public rooms, was now quite broken. This gave an early and general disgust. The gaiety and diversions of a court disappeared.

When Mary died, the plan for a complete rebuilding of the palace was abandoned, or at least slowed down. When he was in England, William continued to spend as much time as possible in his favourite palace. And it was there that he had the encounter with a mole-hill that eventually killed him. He described it himself:

I was riding in the park at noon and while I endeavoured to make the horse change his walking into a gallop, he fell upon his knees. Upon that I meant to raise him with the bridle, but he fell forward to one side, and so I fell on my right shoulder upon the ground. 'Tis a strange thing, for it happened upon a smooth level ground.

Hampton Court's chief impact upon history under Queen Anne was as the scene for that curious quarrel over coffee-cups about which Alexander Pope wrote 'The Rape of the Lock':

> Close by those meads, for ever crown'd with flowers,
> Where Thames with pride surveys his rising towers,
> There stands a structure of majestic frame,
> Which from the neighb'ring Hampton takes its name.
> Here Britain's statesmen oft the fall foredoom
> Of foreign tyrants, and of nymphs at home;
> Here thou, great ANNA, whom three realms obey,
> Dost sometimes counsel take – and sometimes tea.

Here, for some inexplicable reason, screams of horror rent the affrighted skies, because Belinda, alias Arabella Fermor, had her hair cut.

Queen Anne seldom visited Hampton Court. But Swift recorded a ceremonial meeting in her bedroom there, which illustrates the notorious and excruciating tedium of these non-events:

There was a drawing-room today at Court: but so few company, that the Queen sent for us into her bedchamber, where we made our bows, and stood about twenty of us around the room, while she looked at us round with her fan in her mouth, and once a minute said about three words to some that were nearest her, and then was told dinner was ready, and went out.

Surprisingly, for a man with his views about 'all Boets and Bainters', George I converted the Great Hall at Hampton Court into a theatre, and there often watched plays by Shakespeare brought down from London by Colley Cibber. The King used the palace to get away from the English, and as a retreat for his peculiar private life, with his various unpopular German mistresses, Schulenberg, who was promoted Duchess of Kendal, and others. Schulenberg persuaded him to dismiss Sir Christopher Wren, who had been the royal Surveyor General for five successive reigns, and replace him with an undistinguished protégé of her own. When the King was away in Hanover (which was as often as possible), the Prince of Wales and Caroline were allowed to live at Hampton Court, and kept a gay young court there, much praised by participants in it for its intellectual brilliance, its romantic ambiance, and the beauty of the maids of honour, who included the much-exposed-to-poets Molly Lepell:

> So powerful her charms, and so moving,
>     They would warm an old monk in his cell;
> Should the Pope himself ever go roaming,
>     He would follow dear Molly Lepell.

Brightness fell from the air once George I came back. Pope wrote:

. . . I can easily believe no lone house in Wales, with a mountain and a rookery, is more contemplative than this court; and as a proof of it, I need only tell you Miss L[epell] walked with me three or four hours by moonlight, and we met no creature of any quality, but the King, who gave audience to the Vice-Chamberlain, all alone, under the garden wall.

Nor did the magic return when the Prince of Wales came back to Hampton Court as George II. He used to stay in the palace for some months every summer at the beginning of his reign. But Mrs Howard (later the Countess of Suffolk), one of the Queen's women of the bedchamber, who was even more popular in the King's bedchamber, wrote sadly to Molly Lepell:

Hampton is very different from the place you knew . . . *Frizelation, flirtation* and *dangleation* are now no more, and nothing less than a Lepell can restore them to life; but to tell you my opinion freely, the people you now converse with [books] are much more alive than any of your old acquaintances.

In the day time there was hearty hunting. Mrs Howard wrote: 'We hunt with great noise and violence, and have every day a tolerable chance of having a neck broken.' In the evening the King walked up and down, holding forth interminably on military or genealogical matters, 'while the queen knotted and yawned, till from yawning she came to nodding, and from nodding to snoring'. The only dramatic event to disturb the smooth-flowing tedium was the King's hereditary Hanoverian quarrel with his eldest son, Frederick or Fitz. From Hampton Court Frederick drove his wife in a carriage when she was in labour, for the malicious pleasure of preventing his mother being present at the birth of her eldest grandchild. When eventually Lady Suffolk gave up the post of royal mistress, there were discussions at Hampton Court about finding a suitable replacement, so as to make the King less impossible to live with. The Prime Minister, Sir Robert Walpole, pointed out that you could hardly expect the King to spend the evenings with his own daughters, 'after having tasted the sweets of passing them with other people's wives'.

One of his daughters wrote from Hampton Court: 'I wish with all my heart he would take somebody else, that Mamma might be a little relieved from the *ennui* of seeing him for ever in her room.'

After the Queen died, George's visits to Hampton Court became rare and brief. On one of them he lost his always elusive temper, and boxed the ears of one of his grandsons. And after that grandson came to the throne in 1760 as George III, he never set foot in Hampton Court again. According to one of his sons, the ignominy of the boxed ears rankled so sorely and so persistently that it made the palace unbearable. Whatever the reason, George III removed most of the furniture, and started the custom which still survives of granting grace and favour residences in the palace to deserving people. William IV described it, inelegantly, as 'the quality poor house'. Victoria threw open the state rooms to the public. Almost a thousand rooms in the rest of the palace are grace and favour apartments today.

# X

# ST JAMES'S PALACE

AMBASSADORS to London are still officially accredited to the Court of St James's. And although for a century almost nothing has happened in the ancient red brick palace that a Stuart or Hanoverian king would recognise as a court function, although no king or queen has lived in it since George III, because of British reluctance to tamper with tradition St James's Palace is still, in a curious, vestigial way, for some purposes the formal and symbolic royal headquarters in London.

The palace started its architectural life almost a thousand years ago, paradoxically as a leper hospital. Leprosy, as a sort of Saracen's revenge, was imported from the middle east by the crusaders. Probably some time shortly after 1066 and all that, charitable London citizens endowed an isolation lazar-house on the site of St James's, which in those days was a desolate, wild waste of swampy Westminster, safely out of range of the walls of London. It was for the quarantine of 'fourteen leprous maiden sisters, living chastely and honestly in divine service', and was dedicated to St James the Less, Bishop of Jerusalem. Little St James's day is May 1, and the hospital was later granted the profitable privilege of holding a May Fair in the neighbouring fields adjacent to it. This old charity fair in aid of lepers has handed down its name to one of the most expensive and salubrious districts of London.

There were perpetual and scandalous squabbles about jurisdiction between the Master of the hospital and the Abbot of Westminster, until Henry VI in despair transferred the custody of St James's to his favourite new foundation, Eton College. Leprosy began to disappear from western Europe during the fifteenth century. By the time Henry VIII came to the throne there were only four inmates in the convent of St James, three of them widows. They each received an annual allowance of £2 12s, and a quarter barrel of beer. Henry bought the 'hospital of St James's in the Fields' from Eton in exchange for other land. He pensioned off the beer-drinking widows, and on the site of the old leper-house he built a turreted hunting-lodge, manor-palace of four courts, of red brick inset with blue brick patterns, as a hideaway sanctuary for Anne Boleyn. The initials 'H' and 'A' were duly carved on every available surface in the palace, and can still be seen. Holbein did some of the interior decoration. Ever since Boleyn, one of the traditional functions of St James's has been as a convenient *pied-à-terre* for the favourite royal concubine of the moment, as well as the home of the heir to the throne. After Anne Boleyn's strange, solitary coronation, with her long black hair hanging down her back, she joined Henry, who was waiting impatiently for her in St James's, 'where shee rested that night'.

The arrangement for running the household at St James's and the other royal residences had just been reorganised and modernised, mainly by Wolsey. One of the most famous of the new ordinances is the laborious procedure for making the King's bed:

A groom or page with a torch to stand at the bed's foot, they of the wardrobe opening the King's stuff of the bed upon a fair sheet between the Groom and the bed's foot. Two yeomen of the Chamber on each side to make the bed, and a Gentleman Usher to direct them. A yeoman with a dagger to search the straw of the bed, and then to cast up the bed of down upon that; and one to tumble over it for the search thereof, &c., lastly, making a cross and kissing it, the two yeomen next to the foot making the fires, and so every of them to stick up the angels about the bed, and let down the curtains of the said bed.

A squire for the body, or Gentleman Usher, ought to set the King's sword at the bed's head, also to charge a secret groom or page with a light to keep the said bed till the King be disposed to go into it. A groom or page to take a torch or light while the bed is making, to fetch a loaf of bread, a pot with ale, a pot with wine for them that make the bed, and every man drinketh.

Uneasy lies the head that wears a crown.

After Anne Boleyn's 'little neck' had been chopped on Tower Green, Henry did not often use St James's again, except for occasional hunting expeditions. Perhaps old unhappy memories, and those frequent lovers' initials entwined with Tudor roses, gave the place an uncomfortable aura, even for rhinoceros-hided Henry. However it was his daughter Mary's favourite private residence, as an escape from the public life of Whitehall. There is a remarkable and improbable account of a science-fiction attempt to assassinate Mary while she walked in St James's Park. Francis Bacon reports, with no apparent bulge of tongue in cheek, that it was to be done 'by means of a burning-glass fixed on the leads of a neighbouring house' – the original laser-beam, death-ray. Mary took refuge in St James's during

Thomas Wyatt's anti-Papist rebellion. The rebels halted 'to insult the gates of the palace', and a bloody skirmish was fought at its walls. In the early part of her reign St James's was the scene of brilliant receptions for the visiting Spaniards, and of stately religious functions, and sung Masses. At the wretched end of it, deserted by her husband Philip of Spain, alienated from her persecuted Protestant subjects, clinging to the wishful-thinking delusion that she was pregnant with an heir instead of swollen with dropsy, Mary crept to St James's to die. There she signed the treaty between England and France which surrendered Calais, the fatal word which was written on her heart. After a last Mass in her bedroom, she died in St James's in 1558.

In the macabre custom of the time (recently revived by heart-transplant surgeons), 'she was opened by her Physicians and Surgeons, who took out her bowels, which were coffined and buried solemnly in the Chappel [at St James's], her Heart being separately enclosed in a coffin, covered with purple velvet, bound with silver'. The rest of her was buried in Westminster Abbey, possibly in a nun's habit instead of the usual royal rig, because of a last request that the crown which had weighed on her in life should not lie heavy on her corpse in death.

Elizabeth rarely used St James's. It had bitter associations of her mother. Her only major visit there was during the *annus mirabilis* of 1588, Armada-year, when she moved into St James's as a good jumping-off place for any emergency. From there she left to inspect her troops at Tilbury, marching gloriously through the ranks, swinging a truncheon, and making her defiant speech: 'I know I have the body of a weak, feeble woman; but I have the heart and stomach of a king – and of a King of England too, and think foul scorn that Parma or Spain, or any prince of Europe, should dare to invade the borders of my realm.'

The first extant description of St James's was made during Elizabeth's reign:

Not far from this . . . another of Her Highnes houses descryeth itself, of a quadrate forme, erected of brick, the exterior shape whereof, although it appears without any sumptuous or superfluous devices, yet is the spot very princelye, and the same with art contrived within and without. It standeth from other buyldinges about two furlongs, having a farme house opposite to its north gate. But the situation is pleasant, indued with a good ayre and pleasant prospects. On the east, London offereth itself in view; in the south, the stately buyldings of Westminster, with the pleasant park, and the delights thereof; on the north, the green fields. It was buylt by King Henry VIII.

When shambolic James I arrived in London to take over, he appointed

St James's Palace as the official residence of his eldest son, Henry, then aged ten. The Prince of Wales kept a brilliant court there, with a staff of 426 officials. He started the great Stuart art collection and library. He also managed his own accounts, and seems to have run a fairly strict household, installing a swear-box, and forcing 'all those who did swear in his hearing to pay moneys to the same, which were after duly given to the poor'.

The young prince was cultured, handsome, athletic, interested in 'building and gardening, and in all sorts of rare musique, chiefly the trumpet and drumme'. Above all, he was a keen Protestant. It all made an unfortunate contrast with his father James, who made a poor impression on London. Sir Anthony Weldon, a historical writer at his court, wrote:

He was of middle stature . . . fat enough, his doublets quilted for stelletto proof, his breeches in great plaits . . . his eyes large, ever rowling after any stranger that came into his presence . . . his beard very thin: his tongue too large for his mouth . . . hee never washt his hands . . . his walke was ever circular, his fingers ever . . . fiddling about his cod-piece.

And M. de Fontenoy:

His manners . . . are aggressive and very uncivil . . . He never stays still in one place . . . his steps erratic and vagabond . . . He has a feeble body even if he is not delicate. In sum . . . he is an old young man.

By comparison Henry was so popular, his levées were so congested, that his father grumbled sulkily: 'Will he bury me alive?' There was great public grief when Henry died at the age of nineteen, and a rustling of cruel rumours that jealous James had poisoned him, either in a bunch of grapes, or by 'the venomous scent' of a pair of gloves.

The Prince was taken ill with a violent fever (probably typhus) after a game of tennis, and put to bed at St James's. For the next fortnight medical experts tried all the gruesome remedies of the period, from enemas and bleedings to shaving his head and applying pigeons to draw away superfluous blood; 'this day a cock was cloven by the back, and applied to the soles of his feet. But in vain'. Sir Walter Raleigh from the Tower sent round his own patent medicine guaranteed to cure everything except poison. It appears to have had a basis suspiciously like whisky. Prince Henry had once said of Raleigh's incarceration that 'no King but his father would keep such a bird, in such a cage'.

After Henry's long drawn-out death, his brother Charles as heir to the throne occupied the palace. He moved across the park into Whitehall when his father died, but his stubborn, self-willed little French wife Henrietta Maria made St James's her favourite royal nest. Most of her children were born here. She and Charles built up in St James's their splendid collections of tapestries, interior decorations, paintings, and furniture. And her French staff of 440 cost £240 a day and caused perpetual chauvinist ill-feeling – especially her Catholic Bishop in his twenties, and her twenty-nine resident priests, half of whom were scholars, and half Friars 'whose principal occupation was singing of Psalms'.

Eventually public opinion and religious prejudice forced Charles, with the heavy-lidded eyes and the world-weary look of the Van Dyck portraits, to repatriate his wife's French household compulsorily. There was an appalling scene. In a materialistic stampede the French courtiers stripped the palace bare, submitted bogus bills, seized everything they could lay their hands on, jewels, clothes, furniture, and did not leave the Queen 'even a change of linen'. The juvenile French Bishop was carried away standing up and protesting in a coach. 'The women howled and lamented as if they had been going to execution.' The whole expulsion cost £50,000. And the native housekeeper at St James's went on the record with bulldog British bigotry that the French 'had so defiled that house, as a week's work would not make it clean'.

In 1638, to add to Charles's growing troubles, his formidable mother-in-law, the Queen-Dowager of France, Marie de Médicis, came on a visit to St James's, which provoked the Puritans to ecstasies of outraged protest. She brought with her six coaches, 170 horses, 160 attendants, and a whiff of Popish provocation. Three people were killed in a non-violent demonstration outside the gates of St James's. And an impassioned anonymous letter to the King promised '. . . to chase the Pope and the Devil from St James's, where is lodged the Queene, Mother of the Queene'.

The Sieur de la Serre, a French historian in the train of Marie de Médicis, wrote a detailed impression of St James's on this visit:

This place is situated in the same suburb as that wherein the castle of Whitehall stands, from which it is distant only the extent of a park that divides them. Near its avenues is a large meadow, always green, in which the ladies walk in summer. Its great gate has a long street in front, reaching almost out of sight, seemingly joining to the fields. This castle is very magnificent and extremely convenient. It is built with brick, according to the fashion of the country, having the roof covered with lead, in form of a floor surrounded on all sides with battlements which serve for an ornament to the whole body of the building . . . To express the great number of chambers, all covered with tapestry, and superbly garnished with all sorts of furniture, where the Court was to be lodged . . . would be impossible. You shall

Hampton Court Palace from the east and the air

*Photo B.O.A.C.*

18th century engraving of St. James's Palace from Pall Mall

St. James's Palace in the 18th century, painted by Samuel Scott. Original in the collection of Lord Stanley

only know that Sieur Labat, who continued to execute the office of quarter-master, had liberty to mark with his chalk fifty separate chambers of entire apartments.

After two years' crescendo of unpopularity, Parliament voted the Queen's mother £10,000 on condition that she left the country at once. William Lilly, the astrologer, claimed tears in his eyes, 'to see an aged, lean, decrepit, poor Queen, ready for the grave, necessitated to depart hence, having no place of residence in the world left her, but where the courtesy of hard fortune had assigned it'.

Early in the Civil War the Parliamentarians, whose power base was London, seized St James's Palace, and turned it into a remarkably insecure prison for the royal children. First of all Princess Henrietta escaped from the palace disguised in rags as a boy. Then James, Duke of York, later James II, made an equally hair-breadth and transvestite getaway, dressed as a girl in petticoats especially made for him by a London tailor (who found his customer's measurements startling). James lulled the suspicions of his jailers for a fortnight before the escape by playing hide-and-seek every evening, and hiding himself away in impossible crannies. People got used to hunting for him for half an hour every night through the golden maze of corridors and tapestries.

On the night of the attempt James locked up a little dog that followed him everywhere, slipped away down the back stairs, and let himself out into the park with a treble key. Everybody thought that 'hee was butt att the usuall sport'. By the time the alarm was raised by tired hide-and-seekers half an hour later, James was in his petticoats, and on his way to the coast and a boat to Holland.

Charles I was brought back to St James's to spend his last night on earth before his 'second Marriage-Day'. A contemporary French account of the behaviour of his guards during the night is picturesque with passionate propaganda, but deficient of facts:

*Et comme il auroit une adversion extrême pour le tabac, et qu'il les prioit de n'en point prendre, ces infâmes luy répondirent qu'ils n'estoient pas là pour luy obéir, et pour luy accorder ses plaisirs; ils tiroient les rideaux de son lict; ils luy crachoient au visage; ils le découvroient: bref, imaginez-vous une troupe de démons dans la cellule de Sainct Antoine. Ainsi ce Prince passa toute la nuict entre les mains de la plus sordide et la plus enragée canaille que l'Enfer ait jamais vomy . . .*

Propaganda apart, Charles slept soundly for four hours, with a great cake of wax flickering all night in a silver basin. Another famous myth which probably originated in the French fiction factories is the story that after the execution a tall figure muffled in a mask and cloak came by night to stare at the King's corpse, which was lying on view at St James's. The stranger was heard to mutter to himself: 'Dreadful necessity', and was, *naturellement*, Oliver Cromwell. Later in the Commonwealth St James's was used as a military prison and a barracks. The superb collection of Titians, Raphaels, Holbeins, Van Dycks was carelessly sold off at Puritan prices, which would make the hair of a modern ring of art dealers stand on collective end like quills upon a herd of fretful porpentines.

After the Restoration most of Charles II's mistresses had apartments at St James's. Pepys, as usual drooling about women, reports seeing Lady Castlemaine there, 'who looked prettily in her night clothes'. Hortense Mancini, the sensational Duchess of Mazarin, '*Marazin, des amours Déesse tutélaire*', arrived to take up residence with a magnificent sense of publicity, and an empty purse. She rode up to St James's dressed as a gentleman of fashion, escorted by liveried retainers, her spaniels, and her photogenic little black page.

James, Duke of York, had his official residence in his former prison at St James's, and kept a separate court there. Charles, apart from nocturnal assignations at St James's after official bed-time at Whitehall, spent more time in the park than the palace of St James. The famous French gardener Le Nôtre laid it out and planted it for him, and it was stocked with an astonishing assortment of wild life:

The Parke was at this time stored with numerous flocks of severall sorts of ordinary and extraordinary wild fowle, breeding about the Decoy, deere of severall countries – white; spotted like leopards; antelopes; an elk; red deere; roebucks; staggs; Guinea goates; Arabian sheep, &c.

Exotic birds in gilded cages twittered along the length of Birdcage Walk. The picture of Charles playing with his dogs, feeding his ducks, chattering with his courtiers in their gaudy plumage in St James's Park is a cliché. An evocative advertisement of the period in the *London Gazette* announces as lost in St James's Park:

A little Spaniel Dog of his Royal Highness; he will answer to the name Towser, he is liver colour'd and white spotted, his legs speckled with liver colour and white, with long hair growing upon his hind legs, long ears, and his under lip a little hanging; if any can give notice of him they shall have five pounds for their pains.

It was in the park that Charles made his famous retort to James, who had warned him of the hazards of walking there without a body-guard: 'Brother James, take care of yourself, for no man will kill me to make you king.'

Pepys saw orange trees for the first time in the park, and the new game of sliding on ice with 'skaits', which he did not much like.

When James II succeeded, he left St James's for Whitehall. His wife, Mary of Modena, made the calamitous and inexplicable misjudgement of returning there hurriedly at the last minute, at midnight, to give birth to her son James Francis Edward, doomed for seventy-seven years to walk the earth in exile, as the Old Pretender. People were suspicious enough already about the authenticity of the Queen's pregnancy, and depressed enough at the prospect of a Catholic heir to the throne. Princess Anne was sure her step-mother had a 'false belly', and tried unsuccessfully to feel it. The labyrinthine passages of St James's were the perfect setting for hocus-pocus with changelings; 'much the properest place to act such a cheat in,' wrote Anne. James himself should have remembered that from his games of hide-and-seek as a boy.

Out of these faintly dubious circumstances the fantasy sprouted that a spurious child had been smuggled into the Queen's bed in a warming-pan, in place of the hot coals. Ingenious maps were published showing the secret passage of the warming-pan through the palace. Although no less than sixty-seven interested spectators of both sexes were present at the birth, many of them were Catholics, and obtuse James had not made sure that any really hostile and reliable witnesses attended – Princess Anne, the Dutch ambassador, or one of the Seven Bishops, who were by a strange coincidence all locked up in the Tower. The warming-pan myth was the final spark that set off the Glorious Revolution.

When William of Orange arrived in London with tramp of Dutch troops on a pouring wet day, he went to St James's by a roundabout route to avoid the cheering crowds. Evelyn wrote in his diary:

All the world goes to see the Prince at St James's, where there is a greate Court. There I saw him, and several of my acquaintance who came over with him. He is very stately, serious, and reserved. The English soldiers sent out of town to disband them; not well pleased.

William and Mary's official London palace was Whitehall; but after it was burnt down, St James's became the court for those essential alien ceremonies from which William, preoccupied with international politics rather than British pomps, could not escape. After Mary died of smallpox at the age of thirty-two, William partly made up his feral quarrel with her sister Anne over politics and the Marlboroughs, and gave St James's as their residence to Anne and her plump, dull, bibulous, but amiable husband, George of Denmark. Under Queen Anne 'Our Court of St James's' became for the first time the formal royal palace in London.

Anne had a strong sense of her royal dignity, but she was shy. Her court at St James's was brilliant, but stiff. There tended to be awkward silences full of nervous coughing. Anne admitted herself that she was no good at making royal small talk, 'having little to say to them, but that it was either hot or cold'. She frequently received company in her bedroom, where she was often ill with gout, her face red and spotted. For everyone else at St James's court etiquette was inflexibly rigid.

Unfortunate strangers who turned up at Anne's drawing room improperly dressed, without the huge, full-bottomed court wig, were smartly sent home to change. The Queen 'was quick to spy out these irregularities'. Prince Eugene of Savoy upset her dreadfully by arriving in a modest tie-wig. 'I know not what to do; I never had a long periwig in my life,' he cried in despair, having tried unsuccessfully to borrow one from all his valets and footmen. Anne grudgingly agreed to see him because he was a Prince, but said firmly 'it should not be drawn into precedent'. The wig regulations were presumably also lifted for the public audience of the four 'Indian Kings', feathered Mohawk chiefs from North America, who called on the Queen in St James's to ask for help against the French, so that they might 'enjoy peaceable hunting, and have much trade with our Great Queen's children'. Anne entertained them lavishly, and asked the Archbishop of Canterbury to arrange for missionaries to be sent back with them to cultivate 'that good disposition those Indians seem to be in for receiving the Christian faith'.

Spectacles were banned in the royal presence, and smoking in the Mall. The one relaxation allowed in the formality of St James's was cards. Rather jolly glimpses of the animated gambling at Anne's drawing-rooms survive in contemporary letters.

For instance a lady at court writes:

There was a prodigious crowd and the table quite full before she [the Queen] saw me, yet she was not at rest till they brought me a stool over everybody's head and made them set quite close to her own chair; yet with all that I was forced to sit behind, where I had room but for one hand.

Pious, greedy, stolid, and snuffy, Anne was also a voracious reader of precedents and etiquette-books. She appointed the first court jester for more than a century. Her servants spent their time jumping on and off their knees before performing some simple job for the Queen. The protocol of getting her up in the morning has been recorded in exhausting detail, and is a careful copy of Henry VIII's ritual:

. . . when the Queen washed her hands, the page of the backstairs brought and set down upon a side table the basin and ewer; then the bedchamber woman set it before the Queen, and knelt on the other side of the table over against the Queen, the bedchamber lady only looking on. The bedchamber woman poured the water out of the ewer upon the Queen's hands . . . the page of the backstairs was called in to put on the Queen's shoes . . . etcetera.

The household atmosphere at St James's was corroded by the sabre-toothed feud between Sarah, the 'termagant and tempestuous Duchess', and her cousin, Abigail Masham. Beautiful, brilliant Sarah had been Anne's best friend since childhood. Anne conducted a gushing correspondence under the pen-name of 'Mrs Morley' to her 'dear, dear Mrs Freeman'. Anne's quarrel with her sister Mary and William III, for which she was sent into bitter Coventry by the court, was almost entirely over her friendship with Sarah. But after Anne became Queen, the timid worm turned, and she gradually became tired of Sarah's domineering bossiness. Anne, a natural-born Tory, was irritated by Sarah's persistent campaigning on behalf of the Whigs, and turned to Abigail, whose politics were conveniently Tory, and who was more tactful, less arrogant than her cousin. The atmosphere at court was Antarctic. When Anne's husband George died, Sarah dragged her away from what she unsympathetically described as 'that dismal body' at Kensington, to St James's, fed her with therapeutic broth, and noted jealously:

. . . at night I found her at a table again, where she had been eating, and Mrs Masham very close by her, who went out of the room as soon as I came in, but with an air of insolence and anger, and not in the humble manner she had sometimes affected of bedchamber woman.

Sarah went on:

I attended the Queen upon this affliction with all the care that was possible to please her, and never named Mrs Masham to her; and she would make me sit down, as she had done formerly, and make some little show of kindness at night, when I took my leave; but she would never speak to me freely of anything, and I found I could gain no ground, which was not much to be wondered at, for I never came to her but I found Mrs Masham there, or had been just gone out from her, which at last tired me, and I went to her seldomer.

After the final rupture between the Queen and her red Duchess, Sarah hurled her golden keys as Mistress of the Robes and Groom of the Stole on the floor, and stormed out of St James's into the newly finished Marl-borough House. She 'left that part of the palace, which had been her headquarters for years, in a state as if it had been sacked by a destructive enemy – the locks torn off the doors, marble slabs forced out, and looking-glasses and pictures rent from their panels'.

Anne was so furious that she refused to sign a warrant for money to continue building Blenheim, which was the nation's gift to the Marl-boroughs. She said 'she would not build a house for one that had pulled down and gutted hers, and taken away even the slabs out of the chim-neys'. As a final gesture Sarah claimed £18,000 in back pay, which Anne immediately paid. Sarah wrote that she 'did not much like doing this', but comforted herself with the catty thought that she had earned the money by so many hours of boredom.

The most important public political event at St James's during Anne's fortuitously brilliant reign was the completion of the Act of Union between England and Scotland. One of the Scottish commissioners describes the stately procession into the Queen's council chamber congested with the bewigged court and diplomatic corps: 'One of us and one of the English walkt togither, and so on; we on the left hand as we walkt but we were on the Queen's right hand.' The Lord Keeper 'miserably mangled' his speech, and eventually had to take it out of his pocket and read it. Anne replied 'with a very graceful pronunciation and tone of voice'.

When, after so many false alarms, the last of the Stuarts died, the improbable new King was the obscure ruler of a minor European state, who never learned to speak English. George I imported a complete Hanoverian household of a hundred into St James's: chaplains and trumpeters, plate-cleaners and a washerwoman, two Turkish attendants Mustapha and Mahomet (whose backstairs duty was to organise the King's strenuous sex life), political advisers, and his German head-mistress, Ermengarda Melusina von der Schulenberg, whom he made Duchess of Kendal, and installed in splendid apartments in St James's. She was described sourly by English who spoke no German as 'very little above an idiot'. There was no Queen in the palace because Sophia Dorothea was divorced and locked up in a German castle. George apparently had this curious primitive passion for steatopygous women – 'No woman came amiss to him, if she were but very willing and very fat'. Schulenberg was an exception to this rule, having a lean, hungry, and pachydermatous look. In general, however, the regime introduced a new fashion for female fatness at court. 'These standards of His Majesty's taste made all those ladies who aspired to his favour strain and swell themselves like the frogs in the fable. Some succeeded, and others burst.'

George spent half the year in Hanover, and was not interested in English affairs, which he found irrational. He said himself:

The first morning after my arrival at St James's, I looked out of the window and saw a park, with walks, and a canal, which, they told me, were mine. The next day Lord Chetwynd, the Ranger of my Park, sent me a fine brace of carp, out of my canal, and I was told I must give five guineas to Lord Chetwynd's servant for bringing me my own carp, out of my canal, in my own Park.

Because of the Jacobite threat, the main political result of his reign was to put the government of Britain firmly into the hands of the Whig grandees, and of Sir Robert Walpole, who discussed business with the King in atrocious Latin. The latent British hostility to this German court is shown by the anecdote, possibly too feeble to be true, of a couple of the King's Mont-Blanc-bosomed, hippopotamus-buttocked, Teutonic mistresses riding back to St James's in a groaning coach. A large crowd surrounded them, booing, and shouting impolite advice. One of them put her head out of the window, and cried: 'Goot people, vy do you abuse us? We only come for your goots.' A voice from the crowd, with the heavy emphasis of an old *Punch* caption: 'Aye, damn ye, and for our chattels too.'

The Prime Minister's youngest son Horace at the age of ten was presented to George and the Duchess of Kendal at St James's:

I knelt down and kissed his hand. He said a few words to me, and my conductress led me back to my mother. The person of the King is as perfect in my memory as if I saw him but yesterday. It was that of an elderly man, rather pale, and exactly like his pictures and coins; not tall; of an aspect rather good than august, with a dark tie-wig, a plain coat, waistcoat and breeches of snuff-coloured cloth, with stockings of the same colour, and a blue ribbon over all.

In addition to swag-bellied mistresses, the other tiresome new tradition introduced into St James's by the Georges was that of purple turkey-cock quarrels between each King and his eldest son, which regularly split the court into two rival factions not even on screaming terms with each other. Kings have often felt uneasy in the gravestone presence of their expectant successors, but the Hanoverians carried this sentiment to absurdity.

The final break between George I and the Prince of Wales, later George II, happened at the christening of the Prince's second son in St James's. The King insisted on nominating as godfather the Duke of Newcastle, one of his friends, but a well-known *bête noire* of the Prince's. The Bishop had hardly uttered the last Amen, when the Prince rushed up to the god-father in a rage, shook his finger in his face, and shouted in thick Teutonic accents: 'You are a rascal, but I shall find you' (meaning, presumably, 'I shall find a time to get my own back'). Uproar and outrage. The Duke understood the Prince to have said: 'I shall *fight* you', and was stiffening his sinews for a duel. The King took the incident as a personal insult, and had the Prince arrested and locked in his rooms. The Princess of Wales, Caroline of Ansbach, insisted on being locked up with her husband. The Jacobites were delighted. The next day the Prime Minister had to tell the King 'that something must be done, as the present situation was clearly impossible; the heir to the throne could not be kept shut up in his room as if he were a recalcitrant schoolboy'. It is a shame that the dog Latin on this occasion has not been preserved. But the second George was ordered out of St James's by nightfall, deprived of all honours, excluded from the regency, and forbidden the custody of his own children.

And for the next ten years those who could scrounge no favours from the King at St James's, went down the road to Leicester House to see what future promises could be extracted from the Prince of Wales. As the Prime Minister himself said: 'Everybody come to court to get, and if they find there is nothing to be got in present, it is natural to look out for reversions . . . Everyone who can get no ready money had rather have a bad promissory note than nothing.'

On rare occasions afterwards when the two parties eventually met at St James's, according to an eye-witness the animosity

made the whole Thing look like two Armies drawn up in Battle array; for the King's Court was all at the Top of the Room, behind the King, and the Prince's Court behind him. The prince looked down, and behaved prodigious well. The King cast an angry Look that way every now and then; and One could not help thinking 't was like a little Dog and a Cat – whenever the Dog stirs a Foot, the Cat sets up her Back, and is ready to fly at him.

During George I's reign Daniel Defoe published his *Tour of the Whole Island of Great Britain*, which included a visit to St James's:

The Palace . . . though the winter receptacle of all the pomp and glory of this kingdom, is really mean in comparison of the glorious Court of Great Britain. The splendour of the nobility, the wealth, and greatness of the attendants, and the real grandeur of the whole Royal Family, outdo all the Courts of Europe, and yet this palace comes beneath those of the most petty princes in it.

Another eighteenth-century critic wrote:

The buildings that compose this merely nominal palace, (for by all rules of architecture it has no claim to the title), are low, plain, and ignoble, devoid of any exterior beauty to attract and fix the beholder's eye. It reflects no honour on the kingdom, and is the jest of foreigners.

George II carried on the heroic Hanoverian tradition of a vigorous feud with his heir Frederick. 'My dear first-born,' the King said, 'is the greatest ass and the greatest liar and the greatest *canaille* and the greatest beast in the whole world, and I heartily wish he were out of it.' With equally refreshing honesty the Queen said: 'Fred is a nauseous little beast, and he cares for nobody but his nauseous little self.'

Once again the vendetta came to a climax at St James's. In 1737 Fred announced that his wife was about to produce a child. Queen Caroline, who wanted the succession to fall to her second son, William, was sceptical about the announcement, and decided to be present at the birth to keep an eye on the warming-pans. The lamentable Frederick took the huff, and determined to thwart her. On the night that the baby started to arrive the royal family were all at Hampton Court. The Prince of Wales hustled his labouring wife secretly into a coach, and galloped her screaming through the night to St James's. Nothing was ready there, and the Princess was put to bed between two tablecloths. Less than an hour after her melodramatic arrival at the palace, 'she was delivered of a little rat of a girl about the bigness of a good large toothpick case', according to the gossipy memoirs of John, Lord Hervey, the confidant of Queen Caroline, and with Horace Walpole the principal source for the private court history of this reign. The baby was wrapped in napkins and an old red cloak.

News of the baby's arrival was broken to the King and Queen at Hampton Court at two a.m., and within half an hour a furious Queen was on her way to St James's. She refused to speak to her son, but visited the Princess, and kissed the baby, saying: '*Le bon Dieu vous bénisse, pauvre petite créature, vous voilà arrivée dans un désagréable monde.*'

After this adventure Frederick and his family, like his father before him, were expelled from St James's. 'I thank God tomorrow night the puppy will be out of my house,' said the King. 'I hope in God I shall never see him again,' said the Queen. Her hope was granted. Later in the same year Queen Caroline died in St James's, after keeping quiet for too long about a rupture. She was dosed with 'Daffy's Elixir, mint-water, usquebaugh [whisky], snake root, and Sir Walter Raleigh's cordial', which all increased her fever without reducing the pain. When it became clear she was going to die, she spoke of Frederick: 'At least I shall have one comfort in having my eyes eternally closed – I shall never see that monster again.'

She took off the ruby ring which the King had given her at her coronation, and put it on his finger, saying:

This is the last thing I have to give you . . . naked I came to you, and naked I go from you . . . I had everything I ever possessed from you, and to you, whatever I have, I return. My will you will find a very short one. I give all I have to you.

She then urged the King to marry again.

Upon which his sobs began to rise, and his tears to fall with double vehemence. Whilst in the midst of this passion wiping his eyes and sobbing, he got out this answer: '*Non – j'aurai – des – maîtresses.*' To which the Queen made no other reply than: '*Ah, mon Dieu, cela n'empêche pas.*'

Hervey writes: "I know this episode will hardly be credited, but it is literally true."

Lord Hervey, who took such a feline interest in the intimate private life of everybody else, particularly if they were royal, had his own intimate adventures at St James's. In spite of his epicene appearance ('pretty little Master-Miss' was William Pulteney's description of him, a phrase that cost him a duel) Hervey appears to have been adequately heterosexual. As well as being married, and the father of eight children, he made the Hon. Anne Vane, one of Queen Caroline's maids of honour, his mistress. In due course, as mistresses will, Miss Vane moved on to an even more promising and profitable paramour, Frederick, the Prince of Wales. Hervey, whose ruling passion was gossip and being an insider at court, seems to have been more upset about being supplanted in Frederick's favour by Miss Vane than vice versa. He created a furious scene, and fell heavily from favour with Frederick. Four years later, the Prince of Wales was evidently cooling rapidly in his sentiments towards Miss Vane, so she and Lord Hervey secretly took up their old relationship where they had left off. Hervey's wife, by a convenient coincidence, had gone to France, so the coast was clear for Miss Vane to come round to his lodgings at St James's. With ruthless confession and self-exposure Hervey takes up the curious story:

Miss Vane used to walk thither, Lord Hervey himself letting her in and out; and in this manner they used to pass whole nights together, as little apprehensive of danger as if no eyes had been upon them and that at this juncture it would not have been as convenient to the Prince as destructive to her to have traced this commerce and proved it upon her. Miss Vane, who had for several years been subject to fits, was at this time extremely ill, and one night when she was in bed at St James's was taken suddenly with so violent a fit of the cholic that in a quarter of an hour she fell into convulsions. Lord Hervey in vain to recover her crammed cordials and gold powder down her throat; her convulsions grew stronger and at last she fell into a swoon that lasted so long he thought her absolutely dead.

What confusion and distress this put his Lordship into is easier to be imagined than described. He did not dare to send for any assistance, nor even to call a servant into the room, for no one was trusted with the secret. What to do he could not tell, nor what would or would not be said when it should come out, and to conceal it was impossible, that Miss Vane was found dead in his lodgings. Whilst he was agitated with these thoughts and apprehensions she came to herself, and by the help of more cordials, more gold powder, and hot napkins to her stomach, he got her up, dressed her, and led her to a chair in Pall-Mall, not daring to have one brought to take her up at his lodgings.

But even this accident did not prevent these indiscreet people from exposing themselves in the same manner to the same dangers, or from meeting as frequently as they had formerly done.

Under George II the full routine of the court at St James's as a public spectacle was resumed. Visitors could buy tickets for a public enclosure from which they could watch the King and his family eat their Sunday dinner off magnificent plate, served on bended knee by liveried officials. There were frequent audiences, drawing-rooms several times a week, and court balls at every opportunity. Heavy gaming was the normal evening's entertainment, with the King and Queen losing or winning hundreds of guineas a night at ombre, basset, or 'lottery tickets', which was a primitive version of bingo.

Throughout his reign, like his father, George was unpopular because of his preference, which he was not diplomatic enough to camouflage, for spending as much time as possible in Hanover. Satirical notices were stuck on the gates of St James's:

Lost or strayed out of this house, a man who has left a wife and six children on the Parish. Whoever will give any tidings of him to the Churchwardens of St James's Parish, so as he may be got again, shall receive 4s 6d reward. N.B. – This reward will not be increased, nobody judging him to deserve a crown.

And another sarcastic poster:

It is reported that His Hanoverian Majesty designs to visit his British Dominions for three months in the Spring.

The conventional image of George II as a pugnacious, strutting, pompous, irascible little man, who 'looked on all the men and women he saw as creatures he might kick or kiss for his diversion', is softened by two trivial but touching anecdotes towards the end of his life as St James's. A stranger in the palace,

when on a visit to some of the retinue of King George II, slipped down a flight of stairs, and bursting open the door of a room in his fall was precipitated, stunned upon the floor. When the man came to his senses, he found a severe little old gentleman, with white eyebrows and a red face, carefully washing his bald head and applying bars of sticking plaster to the cuts. The amateur surgeon then picked up the wig of the injured man and replaced it on his head. The man rose to express gratitude, but the little man with the sponge frowned and pointed to the door. It was the King, and the room so abruptly entered was the Royal Closet.

And at a drawing-room at St James's a feather-headed Duchess, making nervous small-talk to the old King, chattered tactlessly: 'I have seen so much, your Majesty, that there is only one sight in the world which I would wish to behold, and that is a Coronation.' The King took her hand instead of umbrage, and said with a sigh: 'I apprehend you have not long to wait. You will soon have your desire.'

In 1760 George III succeeded his grandfather, and moved into the official royal residence. In the next year the plain, good, sensible, Protestant Princess, Charlotte of Mecklenburg-Strelitz, aged eighteen, came to St James's to marry him. She had already been symbolically married to the King's representative in Germany, in an interesting ceremony in which she lay down on a sofa, and the representative formally put his foot on the sofa, to represent the invasion of her bed. After a hideous crossing she arrived in London without realising that she was to be married that evening. She was dressed in an ugly 'blue satin quilted jesuit', and her hair was twisted into unflattering little bunches in a style known, appropriately, as *tête de mouton*. When she was told that the wedding was to happen as soon as she arrived, when she heard the yelling crowds, and saw St James's jogging into sight, she turned pale and trembled. The Duchess of Hamilton sitting beside her smiled. 'My dear Duchess,' said Charlotte, 'You may laugh, for you have been married twice; but it is no joke to me.' Horace Walpole was in the drawing-room of St James's for the wedding, and took a careful, gossip columnist's note of the new Queen:

She looks very sensible, cheerful, and is remarkably genteel. Her tiara of diamonds was very pretty, her stomacher sumptuous; her violet mantle of ermine so heavy, that the spectators knew as much of her upper half as the King himself. . . While they waited for supper, she sat down, sang and played. Her French is tolerable . . . They did not get to bed till two.

The next year George, who had no taste for court ceremony, bought Buckingham House, which gradually became the London home of the royal family. But St James's was still used for drawing-rooms, levées, state balls, royal weddings and christenings. In his unconventional later years George attended his levées at St James's out of a sense of duty. Once a Scots Colonel was presented, and bowed so low that his kilt rode up at the back to an alarming height. In a cheerful moment of lucidity the King shouted out: 'Keep the ladies in front. Keep the ladies in front.'

When the plump Prince of Wales, later George IV, was driven unwillingly to the altar by his debts and the need to provide an heir, he came to St James's for his disastrous, Marx-Brothers wedding. His father, George III, with whom he had the usual rancorous Hanoverian enmity, chose as his bride Princess Caroline, daughter of the Duke of Brunswick. She was short, lively, flirtatious, pretty in a flashy way, with a pile of blonde hair, 'a good bust', rather coarse, vulgar, and brash. According to the British ambassador's sniggering private diary she did not wash much, and did not change her underwear often, and as a result smelt strong enough to alarm her best friends. The Prince never forgave the ambassador for not warning him about her.

When she arrived, by calculated malice Lady Jersey, the forty-two-year-old grandmother who was the Prince's latest mistress, was appointed her chief lady-in-waiting. The first meeting was not rosy. The Prince greeted his bride, and then turned to the ambassador and said: 'Harris, I am not well; pray get me a glass of brandy.' After the Prince had left the room, Caroline said: ' *Je le trouve très gros.*'

In fact at this point he weighed seventeen stone in his boots. Gossip reported that Lady Jersey fed the Princess with green onions to make her smell even more unattractive than usual, and that she dosed her with a powerful and agonising laxative just before the wedding. She also took an intimate survey of Caroline while helping her to change, and gave the Prince a malicious blow-by-blow account. The wedding at St James's was farce, fiasco, and tragedy. A guest wrote that the Prince 'looked like Death, and full of confusion, as if he wished to hide himself from the looks of the whole world'.

Apart from embarrassment about Caroline who was 'in the highest spirits . . . smiling and nodding to everyone', the Prince's conscience may have been itching about the just cause and impediment of his previous 'marriage' to Mrs Fitzherbert, 'my wife, the wife of my heart and soul'. Another observer wrote in her diary: 'He was like a man in despair,

half crazy. He held so fast by the Queen's hand she could not remove it.'
Rumour said that the Prince had braced himself for his wedding with more
than even his usual ration of brandy. After the wedding dinner he went out
and drank twelve glasses of Maraschino straight off. In the circumstances,
the honeymoon was predictably short. In less than a year the Prince was
trying to get a separation, and saying: 'I would rather see toads and vipers
crawling over my victuals than sit at the same table with her.'

In 1809 the wing of St James's which had been the scene of the notorious
warming-pan incident was burned to the ground. 'The inhabitants of the
palace were seen issuing in all directions from their apartments half-naked,
and every effort was made to save the furniture and effects.'

In 1840 Victoria came to St James's to marry Albert in, for a change, a
totally successful royal wedding. Contemporary newspapers give long,
ecstatic accounts of the ceremony, the decorations distinguished 'for
simple Chastity combined with Elegance', and, with sentimental hyperbole, the tears in the young Queen's eyes. A guest wrote:

The Queen's look and manner were very pleasing, her eyes much swollen with tears,
but great happiness in her countenance, and her look of confidence at the Prince,
when they walked away as man and wife, was very pretty to see.

Victoria, in her diary, particularly enjoyed the simple way 'in which we
were called "Victoria, wilt thou have &c", & "Albert, wilt thou &c" . . .'.
Her happiest moment was when Albert put on the ring. As usual, a tart
note of reality among the Cinderella tinsel and orange-blossom was
provided by Charles Greville in his memoirs:

She [the Queen] had been as wilful, obstinate, and wrong-headed as usual about her
invitations, and some of her foolish and mischievous Courtiers were boasting that
out of above 300 people in the Chapel there would only be five Tories . . . The
wedding on Monday went off tolerably well.

For some time Victoria continued to use St James's for drawing-rooms
and levées, until she built the new wing on to Buckingham Palace, and
most royal ceremonies were transferred there. The occasional levée still
took place in St James's until the reign of George VI. Today the Palace has
become an architectural fossil of its past, full of minor court bureaucracy,
and apartments for junior members of the royal family. Clarence House, to
all intent a part of the Palace, is still the residence of the Queen Mother.
And St James's is still one of the places where the heralds proclaim the
accession of a new monarch. Mrs Wallis Simpson, as she then was, caused

a considerable stir by appearing at a window looking out on to Friary Court to watch the proclamation of Edward VIII. The new King himself joined the party of sight-seers at the window, having decided at the last minute that he would like to see himself proclaimed King. He wrote later:

As the tremendous words rolled out, the symmetrical polished words of sovereignty and dominion, I was swept by conflicting emotions. There was a flash of pride in becoming King-Emperor of the vast and liberal Commonwealth I knew so well. At the same time these words seemed to tell me that my relations with Wallis had suddenly entered a more significant stage.

As they made their way down from the unused apartment, the future Duchess of Windsor said: 'How thoughtful of you to bother thinking of me and to ask me here.' The King, gently pressing her arm, said: 'Wallis, there will be a difference, of course. But nothing can ever change my feelings towards you.' Then with a sudden smile, he was gone.

# XI

# HOLYROODHOUSE

'ROOD' is a medieval word for 'cross'. Holyrood Abbey, and so Holyrood-house, derive their names from a legend which is recorded in a fifteenth-century manuscript called the Holyrood Ordinale. The miraculous story runs that David I, King of the Scots, who was staying at Edinburgh Castle in the autumn of 1128, decided, against the advice of his confessor, to go hunting on the day of the Exaltation of the Holy Cross. He set off with 'sic noyis of rachis [hounds] and bugillis [horns] that all the beastis war reisit fra their dennys'. As he rode east of the Castle near Salisbury Crag (where there was in those days 'ane gret forest full of hartis, hyndis, toddis [foxes], and siclike maner of beastis'), a stag 'with awful and braid tyndis [broad antlers]' suddenly charged at him, threw him off his horse, and wounded him in the thigh. The King tried to grab the stag's horns to protect himself, and clutched a crucifix which suddenly appeared between the antlers. The stag, which was of course the Devil in disguise, ran off 'with gret violence', leaving the King holding the rood. In recognition of the miracle, David founded the monastery of the Holy Rood on the spot.

Unfortunately this report is not particularly persuasive. The identical adventure is said to have happened to Saint Hubert, the Bishop of Liége, in 727. And by a curiouser and curiouser coincidence Saint Eustache, the first patron saint of hunters, experienced the same remarkable accident in the second century.

But at least there is no doubt that David I founded the Augustinian Abbey of Holyrood in 1128 in a wild landscape of loch and crag to the east of Edinburgh Castle. The steep path by which the canons of the Abbey used to commute between the Castle and their Abbey a mile away is still called Canongate, the road of the canons. In the Middle Ages the vital attribute of a royal residence was to be impregnable. So when Kings of Scotland came to Edinburgh, they tended to stay in Edinburgh Castle, which had perched precipitous on top of its beetling grey rock long before

St. James's Palace

*Photo The Times*

The Palace of Holyroodhouse from the air

*Photo The Times*

the city sprang up around its feet; for the same motive the uneasy early Kings of England used to stay in the Tower of London, where they could be reasonably sure of a secure night's sleep. As Scottish Kings became less vulnerable, they began to lodge in the guest house of Holyrood Abbey, which was less spartan than the Castle, and gradually grew into a considerable but haphazard royal residence. The guest house stood to the west of the main Abbey buildings on the road to Edinburgh.

James IV made Edinburgh the definite capital of Scotland, and began to turn Holyroodhouse into a definite palace. He built the north-west tower, which still stands with its distinctive pointed turrets inside a crenellated parapet. The accounts show continual entries for building at Holyroodhouse between 1496 and 1505, when the great tower was completed. James's wedding in 1502 to Margaret the daughter of Henry VII of England, the momentous alliance of what William Dunbar called 'the Thrissil and the Rois', was celebrated in Holyrood Abbey, and the festivities continued in the palace of Holyroodhouse for a week afterwards. The accounts show that £12 was spent in arras for the great bed. A contemporary description tells how, after the service, the 'King transported himself to the pallais, through the clostre, holdinge allwayes the quene by the body, and hys hed bare, tyll he had brought her within her chammer'. Life for a sixteenth-century wedding guest was rugged: a man was paid 35s for providing straw for the guests to sleep on. However, a young poet at court, Sir David Lindsay, tactfully found life at Holyrood under James IV brilliant:

> And of his court, through Europe sprang the fame
> Of lustie Lordis and lufesom Ladyis ying,
> Tryumphand tornayis, justing, and knychtly game,
> With all pastyme, accordyng for ane king.

James made the fatal error of quarrelling with his belligerent brother-in-law, Henry VIII, crossing the Tweed, and losing his army, the flower of Scotland's nobility, and his own life on Flodden Field.

Under his young son, James V, building went on at Holyroodhouse: a south wing was added to James IV's great tower. The main entrance to the palace was in the middle of the new wing, facing west, flanked by two jutting semi-circular towers which are called, technically, 'engaged rounds'. The top of the steep roof ridge of this new façade was decorated with a row of thistles wearing crowns. And the whole roof of the palace was spiky with weather-vanes, turret-tops, and metal finials. But the plan of the palace, with a matching, protruding great tower in the south-west to balance the north-west tower was not completed.

Holyroodhouse was considerably damaged by English armies during the savage Border raids which Henry VIII launched upon Scotland. The vindictive, opinionated old man was provoked by the refusal of the infant Mary Queen of Scots as a bride for his son Edward. He was alarmed by her engagement to the Dauphin of France instead, with its concomitant renewal of 'the auld alliance', and its encouragement of the French and Catholic factions in Scotland. His brother-in-law the Earl of Hertford (later Duke of Somerset and Lord Protector) was sent north in 1544 and 1547 with savage instructions: 'Sack, burn and slay . . . and extend like extremities and destructions to all towns and villages whereunto ye may reach.' In particular he was told to do his best 'without long tarrying' to burn Edinburgh, beat down the Castle, and sack Holyroodhouse. He inflicted some damage on the new façade, but the great tower survived the English invasions unscathed.

It was, of course, under Mary Stuart, Queen of Scots, that Holyroodhouse chiefly impinged upon history, acting as a suitably forbidding stage for murky melodrama, murder, dissimulation, and jealous factions whispering in draughty corners. Mary, widowed by the death of Francis II of France, arrived back in her northern kingdom in 1561 in dismal haar, to a cold reception. John Knox was as dogmatic about this typically foggy Edinburgh weather as he was about everything else:

The very face of heaven did manifestly speak what comfort was brought into this country with her; to wit, sorrow, dolour, darkness and all impiety; for in the memory of man, that day of the year, was never seen a more dolorous face of the heaven, than was at her arrival, which two days after did so continue: for besides the surface wet, and corruption of the air the mist was so thick and dark that scarce might any man espy another the length of two pair of butts; the sun was not seen to shine two days before nor two days after. That forewarning God gave unto us; but alas! the most part were blind!

The young Queen rode in procession to Holyroodhouse, which had been newly furnished. The elegant French courtiers with her were not impressed with the palace nor with the welcome. The Abbé de Brantôme wrote of their arrival at Holyroodhouse:

. . . there came under her windows five or six hundred citizens, who gave her a concert of the vilest fiddles and little rebecs, which are as bad as they can be in that country, and accompanied them with singing psalms, but so wretchedly out of tune and concord that nothing could be worse.

In Holyroodhouse Mary had her famous interviews with Knox, the implacable little Calvinist with the ferocious beard and bigotry of one of the sterner Old Testament prophets. Knox had already published in Geneva the *First Blast of the Trumpet against the Monstrous Regiment of Women*. He had stirred up continual rebellion against Mary's mother. He disapproved of the new Queen's religion, her sex, her court culture at Holyroodhouse ('vices of the court; the immoderate dancing, and the vast whoredom, that thereof ensued'), and her French connections.

Soon after her arrival he delivered a virulent sermon against all she stood for. Mary sent for him, and they had the first of a series of dramatic debates. It started with a general and topical discussion of whether people had a right to oppose their rulers. Certainly, said Knox; look at the Israelites in Egypt, Daniel under Nebuchadnezzar, and the early Christians in Rome.

Mary: 'Yes, but none of these men raised the sword against their princes.'
Knox: 'God, madam, had not given unto them the power and the means.'
Mary: 'Think ye that subjects having power may resist their princes?'
Knox: 'If their princes exceed their bounds, Madam, no doubt they should
be resisted, even by power. For there is neither greater honour nor greater obedience to be given to Kings or princes than God has commanded to be given to father and mother. But, Madam, the father may be stricken with a frenzy, in which he would slay his own children. Now, Madam, if the children arise, join themselves together, apprehend the father, take the sword or other weapons from him, and finally bind his hands, and keep him in prison, until his frenzy by overpast; think ye, Madam, that the children do any wrong?'

And in full spate, without giving anybody else a chance to utter, he thundered on:

It is even so, Madam, with princes that would murder the children of God that are subject unto them. Their blind zeal is nothing but a very mad frenzy: and therefore, to take the sword from them, to bind their hands, and to cast them into prison until they be brought to a more sober mind, is no disobedience against princes, but just obedience, because it agreeth with the will of God.

Long pause. 'The queen stood still as one amazed more than a quarter of an hour,' Knox records, complacently. At last she said:

Well, then, I perceive that my subjects shall obey you, and not me; and shall do what they like, and not what I command; and so must I be subject to them and not they to me.

After some more brisk dialogue, in which Knox dealt faithfully with the scarlet harlot of Rome, and the iniquity of the Mass, Mary was called away to dinner. Knox summed her up ominously:

If there be not in her a proud mind, a crafty wit, and an indured heart against God and His Truth, my judgement faileth me.

Knox was summoned back again to Holyroodhouse four times, arguing with Mary, and citing with relish lurid passages from the Old Testament. Of her craze for dancing he told her:

I do not utterly damn it, provided two vices be avoided: the former, that the principal vocation of those that use that exercise be not neglected for the pleasure of dancing; and second, that they dance not, as the Philistines their fathers, for the pleasure that they take in the displeasure of God's people.

At the last of these deadlocked dialogues the intransigent disapproval of the grim reformer wore down Mary. She burst into bitter tears, and cried:

I have born with you in all your rigorous manner of speaking, both against myself and against my uncles; yea, I have sought your favour by all possible means: I offered unto you presence and audience, whensoever it pleased you to admonish me, and yet I cannot be quit of you: I vow to God I shall be once revenged.

Afterwards Knox reported happily: 'Scarce could Marnock, her secret chamber boy, get napkins to hold her eyes dry, for the tears and the howling, besides womanly weeping, stayed her speech.' Knox was dismissed to the outer chamber to wait until the Queen recovered and decided what to do with him. He seized the opportunity to preach a characteristically dour sermon to the elegant ladies of court who were also waiting there:

Oh, fair ladies, how pleasant were this life of yours if it should endure, and in the end ye might pass to heaven with all this gay gear. But fie upon that knave Death, which will come whether we will or not. And when he hath layed on the arrest, the foul worms will be busy with this flesh, be it never so fair or tender; but the silly soul, I fear, sall be so feeble, that it can neither carry with it gold, targetting, nor precious stones.

Mary tried to get her revenge by summoning Knox before the Privy Council in Holyrood house on charges of stirring up riots against Roman Catholics. When the Queen came into the crowded council chamber and saw Knox standing bare-headed at the end of the table, she laughed, and said: 'This is a good beginning. But know ye why I laugh? Yon man gart me greet and grat never tear himself. I will see if I can gar him greet.'

However she made the mistake of trying to conduct the case herself. Knox's granite dialectic and sense of his own infallibility were invincible.

And he was acquitted, leaving Holyrood with the pious if slightly ungrateful parting shot: 'Madam, I pray God to purge your heart from Papistry and to preserve you from a council of flatterers.'

Chastelard met his romantic-farcical end at Holyroodhouse. He was a pupil of Ronsard's, a young French poet about court, who fell for the Queen in a more practical way than the idealised romance expected of courtiers. Knox, not necessarily a reliable witness, says Mary always chose him as a partner at the court dances, and in her cabinet 'would lie upon Chastelard's shoulder, and sometimes privily she would steal a kiss of his neck'. Whether encouraged or not, Chastelard misunderstood the formal, fairy-tale nature of court romance, and hid underneath the Queen's bed. He was caught there, unromantically asleep. Chastelard was banished from the Queen's presence, but a few days later Mary found him hiding in her bedroom again. She called hysterically for someone to stab the persistent poet. Chastelard was tried, condemned, and beheaded in view of Holyroodhouse. He carried a copy of Ronsard's 'Hymn to Death' on to the scaffold, and at the last moment is said to have turned toward Holyrood and said: 'Farewell, most cruel and most beautiful of princesses.' He himself summed up the cause of his death admirably: *'Pour estre trouvé en lieu trop suspect.'*

Knox hinted maliciously: 'Chastelard died that the secret of the Queen might not be betrayed.'

But the indelible episode in the history of Holyroodhouse is the melodramatic and midnight murder there of David Rizzio (or Riccio), the Italian musician who had become the Queen's secretary. He was suspect anyway because he was a Catholic and a foreigner. The rebel Protestant Lords of the Congregation wanted to remove his influence from the Queen, and to avoid banishment and forfeiture of their land and goods in Scotland. And Henry Darnley, the tall, good-looking, Tudor-blooded and disastrous husband whom Mary had married in an impatient aberration, was jealous of Rizzio's influence, and, as rumour ran wild, of his even more intimate association with the Queen. He was also furious at being refused the 'Crown Matrimonial', which would have made him King of Scotland. Darnley and various disgruntled lords signed a secret bond or contract to murder Rizzio as the first step to obtaining their assorted political and personal ambitions.

On the evening of March 9, 1566, the Queen, Rizzio and four others were having supper in a small room on the second floor of the north-west tower. The Queen was seven months pregnant. Rizzio sang; as it happened for the last time. Presently Darnley came in. Then Lord Ruthven, risen from his sick-bed, a dying man, 'lean and ill-coloured', wearing armour over his night-shirt, and holding a drawn sword. Behind him crowded the other conspirators.

Mary asked the meaning of this grotesque apparition. Ruthven replied that they meant her no harm; their business was with 'yonder poltroon, David'. The confusion of what happened in the flickering candle-light in that room is recreated in the confusion of the different accounts. Rizzio is said to have cowered down behind the Queen's skirts. Feeble Darnley typically denied that he knew anything about the invasion. Mary's own version, which she sent for official distribution to the French court, says that the conspirators

cast down our table upon ourself, put violent hands on him, struck him over our shoulders with whingers, one part of them standing before our faces with bended daggs, most cruelly took him forth of our cabinet, and at the entry of our chamber gave him fifty-six strokes with whingers and swords, in doing whereof we were not only struck with great dread, but also by sundry considerations, were most justly induced to take extreme fear of our life.

Ruthven's account, from an understandably different angle, was that no violence or threats were offered to Mary, but Rizzio was dragged off next door, where there were a great number, 'who were so vehemently moved against the said David that they could not abide any longer, but must do him in at the Queen's far door in the upper chamber'.

Yet another version says that Rizzio was dragged from the Queen uttering great skirls and cries.

After the butchery, according to Ruthven, by Darnley's command

Davie was hurled down the steps of the stairs from the place where he was slain, and brought to the porter's lodge; where the porter's servant, taking off his clothes, said, 'This hath been his destiny; for upon this chest was his first bed when he entered into this place, and now here he lieth again, a very ingrate and misknowing knave.'

Ruthven also reports that

the King's wynyard [dagger] was found sticking in David's side after he was dead, but always the Queen enquired of the King where his wynyard was, who answered that 'he wit not well'. 'Well,' said she, 'it will be known thereafterwards.'

Since the main participants in the affair were as careless with truth as they were with life, the precise details of the murder will never be known.

It remains suitably blurred and macabre. Knox considered the murder 'worthy of all praise'. Mary is said in some versions to have threatened revenge: she told Darnley she would never be content 'till I gar you have as sore a heart as I have presently'. The story of the blood-stain on the floor which would never wash out, although a purple patch in the repertoire of generations of Holyrood guides, has an even flimsier foundation than might be expected. The rooms, including the floors, in the north-west tower were all heavily altered and renovated under Charles II.

After lulling the suspicions of the conspirators, and seducing her husband from his compact with them, Mary escaped from Holyroodhouse secretly by night, going through the kitchens, and 'the back door that passed through the wine cellar'. Not surprisingly after her grim memories of Holyrood she chose Edinburgh Castle for the birth of her son, James VI. In the next year Darnley himself was mysteriously murdered in a house outside Edinburgh wall in Kirk o' Field. The house was blown sky-high in the middle of the night with an explosion, as the French ambassador described it, 'like that of twenty-five pieces of cannon'. Darnley's corpse was found some distance from the house in a shirt, without a mark on him, having probably been smothered. Mary had visited him that evening, but at the time of the explosion was dancing in Holyroodhouse at the wedding of one of her servants. She was at once suspected of foreknowledge, if not worse; of, in the contemporary jargon, 'looking through her fingers at' the convenient removal of her increasingly inconvenient husband. She had certainly persuaded Darnley to leave the comparative safety of his family stronghold in Glasgow, and to come to convalesce in the improbable and sinister house at Kirk o' Field. And she did not exactly discourage the rumours nor improve her reputation by marrying the Earl of Bothwell, the man chiefly suspected of disposing of Darnley, within three months of being so noisily widowed.

The enigma – whether Mary was a tigerish Lady Macbeth with indelible blood on her hands, or a tragic, persecuted, unlucky princess – depends largely on the notorious 'Casket Letters', which were alleged to have been written by her to Bothwell plotting something distinctly unpleasant for Darnley. Mary herself at the time, and her supporters ever afterwards, declared that the letters were 'false and feigned, forged and invented only to my dishonour and slander'. She is a character about whom it is evidently impossible to be neutral, but innocent or guilty, her memory, the great skirls of Rizzio, and the suffocating, unreal atmosphere of betrayal, conspiracy, and assassination in the dark are the influences that still haunt the gaunt tower of Holyroodhouse.

Mary's son, James VI, called Solomon because of his pedantry and because, scurrilously, he was said to be 'the son of David', kept court mainly at Holyroodhouse until he was summoned south in 1603 to become James I of England. He had some repairs done to the palace before his last visit in 1617 in order not to lose Scottish face in front of the visiting English. They were apparently reasonably successful; an English tourist in this year wrote:

I was at His Majesties Palace, a stately and princely seat, wherein I saw a sumptuous chapell most richly adorned with all the appurtenances belonging to so sacred a place or so Royale an owner.

But Holyroodhouse was not much used by the Stuarts, nor indeed by subsequent Kings. During the Civil War it was transformed into a barracks by Cromwell's troops, and suffered a certain amount of damage. Charles II built the palace as it exists today, at last erecting a twin tower to the south-west to balance the original medieval tower; and making the main body of the palace linking the two towers in the fashionable Palladian style, with its classical crescendo of Doric, Ionic, and Corinthian pilasters. Charles also provided for the interior decoration of Holyroodhouse with one of the most extraordinary commissions ever given to an artist. Jacob de Wet, a Dutch painter, was ordered for a fee of £120 a year to produce 111 portraits 'in large royall postures' of all the Kings of Scotland, starting from the legendary Fergus, *circa*, if ever, A.D. 330, appearance unknown, and carrying on for some centuries with equally improbable characters. He churned them out at the rate of about one a week, presumably relying heavily on his imagination, though he was given the use of some traditional old portraits.

A contemporary wrote:

In our gallery of the abbey there is set up the pictures of our one hundred and eleven kings since Fergus I, 330 before Christ, [*sic*] which make a very pretty show, and the eminenter of them are done *ad longum*. They have guessed at the figures of their faces before James I. They got help by those pictures that were used at Charles I's coronation in 1633, where they all met and saluted him, wishing that as many of their race might succeed him in the throne as had preceded him.

Charles II never visited his new palace, though his brother James II did, as Duke of York, when it was necessary to have him out of London during the bitter sectarian struggle over the Exclusion Bill.

The next, and spectacular, royal resident at Holyroodhouse was James's grandson, Charles Edward Stuart, the Young Pretender, who arrived in 1745 to reclaim his grandfather's lost palace and kingdom. And once again Holyroodhouse was filled with glitter of candles, and with the fatal theatrical ambiance which always seems to have been its favourite prevailing atmosphere. Greeted with an unfriendly salute from the cannon in the Castle, Bonnie Prince Charlie rode into Holyrood park with eighty cavaliers. He was wearing a Stuart tartan jacket, the blue sash of the Garter, red breeches, and a green bonnet with a white cockade on it – 'a gentleman and a man of fashion, but not like a hero or a conqueror,' wrote a prophetic witness. James Hepburn of Keith, who had been out with the Old Pretender in 1715, drew his sword to lead the last of the Stuarts up the grand staircase. In the day-dream five weeks around his surprising victory at Prestonpans, the Prince held tartan court at Holyroodhouse, before his doomed descent into England. He touched for the King's Evil, and dined in public. There was a state ball crowded with Jacobite ladies in white cockades and gowns they had not worn for years, heavy with the scent of moth-balls and impending disaster.

Pipes played 'When the King enjoys his own again'. Whisky flowed. The Prince himself refused to dance: 'It is very true I like dancing, and I am glad to see the ladies and you divert yourselves, but I have now another air to dance, and until that be finished I'll dance no other.' Tradition also says he pointed to one of his hairy Highlanders and said: 'These are my beauties.' Sir Walter Scott used this famous and romantic ball as a scene in *Waverley*. Edward Waverley is 'dazzled at the liveliness and elegance of the scene now exhibited in the long-deserted halls of the Scottish palace'. He has a conversation with the Chevalier, who ends the evening with:

Good night, fair ladies, who have so highly honoured a proscribed and banished Prince – Good night, my brave friends; may the happiness we have this evening experienced be an omen of our return to these our paternal halls, speedily and in triumph, and of many and many future meetings of mirth and pleasure in the palace of Holyrood.

It was a brilliant, ephemeral, neurotic court:

One would have thought the King was already restored, and in peaceable possession of all the dominion of his ancestors, and that the Prince had only made a trip to Scotland to show himself to the people and receive their homage; such was the splendour of the court, and the satisfaction that appeared in everybody's countenance.

'An infinite crowd' gathered at Holyroodhouse to see the Prince off on his unfortunate crusade. In the next year the Duke of Cumberland stayed in the palace *en route* for Culloden and the nickname of 'Butcher'.

After the Stuart cause had set for ever on the bleak reality of Culloden moor, Holyroodhouse was deserted as a royal residence. Then in 1822, as a relief from all its intense melodrama, George IV came to give the palace its first ration of farce. He arrived in Edinburgh on his Scottish tour, the first Hanoverian monarch to set foot on the soil of Scotland. The King did not stay in Holyroodhouse, which was in a state of some dilapidation, but he held a levée in the palace. For this remarkable occasion he wore a kilt of Stuart tartan, and full Highland trimmings, which were said to give him 'quite a martial air'. Always enthusiastic about dressing up, George was the first of the British royals to be infected with tartanitis; and indeed actually made his first appearance in Highland dress in 1789, the very year after the death of Bonnie Prince Charlie. The various panegyrical accounts of the visit record that the King himself looked down at his lower half and said: 'I cannot help smiling at myself.' His outfit inspired satirical verse:

> With his tartan plaid and kelt so wide,
> The ladies blush who stand beside;
> And as he bows, behind each fan,
> Exclaim – O gallant Highlandman.

In fact George preserved his modesty by wearing flesh-coloured tights under his kilt. The ludicrous undertones of the occasion were greatly enhanced by Sir William Curtis, an immensely rich and jolly Londoner, companion of and even fatter than the King. He was seized with an irresistible urge to wear the kilt as a gesture of loyalty. His appearance at the levée also in Stuart tartan, to which he was even less entitled than George, as a sort of beaming, grotesque caricature or *Doppelgänger* of the King was the sensation of the day. 'A portentous apparition' was the verdict of Sir Walter Scott, who was organising the ceremonial. Another unconventional feature of the levée was the reaction of some of the Scots, who, when told to kiss hands, bowed and kissed their own hands to the King. But in spite of such minor solecisms, the state visit was an immense success. George's ceremonial drives to and from Holyroodhouse were ecstatically cheered by crowds estimated to be a million. At a banquet with the Lord Provost and Corporation the King told them he would 'ever remember as one of the proudest moments of my life the day I came among them, and the gratifying reception which they gave me'. He proposed a toast in whisky: 'Health to the Chieftains and Clans, and God Almighty bless the Land of Cakes. Drink this three times three, gentlemen.'

In 'Don Juan' Byron mocked the visit:

> Teach them the decencies of good threescore;
>     Cure them of tours, hussar and highland dresses;
> Tell them that youth once gone returns no more,
>     That hired huzzas redeem no land's distresses;
> Tell them Sir William Curtis is a bore,
>     Too dull even for the dullest of excesses –
> The witless Falstaff of a hoary Hal,
> A fool whose bells have ceased to ring at all.

Victoria stayed in Holyroodhouse for a state visit, and wrote that the palace remindered her 'forcibly and sadly of former days'. She inspected the little turret room where 'poor Queen Mary was supping when poor Riccio was murdered'. And afterwards she used the palace quite often to spend a night in to break the journey to or from Balmoral.

Subsequent Kings and Queens have made periodic and usually brief visits to Holyroodhouse, which is still a royal palace. Once a year at the General Assembly of the Church of Scotland it is the official residence of the Lord High Commissioner, and so recaptures some of the first fine ceremonial rapture for which it was built. But melodrama and Mary Queen of Scots still dominate the historical atmosphere of the palace of the Scottish kings.

# XII

# NONSUCH

NONSUCH is an attractive, archaic noun or adjective meaning unique, unparalleled, nonpareil, like nothing else on the wide earth. 'Job was a nonsuch in his day for holiness,' according to a seventeenth-century author. The vanished palace of Nonsuch, in what are now the sedate Surrey suburbs of London ten miles south of the Thames, did its best to live up to its vainglorious name. It was a prodigy of an ornate pleasure dome, glittering with gilt and white stucco, with bas-reliefs and cartouches plastered thick on the walls, swarming with serried statues, congested with monstrous regiments of Roman Emperors, with every inhabitant of classical mythology, with assorted allegorical and metaphysical creatures; a vast pantomime-pile of cupolas and towers corbelled out into great pot-bellies high above ground, rampant with heraldic beasts above every battlement, golden onion-domed, extravagantly oriel-windowed, tall-turreted, scaly as an armadillo with Parisian slates, artificial-wildernessed, many-fountained, such stuff and nonsense as dreams, or perhaps oriental nightmares, are made on, out of this world, and certainly out of the rolling Surrey plain. A thunderstruck visitor in 1598 wrote, with deadpan understatement: 'One would imagine that everything that architecture can perform to have been employed in this one work.'

Henry VIII began to build Nonsuch in the last decade of his reign, when his youthful athletic mania for jousting and tennis (particularly for winning at jousting and tennis), and for 'doing marvellous things, both in dancing and jumping', had worn itself out into less strenuous forms of exhibitionism, like architecture. Instead of prancing before the ladies between all the courses of a tourney, 'making a thousand jumps in the air', wearing out horse after horse, he became what a contemporary described as 'the only Phoenix of his time for fine and curious masonry'. In all, Henry built from scratch, rebuilt, or made extensive alterations to thirteen major palaces in or near London. The immense development of royal residences under the Tudors is an outward and visible expression of the inexorable increase of the power of the crown under the formidable dynasty. Nonsuch was the favourite building enterprise of the last years of Henry's life, an unparalleled expression of the cultural vanity of a Renaissance King. He built it 'for his solace and retirement'.

The official purpose of Nonsuch was as yet one more lavish and secluded hunting lodge, in a great deer park of 1,700 acres stocked with a thousand head of deer, a day's ride from London, and close to his riverside palace of Hampton Court. The unofficial reason for building the extravaganza was Henry's ingrained and ancient rivalry for glory with the French King, Francis I.

Each of the two Kings saw himself as the prototype and personification of the Renaissance prince, one of whose functions was to employ the greatest artists of his age in ambitious building programmes. As a young man Henry had been emerald-eyed with envy about Francis's military triumphs, about his physical feats, even about the rugged shapeliness of the French royal legs. He had difficulty in suppressing tears of jealousy when he heard that Francis had won the battle of Marignano in Italy. The unsuccessful wrestling match between the two young Kings on the Field of Cloth of Gold, when Francis won by a surprise attack, was mortification and bitter memory to Henry, and is tactfully ignored in the official English accounts.

In his old age Henry decided to build a palace which would astonish and humiliate the French ambassadors, and which would make Francis's magnificent hunting lodges, his Château of Chambord, his spectacular Renaissance palace of Fontainebleau, look dingy, old-fashioned, one-star, second-rate. The supreme egotist, Henry was always determined to be top in whatever he took up. Nonsuch was to make permanent the fantastic and ephemeral decoration of the buildings erected at Guisnes for the Field of Cloth of Gold.

A fascinating correspondence between Henry and his ambassador to France, Sir John Wallop, survives, spicy with undertones of architectural jealousy, and of keeping up with the Valois. The ambassador describes in detail the French King's latest fashion of interior decoration at Fontainebleau, and reports Francis's interest in what Henry is building:

He heard say that your Majesty did use much gilding in your said houses, and especially in the roofs, and that in his buildings he used little or none, but made the roofs of timber finely wrought with divers colours of wood natural.

Both Kings competed vigorously to attract from Italy the new school of artists and craftsmen to decorate their courts in the revived classical style. In a master *coup* and scoop, Henry managed to lure from Fontainebleau to Nonsuch Nicholas Bellin, the expert *stuccatore* from Modena, who was referred to patronisingly in his letters as 'Modon'. Bellin came to England in 1537, possibly to avoid punishment for embezzling money from Francis I. Henry firmly resisted the French King's requests to extradite him. And Bellin was almost certainly responsible for the most revolutionary feature of Nonsuch, the fantastic scheme of huge stucco reliefs framed in ornate patterns of slate, which was spread around the walls of the inner court, and along the south front of the palace, like an exuberant wedding cake.

Here is ambassador Wallop reporting again on Fontainebleau and Bellin:

And after that I had wel behold the said gallery, me thought it the most magnifique that ever I saw the lengt and bredthe no man canne better showe Your Majestie than Modon who wroughte there in the begynnynge of the same . . . upon the fourthe part is all antique work of such stuff as the said Modon makith Your Majesties chemeneys; and betwixt every windowe standes grete anticale personages entier . . . His bedde chamber is very singulier as wel with antycale borders, as costly seeling and a chemeney right wel made.

Bellin's end product at Nonsuch may have seemed a piece of puffing and blowing bullfrog architectural megalomania, ostentatious and vulgar to some refined and traditional connoisseurs. In Hoefnagel's famous sketch of Elizabeth arriving outside in a Cinderella coach, Nonsuch looks enchanting, fantasy fairy-tale, a distinctly improbable object to find in Surrey.

In April of 1538 Henry acquired the village of Cuddington between Ewell and Epsom, giving the manorial lord, Richard Codington, some royal land in Norfolk in exchange. With a typically Tudor high hand he ordered the village, the church, and the old manor house to be pulled down. Hundreds of tons of thirteenth-century stone for the foundations, much of it carved and decorated, began to be carted five miles to the site from Merton Priory, which by a convenient coincidence had just been suppressed, and had begun to be demolished only a week before. An army of 520 workmen camped in tents on the site of the prospective palace. Masons and craftsmen were recruited from all over England, artists and sculptors from all over Europe. An Oxfordshire cowman was prosecuted for seditious speech for spreading a rumour that the workmen at all other royal palaces had been dismissed, since 'His Grace hath begun one other new work which shall be named None Such'. In six years £23,000 was spent on the palace. Its basic plan was the traditional collegiate one of two-storey buildings arranged around two interconnecting open-air quadrangles. On to this medieval basis (less than 150 yards long) was plastered the lush marzipan and icing-sugar exuberance of Renaissance decoration, more fantastic and elaborate than in any other palace in Europe.

'O Gods. What labour, what workmen, what axes, what crowbars, what artists, what sums of money were needed for so great a task,' wrote (in Latin) the rector of the neighbouring parish of Cheam, Dr Anthony Watson, with rather too much obsequious sycophancy, and rather too little concern for the demolition of the church next door. But even Henry, 'that majestic lord that broke the bonds of Rome', who stood up to France and Spain, whose whim was law, was helpless to hurry the unhurrying chase and unperturbed pace of the British workman. There is a pathetic letter from Henry to the Privy Council complaining about his plasterer at Nonsuch, Giles Gering. He suspected Gering of hiring himself out elsewhere, since he did not turn up on the building site for weeks at a time, and when he did he 'brabbled' with the royal overseers. 'We may,' wrote Henry, 'as occasion shall rise, charge both him and others;' adding bitterly, 'He is a fellow that glorieth much in himself and his doings.'

Gering never appears to have been charged. Presumably he was indispensable, and knew it; and finished his work in his own deliberate time, with all the statutory tea-breaks and restrictive practices of the British building site.

The rich inner court was completely finished, and the rest of the palace nearly finished, when Henry died nine years later. More than £24,000 had been spent on it. But Henry seems never to have spent a night at the palace he intended to be the elaborate monument of his cultural and dynastic ambitions. Probably in his last years riding and hunting had become too painful for him. It seems likely that he made day trips to Nonsuch from Hampton Court. His last wife Katherine Parr paid a brief visit in 1544.

Mary did not like Nonsuch. It may have reminded her of sides of her father's character which had soured the lives of her mother and herself. In any case she disliked hunting, which was the chief raison d'être and amenity of Nonsuch. She considered pulling down the unfinished place, to save the bills for 'Kepying the Queene's place & parkes, gardeyn, & wardrobe' at Nonsuch. But Henry Fitzalan, the Earl of Arundel, persuaded her to give him the palace in exchange for lands in Suffolk, and he completed it according to Henry's plans, and laid out the gardens, filling them with classical statues. He gave as his improbably sentimental and unmercenary motive 'the love and honour that he bare to his old master, his godfather'. When Elizabeth came to the throne, Arundel was one of her earliest suitors, though something of an outsider, in the interminable dithering of the marriage-stakes. He came hurrying home from the continent, and the sardonic Spanish ambassador noted that his tears of joy 'floated the ship in'. Walsingham observed that Elizabeth was 'the best marriage in her parish, and brought a kingdom with her for dowry'.

However Arundel himself was not exactly a brilliant catch. He was nearly fifty, no beauty, rather stupid and uncouth, twice married already, and with two married daughters. In any case, his rank was not high enough for him to aim at a Queen, especially so class-conscious a Queen as Elizabeth. Nevertheless for a short time Londoners fancied his chances, and placed bets on him. When her first Parliament urged Elizabeth to marry from among her own subjects, Arundel was possibly the 'English spouse' at the back of their minds. In this gossipy and romantic ambiance, Elizabeth went to stay with him at Nonsuch in the first summer of her reign, during her summer progress of 1559. There was a week of revelry by night, masques, a midnight tattoo, concerts. By day, from a raised stand in the park, the Queen watched the ageing Earl galloping after stags as gallantly as Alice's White Knight. At night the choristers of St Paul's acted a new play lasting until three a.m. There was, according to an eye-witness whose grammar seems to have been overcome by the rich food, 'a grett bankett at ye cost as ever was sene, for soper, bancett, and maske, wth drums & flutes & all ye mysyke yt cold be, tyll mydnyght; & as for chere has not bene sene nor heard'. At the end of the gala visit, Arundel gave Elizabeth a leaving present of a cupboard of gilt plate. But no engagement was forthcoming. Six months later the discarded and dis-appointed Earl sent in his bill for the party, and for once Elizabeth did not quibble about paying it.

The Queen may not have fallen for the Earl, but she was much taken with his house. Arundel went off to the therapeutic baths at Padua in a fit of gout and sulks, and while he was away, Elizabeth made a sudden surprise visit to Nonsuch.

She wrote to the owner:

In the meane tyme, we have in the later end of this winter seeking to take the ayre for a small tyme in Surrey, visited your house at Nonesuch. Where we had dyvers wayes very good contentation. And did so well ayre every parte of your house as at your comming we thinke you shall fynde it seasonable for you. And so we wishe yow to fynde it.

Nonsuch Palace. The original watercolour painted in 1568 by the Flemish artist Joris Hoefnagel. The great octagonal towers are almost certainly Italian in design. Drawings of identical structures were made by Leonardo da Vinci. The painting is in a private collection in England

*Photo The Times*

Nonsuch Palace. Print by Joris Hoefnagel showing Queen Elizabeth arriving at Nonsuch in 1582

*Photo Mansell Collection*

Ram's head from Nonsuch. A relic of one of the panels of plaster moulding which, framed in carved and gilded slate, decorated the outside of the palace

*Photo London Museum*

Cherub's head from Nonsuc[
One of the few survivir
fragments of the vast stucc
frieze that covered the façac
of the palace

*Photo London Muse*

Elizabeth returned for many summers to Nonsuch, and in 1592 she bought back her father's palace from Arundel's son-in-law John, Lord Lumley, who had inherited it, and who had fallen inextricably into debt. During the last ten years of her reign Nonsuch was her favourite country seat, a masquerade world where she could hide away from creeping old age, from time's hurrying footsteps, among the gilt and the glitter, the games and the private dances with her favoured few friends, the outrageous flatteries of everybody. 'Her Majesty is returned again to Nonsuch, which of all places she likes best,' wrote a courtier.

There are several contemporary descriptions of the palace. The trouble is that they are mostly long on hyperbole and astonishment, and short on factual detail. Louis Frederick, Prince of Württemburg, penned an enthusiastic account of his impression of the life of the palace, the beauty of its fittings, and the fountains in the gardens, which has never been published. Camden, the antiquary, wrote:

Here Henry VIII, in his magnificence, erected a structure so beautiful, so elegant, and so splendid, that in whatever direction the admirer of florid architecture turns his eyes, he will say that it easily bears off the prize. So great is the emulation of ancient Roman art, such are its paintings, its gilding, and its decoration of all kinds, that you would say that it is the sky spangled with stars. Long life to a king who spares no expense that the ingenuity of his artists may exhibit such wonders, which ravish the minds and the gaze of mankind by their magnificence.

And Philemon Holland in Camden's *Brittannia* commented:

As for the very house it selfe, so environed it is about with Parkes full of Deare, such dainty gardens and delicate orchards it hath, such groves adorned with curious Arbors, so prety quarters, beds, and Alleys, such walkes so shadowed with trees, that Amenitie or Pleasantnesse it selfe may seeme to have chosen no other place but it.

However it is possible to reconstruct pretty accurately what Nonsuch looked like, partly by gleaning facts from among the purple superlatives of visitors; often foreign ones, attracted by its reputation; partly from a handful of drawings of the palace; and partly from the excavations of 1959 which uncovered the foundations and ground plan. It was 355 feet by 170 feet in size, and its basic shape was a northern outer court in the plain Tudor style leading into an inner court which was decorated with all the Christmas cake exuberance of the French Renaissance.

The visitor entered the outer court through a three-storey gatehouse with octagonal angle turrets like those at Richmond and Hampton Court.

The outer quadrangle was plain, built of freestone, two storeys high. Courtiers lodged on the top floor; servants, cellars, and buttery underneath. The cobbled yard was crossed with flagged footpaths. To the left an archway led to a smaller kitchen court. To the right, another archway led to the stables. The visitor, at least if he was the Vicar of Cheam, gasped in pseudo-Ciceronian periods at 'the size of the rooms, the splendour of the windows, the manifestly Royal form of the building, the pinnacles aloft in the sky, which at the bottom are held up by little animals, and at the top bear dogs and griffins and lions resting on decorated shields'. Straight ahead was a second, taller gatehouse, 'which outdoes the first by one tower, a clock, a symphony, and six gilded horoscopes'. The triple oriel window over the archway seemed 'as if the delicate hand of Praxiteles had hewn the manifold projection of the windows'.

Between the towers on top of the inner gatehouse protruded the belfry, clock, and musical concourse of bells, 'of most excellent workmanship, a verie speciall ornament to Nonesuch House'. Through the archway gleamed the astonishing white and gold ornamentation of the inner court. 'When you have greeted its threshold,' said the glowing Dr Watson, 'and seen with dazzled eyes the shining lustre of the stone, glittering with purest gold, it is not surprising if it should hold you senseless.' When you came back to your senses, you would notice in the middle of the courtyard a white marble fountain, over which impended a galloping white marble horse. The three Graces, arms entwined, poured streams of water into a marble basin, held up, for no immediately obvious symbolic reason, by a brace of golden griffins. Beyond the fountain, against the wall facing the goggle-eyed visitor, sat a heroic statue of Henry VIII, gleaming on a burnished throne. All the inside walls of this quadrangle, and the three outside faces on the west, south, and east sides were covered with white stucco-duro (a very hard, stone plaster), moulded into life-size bas-reliefs five inches deep. To Henry's right hand, the façade of his own apartments featured the whole of Mount Olympus and the Labours of Hercules, down to the last gory detail. A bronze statue of Scipio for some swollen-headed and inapposite reason stood at the entrance to the King's apartments. On Henry's left the outer walls of the Queen's rooms swarmed with a bewildering multitude of theological, symbolic, classical, and assorted plaster females.

Around the upper floor of the courtyard thirty-one Roman Emperors from Julius Caesar to the brutish and short-reigned Aemilianus were paraded between the windows 'in most pleasing concord'; the visitor noted: 'All places are full of Kings, Caesars, Sciences, Gods.' The timber-work between these frequent plaster creatures was lavishly gilded, and decorated with imported French slates arranged in the latest, intricate patterns from France. Any odd blank spaces were filled in with emblems and cartouches. At the far corners of the quadrangle two fat polygonal towers soared up five storeys bristling with oriels, bulged out into fat corbels for one storey, and then receded again, to splutter out in a final gesture of domes, battlements, heraldic beasts, turrets, pennants, cupolas, and creaking weather-vanes. These towers were 'the chief ornament of the whole house of Nonsuch'. One exhausted visitor, over-whelmed by his guided tour, called Nonsuch 'the eclipse and glory of its kind'; and another, 'the very pearl of the realm'.

The gardens at Nonsuch were as famous and unique as the palace, and contained a maze, an aviary, knot gardens, summerhouses. The central attraction was the grove of Diana, with a great marble fountain featuring the sporting Goddess, and Actaeon being transmogrified into a stag because of his unfortunate Peeping Tom accident. There is a very old tradition that this was the bathroom of the palace, and that Elizabeth used to come down here for her ablutions. More statuary, 'which seemed to rival the perfection of Roman antiquity', lurked behind every bush.

There were the popular Tudor practical joke pieces: the pyramid of marble 'full of concealed pipes, which spirt upon all who come within their reach'.

Dr Watson admired the nymph fountain in the Privy Garden:

A shining column which carries a high statue of a snow-white nymph, perhaps Venus, from whose leaden breasts flow jets of water into the ivory-covered marble.

The dream-like, Alice in Wonderland atmosphere was increased by the crouching presence of all kinds of marble animals in the bushes, 'most artfully set out, so that from a distance one would take them for real ones'. There was, inevitably, a maze, and an orchard, as well as the 140 fruit trees growing haphazard around the main garden. In one corner there was a man-made wilderness, where visitors sat, made conversation, and listened to the birds singing beside them in the wilderness. In another corner was a deep, dark wood, pierced with alleys lined with boards for tennis and other ball games. Here one guest was particularly pleased with 'the delicious song of the birds in the tall trees, densely planted along the sides in ordered array'. There were shrubs and plants sown in intricate circles, 'as though by the needle of Semiramis', flocks of 'ewe' trees, and the famous and unusual 'lelacks, which trees beare no fruit, but only a verie pleasant flower'.

Diana's fountain was surrounded by these lilacs, which prevented the Queen from being surprised in her bath by any itinerant Actaeons at court. On the edge of the gardens, 400 yards west of the palace, pirouetted the Banqueting Hall, built in the same flamboyant idiom as the palace. It was a two-storey balconied hall, standing on high ground, with a view in all directions. On top of it there were balconies at each corner from which spectators could watch the court hunting. It was probably also used for masques.

In 1599 Thomas Platter visited Nonsuch to sight-see on a Sunday while the Queen was in residence. And like all good German tourists he kept a voluminous journal. The party was taken into the Presence Chamber, and 'placed well to the fore, so as better to behold the Queen'.

They noted admiringly the tapestries, and the floor, 'strewn with straw or hay, only where the Queen was to come out and up to her seat were carpets laid down worked in Turkish knot'. The throne was of red damask embroidered with gold, so low 'that the cushions almost lay on the ground'. Overhead a great canopy was 'fixed very ornately to the ceiling'. From noon onwards a trickle of officials holding white staffs began to emerge from an inner chamber. Then a pride of Lords stalked in. And finally the Queen herself, 'alone without escort, very straight and erect. She was most lavishly attired in a gown of pure white satin, gold-embroidered, with a whole bird of Paradise for panache, set forward on her head studded with costly jewels; she wore a string of huge pearls about her neck and elegant gloves over which were drawn costly rings. In short she was most gorgeously apparelled, and although she was already seventy-four' (sixty-six, to be pedantically precise) 'she was very youthful still in appearance, seeming no more than twenty years of age. She had a dignified and regal bearing'.

A sermon was then delivered by 'a preacher in a white surplice, merely standing on the floor facing the Queen'. But since it was very warm and very late, Elizabeth had soon had enough, and sent word to the preacher to finish. She then immediately withdrew from the Presence Chamber. Preaching to a congregation that included Elizabeth was a hazardous business at the best of times. There was always the distinct possibility of being interrupted by a furious shout of: 'To your text, Master Dean. To your text. Leave that. We have had enough of that', if the Queen happened to disagree with some passage in the sermon.

The most famous occasion of an indiscreet, or perhaps an intrepid preacher before Elizabeth, was when Bishop Aylmer of London 'seemed to touch on the vanity of decking the body too finely'. The atmosphere crackled with rage. 'Perchance the Bishop hath never sought Her Majesty's wardrobe, or he would have chosen another text,' wrote Sir John Harington, Elizabeth's witty godson. Elizabeth remarked icily afterwards that 'if the Bishop held more discourses on such matters, she would fit him for Heaven, but he would walk there without a staff, and leave his mantle behind him'.

After the hastily truncated sermon at Nonsuch, trestle tables were set before the throne. A stately procession of guards and gentlemen marched into the chamber, bowed three times, and set cloth, knives, salt and bread upon the tables, 'with honours performed as if the Queen herself had sat there'. Then followed another procession of forty of the guard in red tabards: 'they are all very tall, fine young men, and all similarly attired, so that I never in my life saw their like.' Each of them carried a dish, 'and I observed amongst them some very large joints of beef, and all kinds of game, pastries and tarts'. Elizabeth herself did not emerge. A lady-in-waiting carved, and the helpings were carried in to the Queen in her private chamber; 'and she ate of what she fancied, privily however, for she very seldom partakes before strangers'. Three courses were served in the same way. Then 'the Queen's musicians appeared in the Presence Chamber with their trumpets and shawns, and after they had performed their music, everyone withdrew, bowing themselves out just as they had come in, and the tables were carried away again'.

The tourist, as tourists usually are, was particularly pleased with the thrice-gorgeous general ceremony of Court, and most of all by the business of kneeling to talk to Elizabeth. 'I am told that they even play cards with the Queen in kneeling posture.'

It was in the autumn of this same year of 1599 that Nonsuch was the stage for its one major historical scene, a set-piece sufficiently surrealist and melodramatic even for such a melodramatic and surrealist stage. This was when the Earl of Essex, thirty-three years old and impossibly temperamental, came hurtling home from Ireland in highly questionable circumstances, and burst in upon Elizabeth still distinctly in her déshabillé in her bedroom at Nonsuch, unpainted, without her wig, her grey hair hanging in wisps about her wrinkled face, her eyes starting from their sockets. This fatal entrance under the battlements of Nonsuch set in motion the collapsing dominoes of events which ended with Essex, the man of blood who did not live out half his days, being 'spewed out of the realm' by a grisly, botched execution in the Tower.

Essex's Irish expedition as Lord Lieutenant against the intractable rising led by 'the great O'Neill', the rebel Earl of Tyrone, had been unmitigated disaster from the beginning. Essex, 'Great England's glory and the world's wide wonder', had promised so much in Council before he left, had criticised his predecessors so arrogantly, that he had left himself no possible excuse for failure.

As soon as he arrived in that 'moist, rotten country', and against explicit instructions, he started knighting his young followers prodigally and defiantly, so building up his formidable military *clientèle*, which already looked sinister to wary eyes at Court. Instead of going after Tyrone in Ulster, he frittered away the summer in a fruitless expedition into Leinster, which Elizabeth compared to the track of a ship at sea: like the waters of the ocean the guerilla rebels just opened before the passage of Essex, and closed behind him. 'I give the Lord Deputy a thousand pounds a day to go on progress,' snarled Elizabeth, and sent him devastating, stinging letters, ordering him to march against Tyrone at once, and commanding him on his duty not to return to England without permission. Essex by now was almost insane with the sour smell of failure, and with wounded pride. He was tortured by tyrannical jealousy and vindictive hatred of his rivals at Court, and blamed all his troubles on his 'enemies', the party around Robert Cecil.

So Essex committed the one unpardonable imbecility, against which Elizabeth had warned him months before, when she told him that he should 'beware of touching her sceptre'. He had treasonable discussions with his reckless followers about a desperate *coup d'état*. The project was to march with part of his army to court, not explicitly to overthrow the Queen, though it might come to that, but to remove his enemies. Essex marched against Tyrone, not to battle, but to a most suspicious half-hour's private parley at a ford, which ended, against all his strict instructions, in a truce. There may have been wild talk of one becoming King of England, the other Viceroy of Ireland.

Then on September 24 Essex set out from Dublin with 'a competent number' of choice men. The troop galloped fiery-footed across England, and arrived in London on Friday morning, the 28th. By now the plan of instigating a deliberate revolt had faded in the wild and woolly recesses of Essex's brain. His one idea was to get to the Queen as quickly as possible, and argue, bully, coax, sulk, rodomontade, flatter his way out of a scrape and into the sunshine of her favour again, as he had done so often before. He left most of his cavalcade behind in London, from where if necessary they could do something to rescue him. With an escort of six friends he crossed the ferry from Westminster to Lambeth, and took horses on the far side. As they rode wearily on the last leg towards the golden domes and minarets of Nonsuch, Lord Grey of Wilton, one of the Cecil party, over-took them on a faster horse. One of Essex's companions, Sir Thomas Gerard, hurried after him, and shouted: 'My Lord, I beg you will speak with the Earl.'

Grey: 'No, I have business at Court.'

Gerard: 'Then I pray you let my Lord of Essex ride before, that he may bring the first news of his return himself.'

Grey: 'Doth he desire it?'

Gerard: 'No, nor I think will desire anything at your hands.'

Grey: 'Then I have business;' and vanished in a cloud of dust, leaving the panicky little group debating whether they should chase after and kill him.

Lord Grey arrived at Nonsuch, and told Cecil the astounding, the alarming news that Essex was back. Little, hunch-backed spider Cecil, nicknamed 'Robertus Diabolus', did nothing, sent no word to the Queen who was dressing in her upper chamber, but sat quietly in his chair, waiting. A quarter of an hour later Essex arrived at the gate. It was ten a.m. His whirlwind irruption into Nonsuch is best described in a letter written the next day by an eye-witness at Court, Rowland Whyte, the agent of Sir Robert Sidney, who was one of Essex's faction:

Nonsuch, Michaelmas Day at Noone 1599 –

On Michaelmas Eve, about 10 o'clock in the morning, Lord Essex 'lighted at Court Gate Post, & made all haste up to the Presence, & soe to the Privy Chamber, and staied not till he came to the Queen's Bedchamber, where he found the Queen, newly up, her Hare about her Face; he kneeled unto her, kiss'd her Hands, & had some private speach with her, which seemed to give him great contentment; for coming from her Majestie to go shifte himself in his Chamber, he was very pleasant, & thanked God, though he had suffered much troubles and Storms Abroad, he found a Sweet Calm at Home. 'Tis much wondered at here that he went so boldly to her Majestie's Presence she not being ready, & he so full of Dirt and Mire, that his very face was full of yt. When ready he went up againe for half an Howre after 12. As yet all was well, & hr Usage very gracious towards hym.

But when, after dinner, he againe went in to her Presence, he found her much changed, for she began to call hym to question for his Return, & was not satisfied in the Manner of hys coming away & leaving all things at so great hazard. She appointed the Lords to heare hym, a soe they went to Cownsell in the Afternoone. Yt is mistrustful that for hys Disobedience he shall be comytted. On the same evening a Commandment came from the Queen to my Lord of Essex, that he should keepe his Chamber.

In the first frightening turbulence of Essex's arrival at Nonsuch, Elizabeth as usual took refuge in dissimulation and procrastination. What did this unannounced, forbidden return mean? How many men had he brought from Ireland, and where were they? 'As God help me,' wrote one of those present during that long, doom-laden week-end, oppressive with the shadow of that two-handed engine at the door, 'it is a very dangerous time here; for the heads of both factions being here, a man cannot tell how to govern himself towards them.'

Gradually, after consultation with Cecil, Elizabeth felt strong enough to put Essex under house arrest. The desperate gamble of the invasion of the Queen's bedroom at Nonsuch had failed. Essex's character being what it was, Nemesis followed as inexorably as in Aeschylus.

His 'injuries' and his pride suppurated in disgrace. With suicidal recklessness he spoke of Elizabeth in public, that being now an old woman, the Queen 'was no less crooked and distorted in mind than she was in body' – only a year before he had written to her in ludicrously euphuistic love letters, as hunting like Diana, walking like Venus, a nymph, a goddess, an angel. Within a few months he blundered with his supporters in London into an inept and madcap rising. Elizabeth declared bitterly that 'a senseless ingrate had at last revealed what had long been in his mind'. And Essex took the long, inevitable walk of all great state criminals to the scaffold in the courtyard of the Tower, to which everyone except himself had seen him heading for so long.

James I disliked Nonsuch, 'a lavish place of nonsense'. He went coursing and hunting in the great deer park in his significant and sanguinary passion for the death of animals, leaping off his horse to cut the stag's throat, ripping its belly open, putting his hands and sometimes his feet inside, and splashing his companions with blood. But the palace he assigned to his Queen, blonde Anne of Denmark. Charles I spent considerable sums on repairing the palace, and gave it as a dower-house to Henrietta Maria as part of her jointure.

During the Civil War Parliament stripped Nonsuch of its furniture. When Charles was executed all the royal properties including Nonsuch were confiscated and sold one by one. The Parliamentary Commissioners made a survey of Nonsuch and its grounds in 1650, and valued the estate at £14,158 12s. This survey, which is one of the main sources for knowledge of Nonsuch, described everything with dry and faintly disapproving detail. For instance, the famous fountain in the inner court:

In the sayd inner Court . . . is placed one fayer fountayne of whyte marble supported with two brass dragons under which is a large square cesterne of lead sett within a frame of whyte marble.

Nonsuch was bought by John Lambert of Wimbledon, Major General of the Parliamentary armies, a faintly improbable dragon in his pleasant palace. He enjoyed it until Charles II's restoration (Charles sailed home from Brussels with a ship named *Nonsuch* after his Surrey hunting estate).

Nonsuch never recovered its lost glory after the Restoration. It was returned to the Queen Mother, but she never visited it. During the plague winter of 1664-65 the Exchequer money was evacuated from Westminster, put into vessels, and carried to Nonsuch. John Evelyn wrote in his diary:

I supped in Nonsuch House, whither the Office of Exchequer was transferred, and took an exact view of the plaster statues and bassrelievos inserted betwixt the timbers and puncheons of the outside walls of the court. I much admired how they had lasted so well and entire since the time of Henry VIII, exposed as they are to the air; and pity it is that they are not taken out and preserved in some dry place . . . The Palace consists of two courts, of which the first is of stone, castle-like, by the Lord Lumleys (of whom it was purchased), the other of timber, a Gothic fabric, but these walls incomparably beautified. I observed that the appearing timber puncheons entrelices, etc., were all so covered with scales of slate, that it seemed carved in the wood and painted, the slate fastened on the timber in pretty figures, that has, like a coat of armour, preserved it from rotting.

In the autumn of 1665 the indefatigably curious Samuel Pepys journeyed there to pay money into the Exchequer, and wrote:

A great walk of an elme and a walnutt set one after another in order. And all the house on the outside filled with figures of stories, and good painting of Rubens' or Holbens' doing. And one great thing is, that most of the house is covered – I mean, the posts and quarters in the walls, with lead, and gilded. I walked, also, into the ruined garden.

A month later he is complaining about the discomfort of riding to Nonsuch on Exchequer business on a wet November day: 'The ways very bad, and the weather worse, for wind and rain.' So next week instead of riding, he took 'a hackney-coach appointed with four horses . . . so we, the way being very bad, to Nonsuch'.

In 1670 Charles II gave Nonsuch to Barbara Villiers, Lady Castlemaine, his notorious, odious, Philistine, prodigal, and predatory mistress, and at the same time created her Baroness Nonsuch (later she was made Duchess of Cleveland). The new Baroness had no intention of living in a house which in her eyes seemed provincial and old-fashioned – she was no huntress, except metaphorically, and preferred to divide her fashionable, metropolitan time between Whitehall and Paris. In 1692 she leased the palace for demolition and building materials to property developers. It was pulled down, and crumbled on its own, so that by the end of the century only a ruin was left.

The fair, frail palace dissolved and disappeared, an insubstantial pageant of memory and legend for nearly 300 years. In 1959 and 1960 the site was excavated, and back from their subterranean oblivion many thousands of evocative fragments were disinterred: marble, sculpture in stone, heads of rams and cherubs in stucco, Delft pottery and Venetian glass, masonry and lead, carved slates from France with assembly instructions on them in French for the imported workmen, wine bottles, the foundations of old Cuddington church, a shell used for mixing cosmetics on which traces of rouge are still visible, strips of gilded lead which were used with *papier mâché* to decorate ceilings, a perfume bottle, pewter plates stamped with Lumley's badge of three popinjays, chamber pots, Tudor roses made of lead. The excavation had to be filled in again almost at once. Bulldozers pushed back the 6,000 tons of earth and rubble, and levelled off the site. Nothing beside remains of that colossal wreck, except for a chalk-pit from which Henry's workmen cut blocks for the foundations, and a grass-covered mound beside the avenue through Nonsuch Park – and the mirage in the old drawings of a fairy-tale palace like nothing else on earth.

# XIII

# KENSINGTON

'SLOTHFUL and sickly', wrote the Tory Evelyn. The Spanish ambassador Ronquillo reported happily to Madrid that whenever he saw him the King was gasping for breath, and coughing till the tears ran down his cheeks. His doctors pronounced that he could not last until the end of the year.

As soon as William and Mary were settled in London by the bloodless revolution of 1688, it became clear that they could not live at Whitehall, where the fog, smog, fumes, smoke, stench, and damp of the river, as well as the perpetual public press of court aggravated his chronic asthma and shyness. They moved out to the cleaner air and quieter atmosphere of Hampton Court. To a metropolitan grumbler about this anti-social isolation William growled: 'Do you wish to see me dead?' But he began to look around for a residence nearer to his capital for the transaction of business, 'but not near enough to be within that atmosphere in which he could not pass a night without risk of suffocation'.

He had a look at Holland House, but eventually settled on the house and park in Kensington of the Earl of Nottingham, his trusted Secretary of State, which he bought for 18,000 guineas. Sir Christopher Wren was commissioned to enlarge Nottingham House, and to make it fit for royalty in a hurry. The work seems to have gone too quickly: in November 1689 one of the new buildings just covered with lead, 'suddenly fell flat to the ground, killing seven or eight workmen and labourers. The Queen had been in that apartment but a little while before'.

Mary was anxious to move in. She wrote:

I could not do as I would. This made me go often to Kinsington to hasten the workmen, and I was to impatient to be at that place, imagining to find more ease there . . . [but] part of the house which was new built fell down. The same accident happened at Hampton Court.

While William was away routing his father-in-law James at the Boyne,

Mary wrote to him often and impatiently reporting progress on the new palace:

The outside of the house is fiddling work, which takes up more time than can be imagined; and while the schafolds are up, the windows must be boarded up, but as soon as that is done, your own apartment may be furnished.

And the next week:

I have been this day to Kensington, which looks really very well, at least to a poor body like me, who have been so long condemned to this place [Whitehall] and see nothing but water and wall.

Wren's conversion of Nottingham House was a workmanlike effort in a hurry, without any attempt at classical ornament or royal grandeur. Essentially what he did was to add four wings, one at each corner to the old oblong Jacobean house (built about 1605); and to reorientate the building by making the entrance, courtyard, and portico on the west side. The distinctly domestic and unostentatious character of what a contemporary described as 'the only retreat near *London*, he [William] was pleas'd with', is indicated by the fact that it was never described as a palace, always as Kensington House.

In the spring of 1690 John Evelyn wrote in his diary:

I went to Kensington, which King William has bought of Lord Nottingham, and altered, but was yet a patched building, but with the garden however it is a very sweete villa, having to it the Park and a straight new way through this Park.

This straight new way was the '*Route du Roi*', 'Rotten Row', an essential item in those days when Kensington was in the country outside London, along paths thick with mud and highwaymen, through foggy nights without lamps. This private road was 'perfectly straight and so wide that three or four coaches can drive abreast . . . and has posts put up at even distances, on the tops of which lanterns are hung and lamps placed in them, which are lighted every evening when the Court is at Kensington'.

In the next year a fire in the night burned down a new wing of the palace (part of the southern range of the courtyard). An eye-witness described William and Mary (who had first of all been frightened that it was an assassination plot) standing in the garden,

laughing heartily as the ladies of the court rushed about *en chemise* with needless alarm. The King was walking about looking at the bundles of goods which had been packed up by each person and was especially amused at a heap of Dutch cheese, bottles and bread which someone had got together as if to withstand a siege.

The fire gave an opportunity for a complete remodelling of the approach to the royal apartments, with the King's staircase rebuilt in marble, and an ornate Guard Chamber at the foot of the stairs.

In all more than £100,000 was spent in turning the house into what was in fact though not in name a palace. Wren added four new 'pavilions' or blocks at the corners of the old house, and a new main entrance, gate-tower, and large, two-storied courtyard to the west. The pay books record in meticulous detail the wages and work done at Kensington. Carpenters were paid at the rate of 3s and 2s 8d a day; ordinary labourers got 2s, 1s 8d, or 1s. Lavatory matters were faithfully recorded:

To Isaac Thompson, Engine Maker, for making a forcing Engine to force ye Water into ye Cisternes by ye King's Kitchin, & into ye Q's stoole. For making a Stoole for ye Queene, for making a Seate & covering it with Velvet, for a washer for ye Cistern and a ring in it in ye Stoole roome.

The gardens of the palace covered twenty-six acres, and between 1689 and 1696 nearly £11,000 were spent on them. Building and gardening were William's main relaxations from politics and campaigning. 'In the least Interval of Ease, Gard'ning took up a great part of his Time, in which he was not only a Delighter, but likewise a great Judge,' wrote Stephen Switzer, gardener to the aristocracy, and horticultural scribe.

Two private glimpses of William at Kensington show the warmth behind the cold, austere, rather inhuman mask of the international statesman. Both involved children, of whom William, who had none of his own, was fond. A child, Lord Buckhurst, was taken to tea in the royal apartments at Kensington. The King was late. The Queen was impatient. Young Lord Buckhurst waddled along the corridor pulling his toy cart, and banged on the sacrosanct door of William's study.

'Who is that?'

'It's Lord Buck.'

'And what does Lord Buck want with me?'

'The Queen says you're to come to tea now.'

The King emerged, sat Lord Buck in his cart, and ran to tea pulling him behind. He then collapsed in a hacking fit of coughing, from which he recovered in time to stop the small boy being punished.

On another day his sister-in-law Anne's short-lived son, the Duke of Gloucester, aged four, paraded an army of little boys at Kensington for the King's inspection. William performed magnificently. And Gloucester told him: 'My dear King, you shall have both my companies with you to Flanders.'

Two years later Gloucester appeared with a toy musket, presented arms to his uncle, and said: 'I am learning my drill that I may help you to beat the French.' The King laughed loud, and a few days later rewarded the boy who was likely to be his eventual heir with the Garter.

Mary died of smallpox at the age of thirty-two at Kensington in 1694. As soon as she heard what was in those days the terrible diagnosis, she ordered everybody who had not had smallpox out of Kensington, locked herself in her closet, burned some papers, and calmly awaited her death. The King moved into her room on a camp bed. Mary saw her impassive husband weeping, and said: 'Why are you crying? I am not very bad.' William took Bishop Burnet aside, and said: 'There is no hope. I was the happiest man on earth; and I am the most miserable. She had no fault; none: you knew her well: but you could not know, nobody but myself could know, her goodness.' Towards the end William collapsed in some sort of nervous breakdown and depression from which he did not recover for months.

After Mary's death William gave up his project for the complete rebuilding of Hampton Court, and instead made Kensington his principal residence. Evelyn visited the palace again in April 1696:

The House is very noble, tho not greate; the Gallerys furnished with all the best Pictures of all the Houses, of Titian, Raphel, Corregio, Holben, Julio Romano, Bassan, V: Dyke, Tintoret, & others, with a world of Porcelain; a pretty private Library; the Gardens about it very delicious.

William was a considerable connoisseur of painting as well as of gardening.

A more unusual visitor was Peter the Great, Tsar of Russia, on his extremely unconventional royal visit of exploration to London in 1698. Because he so detested gaping crowds, he was let into Kensington by a back door. Once inside Peter was particularly impressed with the wind-dial over the fire-place in the King's gallery, which 'by an ingenious machinery indicated the direction of the wind; and with this plate he was in raptures'. The pointer, connected with a wind-vane on the roof, showed the direction of the wind over a map of north-west Europe, and is still there today. Even though it was about as unreliable as most modern weather forecasts, the contraption was of considerable strategic import-ance to William, helping him to predict and plot the movement of fleets and the arrival of messengers from the continent. He had, after all, arrived on the throne on the wings of a helpful Protestant wind.

The next major event at Kensington was William's own death. While he was riding in Hampton Court Park, his favourite horse Sorrel stumbled on a mole-hill, and went down on his knees. The King fell off and broke his collar-bone. While optimistic Jacobites drank the health of the little gentleman in black velvet who had dug the mole-hill, William was taken to Kensington in a jolting coach to recover. There he fell asleep by an open window looking out over the park, and caught a chill which turned to pneumonia. His old Dutch friend Van Keppel, the Earl of Albemarle, hurried home from the negotiations over the Grand Alliance in Holland, and William told him: ' *Je tire vers ma fin.*' He said to the doctors: 'I know that you have done all that skill and learning could do for me: but the case is beyond your art; and I submit.' He handed the keys of his closet and his private drawers to Albemarle. No longer able to speak, he took the hand of William Bentinck, the Duke of Portland, his earliest and most jealous friend, and pressed it to his heart. And so he died. After his death a gold ring containing a lock of Mary's hair was found tied to his left arm by a black ribbon. The tactless lords in waiting ordered it to be taken off.

Queen Anne, Mary's younger sister, came to the throne, to Kensington, and to an unexpectedly glorious reign at the age of thirty-seven. She was untidy, crippled by arthritis, growing fat, with a 'red and spotty' face, and her foot often wrapped in 'nasty bandages' because of frequent attacks of gout. Her enemies gossiped that the gout was caused by alcohol, the Queen's 'cold tea', and nicknamed her 'Brandy Nan'. In fact there seems to have been no foundation for the gossip. Her intimate former friend and favourite Sarah, Duchess of Marlborough, after they had quarrelled, and after there was no longer any need to conceal the malicious truth, wrote:

I know that in some libels she hath been reproached, as one who indulged herself in drinking strong liquors, but I believe this was utterly groundless, and that she never went beyond such a quantity of strong wines as her Physician judged to be necessary for her.

She was certainly a good eater. Walter Bagehot said that (spiritually rather than physically) Queen Anne was one of the smallest people ever set in a great place. But although she was adequately stupid, stubborn, timid, and with a farcical passion for etiquette, she was also basically kind, charitable, devout, and as she boasted in her first speech to Parliament, 'I know my heart to be entirely English'. There are grounds for calling her 'Good Queen Anne'.

She made Kensington rather than St James's her main residence because like William, whom she detested cordially, she liked gardening and seclusion; and also because Kensington's country air was better for the asthma of the plump, bibulous husband she adored, Prince George of Denmark. Her uncle, Charles II, said he had tried George drunk and tried him sober, but, God's fish, there was nothing in him. He advised the Prince: 'Walk with me, hunt with my brother, and do justice to my niece, and you will never be fat.' George followed his advice almost too conscientiously, but it did not have the slightest effect on his bulging waist-line.

Anne's chief contribution to Kensington was her alteration and enlargement of the palace gardens. She had William's symmetrical Dutch box hedges, immaculate borders, and separate compartments unprooted and replaced with something wilder, greener, and more English. 'Her first Works were the Rooting up the Box (the smell of which she apparently disliked), and giving an *English* Model to the Old-made Gardens.'

Joseph Addison in the *Spectator* in 1712 called her gardeners

our heroick poets; and if, as a critic, I may single out any passage of their works to commend, I shall take notice of that part in the upper garden, at Kensington, which was at first nothing but a gravel pit. It must have been a fine Genius for gardening, that could have thought of forming such an unsightly hollow into so beautiful an Area, and to have hit the eye with so uncommon and agreeable a scene as that which it is now wrought into . . . To give this particular Spot of Ground the greater Effect, they have made a very pleasing Contrast . . . for as on one Side of the Walk you see this hollow Basin, with its several little Plantations . . . on the other Side of it there appears a seeming Mount, made up of Trees rising one higher than another in Proportion as they approach the Center.

At the same time Anne built a 'stately Green House', otherwise the Orangery, to the north of the palace, where the green-fingered Queen could potter with her precious exotic plants, and sometimes counsel take, and sometimes tea. It is the perfect specimen of Queen Anne style, and has been called 'one of the most beautiful examples of the art of the Renaissance in London, if not in England'.

Designed by Hawksmoor, modified by Vanbrugh, with its elegant centrepiece and Corinthian columns, it was easily the best bit of architecture yet built at Kensington. Anne often used the Orangery for tea and dinner parties, as a 'Summer Supper House', with music from the end rooms drifting romantically through the lemons and gum trees to the Queen, dutifully making painful small talk to a circle of brocaded robes, hoops, flycaps, fans and formal wigs.

Kensington was the stage for the tragical-comical-historical-pastoral disintegration of the beautiful friendship between the Queen and the Duchess of Marlborough. Anne had been dominated since she was six by

Kensington Palace. The formal gardens as altered for Queen Anne. In the distance are the new gardens; on the right, the deer paddock

*Photo Mansell Collection*

Kensington Palace from the east. The King's Gallery, now believed to have been designed by Wren's assistant Nicholas Hawksmoor. The statue of William III is Edwardian

*Photo The Times*

Nash's reconstruction of Buckingham Palace, with the entrance through the Marble Arch, from an engraving of about 1840

*Photo Mansell Collection*

The private face of Buckingham Palace, from the gardens

*Photo The Times*

the dazzling but dictatorial Sarah. Intimate, fussy, boring letters went from 'Mrs Morley' to 'Mrs Freeman' as often as twice a day. After Anne became Queen, the passionate, probably unconsciously Lesbian relationship cooled, mainly because of Sarah's violent and tactless lobbying on behalf of the Whigs.

By 1707 Sarah discovered that she had a rival in the Queen's affections, who 'came often to the Queen when the Prince was asleep'. This was Abigail Masham, née Hill, a poor cousin of the Duchess herself, whom she had introduced to the Queen in an unfortunate fit of charity. Abigail was no beauty. Her red nose was unkindly lampooned by the satirists of the day. Swift wrote that she was 'extremely like one Mrs Malolly, that was once my landlady in Trim'. But her great attraction was that she was a Tory, and that she did not bully the Queen. From now on the court was increasingly torn by triangular jealousy, sarcasm, and coldness. The quarrel snarled to a climax when Prince George was dying of gout and asthma at Kensington. Sarah travelled through the night to be with her royal mistress, but was received 'very coolly and like a stranger'.

After the Prince had died, Sarah knelt beside Anne and tried to console her as she 'clapt her hands together with other marks of passion'. The Duchess's cold concept of consolation was to tell the widow that

nobody in the world ever continued in a place where a dead husband lay, and I did not see where she could be but without a room or two of that dismal body; that if she were at St James's she need not see anybody that was uneasy to her, and that she might see any person that was any comfort to her as well there as anywhere else.

As she dragged the reluctant widow away from Kensington, Sarah noticed suspiciously that 'she had strength to bend down towards Mrs Masham like a sail and in passing by went some steps more than was necessary to be nearer her'.

Anne asked the Lord Treasurer to 'give directions there may be a great many yeomen of the guards to carry the Prince's dear body, that it may not be let fall, the great stairs being very steep and slippery'.

Sarah thought this funny. It was not altogether surprising that the Queen found Mrs Masham a more comfortable and sympathetic companion.

After a few more years of bickering and mutual reproaches, the final confrontation between the two life-long friends took place in one of the Queen's little rooms at Kensington. Sarah, after being kept waiting 'like a Scotch lady with a Petition waiting for an answer', attacked the Queen with arguments, reproaches, entreaties. With magnificent and infuriating stubbornness, using a phrase Sarah had once said to her in an entirely different context, Anne stonewalled by repeating over and over again: 'You said you desire no answer, and I shall give you none.' Sarah burst into tears, and said that Anne would suffer for her inhumanity. 'The Queen answer'd, that will be to myself.' The two friends never met again.

Anne died at Kensington. 'Her life would have lasted longer,' wrote a contemporary, 'if she had not eaten so much . . . She supped too much chocolate, and died monstrously fat; insomuch that the coffin wherein her remains were deposited was almost square, and was bigger than that of the Prince, her husband, who was known to be a fat, bulky man.'

In spite of Anne's crypto-Jacobite sympathies out of loyalty to her own father and family, in spite of some death-bed alarm and drama, the succession passed unexpectedly smoothly to the German but Protestant House of Hanover. In this way Anne's death-bed at Kensington was 'the last serious battle-ground of the Stuart cause'.

The new King, 'a short, round-featured, ease-loving, selfish, dull man; not ill-natured, where not thwarted, but capable of hating stubbornly', liked Kensington's green felicity, because it reminded him of his country home of Herrenhausen in Hanover. George had a healthy sense of his own importance, and decided to make Kensington worthy of himself by adding an ornate new suite of state apartments. Wren was dismissed from his post as surveyor, and replaced by William Benson, who had worked for the King in Hanover before he came to the throne. And the fashionable new artist, William Kent, rage of the smart set, was engaged to decorate the new rooms:

Kent was then the only oracle; and such was his reputation, that he was applied to by all who were emulous for distinction, by an ostentatious display of their consequence or wealth. He not only projected alterations in their mansions, and metamorphised their pleasure-grounds and gardens, but changed the fashions of their chairs and tables and gave new designs for picture and glass frames and other furniture; he new-modelled their plate, and even ladies of rank consulted his tasteful fancy for the design of their court-dresses.

Kent decorated the new 'Cube' or 'Cupola' room at Kensington, the principal state room of the palace, with giant Ionic columns, gilded statues of Roman gods and goddesses roosting on pedestals, frequent chandeliers, and marble grandeur in the slightly overpowering vulgarity of the period. The theme of the room was the grandeur that was Rome, combined, improbably, with the alleged heroic virtues of the Hanoverian dynasty. On the ceiling Kent painted the Star of the Order of the Garter. The Treasury sent a commission of artists to inspect his work when it was half finished. Their report still rings with echoes of professional sour grapes:

. . . 'tis our opinion that the Perspective is not just; that the principal of the work, which consists in ornaments and architecture, is not done as such a place requires. Mr Nesbot adds that the Boys, Masks, Mouldings, etc., far from being well, he has seen very few worse for such a place: and Mr Rambour affirms that the said work, far from being done in the best manner, as mentioned in your letter, it is not so much as tolerably well perform'd.

For painting and gilding the sides of the Cupola Room Kent was paid £344 2s 7d, but he had difficulty in getting his bill for work on the ceiling settled.

But his most flamboyant operation at Kensington was his transformation of Wren's entrance into a Grand Staircase, and his painting on the walls and ceiling groups of recognisable real people, looking down to welcome George. They included the King's two Turkish servants, Mahomet and Mustapha, who had saved George's life when he was the Electoral Prince of Hanover and was wounded at the raising of the siege of Vienna in 1685 (they had been taken into his service, as a dubious reward); some Yeomen of the Guard; a Polish page called Ulric; and Peter the Wild Boy, who had been found living rough on all fours, climbing trees like a monkey, eating grass and roots in the woods near Hanover. George brought him to England in his motley household as a curiosity. 'He could not speak . . . and much difficulty was found in making him lie on a bed . . . he resisted all instruction.'

On the ceiling over the staircase Kent painted himself looking down, and by his side 'a female of very pleasing countenance, which is supposed to be a resemblance of an actress with whom he lived in the habits of peculiar friendship, and to whom he left a part of his fortune'. The lady's name was Elizabeth Butler.

Kent also had his hand in the beginning of the landscape gardening of Kensington Gardens and Hyde Park, with its Broad Walk, and avenues, and Round Pond. The new fashion was to admire grass and nature in the comparatively raw, so the unfashionable artificial gardens to the south of the palace were replaced by lawns. Under George I the gardens first became a place for fashionable promenade and mutual inspection of hats and companions by smart society. The gardens were opened to the public only on Saturdays, when the court moved to Richmond. Thomas Tickell wrote a long poem about the new custom in 1722, in imitation of Pope's 'The Rape of the Lock';

> . . . The dames of *Britain* oft in crowds repair
> To gravel walks, and unpolluted air,
> Here, while the Town in damps and darkness lies,
> They breathe in sun-shine, and see azure skies.

George II, 'shorter than his short father, smart, strutting, decided-looking, with higher features and an underhanging jaw, was fond of being seen'. He was also fond of Kensington. The bizarre domestic details of his life there come alive in the spicily malicious memoirs of John, Lord Hervey, and Horace Walpole, who could be considered the original ancestors of newspaper gossip columnists, and to have the same preference for a good story rather than the stodgy truth.

Hervey was the repository for royal tattle. For instance, gossiping cosily in the Princess Royal's apartment at Kensington one day, he wondered why the King was so abominably cross, and supposed it must be bad political news. 'My God,' replied the Princess Royal, 'I ashamed am for you, who have been so long about Papa, to know so little of him as when he is the most peevish and snappish to think it is the most material things that have made him so. When great points go as he would not have them, he frets and is bad to himself; but when he is in his worst humours, and the devil to everybody that comes near him, it is always because one of his pages has powdered his periwig ill, or a housemaid set a chair where it does not use to stand, or something of that kind.'

Or here he is, in another turkey-cock temper, snapping off the head of Hervey, who always wrote about himself in the third person. Hervey, who was Queen Caroline's close confidant and friend, had at her request moved some very ugly pictures out of the great drawing-room at Kensington, and replaced them with some very good ones. The King, out of contrariness, or 'from his extreme ignorance in painting', ordered him to change them all back again. The faintly epicene Hervey, sticking up for the Queen, asked if at least the two Van Dycks on either side of the fireplace might stay.

George: 'My Lord, I have a great respect for your taste in what you understand, but in pictures I beg leave to follow my own. I suppose you assisted the Queen with your fine advice when she was pulling my house to pieces and spoiling all my furniture. Thank God, at least she has left the walls standing. As for the Vandykes, I do not care whether they are changed or no; but for the picture with the dirty frame over the door, and the three nasty little children, [probably Van Dyck's portrait of Charles I's children] I will have them taken away, and the old ones restored; I will have it done too tomorrow morning before I go to London, or else I know it will not be done at all.'

Hervey: 'Would your Majesty have the gigantic fat Venus restored too?'

George: 'Yes, my lord, I am not so nice as your Lordship. I like my fat Venus much better than anything you have given me instead of her.'

Lord Hervey thought, though he did not dare to say, that 'if His Majesty had liked his fat Venus as well as he used to do, there would have been none of these disputations. . . .'

While Hervey was telling the crestfallen Queen about the new picture-removals, the King came in and stayed about five minutes in the gallery, 'snubbed the Queen, who was drinking chocolate, for being always stuffing, the Princess Emily for not hearing him, the Princess Caroline for being grown fat, the Duke [of Cumberland] for standing awkwardly, Lord Hervey for not knowing what relation the Prince of Sultzbach was to the Elector Palatine, and then carried the Queen to walk, and be resnubbed, in the garden'.

This Princess Emily played a practical joke on Lady Deloraine, one of the King's mistresses, one night at Kensington, by pulling away her chair just as she was going to sit down to cards. She sprawled on the floor. The King roared with laughter. So brave Lady Deloraine entered into the party spirit by pulling away the King's chair a moment later. 'But alas, the Monarch, like Louis XIV, is mortal in the part that touched the ground.' Lady Deloraine was not invited back to court for some time.

Life was equally preposterous, and occasionally macabre for the staff. A contemporary newspaper reports:

Last Week a Centinel who was just come off of Duty at Kensington, going to the Guard-Room, dropt down as dead. Upon which Notice being sent to his Colonel, he ordered them to take Care and bury him; which was indiscreetly done within a few Hours. But their Majesties hearing of the Affair, as they were at supper, out of their singular Compassion and great Humanity, immediately ordered him to be taken up again and put into a warm Bed. He bled a little, upon having a Vein open'd, but he had lain too long to be recovered.

Queen Caroline had a passion for landscape gardening, and is mainly responsible for the creation of Kensington Gardens as they are today. The 'Basin', or Round Pond, was finished and filled. The ribbon of marshy ponds of the West Bourne was joined into the Serpentine. Long avenues of trees intersecting the park in geometrical vistas were laid out. And a new sort of ditch with a low wall was made so unobtrusive that the unwary pedestrian stumbling into it cried out 'Haha'.

The common theory was that Caroline wore the trousers. The King, who had an uneasy and correct feeling that she was more intelligent and cultured than he was, was infurated by sarcastic rhymes:

> You may strut, dapper George, but 'twill be all in vain;
> We know 'tis Queen Caroline, not you that reign –
> You govern no more than Don Philip of Spain.
> Then if you would have us fall down and adore you,
> Lock up your fat spouse as your Dad did before you!

But in spite of his long procession of fat mistresses, George never really recovered from Caroline's death. His obvious grief made him more popular than before. After he had led his army to victory at Dettingen, an excited little red-faced gentleman waving his sword on an equally excited horse and getting in the way of the generals, the people 'almost carried him into the palace on their shoulders, and at night the whole town was illuminated and bonfired'.

When news reached Kensington that Bonnie Prince Charlie had landed stout George stoutly said: 'Is it so, my lords and gentlemen? Take care of yourselves, but for me, it is my resolution to live and die King of England.'

He spent more and more time at Kensington, growing, if possible, steadily more irritable, and blinder. Everybody's face looked, he said, as if it was covered with black crêpe. On October 25, 1760, he died after an apoplectic fit at Kensington. Walpole's description is famous:

He went to bed well last night, rose at six this morning as usual, looked, I suppose, if all his money was in his purse, and called for his chocolate. A little after seven, he went into the water-closet; the German *valet de chambre* heard a noise, listened, heard something like a groan, ran in, and found the hero of Oudenarde and Dettingen on the floor, with a gash on his right temple, by falling against the corner of a bureau. He tried to speak, could not, and expired.

The state rooms at Kensington were locked up and deserted after George II's death. Assorted royal relations were billeted in Wren's red brick palace. The most exotic resident was the flighty Caroline of Brunswick, after she had separated from the Prince of Wales. After her morals, if not her discretion, had been cleared by the 'delicate investigation', she was given apartments at Kensington, and kept what she called 'knife and fork' company. 'She kept a sort of open house, receiving visitors in a dressing-gown, and sitting and talking about herself with strangers, on the benches in the garden, at the risk of being discovered.' Her dinner parties were the gayest in town. One of her ladies wrote:

Very frequently she will take one of her ladies with her to walk in Kensington Gardens . . . dressed in a costume very unsuitable to the public highway; and all of a sudden she will bolt out of one of the smaller gates and walk all over Bayswater and along the Paddington Canal, at the risk of being insulted, or if known, mobbed.

The most significant occupants of Kensington were the impoverished Duke and Duchess of Kent, who were grudgingly given apartments there by a reluctant Prince Regent. After a life-time's devotion to his Canadian mistress, Madame Julie de St Laurent, Edward, Duke of Kent, married the widowed Princess Victoria of Leiningen out of a sense of dynastic duty. It was part of the great matrimonial marathon or succession stakes with his brothers to produce a legitimate heir for the huge but singularly un-lucky family of George III. And early in the morning of May 24, 1819, Princess Victoria was born in Kensington Palace. Her proud father was quite convinced that the crown would come his way, in spite of all his older brothers. He showed off the pretty little princess, 'plump as a partridge', to his friends, and said: 'Take care of her, for she will be Queen of England.' In reply to a letter consoling him that he had got a daughter, not a son, he wrote:

As to the circumstance of that child not proving to be a son instead of a daughter, I feel it due to myself to declare that such sentiments are not in unison with my own; for I am decidedly of opinion that the decrees of Providence are at all times wisest and best.

He boasted that his Duchess gave the baby 'maternal nutriment', and that she was 'most happy that the performance of an office, most interest-ing in its nature, has met with the wishes and feeling of society'.

There was a mortifying, Almanac de Gotha scene at the baby's christening in the Cupola Room upstairs. The Prince Regent was god-father, and it was proposed to call the baby Georgiana Charlotte Augusta Alexandrina Victoria. Georgiana was for the Prince Regent, and Alexan-drina for the other godfather, Tsar Alexander I of Russia, whom George loathed. At the last minute the Prince Regent sent a note, 'that the name of Georgiana could not be used – as He did not chuse to place His name before the Emperor of Russia's, – and He could not allow it to follow'. There was an awful silence as the Archbishop of Canterbury stood holding the baby, waiting for the Prince to pronounce her names. At last he growled 'Alexandrina'. Another long pause. The Duke of Kent prompted,

'Charlotte'. The Prince shook his head violently; it was the name of his own dead daughter. 'Augusta': certainly not. The Duchess was quivering in a monsoon of tears. At last the Prince said: 'Let her be called after her mother', adding rudely that the Alexandrina must always come before the Victoria. And so the child was known as 'Drina' until she was nine.

The Duke died of a cold caught sight-seeing in Salisbury Cathedral nine months after the birth of his daughter. The Duchess of Kent, accompanied by the incompetent but sinister Svengali-figure of her husband's equerry, John Conroy, returned to Kensington Palace to bring up the little girl to be Queen. For this purpose they gradually formed what became known as 'the Kensington system', to manipulate the Princess as a political pawn. The clandestine objects of the system were: to give Victoria an education supposed to be fit for a Queen; to keep her away from the rest of the royal family, especially from the morals and politics of the other royals, so as to make her popular; to make sure that her mother was made Regent, if Victoria succeeded before she came of age; to make Conroy Victoria's private secretary when she became Queen.

The world suspected the worst about the relationship between Victoria's mother and Conroy. Greville described Conroy as 'a ridiculous fellow, a compound of "Great Hussy" and the Chamberlain of the Princess of Navarre'. To the Duke of Wellington, 'I [Charles Greville] said I concluded he was her lover. And he said he supposed so'. Most people supposed so. But Victoria herself, although her diary is full of recriminations about 'that FIEND' (heavily underlined), and 'a certain wicked person', never believed it herself, and implicitly denied it. Her complaint was about Conroy's deceit, his cruelty, and his attempt to dominate her and divide her from the rest of her family. On Conroy's death the Duchess of Kent wrote an obituary, which does not read like words for a lover: '. . . this man, who has been for MANY, MANY years with me . . . and who has been of great use to me, but unfortunately has also done great harm.'

Victoria's only ally in the neurotic atmosphere of the Kensington system was Fräulein, later Baroness, Louise Lehzen, who had her oddities (a passion for chewing caraway seeds), but was tigerishly devoted to the Princess. There is a monstrous cornucopia of loyal anecdotes about Victoria's childhood at Kensington: the little girl saying to a friend: 'You must not touch those, they are mine; and I may call you Jane, but you must not call me Victoria;' the Duchess of Kent saying: 'When you are naughty, you make me and yourself very unhappy.' Victoria: 'No Mama, not *me*, not myself, but you.' The piano master telling her: 'There is no royal road to music, Princess. You must practise like everybody else.' Victoria banged the piano lid down; 'There. You see there is no <u>must</u> about it.'

When she was eleven it was broken to her how close she was to the throne. During a history lesson Lehzen slipped an extra page into her genealogical tables of the Kings and Queens of England. Victoria studied it, saw her own name sitting there naked and alone, after the names of her two uncles George and William, and burst into tears. After the 'little storm', she raised the forefinger of her right hand and spoke the immortal words: 'I will be good.'

Victoria herself wrote that she was 'brought up very simply', and 'always slept in my mother's room till I came to the Throne'. Breakfast was at seven, lunch at half past one, dinner at seven, 'to which I came generally (when it was no regular large dinner party) – eating my bread and milk out of a small silver basin'.

Greville saw Victoria at her first formal appearance at court, and, always preferring a sour to an obsequious phrase, at least in his private diary, described her as 'a short, vulgar-looking child'. A year or two later his verdict is becoming marginally more charitable: 'If she had a better mouth and did not show her gums, and had more shade in her face, she would be pretty.'

The Duchess of Kent extended her apartments without royal permission and to the King's thunderous annoyance into the abandoned state apartments of Kensington. Princess Victoria, however, approved of the new arrangements:

Our bedroom is very large and lofty, and is very nicely furnished, then comes a little room for the maid, and a dressing-room for Mamma; then comes the old gallery which is partitioned into 3 large, lofty, fine and cheerful rooms. One only of these is ready furnished; it is my sitting-room and is <u>very</u> prettily furnished indeed . . . The next is my study, and the last is an <u>anteroom</u>.

On her eighteenth birthday King William, who was intensely irritated by the tug-of-war between Kensington and the court over his heir, the 'royal progresses', the 'continual popping' of salutes which Conroy organised for her, sent a messenger with a letter to Victoria in her newly occupied apartments at Kensington. Conroy and the Duchess both tried unsuccessfully to intercept the letter before it reached Victoria's hands. The King offered Victoria £10,000 a year of her own, entirely free from her mother's control; an independent Privy Purse; and the right to appoint her own ladies. It was a devastating blow to the Kensington system, and there was a furious scene. The Princess retired to her room, and wrote: 'Felt very miserable & agitated. Did not go down to dinner.'

By the morning Conroy had concocted a reply for her, gratefully accepting the money, but declining the offer of independence. When he read it William growled: 'Victoria has not written that letter', and 'The real point is the Duchess and King John want money'.

A month later William died, and at crack of dawn the Archbishop of Canterbury, the Lord Chamberlain, and the King's doctor galloped a carriage from the royal death-bed at Windsor to Kensington with the news. With some anti-climax they could not get in. The Duchess refused to wake Victoria until they demanded to see 'the Queen'. Then her mother 'awoke the dear Child with a kiss'. Victoria came down in her dressing-gown and slippers, and as soon as she heard the words 'Your Majesty', shot out her hand to be kissed, and to grab her freedom. At eleven a.m. the young Queen held her first crowded Privy Council, 'quite alone', as she keeps on repeating with satisfaction in her journal. Even Greville was impressed:

She . . . read her speech in a clear, distinct, and audible voice, and without any appearance of fear or embarrassment . . . She seemed rather bewildered at the multitude of men who were sworn, and who came one after another to kiss her hand, but she did not speak to anybody, nor did she make the slightest difference in her manner, or show any in her countenance, to any individual of any rank, station, or party.

It was approved that she got out of her chair, and approached her old uncle, the Earl of Sussex, rather than let him come to her.

During her formidably efficient first day as Queen, Victoria dismissed Conroy from her Household, appointed Baroness Lehzen to the vague title of Lady Attendant on the Queen, and had her bed moved out of her mother's room. She saw her Prime Minister, Lord Melbourne, twice, 'of COURSE quite ALONE as I shall always do all my Ministers'.

In her diary she wrote: 'I am very young and perhaps in many, though not in all things, inexperienced, but I am sure, that very few have more real good will and more real desire to do what is fit and right than I have.'

On July 13 Victoria finally broke the umbilical cord with Kensington and the past:

Got up at 8. At ½ p. 9 we breakfasted. It was the last time that I slept in this poor old Palace, as I go into Buckingham Palace today. Though I rejoice to go into B.P. for many reasons, it is not without feelings of regret that I shall bid adieu <u>for ever</u> (that is to say <u>for ever</u> as a DWELLING), to this my birth-place, where I have been born and bred, and to which I am really attached. . . . I have gone through painful and disagreeable scenes here, 'tis true, but still I am fond of the poor old Palace . . . the poor rooms looks so sad and deserted, everything being taken away . . .

Kensington was restored, and the state rooms opened to the public on the Queen's eightieth birthday in 1899. It remains a royal palace, with all except the public state rooms still being used as apartments for members of the royal family.

# XIV

# BUCKINGHAM PALACE

THE ugliest royal residence in Europe? 'A monstrous insult upon the nation'? These and sundry other harsh criticisms of an undistinguished but inoffensive pile of masonry may seem hyperbolic and hysterical to the swarms of tourists who turn out to watch them changing guard at Buckingham Palace today. But ever since it became a royal palace, the unhappy building has been savagely denounced for its expense, ugliness, erratic architecture, and lack of style. Another grumbler wrote that the only hope for the place would be 'if Aladdin, with his magic lamp, would come and transport it into an African desert'. Queen Victoria complained that its exterior was 'a disgrace', heavily underlined, 'to the country'. And Edward VII, who associated it with sixty years of frustrated waiting as heir apparent, always called it 'The Sepulchre'. In fact the architectural growth of Buckingham Palace was so disjointed that it never had a chance from the start.

The site of the palace first impinged on history as the scene of a disastrous experiment sponsored by James I to produce raw silk in Britain, by breeding patriotic British silk-worms. The land where Buckingham Palace now stands was planted with 30,000 mulberry trees to feed the little creatures. Either in ignorance, or in a daring entomological innovation, black mulberries were planted, instead of the white mulberries which are the normal menu of silk-worms. The silk-worms were not amused. The experiment was not a success. And the Mulberry Garden eventually became a popular and disreputable pleasure garden and night-club, where cruising gallants boarded loitering masked beauties with hearty cries of 'S'Death' and 'Egad'. In 1654 Evelyn was treated at the Mulberry Garden, 'now the only place of refreshment about the town for persons of the best quality to be exceedingly cheated at'; and observed disapprovingly 'how women began to paint themselves, formerly a most ignominious thing, and used only by prostitutes'.

Pepys was equally unimpressed at his first visit a few years later: 'a very silly place, worse than Spring-Gardens, and but little company, and those of a rascally, whoring, roguing sort of people, only a wilderness, that is somewhat pretty, but rude. Did not stay to drink.' However John Dryden, before he became famous, was a regular cormorant of mulberry tarts in the garden, with his favourite actress, Mrs Reeve.

Meanwhile beside the Mulberry Garden a series of mansions were built, one on the foundations of another as they were burnt down, by a rapid succession of political magnates. First it was Goring House, built by George Goring, the devoted royalist, who is remembered for his enthusiastic phrase in the Civil War: 'Had I millions of crowns or scores of sons, the King and his cause should have them all.' Then it was bought and extravagantly rebuilt as Arlington House by Henry Bennet, Earl of Arlington, the pompous Restoration politician with a strip of black plaster always over the scar on his nose, a member of the Cabal.

It soon went up in flames again, and was bought by John Sheffield, Duke of Buckingham and Normanby, nothing to do with the Villiers father and son, but the politician and minor poet who remained loyal to James II after 1689. He was an old flame and writer of love songs to Princess, later Queen, Anne, when she was seventeen. Indeed, 'some believe his proceedings so far as to spoil her marrying anybody else, and therefore the town have given him the nickname of King John'. When Anne came to the throne, she gave him his title, and a slice of St James's Park to enlarge his estate. The house he built there was generally agreed to be the finest private palace near London. The proud owner describes its delights in minute detail in a long letter. The walls of the great staircase were painted with the story of Dido, 'who though the Poet was obliged to dispatch away mournfully in order to make room for Lavinia, the better-natured Painter has brought no further than to that fatal cave, where the lovers appear just entering, and languishing with desire'.

He was also particularly pleased with his library in a greenhouse, where the books were arranged by a system, so 'that by its mark a very Irish footman may fetch any book I want'. Under the windows of the library was 'a little wilderness full of black birds and nightingales'.

Buckingham's third wife was the illegitimate daughter of James II by Catherine Sedley, that incredibly unattractive mistress who, according to Charles II, was inflicted on his brother as a penance for lechery by his priests. When Buckingham died, his last Duchess lived on in his house and a state of considerable eccentricity for twenty-one years. She was an odd woman, and a crashing snob about her bastard royal blood. Contemporaries called her 'Princess Buckingham'. She commemorated the anniversaries of the execution of her grandfather Charles I, and the decampment and deposition of her father James II, by putting her court of ladies into blackest mourning. Buckingham House became the centre of a notorious network of lurid and inept Jacobite intrigue. On her death-bed the Duchess made her attendants swear not to sit down in her royal presence until they were absolutely sure she was dead.

As early as 1723 the Prince of Wales (the 'Little Captain', later George II) made tentative inquiries about buying Buckingham House. The Duchess replied enthusiastically that 'all His Majesty's revenue cannot purchase a place so fit for them, nor for less a sum,' and asked £60,000. Her price seemed optimistic, and the negotiations were abruptly dropped.

When the Duchess died, an illegitimate son of her Duke inherited the place. In the second year of his reign George III bought Buckingham House from him for £21,000 as a domestic retreat from the ceremonial pomp of St James's for his shy new bride with the huge mouth, who was never able to express herself grammatically in English, Charlotte. It was renamed 'the Queen's House' in 1775. Here the King and Queen retired into what was almost a rural retreat in those days, surrounded by meadows full of cud-chewing cows, to produce their fifteen children with remorseless regularity, and at the shortest conceivable intervals; and to lead their life of virtuous monotony which so disgusted fashionable society, and so gratified the rising middle classes.

A critic complained that in their court there were 'constant avocations without any employment, and a great deal of idleness without any leisure; many words pronounced, and nothing said; many people smiling, and nobody pleased; many disappointments and little success; little grandeur and less happiness'. Etiquette in the Queen's House was Germanic and stiff. Nobody was allowed to pass a room in which one of the royal family was present unless the door was shut. Knocking on the Queen's door was forbidden: the handle had to be rattled instead. The gentlemen were dressed in the Windsor livery of blue with scarlet and gold facings, specially designed by sartorially-sensitive George, who had an expert passion for uniforms. And here Charlotte introduced from Germany the Christmas tree, for the first time in England. At the surprise house-warming cum King's birthday party on June 6, 1762 the grounds were illuminated with 4,000 coloured lamps, and a huge, unprophetic picture showing

George giving peace to all parts of the earth. For this party a new court dress of stiff-bodiced gowns and bare shoulders was introduced. 'The old ladies will catch their deaths,' wrote acid Horace Walpole; 'What dreadful discoveries will be made, both of fat and lean! I recommend to you the idea of Mrs Cavendish when half-stark.'

Various alterations were made to the house. The leaden classical figures were removed from the parapet, because in a high wind they were likely to be as lethal as the tortoise that killed Aeschylus. New wings were added. And at once the first of a long chorus of critics gave tongue:

Originally this building had an air of elegant uniformity, but though the front view is not yet damaged, so many irregular additions have been made on each side, as to inspire the spectator with the idea of a country parsonage house, to which every incumbent has added something, one a wash-house, another a stable, another a hen-roost, etc., till the whole is made a mere jumble of patchwork.

The most important addition was George's superb library, which he built up steadily during his long reign, and which after his death was presented to the British Museum. The King's omnivorous passion for collecting books and manuscripts conflicts with his celebrated views on Shakespeare, and the fact that he never acquired the habit of reading. What he actually said to Fanny Burney was:

Was there ever such stuff as great part of Shakespeare? Only one must not say so! But what think you? What? Is there not sad stuff? What? – What? . . . Oh, I know it is not to be said! But it's true. Only it's Shakespeare and nobody dare abuse him.

Dr Johnson was a frequent visitor to browse through the books of the library at the Queen's House. In February 1767 the King had a long private conversation with him there. Johnson loved repeating the commonplace details of this meeting at length and *ad nauseam* to his friends: a habit which is as revealing of an Achilles' heel in the great, garrulous pundit's armour as his insistence on using his honorary title of Doctor of Laws. The librarian brought the King quietly up behind Dr Johnson, who was still in a profound study. They talked at length and learnedly about books, from Lord Lyttelton's new history to the *Philosophical Transactions*. The King asked if Johnson himself was writing anything. Johnson replied that he thought he had already done enough as a writer. George III: 'I should have thought so too, if you had not written so well.'

In later years, describing the dialogue, Johnson said: 'No man could have paid a handsomer compliment; and it was fit for a King to pay. It was decisive.' Did he reply to the King, his breathless audience asked.

'No, Sir,' said Dr Johnson. 'When the King had said it, it was to be so. It was not for me to bandy civilities with my Sovereign.'

Later the King suggested that Johnson should write the literary biography of England. Johnson agreed, and eventually wrote his *Lives of the Poets*. Throughout the interview 'Johnson talked to his Majesty with profound respect, but still in his firm manly manner, with a sonorous voice, and never in that subdued tone which is commonly used at the levée and in the drawing room'. Afterwards a gratified Dr Johnson, always at heart a supporter of the Stuarts, said to the librarian: 'Sir, they may talk of the King as they will; but he is the finest gentleman I have ever seen.'

In the Queen's House George put into practice his Spartan and disastrous theories of education upon his children.

He was most anxious to train up his children in the way they should go, but severity was the fashion of the day, and though naturally a tender and affectionate father, he placed his sons under tutors who imagined that the rod of Scripture could mean only bodily punishment. Princess Sophia told me once that she had seen her two eldest brothers, when they were boys of thirteen and fourteen, held by their arms to be flogged like dogs, with a long whip.

'Ignorant, narrow-minded and arbitrary, with an unbounded confidence in his own judgement', the King used to watch these floggings with a virtuous, this-hurts-me-more-than-it-hurts-you satisfaction. The end products were not exactly an advertisement for his system.

Business, electioneering, and George's obstinate attempts to run his own court party of political hacks called the 'King's friends' gradually intruded into the domestic seclusion of the Queen's House. His archaic and catastrophic ideas about the royal prerogative had been drummed into him as a boy by his mother repeatedly urging him to 'be a King'. The Privy Council began to meet regularly in the Queen's House. When the mob yelling for Wilkes and Liberty stampeded through London, breaking windows, the flushed and angry King hoped they would attack Buckingham House, so that he could charge the rioters in person, 'at the head of his Guards'. He sat up all night, 'full of indignation at the insult'.

In 1780 the lunatic Lord George Gordon led the London mob on a burning rampage against Roman Catholics and cheap Irish labour. As the demonstrators surged menacingly towards Westminster, 3,000 troops were called up to guard the Queen's House, and were billeted on the bare ground. It is reported that George walked through the ranks, saying:

My lads, my crown cannot purchase you straw tonight, but depend on it I have given orders that a sufficiency shall be here tomorrow forenoon; as a substitute for the straw my servants will instantly serve you with a good allowance of wine and spirits to make your situation as comfortable as possible; and I shall keep you company myself till morning.

Or words to that effect.

The last years of the reign of George, by now totally blind and totally mad, were spent in the green solitudes of Windsor, where he wandered in a strange ghost world of hallucination.

When the Prince Regent, that obese, elegant *enfant terrible* of fifty-seven, with a grotesque passion for other men's grandmothers, succeeded his father, he decided to turn Buckingham House into a palace worthy of London, and the British monarchy, and himself. Unfortunately he had already spent so many hundreds of thousands of tax-payers' pounds on his spectacular building operations and interior decorations at Carlton House, Brighton Pavilion, and Windsor that Parliament was extremely wary about voting any more. He managed to get the Commons to grant him an estimate of £200,000, not to be exceeded, for what was disarmingly described as 'a repair and improvement of Buckingham House'. In fact the 'repair' was a disingenuous subterfuge for a radical rebuilding from the foundations, but within the shell of the old house, by John Nash, the Welsh architect and particular protégé of George's. In no time at all the estimate was exceeded. More than three times as much had been spent when George IV died in 1830, and the King's House in Pimlico, as it was called for a while, was still not finished. Nash kept on submitting supplementary and unforeseen estimates for 'repairs' as drastic as 'pulling down the wings forming the quadrangle, rebuilding them further apart, and forming a colonnade on each side'.

Indignant grumblings rumbled from Parliament:

At a time when bread can scarcely be found for a large portion of our population it is unjustified to lavish such sums upon such purposes. The Chancellor of the Exchequer when he sees thousands ruined by the pressure of taxation in order to complete this place in a style of unnecessary splendour, it should induce him to pause. . . . The Crown of England does not require such splendour. Foreign countries might indulge in frippery, but England ought to pride herself on her plainness and simplicity.

A Member regretted, several years too late, that George IV's taste in architecture was not 'that simple, chaste and solid English kind'. A select committee was set up to inquire into the affair. George wrote to the Duke of Wellington: 'Mr Nash has been infamously used. If those who go through the furnace for me and for my service are not protected the favour of the Sovereign becomes worse than nugatory.'

Not only the extravagance, but also the style of the building was savagely criticised. People were particularly scathing about the dome on the roof. Lampoons rhymed vigorously about:

> . . . the beautiful Ball in the Cup,
> Which the tasteful Committee in wisdom set up
> On top of the Palace that N——H built.

Nash's palace consisted of a main, western block, with two wings running down towards St James's Park. It has all been blocked from public view by the slabby eastern façade which was built for Queen Victoria, and which turned Buckingham Palace into a hollow square. The main entrance to Nash's palace was from the east, through the Marble Arch, a multi-sculptured memorial to the victories of Trafalgar and Waterloo, which cost £34,350, and was modelled on the arches of the more ostentatious Roman emperors. It was originally planned that an heroic bronze equestrian statue of George would ride on top of the arch. But George died before it was finished, and his statue, riding bare-back in his socks, ended up in Trafalgar Square. The Marble Arch was lugged to its present site as a traffic roundabout and the symbol of an underground railway station when the east front of the palace was begun in 1851.

When George died there was talk of selling the unfinished white elephant, which was sometimes called Pimlico Palace, and sometimes New Palace. Eventually it was finished by a new architect, Edward Blore, whose idiom was as different from Nash's as chalk from Gorgonzola. The repairs had cost £719,000. A German tourist in the summer of 1835 thought it was wasted money:

I never saw anything that might be pronounced a more total failure in every respect. It is said, indeed, that, spite of the immense sums which have been expended, the king is so ill-satisfied with the result, that he has no mind to take up his residence in it when the unhappy edifice shall be finished. This reluctance appears to me very natural. For my own part, I would not live in it rent free.

The disgusted visitor writes of the pillars in the state apartments:

. . . partly red, like raw sausages; partly blue, like starch – bad imitations of marbles which nobody ever saw, standing upon blocks which art rejects, to support nobody knows what.

William IV seems to have been almost as unenthusiastic. When Westminster Palace was burned down, he offered Buckingham Palace as a new permanent home for Parliament. The generous offer was hastily refused. William next suggested that the Palace might be converted into a barracks for the Guards. Finally he decided to move in himself, forthwith, but the interminable contractors procrastinated, and put him off because the gas lighting still had to be installed. While the Palace was in its final stages of furnishing, catty Thomas Creevey the diarist was shown over it:

It has cost a million of money, and there is not a fault that has not been committed in it . . . Instead of being called Buckingham Palace it should be the Brunswick Hotel. The costly ornaments of the State Rooms exceed all belief in their bad taste . . . Raspberry coloured pillars without end, that quite turn you sick to look at; but the Queen's papers for her own apartments far exceed everything else in their ugliness and vulgarity.

Within three weeks of her accession, the eighteen-year-old Queen Victoria escaped from her domineering mother by moving, in the State Coach, from Kensington into Buckingham Palace. The Duchess of Kent was given a suite as far away as possible from her daughter, and immediately complained that there was not enough room for her belongings. Victoria however was delighted with her new home. The rooms were 'high, pleasant and cheerful', and her spaniel, 'dear *Dashy*', liked the gardens. A lady around court wrote:

The little Queen has already shown that she has character and a will of her own. She insisted on getting into the new palace which she is to inhabit, and leaving Kensington last week – In vain they urged the furniture was incomplete and the carpets not down – There was furniture enough for her, and she did not care for carpets. She made good her point and that very evening gave a dinner to her People in Waiting, and some of her Ministers, and sang and played with the Duchess of Kent afterwards.

Spending her own money for the first time, Victoria chose all her new furniture for herself from new green silk draperies for her four-poster, to a new throne (the upholsterer was told that it must not cost more than £1,000).

A number of immediate alterations had to be made to the Palace. A door was banged in the Queen's bedroom wall to give access to Baroness Lehzen, 'dearest Daisy', the inseparable attendant whom Victoria called her 'Mother'. The plumbing was unmentionable. Only a handful of the fifty brand new lavatories worked, and one of them discharged its contents on to the leads in front of the Queen's dressing-room window. A main sewer ran under the Palace, and occasionally seeped up into the kitchens. A hot water pipe was installed, 'for the supply of Her Majesty's moveable bath and for the bedrooms'. During these essential alterations, the opportunity was taken to remove the central dome of contention from the roof of the Palace.

The spiteful scandal over wretched and grossly maligned Lady Flora Hastings, linked with the furious fuss Victoria made when Sir Robert Peel tried to persuade her to have a few Tory Ladies of the Bedchamber, disturbed the early years at Buckingham Palace, and made the young Queen unpopular.

Life at Buckingham Palace does not seem to have been particularly gay or brilliant. Charles Greville gives a devastating account of a dreadful dinner party there in January 1838, where the men huddled round the door in the drawing room 'in the sort of half-shy, half-awkward way people do', until Victoria came up to talk to each in turn. His 'deeply interesting' dialogue with the Queen ran as follows:

Queen: 'Have you been riding today, Mr Greville?'
Greville: 'No, Madam, I have not.'
Queen: 'It was a fine day.'
Greville: 'Yes, ma'am, a very fine day.'
Queen: 'It was rather cold though.'
Greville: 'It was rather cold, madam.'
Queen: 'Your sister, Lady Frances Egerton, rides I think, does not she?'
Greville: 'She does ride sometimes, madam.' (A pause when I took the lead though adhering to the same topic.)
Greville: 'Has your Majesty been riding today?'
Queen (with animation): 'O yes, a very long ride.'
Greville: 'Has your Majesty got a nice horse?'
Queen: 'O, a very nice horse.'

In November 1839 Victoria made her Declaration of Marriage, elegantly composed for her by Lord Melbourne, to a distinguished dodder of eighty-two Privy Councillors packed into the Bow Room at Buckingham Palace. Before she went in she was asked if she was nervous. Victoria: 'Yes, but I did a much more nervous thing a little while ago.'

'What was that?'

'I proposed to Prince Albert.'

In her Journal Victoria wrote that her Coburg cousin was beautiful, underlined, 'such beautiful blue eyes, an exquisite nose, & a pretty mouth with delicate moustachios & slight but very slight whiskers: a beautiful figure, broad in the shoulders & fine waist'. For her declaration she wore a plain morning gown, and Albert's portrait in a bracelet on her arm. The sharp-eyed Clerk of the Privy Council (Greville) noted: 'She read the declaration in a clear, sonorous, sweet-toned voice, but her hands trembled so excessively that I wonder she was able to read the paper which she held.'

Victoria wrote to Albert that it was 'rather an awful moment', but that she felt so happy to do it. She was still shivering with nerves the next day.

After their brisk honeymoon ('. . . strange that a bridal night should be so short; and I told Lady Palmerston that this was not the way to provide us with a Prince of Wales,' wrote Greville maliciously), the newly-marrieds brought gaiety at last to Buckingham Palace. There were waltzes and gallops and quadrilles around the ballroom glittering with its new damask, and mirrors, and gilding. Albert was 'a splendid dancer'. They played duets on two pianos. They held grand concerts at Buckingham Palace. A typical programme featured: 'Duo . . . "Non funestar crudele" . . . Her Majesty and Prince Albert.'

A series of exotic, charity fancy-dress balls was held in the Palace. At the Plantagenet Ball Albert went as Edward III, and Victoria as Queen Philippa, wearing a startling stomacher decorated with more than £60,000 worth of jewels. But it was not all glitter and glamour and bliss. There was frequent unpleasantness about Albert's allowance, Albert's Household, above all Albert's precedence. The royal Dukes, Victoria's uncles, the *old* royal family, supported by the Tories ('infernal scoundrels', scribbled Victoria) were not anxious to give precedence to 'a paper Royal Highness'.

The childish but feral dispute came to a ludicrous head in 1843, with a royal scrum at the wedding in Buckingham Palace of Princess Augusta of Cambridge to the Grand Duke of Mecklenburg-Strelitz. Victoria's wicked uncle Ernest, now King of Hanover, was grimly determined to sign the register before Albert in order to demonstrate his superior status. He pushed Albert off the altar steps, and barged into his place. As Victoria signed the register, the King hovered triumphantly beside her, waiting to pounce on the pen before Albert. Quick as a flash, Victoria dodged round the table to where Albert was standing, scrawled her signature, and handed the pen on to Albert, who signed next.

Albert described the curious scene in a letter to his brother:

It almost came to a fight with the King. He insisted on having the place at the altar, where we stood. He wanted to drive me away, and, against all custom, he wanted to accompany Victoria and lead her. I was to go behind him. I was forced to give him a strong punch and drive him down a few steps, where the First Master of Ceremonies took him and led him out of the Chapel. We had a second scene, where he would not allow me to sign the register with Victoria. He laid his fist on the book. We manoeuvred round the table and Victoria had the book handed to her across the table. Now the table was between us and he could see what was being done. After a third trial to force Victoria to do what he commanded, but in vain, he left the party in great wrath. Since then, we let him go, and happily, he fell over some stones in Kew and damaged some ribs.

As Greville said, with more truth than poetry: 'The Royal Family . . . always fancy any trumpery matter relating to their rank and dignity of greater importance than the gravest affairs.'

Children were arriving thick and fast, and the Palace was becoming crowded. In 1845 the Queen wrote to Sir Robert Peel, reminding him of 'the urgent necessity of doing something to Buckingham Palace . . . and the total want of accommodation for our little family, which is fast growing up'. The Prime Minister replied that it would be tactful to wait for a little, until they could observe the public reaction to the decision to reimpose income tax. In the next year Parliament voted money for alterations to the Palace; a stipulation was made that the Pavilion at Brighton should be sold to help defray the cost. Victoria noted that only one 'very ill-conditioned man' had spoken against the extravagance of the proposal. But a *Punch* cartoon showed the Queen and Prince Consort with their family begging for money outside the Palace. And the east front of the palace, filling in the fourth side of the rectangle, was built with much controversy of architects and Caen stone, which started to crumble almost immediately. The Marble Arch was removed to the site of the old Tyburn gallows to make room for the gloomy new wing. And some of the beautiful chimney pieces from Brighton Pavilion were put into Bucking-ham Palace, in spite of temperamental cries from the architect that they were'utterly worthless' – he was predictably feline about anything built by Nash.

Meanwhile Albert, to compensate for his rigid exclusion from all affairs of state, for which Victoria was subconsciously partly to blame, was busy in his zealous German way reorganising the chaotic internal administration of the Palace. Decades of inefficiency, of domestic pickings and perquisites, were swept away by his necessary but tactless new broom. One servant had the bonus of collecting every day the hundreds of tallow candles, which were never lit, but which had been supplied religiously since George III used them to cure a cold. The most notorious example of the anarchy, overstaffing, and waste was the business of the shivering cold in the Palace. It was a function of the Lord Steward's department to lay the fires, and of the Lord Chamberlain's to light them. The underlings of the two noblemen were never co-ordinated, so fires were seldom, if ever, lit. In the same way the Department of Woods and

Forests cleaned the outside, and the Lord Chamberlain's men the inside of the Palace windows; with the obvious result that both sides were never clean at once. Albert introduced a single central authority, a resident Master of the Household. He also reduced the wages of forty of the housemaids from £45 a year to £12 rising infinitesimally to £18.

The big new balcony looking out over the Mall from the east wing of the palace began to be used on great occasions as a platform for mutual inspection by the royals and the people. Victoria and her family first stood on the balcony to see the Guards marching off to the glittering lunacy of the Crimea. 'A fine morning,' she wrote in her journal, 'the sun shining over the tower of Westminster Abbey and an immense crowd. It was a touching and beautiful sight; many sorrowing friends were there and one saw the shake of many a hand.'

After Albert died in 1861, Buckingham Palace went into a dust-sheeted decline, while Victoria, indulging in her agony of bereavement, turned herself into the Widow of Windsor. The Palace was shut and shrouded in sheets. Albert's rooms were left untouched, and on the rare occasions that Victoria came to the Palace, his evening clothes were laid out every night.

But Buckingham Palace still had its occasional gaudy moments. The Queen had an interview with Charles Dickens there two months before his death. Dickens asked permission to present Victoria with bound copies of his books. The Queen picked up a copy of her *Leaves from the Journal of my Life in the Highlands*, which by an extraordinary coincidence happened to be sitting beside her, autographed it 'To Charles Dickens', and said she was ashamed as one of the humblest of writers to offer it to one of the greatest. During their conversation Dickens told her that in his opinion the division between the classes in Britain would gradually cease. 'And I earnestly pray it may,' the Queen wrote, surprisingly, in her journal.

In 1873 the Palace was loaned to the Shah of Persia for his unconventional state visit. To the Queen's relief he discreetly left three of his wives behind him on the continent, but there were a number of other glamorous ladies in his party, whose functions were unspecified, but distinctly dubious. The Shah agreed to sleep in a bed at the Palace, but insisted on eating on the floor. Holes were burned in the carpets by his cooking tripods, and whole roast lambs were devoured under the table. There were alarming reports about the Shah's lurid night life, and his offhand reluctance to use the Palace lavatories; and even more alarming ones about a member of his staff being executed with a bowstring and buried in the Palace grounds. Victoria was not amused to hear that he had arranged to watch a boxing match in her Palace garden.

The last major structural alterations to Buckingham Palace were made in 1913, when the shabby east front was refaced with 5,757 tons of Portland stone, and had a therapeutic face-lift of its pediments and cornice. The aim was to provide a plain backcloth for the exuberance of the Victoria Memorial.

In this century sovereigns have increasingly been allowed and expected to lead private lives. The ritual display element of monarchy has atrophied to a few state pomps. But it is an odd full circle of history that the house which started life as a private retreat for George III and Queen Charlotte to escape from court ceremonial, has now become the official state palace for most of the surviving court ceremonials. Presumably and probably the wandering British monarchy has finally come to rest, and Buckingham Palace will be the final royal residence in London, eventually, when the fabric is worn out, being replaced on the same site by the first royal skyscraper. In November of 1969 the Duke of Edinburgh, answering questions on American television, raised the possibility of the royal family leaving Buckingham Palace: 'We go into the red, I think, next year. . . . We may have to move into smaller premises, who knows?' This was generally taken at the time as a classic example of the Duke's bluff, bantering, sea-dog act, in extempore reply to inquisition. If in fact it turns out to have been seriously prophetic, there are long precedents for the royal family moving hopefully out of their official London residence into something smaller and more private.

# XV

# BRIGHTON PAVILION

I look through all his life and recognise but a bow and a grin. I try to take him to pieces, and find silk stockings, padding, stays, a coat with frogs and a fur collar, a star and blue ribbon, a pocket handkerchief prodigiously scented, one of Truefitt's best nutty-brown wigs reeking with oil, a set of teeth and a huge black stock, under-waistcoats, more under-waistcoats, and then – nothing.

THACKERAY'S verdict on George IV is famous, unkind, and – superficial. He did not look hard enough.

Not that it was by any means the most beastly thing that was written about poor George in an age which was red in tooth and claw with vicious lampoons and cartoons that make modern satirists look positively vegetarian.

> By his bulk and by his size,
> By his oily qualities,
> This (or else my eyesight fails),
> This should be the Prince of Whales,

mildly contributed Charles Lamb to the avalanche of insult.

The radical journalist Leigh Hunt wrote in his paper, the *Examiner*:

. . . This delightful, blissful, wise, pleasurable, honourable, virtuous, true and immortal Prince was a violator of his word, a libertine over head and ears in debt and disgrace, a despiser of domestic ties, the companion of gamblers and demireps, a man who has just closed half a century without one single claim on the gratitude of his country or the respect of posterity.

For these fighting words he was promptly sent to prison for two years and fined £1,000.

The Duke of Wellington who actually knew Prinny well was more charitable in his analysis, and more profound: 'The most extraordinary compound of talent, wit, buffoonery, obstinacy and good feeling– in short a medley of the most opposite qualities, with a great preponderance of good – that I ever saw in any character in my life.'

The truth about George, as far as it is possible to pin down the truth about anybody, is that inside the gross, spoilt, obese, lachrymose, unpopular, selfish, ridiculous figure, swilling down 'diabolino' and cherry brandy, with his huge buttocks wrapped in tight white inexpressibles, there was a slim, elegant, popular, intellectual, amiable prince in dashing Hussar's uniform struggling to get out. He was the most cultured and witty British King since Charles II, who he himself said was the only one of his predecessors who could be lived with as a gentleman. Genuinely musical, with exquisite taste in pictures and furniture, quoter of Homer in Greek, brilliant mimic, one of the earliest admirers and encouragers of Jane Austen and Walter Scott, pathetic fan of Byron, who retaliated with an excruciatingly rude poem about him ('the sublime of hatred,' said Goethe), George was a more complex, more tragic, more likeable man than the grotesque monster invented by the opposition caricaturists. B. R. Haydon, the painter, called him: 'As thoroughbred an Englishman as ever existed in the country. He admired her sports, gloried in her prejudices, had confidence in her bottom and spirit.'

'National scandal, a national disaster, a national achievement, and national entertainment', one of his several claims on the gratitude of his country and the respect of posterity is his creation of Brighton and of his Royal Pavilion there, that stately pleasure-dome which is the perfect architectural counterpart of the most romantic of poems.

In the middle of the eighteenth century Brighthelmstone, as it was then called, a desolate, decayed fishing village, suddenly started to grow, because of the new discovery of the therapeutic qualities of sea-water. This was taken not only externally by boldly bathing in the sea, but internally as well, heated or with milk. The doctors of the day said that the sea-water around Brighton was particularly beneficial because it was so far from a river mouth, and therefore contained more salubrious salt than at any other watering-place in Britain. Brighton became fashionable. The smart set

> Rush'd coastward to be cur'd like tongues
> By dipping into brine.

In September 1783 the Prince of Wales, just twenty-one, came down to Brighton for the first time to stay with his disreputable uncle, the Duke of Cumberland, and to get away from his father's strict Spartan, or rather German, ideas about discipline for children. He was also advised that sea water might help the swellings in the glands of his neck, to conceal which he wore those ludicrously high collars and stocks, which immediately, inevitably, became fashionable even for young men with unswollen necks.

Young George enjoyed Brighton, the Dress Balls, the sea breezes, and the freedom so much that in the next year he took a house for the summer in the name of his German cook, Weltje. This 'respectable farmhouse' was on the town's main promenade, a broad stretch of grass called the Steine, where visitors walked up and down inspecting each other and the fishermen spreading their nets to dry, and listening to the band. A London newspaper wrote:

The visit of a certain gay and illustrious character at Brighton has frightened away a number of old maids, who used constantly to frequent that place. The story of the gallantries of last season, which is in constant circulation, has something in it so voluminous, and tremendous to boot, that the old tabbies shake in their shoes whenever His R——L H——ss in mentioned.

The attractions of Brighton were not just medicinal. Robert Huish, one of the Prince's more lurid biographers, wrote that George was drawn to Brighton this season 'by the angelic figure of a sea-nymph whom he one day encountered reclining on one of the groins on the beach', and with whom he seems to have had a brief affair.

In the next year, after hysterical flights overseas, passionate pursuits, and melodramatic suicide gestures, the Prince bullied Mrs Maria Fitzherbert, a beautiful, young, golden-haired Roman Catholic widow into a secret marriage with him. Their marriage was valid in the eyes of the Pope, who later privately confirmed it in a Papal Brief. But it was illegal and void in the eyes of the law because of George III's despotic Royal Marriage Act; and, more serious, because of a clause in the Act of Settlement of 1689 which excludes from the throne anybody who 'shall marry a Papist . . . as though he were naturally dead', the marriage could have cost George his crown. The Prince himself in his better moments never doubted that he was really married to Mrs Fitzherbert. Years later in a will he wrote when he thought he was dying, he left all his property 'to my Maria Fitzherbert, my Wife, the Wife of my heart and soul. Although by the laws of this country she could not avail herself publicly of that name, still such she is in the eyes of Heaven, was, is, and ever will be such in mine'.

When he married the Prince was as usual overwhelmed with debts. He owed at least a quarter of a million, and had no prospect, apart from his father's death, of paying. So he sold his stud of racehorses, stopped the rebuilding of his London residence, Carlton House, and set off for Brighton with Mrs Fitzherbert and a hired coachload of good resolutions to turn

over a new leaf and live within his income. To keep up appearances Mrs
Fitzherbert stayed in a house of her own, and the Prince in a rented house
looking out over the Steine to the sea. Around this house his current
architect, Henry Holland, built him the 'Marine Pavilion' Mark 1 in 1787.
It was a classical Palladian building, revolving around the drawing-room,
a central, domed rotunda surrounded by Ionic columns. Wings to north
and south had bow windows and ironwork balconies on both floors. Work
was done in a great hurry. As many as 150 workmen were employed on
the site, and the Pavilion was ready for the eager Prince in five months.
The Prince's bedroom on the first floor was equipped with 'reflecting
glasses, which enabled His Royal Highness, while reclining on his pillow,
to see the promenade on the Steine very distinctly'.

Here the Prince and Mrs Fitzherbert spent a life of elegant, popular
gaiety, with their circle of witty, Whiggish friends:

> 'Tis at Brighton, the mirror of watering places,
> Assemble their Honors, their Lordships and Graces,
> Nay, England's first Prince – and the famous Dame Fitz.
> And old friends meet new friends of fashion and wits.

Fox, Sheridan, Beau Brummell, and all the other fashionables were frequent visitors at the Pavilion. There was hunting, racing, cricket on the
Steine, which the Prince played 'with great affability and condescension',
and bathing, with Martha Gunn to dip the ladies in the sea, and 'Smoaker'
Miles acting as the Prince of Wales's swimming tutor, or 'dipper'. Obsequious local anecdote chuckled that Smoaker once stopped the Prince
from going swimming on a rough day by standing in front of him with
fists raised, and saying: 'What do you think you father would say to me
if you were drowned? He would say, "This is all owing to you, Smoaker.
If you'd taken proper care of him, Smoaker, poor George would still be
alive." '

The Prince's birthday was normally celebrated at Brighton with lavish
public festivities, fireworks, roasted oxen, bell-ringing, illuminations, a
review, and prizes.

During the French Revolution the Prince and Mrs Fitzherbert used to
go down to the beach to welcome boat-loads of aristocrat refugees from
the Terror, and entertained them in the Pavilion. Life was a bit wild and
rackety, though not really wicked. But critics already croaked about the
Prince, who so wanted to be popular, whose character was so unfit to cope
with popularity. One of them once wrote that 'the only respectable thing
in the royal property' was a colony of rooks in an avenue of trees which

had been added to the Pavilion grounds. Even the conventional, inno-cuous original building already attracted that architectural hostility and mockery which buzzed, more predictably, around the later exotic altera-tions; using the *nom de guerre* 'Antony Pasquin', a critic wrote in his *New Brighton Chronicle*: '. . . it is a nondescript monster in building, and appears

like a mad house, or a house run mad, as it has neither beginning middle nor end. . . . The room in which the Prince usually dined may be compared to a sort of oven: when the fire is lighted the inmates are nearly baked or incrusted.

At least the sour writer seems to have been right about the tropical central heating from the Pavilion's patent stove. There is a famous story of Sheridan, the playwright and Whig leader, asking George Hanger, an-other of the Prince's fast hangers-on, at dinner in the Pavilion if he did not feel hot.

Hanger: 'Hot, hot, hot as hell.'
Sheridan: 'It is quite right that we should be prepared in this world for that which we know will be our lot in another.'

Another peculiar feature of Pavilion life in these halcyon years was the air guns. George had a passion for firearms, and tended to fire them over the dinner table to the alarum and excursion of his guests. He and a bibu-lous friend once scattered an entire orchestra, and shot out the lights, although his aim on the whole was not good. After one jolly dinner in the Pavilion, the Prince insisted on his guests having a shot as well. Some made nervous excuses, but 'Lady Downshire hit a fiddler in the drawing-room, Miss Johnstone a door, and Bloomfield [his secretary] the ceiling'.

Music was a regular and more conventional after dinner entertain-ment. The Prince enjoyed showing off his thunderous if not particularly distinguished bass voice. A young guest at the Pavilion, Mr Philip Francis, was once invited to join in singing a trio from *Azioli* with George. As they roared out '*Ritorneremo a Clori, al tramontar del di*', Mr Francis, overcome by nerves, the noise, and the proximity of the Prince's large red face, broke down in a fit of giggles. George was not angry, but showed signs of laughing himself, and just said: 'Come, come Philip.'

A letter from Brighton in 1787 gives a glimpse of the Prince walking on the Steine between the Duchess of Cumberland and Mrs Fitzherbert:

Each had hold of an arm, and in that manner went tugging him along; his new house is very handsome, a grand Dome in the Centre, with Wings, and a good deal of ground before with a Ha! Ha! and behind is a noble square, with Pillars and Lamps between, the stables are not yet finished; I think he has strong Marks of his late Illness, as to Mrs Fitz-t. She has not the least appearance of the Mistress of a young P——. She may be a very entertaining woman, but as to Beauty, to me there is no sign of it, but seems a very good kind of Nurse, the Duchess is at this time of day, in my opinion, a much more desirable person.

Like most of George's good resolutions, the economy campaign faded away. The eternal problem of the Prince's debts reared its hideous Hydra heads. By 1794 he owed £640,000. Much of this was due to his building operations at the Marine Pavilion and at Carlton House. He had borrowed money to be repaid at his father's death, a fact which his father George III with some justice called 'mortifying to my feelings'. Then there was what the Lord Chancellor pompously described as 'Newmarket and other extravagances more referable to profusion than essential to dignity'.

The only condition on which his obstinate and short-sighted father would agree to extricate him from the bottomless bog of debt was if he married somebody suitable, in other words a German princess, and settled down into 'a more creditable line of life'. Debt and the need to provide an heir drove George unwillingly and with a bad conscience to the altar; the old royal way to pay new debts. The Prince is reported to have said 'that one damned German *frow* was as good as another', and accepted the King's niece and candidate in the matrimonial stakes, Caroline of Bruns- wick. In any case he had already broken with Mrs Fitzherbert, and was living openly with the bewitching Lady Jersey.

The marriage was a totally predictable disaster. A daughter, Princess Charlotte, was born, but George had already separated from Caroline. His sensible letter to her said: '. . . our inclinations are not in our power, nor should either of us be held answerable to the other because nature has not made us suitable to each other'; and proposed that they should live the rest of their lives apart 'in uninterrupted tranquillity', and without ever again proposing 'a connexion of a more particular nature'.

In 1800 after much conscience-searching, after much importunity from the Prince, after getting permission from the Pope, Mrs Fitzherbert agreed to return to him. And they came back to Brighton with an in- creased income, and comparatively free from debt. The Prince's building itch was as strong as ever. Massive alterations started at once on the Pavilion. In particular two large, oval-shaped rooms were added at either end of the main eastern front. Through all the constant confusing altera- tions and redecorations of the next twenty years this remained the basic plan of the Pavilion – three large rooms, music-room, domed drawing-room in the middle, and dining-room, connected by saloons, corridors, and ante-rooms.

During these alterations the first exotic virus of the romantic Orient, which was soon to infect the whole building, erupted in the Pavilion. The Prince was given a present of some Chinese wallpaper, and created a Chinese gallery to take it. At the same time, while the mood was on him, he made a small Chinese passage room entirely of glass painted with 'the peculiar insects, fruit, flowers etc. of China'. It was lighted from outside, and said to give the impression of walking through an immense Chinese lantern.

There was nothing startlingly new about this Chinese inspiration. The craze for *chinoiserie*, 'Chinese Chippendale', eastern papers, had raged since England first traded with the east, and reached its peak around the middle of the eighteenth century. The Prince himself had had a Chinese drawing-room at Carlton House for more than ten years. The new thing about his Chinese decorations at Brighton was that they had more barbaric rich-ness and realism than the previous restrained and anaemic British attempts at the Chinese style.

Very rapidly the oriental fantasy spilled over into the rest of the Pavilion, which now entered permanently upon its adventurous 'Cycle of Cathay'. From now on a steady, gaudy stream of Chinese furniture and fittings, ornaments and wallpapers poured down to Brighton. The long lists of imports include 'very handsome Sophas', chairs and stools of bamboo, 'Japan lacquer' cabinets, models of pagodas and junks, Chinese costumes, birds' nests (edible?), a Chinese razor, and 'a miraculous jug'.

Not surprisingly the idea soon occurred to the Prince to give the Pavilion a Chinese exterior to go with its astonishing inside. His architect produced designs for a Chinese façade for the Pavilion, with green pagoda-shaped roofs snarling with gilded dragons at every available point. How-ever it was decided that the Chinese style, though delightful for interior decoration and small summer-houses, was 'too light and trivial' for exteriors.

At this point another unexpected architectural element was blended into the oriental fantasy at Brighton. In 1803 work began on a vast, domed royal stables and riding house behind the Pavilion. The great central cupola was eighty feet in diameter and sixty-five feet high. The horses were housed in forty-four stalls arranged round the circular interior, with a fountain in the middle to water them and cool the romantic atmosphere. The work was eventually finished five years later, and had cost more than £55,000. The astonishing new building with dome, pinnacles, and Omar Khayyam battlements had a strong ambiance not of Chinese crinkum-crankums but of Islam, Moslem mosque, and Moghul court, and a Muezzin from the Tower of Darkness crying.

Early in the new century the Prince was bitten with the bug of Indian romanticism, and infected as completely and touchingly as Toad of Toad Hall with a new enthusiasm. Partly this may have been inspired by a visit to Sezincote, a mansion in the Indian style at Moreton-in-the-Marsh, built by a retired Indian nabob who wanted something more solid than his interminable reminiscences to remind him of the best years of his life spent in India. Partly the Prince himself may have been influenced by childhood memories of Kew, the Indian temple and the Pagoda. In any case a wild wave of excitement about Indian mysticism, mythology and literature was sweeping through Europe in reaction to classical eighteenth-century rationalism. Whatever the inspiration, in 1805 the Prince ordered his architect to draw up designs for converting the Pavilion into an Indian palace. However, the usual financial difficulties made it impossible to start work on the new project for the time being.

A visitor in this year, Lady Bessborough, wrote:

To-day I have been going all over the Pavilion, which is really beautiful in its way. I did not think the strange Chinese shapes and columns could have look'd so well. It is like Concetti in Poetry, in *outré* and false taste, but for the kind of thing as perfect as it can be, and the Prince says he had it so because at the time there was such a cry against the French things, etc., that he was afraid of his furniture being accus'd of Jacobinism.

Meanwhile the Prince fell in love again with a woman who possessed the two indispensable, irresistible qualities to attract him; Lady Hertford was in her forties, and she was a grandmother. George got to know her well through the 'Minnie' Seymour case, Mrs Fitzherbert's long legal struggle as a Catholic to adopt little, Protestant Mary Seymour. Lord Hertford was head of the Seymour family, and solved the deadlock by undertaking to be the child's guardian himself, and than appointing Mrs Fitzherbert to act for him. Mrs Fitzherbert gained an adopted daughter, but she lost her husband, who fell heavily for Lady Hertford. The lady appears to have been distinctly handsome, but to have had a faint air of mutton dressed as lamb; some years later she was described:

All gentle and juvenile, curly and gay
In the manner of Ackermann's *Dresses for May*.

The Royal Pavilion, Brighton, illuminated for Son et Lumière

The oriental geometry of the roof of the Royal Pavilion

*Photo The Times*

The Banqueting Room of the Royal Pavilion

*Photo The Times*

The Prince was only constant in his capricious taste for elderly women. A few years later he made a violent and farcical attempt to transfer his affections to Lady Bessborough, yet another mature grandmother. She was a vivid letter-writer:

He threw himself on his knees and, clasping me round, kissed my neck before I was aware of what he was doing. I screamed with vexation and fright; he continued, sometimes struggling with me, sometimes sobbing and crying . . . vows of eternal love, entreaties and promises of what he would do – he would break with Mrs Fitzherbert and Lady Hertford, I should make my own terms, I should be his sole *confidante*, sole adviser . . . I should guide his politics, Mr Canning [a politician to whom Lady Bessborough was devoted] should be Prime Minister . . .; then over and over again the same round of complaint, despair, entreaties and promises . . . that immense, grotesque figure flouncing about, half on the couch, half on the ground.

Wretched Mrs Fitzherbert was still expected to attend all the functions the Prince held for Lady Hertford at the Pavilion, as a chaperone and smoke-screen to divert gossip. Gradually she refused invitations. The final break came in 1811 when the Prince held a magnificent fête at Carlton House to celebrate becoming Regent. Mrs Fitzherbert was told she would not be seated at the Prince's table as always before, but would have to scramble for her caviare with the general crush of guests at the buffet. She went and asked the Regent face to face where she was to sit.

George: 'You know, madam, you have no place.'

Mrs Fitzherbert: 'None, Sir, but such as you choose to give me.'

And mortified, she withdrew into dignity and seclusion, and never again visited the Pavilion, from which she said she had been 'drove by Lady Hertford', until after George's death.

With the Regency, there was more money available for building. And the Prince's latest architect, John Nash, was commissioned to transform the Pavilion. Over the next ten years Nash, with the Prince breathing down his neck, conjured up the curiously beautiful compound of Indian, Chinese, and Persian styles that is the Pavilion today.

The music-room and dining-room at either end of the main front were rebuilt into great new state apartments with roofs like pagodas, which have been described as 'the apotheosis of the tent'. That inverted bowl the ceiling of the banqueting room was painted like an Eastern sky, and was 'partially obscured by the broad and branching foliage of a luxuriant and fruited plantain tree'. Under this perched a huge and gaudy dragon dangling from its claws 'a magnificent lustre of unparalleled size and beauty', thirty feet long and weighing a ton. This chandelier features a brood of six smaller dragons all biting in their mouths lotus flowers of tinted glass. The wall compartments of the banqueting hall are filled with paintings of Chinese domestic life; underneath the pigtails, some of the Chinese faces have an uncanny resemblance to some of George's good friends.

At the north end of the pavilion the great new music-room also had as domed ceiling, which is covered with innumerable carved and gilded scales. The scales become smaller as the room goes higher so as to give an illusion of greater height. From the apex dangles another monstrous lustre, 'sustaining by its chain-work an immense lamp in the form of the *nelumbium* or water lily'. Out of the lily darts the apparently obligatory covey of flying, ferocious golden dragons.

The walls are decorated with crimson and gold paintings of Chinese landscapes, full of pagodas, plantains, and a surfeit of bamboo. Porcelain pagodas fifteen feet high beetled over their bases. On the floor was a massive bright blue Axminster carpet decorated with golden dragons, birds, stars, serpents, and insects.

The long Chinese gallery connecting the two great rooms is 162 crowded feet of peach-blossom, life-sized Chinese figures, and Oriental *bric-à-brac*. At either end are two slender double staircases, built of cast iron to look like bamboo. The large central skylight portrays on painted glass 'Lin-Shin', the Chinese God of thunder, 'a monstrous human figure having an eagle's beak, talons and wings, and appearing in a circle of eight drums, holding in his right hand a truncheon wherewith to strike the drums and arouse the thunder'. On the ground floor also were George's private apartments, suitably be-dragoned and lotus-flowered. His bathroom was lined with white marble. The bath was an imperial sixteen feet long, by ten feet wide, and six feet deep. It was 'supplied with salt water from the sea by a succession of pipes and other machinery'.

Pretty well the only parts of the Pavilion to avoid the Oriental theme were the chapel and the kitchens. John Wilson Croker, who thought the rest of the Pavilion an absurd waste of money, as well as copied from the Kremlin, found the kitchens and larders admirable:

. . . such contrivances for roasting, boiling, baking, stewing, frying, steaming and heating; hot plates, hot closets, hot air and hot hearths, with all manner of cocks for hot water and cold water, and warm water and steam, and twenty saucepans all ticketed and labelled, placed up to their necks in a vapour bath.

The complete cornucopia of minarets, pinnacles, columns, bulbous domes, ormolu, dragons rampant, Chinese cabinets, chandeliers, mandarins, musical instruments, incense-burners, lanterns, weapons, junk of both sorts, Pekin pots and pipkins beggared all description. This did not stop people trying to describe it, often rudely. A popular verse ran with relish:

> The outside – huge teapots, all drill'd round with holes,
> Relieved by extinguishers, sticking on poles.
> The inside – all tea-things and dragons and bells,
> The show rooms – all show, the sleeping rooms – cells.

William Cobbett said the Pavilion was like the painted end of a large Norfolk-turnip surrounded by four smaller turnips and a promiscuous assortment of narcissus, hyacinth, tulip, and crocus bulbs. William Hazlitt contributed:

The Pavilion at Brighton is like a collection of stone pumpkins and pepper boxes. It seems as if the genius of architecture had at once the dropsy and the megrims. Anything more fantastical, with a greater dearth of invention was never seen.

The most famous sarcasm about the Pavilion is attributed to the Rev. Sydney Smith, who is supposed to have said, delightfully, that 'the dome of St Paul's had come down to Brighton and pupped'. In fact the phrase seems to have belonged, in the first place at least, to the philanthropist William Wilberforce, who wrote: 'The Pavilion in Chinese style – beautiful and tasty . . . though it looks very much as if St Paul's had come down to the sea and left behind a litter of cupolas.'

A considerable factor behind the resentment aroused by the Pavilion was the extravagant expenditure on it in a period of economic depression after a war: 'money extracted from the pockets of the suffering people of England,' as radical orators were fond of declaiming to Parliament. Indeed in 1816 the Prime Minister, Foreign Secretary, and Chancellor of the Exchequer signed a joint memorandum to the Prince stating that the existence of the Government would be jeopardised unless all new expenses on the Pavilion were stopped at once. In view of the general distress of the country, they felt that the unfavourable impressions made by the Prince's demands 'may never be effaced'.

In all, during his life-time George seems to have spent a grand total of £502,797 6s 10d on the estate, buildings, and furnishings of the Pavilion. Byron wrote in 'Don Juan':

> Shut up – no, not the King, but the Pavilion,
> Or else 'twill cost us all another million.

Today long years away from the party passion and resentment of the period, when far more money is spent annually on blank, impersonal office blocks and screaming motorways, it seems a modest sum to pay for such a romantic and dream-like national asset and monument to the Picturesque.

Not just the extravagant hardware, but also the human goings-on inside the Pavilion attracted a shrill tornado of criticism. Princess Lieven, wife of the Russian ambassador, and an intimate friend of the Prince Regent (who at last became King in 1820), wrote in a letter from the Pavilion:

I do not believe that, since the days of Heliogabalus, there has been such magnificence and such luxury. There is something effeminate in it which is disgusting. One spends the evening half-lying on cushions; the lights are dazzling; there are perfumes, music, liqueurs – 'Devil take me, I think I must have got into bad company'. You can guess who said that, and the tone in which it was said.

But then the witty Princess was never exactly one to sacrifice an amusing phrase for strict accuracy. The picture of life in the Pavilion as one continuous round of drunkenness, dissipation, and nameless debauchery was adopted and embroidered by later writers with pursed-lip relish. A Victorian authoress put the typical view in a lurid and prudish purple patch:

The unbridled license the future monarch allowed himself in this sybaritical palace was, however, the cause of grave scandal throughout the country. It is perhaps better to make no more than a shadowy allusion to the character of the company harboured beneath the Pavilion Domes. Riot and unrestrained festivity were the order of the day; and it may also be added of the night.

Now there is something inherently improbable about this popular image of Regency bucks on the rampage like a rugby club on a Saturday night. The Pavilion, with its tinkling elegance and brittle *bric-à-brac*, was not built to stand even one night of such riotous reel and rout. In boring fact, life at the Pavilion in these later years appears to have been humdrum and formal rather than an orgy of unbridled license. Croker was a frequent guest, and in his *Journal* gave descriptions of the bland routine:

The etiquette is that before dinner (at 6.30) when he comes in, he *finds* all the men standing, and the women rise; he speaks to everybody, shakes hands with new comers or particular friends, then desires the ladies to be seated. When dinner is announced, he leads out a lady of the highest rank or when the ranks are nearly equal, or when the nominal rank interferes a little with the real rank, as yesterday, with Lady Liddell and Mrs Pelham, he took one on each arm.

A few days later Croker dined at the Pavilion again:

After dinner there was music as usual. . . . The supper is only a tray with sand-
wiches and wines and water handed about. The Prince played a hand or two at
Patience, and I was rather amused to hear him exclaim loudly when one of the Kings
had turned up vexatiously, 'Damn the King.'

Or another, eminently cultured dinner party: 'In the evening the music
room was lighted and the band played, both magnificent – the band rather
*bruyant*, and the music better heard from the next room in my opinion.'

Greville found an evening in the Pavilion far from riotous or sybaritical:

The gaudy splendour of the place amused me for a little and then bored me. The
dinner was cold and the evening dull beyond all dullness. They say the King is
anxious that form and ceremony should be banished, and if so it only proves how
impossible it is that form and ceremony should not always inhabit a palace. The
rooms are not furnished for society, and, in fact, society cannot flourish without
ease; and who can feel at ease who is under the eternal constraint which etiquette
and respect impose? The King was in good looks and good spirits, and after dinner
cut his jokes with all the coarse merriment which is his characteristic.

William Wilberforce, that pillar of sober respectability, dined at the
Pavilion in 1815, and was pleasantly surprised. He had been warned,

that commonly the talk was such as I should dislike to hear. The direct contrary was
the fact. The Prince is quite the English gentleman at the head of his own table. . . .
Really had I been covered with titles and ribands, I could not have been treated
with more real, unaffected, unapparently condescending and therefore most
unostentatious, civility.

Wilberforce could not resist moralising mildly: 'How ill-suited to the
baptismal engagement to resist the pomps and vanities of this wicked
world.'

About one item the suspicions of the Pavilion's critics were entirely
accurate, and that was the luxury of the food. The Prince gave a dinner
party at least twice a week, and chose the menu himself. The programme
for a typical dinner prepared by his Parisian chef Carême is so succulent
and sybaritic that even in cold print it induces sensations of saturation
and sea-sickness. It started with four soups; followed by four fish courses;
then '*Quatre Grosses Pièces pour les Contre-Flancs*'; then thirty-six assorted
*entrées*, ranging from the polysyllabic poetry of '*les petites croustades de
mauviettes au gratin*' to '*l'épigramme de poulardes, purée de céleri*' (presumably
these were to be eaten concurrently rather than consecutively); then '*pour
extra, dix Assiettes Volantes de Friture*'; '*Huit grosses pièces de Pâtisserie*'; '*Quatre*

*Plats de Rôts*'; '*Trente-Deux Entremets*'; and, yet again, '*pour extra, Dix Assiettes Volantes*'.

One unsurprising result of all this energetic browsing and sluicing was that George became pretty portly. A peer put it more crudely: 'Prinny has let loose his belly which now reaches his knees.' His vanity and dread of ridicule made him hide himself away more and more in the seclusion of the Pavilion to avoid the stares and giggles of the public.

Another aspect of the Pavilion scene which irritated the critics was the King's sex life. This was, as always, unorthodox. He had gradually become bored with Lady Hertford. Nobody was particularly surprised when he transferred his affections to yet another elderly Marchioness. Lady Conyngham was a plump, rather dim, unmusical matron of fifty-one in 1820, with five grown-up children. She and her husband and family all moved into the Pavilion, and were found jobs in the royal household. And for the rest of his life she was the King's lady companion. There is some doubt about their precise relationship. The pamphleteers nourished no such doubts. Here is a typical offering, in which Lady Conyngham features as 'Q' – (she was nicknamed 'The Vice Queen'):

> Give the devil his due, she's a prime bit of stuff,
> And for flesh she has got in all conscience enough.
> He'll never need *pillows* to keep up his head,
> Whilst old Q and himself sleep and snore in one bed.

> 'Tis pleasant at seasons to see how they sit,
> First cracking their nuts, and then cracking their wit;
> Then quaffing their claret – then mingling their lips,
> Or tickling the *fat* about each other's hips.

If this really was the position it is extraordinary that her highly respectable husband and children should connive at it. And Lady Conyngham herself, to outsiders at least, gave a distinctly strait-laced impression. Princess Lieven said that her limited mind was 'occupied with religious questions'. Whatever else she was, she was certainly mistress of the Pavilion. Once when she was staying there she gave orders to light up one of the state rooms. The King came up and said to her, in public: 'Thank you, thank you, my dear; you always do what is right; you cannot please me so much as by doing everything you please, everything to show that you are mistress here.'

There is quite a convincing proposition that the King's relationship with Lady Conyngham was not sexual but affectionate, and sprang from a lonely old man's need for friendship and company. She does seem to have been partly responsible for the melancholy irony that once the Pavilion had been recreated in its flamboyant plumage, George gradually stopped visiting it. She disliked Brighton, where there was little privacy from the crowds, and much public sympathy for Mrs Fitzherbert. The Duke of Wellington said later that the King deserted the Pavilion because Lady Conyngham, having seen 'some words on a window written with a diamond and reflecting severely upon herself, declared in her passion that she would never return to the palace – nor did she, nor the King either'.

Before he left his pleasure-dome for good, he perpetrated there a touching-trivial anecdote which illustrates not only his well-known peacock passion for fine feathers, but also his less well-known compassion. He was always anxious to reprieve condemned criminals. The Home Secretary, Sir Robert Peel, was staying at the Pavilion, when the King, unable to sleep from worry, had him woken up in the middle of the night and brought to him. They had a long interview in which the King persistently begged to be allowed to pardon a condemned man about to be hanged. Having finally persuaded Peel, he kissed him, and then noticing the Home Secretary's plain and functional dressing-gown, said: 'Peel, where did you get your dressing-gown? I'll show you what a dressing-gown ought to be.' And he insisted on Peel trying on one of his large and gaudy collection.

George IV's sucessor, his brother, William IV, the hearty old Admiral, quite enjoyed the staring crowds of Brighton, and spent much time in the Pavilion. Greville sniffed: 'He lives a strange life at Brighton, with tagrag and bobtail about him, and always open house'; and 'very active, vulgar and hospitable; King, Queen, Princes, Princesses, bastards and attendants constantly trotting about in every direction'.

William behaved with considerable sensitivity to Mrs Fitzherbert, and always invited her to the Pavilion when he was in residence. A diary of 1831, kept by Mary Frampton, says:

The magnificence of the parties given by the King and Queen at the Pavilion at Brighton are spoken of as realising the ideas of the entertainments described in the *Arabian Nights*, the dinners consisting daily of about forty persons. The King is very temperate. He consults Mrs Fitzherbert much as an old friend in matters relating to the fêtes, etc.

William had the huge dragon-chandelier in the Banqueting Room taken down, because he 'was fearful lest from its immense weight, the supports should give way, and some dreadful accident occur'. It was said that Queen Adelaide had a dream that the chandelier fell on the King and killed him.

Victoria was not at all amused by the bamboo and dragon world her 'Uncle King' had created. On her first visit she wrote: 'The Pavilion is a strange, odd Chinese looking thing, both inside and outside; most rooms low . . . I only see a little morsel of the sea from one of my sitting-room windows.' The lack of privacy was even more distressing than the bizarre foreign ambiance. Victoria complained: 'The people are very indiscreet and troublesome here really, which makes this place quite a prison.'

Shortly after her marriage the Queen bought Osborne as a suitably secluded sea-side residence for her domestic life. There was a vandal proposition to demolish the Pavilion. But fortunately in 1849 it was agreed to sell it to the town of Brighton for £50,000. The money went towards the enlargement of Buckingham Palace. No less than 143 vanloads of assorted furniture were removed from the Pavilion to other royal palaces. Since then much of it has been restored to the Pavilion, whose gleaming domes and minarets remain one of the most flamboyant and extravagant ornaments and museums of the country.

# XVI

# OSBORNE AND BALMORAL

THERE is a certain irritating irony for subjects when royalty complains, as it often used to complain, about being overcrowded in its numerous vast palaces, and needing to build another. Partly, one of the atavistic functions of a King was to be the national architect, builder, and fashion setter. More often what congested royalty means is that it wants a fine and private place, away from the goldfish-bowl life of state ceremonial. This understandable instinct for a privacy, an obscure nook, was particularly highly developed in Queen Victoria. Spurred on by it she bought and built, with her own rather than public money, Osborne House on the Isle of Wight and Balmoral Castle in the shadow of the Cairngorms, as well as several other smaller sanctuaries.

None of her existing residences was considered suitable for the placid, bourgeois life of domestic bliss she, and particularly Albert, wanted after their children started remorselessly to arrive. At Buckingham Palace the only room for the nurseries was in the attics. At Windsor there was no private garden, nor any asylum from sight-seeing crowds. Brighton Pavilion was the original sea-side home of the sovereign, but again there was no escape from the peering public, and the town had grown so fast that the sea was only dimly visible from the upper windows of the Pavilion. Victoria started to look for a refuge and a holiday home.

She had visited the Isle of Wight twice as a girl, on those notorious 'royal progresses' organised by Sir John Conroy; the 'popping' of royal salutes by the ships at Portsmouth to his heir presumptive infuriated King William. In 1844 the Queen paid a trial visit to Osborne on the recommendation of the Prime Minister, Sir Robert Peel. She liked it. 'It is impossible to imagine a prettier spot,' she wrote in a letter to Lord Melbourne;

valleys and woods which would be beautiful anywhere, but all this near the sea (the woods grow into the sea) is quite perfection; we have a charming beach quite to ourselves. The sea was so blue and calm that the Prince said it was like Naples. And then we can walk about anywhere without being followed or mobbed.

Her doctor, Sir James Clark, the original, fanatical fresh-air fiend, came down to vet the atmosphere, and pronounced it sufficiently bracing and therapeutic. And the next year she bought her 'dear little Home', and its estate of almost 1,000 acres, for the moderate price of £26,000; the Prime Minister again helped in the negotiations.

It is quite clear from the letters that the original motive for Osborne was privacy. Victoria wrote to her uncle Leopold, King of the Belgians, and the first of her collection of father-figures: 'It sounds so pleasant to have a place of one's own, quiet and retired, and free from all Woods and Forests and other charming departments, which really are the plague of one's life.' Albert told his brother that Osborne was a retreat from the 'inquisitive and often impudent people'. However, by the lunatic logic of royal residences, as soon as they had got a 'dear little Home' all of their very own, Victoria and Albert proceeded to pull it down and replace it with a formal palace capable of accommodating a court. Afterwards Victoria regretted the disappearance of the old Osborne: 'The character of that little house is gone.'

In that very first summer of 1845 the foundation stone of the new, grander Osborne was laid. Albert planned the house. And because in his curious and nostalgic facility for unconvincing geographical comparisons he felt that the Solent was like the bay of Naples, the house was designed to look like his idea of an Italian villa, with two tall campaniles (the Clock Tower and the Flag Tower), a first floor balcony or loggia, and terraced gardens leading down to the sea, with a fountain and statues in the Renaissance manner.

Albert's flat-roofed, Italianate vision was translated into masonry by Thomas Cubitt, one of the first of the big, modern building contractors, who used the latest building gimmick, cast-iron beams, in the structure. In the autumn of 1845 Charles Greville visited Osborne for a meeting of the Privy Council, and was characteristically cool:

Osborne a miserable place and such a vile house that the Lords of the Council had no place to remain in but the Entrance Hall, before the Council. Fortunately the weather was fine, so we walked about, looking at the new house the Queen is building. It is very ugly and the whole concern wretched enough. They will spend first and last a great deal of money there, but it is her own money and not the nation's. I know not where she gets it, but Graham told me she had money. . . . Nothing can exceed the universal indignation felt here by people of every description at the brutal and stupid massacre of the deer, which Albert perpetrated, and at which she assisted. It has been severely commented on in several of the papers, and met by a very clumsy (and false) attempt to persuade people that she was shocked and annoyed. No such thing appeared and nothing compelled her to see it. But the truth is her sensibilities are not acute, and though she is not at all ill-natured, perhaps the reverse, she is hard-hearted, selfish, and self-willed.

The inside of Osborne was fussy. Interior decoration was not Albert's most sucessful hobby, although he was a dedicated fiddler and rearranger of furniture and paintings. Lord Rosebery said that he thought the drawing-room at Osborne was the ugliest in the world – until he saw the one at Balmoral. It was supported on immense, pseudo-marble, marmalade-coloured columns. In the Horn Room every stick of furniture including the table tops was made from the antlers of deer. The Prince Consort was a passionate, prolific, though not always successful or good-tempered stalker. The billiard-room, which led out of the drawing-room, provided perches of raised leather seats, where the gentlemen of the household could roost, although they were still technically in the presence of the Queen. The long rooms were congested with frequent tables, and the tables were cluttered with porcelain, portraits, souvenirs, *bric-à-brac*, miniatures of historic building in ivory and silver, vases of flowers, busts, and, disconcertingly, marble replicas of the arms and legs of the royal children. The corridors had elaborate tiled floors, and were lined with Garter-blue recesses, out of which impended busts of imposing German uncles, or plaster reliefs in the style of the frieze of the Parthenon.

The royal bedroom was solid, simple, and in the Queen's favourite adjective, 'cosy', with chintz and mahogany. A stupendous mahogany wardrobe covered the whole of one wall, coyly concealing behind one of its doors what Queen Victoria chose to call the 'little room'. The idyllically entwined initials 'V' and 'A' were broadcast lavishly throughout the house, except over the door of the smoking-room, where there was a solitary 'A'. Greville was just as unimpressed with the end product as he had been with its beginnings: 'Like a small German Principality Palace.'

Albert's efforts at landscape gardening in the park were more successful, or at any rate more in tune with modern taste. Among the much frustrated Prince's keenest frustrations was the fact that he was unable to reorganise the grounds at Windsor or Buckingham Palace, which were administered by the Department of Woods and Forests. Osborne was the Queen's private property, and the Prince was given a free hand to exercise his green fingers.

Down towards the Solent at the foot of the garden, where his wife's big ships slid past, he planted thousands of traditional English trees, oak and elm and beech. Around the house, homesick for his birth-place, the Rosenau, in the green shade of a Coburg forest, he made shrubberies of evergreens, flowering shrubs, and conifers, including novel immigrants from Germany like the Monkey Puzzle and the Christmas Tree. Through the woods he made winding walks, with seats placed at strategic points of view of the sea, where he and Victoria could sit 'away from all the bitterness people create for themselves in London', and Albert could do his imitations of his pleasant voices, his nightingales. Years later Victoria wrote about these early years at Osborne: 'The happy, peaceful walks he used to take with the Queen in the woods, and whistling to them [the nightingales] in their own long, peculiar note, which they invariably answered.'

A scheme of Albert's to convert the sewage from the house into fertiliser for the gardens was less successful than his other horticultural enterprises.

The main 'Pavilion' wing of the new house was finished in a year, and the royal family moved in in September 1846. After dinner Albert said that there was a special Lutheran hymn used in Germany on such occasions, and quoted from it. Everybody felt rather solemn. The two eastern wings of Osborne were not finished until 1851. The whole operation and furnishing cost £200,000, which Albert managed to squeeze out by his thrifty organisation of the Queen's finances. By then the 'little Paradise' had become the Queen's regular holiday home. Here Victoria would venture into the sea in her bathing machine, which rumbled down a sloping pier, and deposited her discreetly into the bracing waves. She wrote in her diary for July 30, 1847:

Drove down to the beach with my maids and went into the bathing machine, where I undressed and bathed in the sea (for the first time in my life), a very nice bathing woman attending me. I thought it delightful till I put my head under water, when I thought I should be stifled. After dressing again, drove back.

After this claustrophobic first launching, the Queen in future sponged her face before going in, and then 'plunged about' in the sea without getting her face wet.

Albert busied himself becoming a model landlord to compensate for his exclusion from state affairs. A lady-in-waiting, Lady Lyttelton, wrote:

It is pleasant to see how earnestly Prince Albert tries to do the best about this place, giving work to as many labourers as possible, but not making any haste, so as to make it last, and keep at a steady useful pitch, not to over-excite the market. His bailiff (I mean, of course, the Queen's) has dismissed quantities of men lately, because it is harvest time, that they may work for others, telling them all, that the moment any man is out of employment, he is to come back here, and will, without fail, find work to do. This is doing good very wisely.

In the grounds a small chalet, imported from Switzerland, was put up, where the children could play and improve their minds according to the Prince's earnest 'Plan'. The princes were supposed to learn gardening and carpentry in the chalet, the princesses housekeeping and cooking on miniature charcoal ranges. The small wheelbarrows and tools were all labelled with the owner's initials, 'PoW', 'PssR', and so on. Around the outside of the black wooden walls of the Hansel and Gretel cottage were carved edifying proverbs and quotations from the Psalms in German.

Behind the Swiss Cottage is a miniature fortress where Prince Arthur, the future Field Marshal the Duke of Connaught, and his brothers could play war games with their wooden cannon and earthworks, ravelin and counterscarps, as delightfully as Tristram Shandy's Uncle Toby. 'How happy we are here!' wrote the Queen, 'And never do I enjoy myself more, or more peacefully than when I can be so much with my beloved Albert & follow him everywhere.'

Significantly, when Albert died at Windsor in 1861, the hysterically wounded Queen took refuge in Osborne, in the widow's clothes she never discarded. There, as in her other palaces, she dedicated herself to preserving everything unaltered so as to remind her of Albert. When the primroses came out at Osborne that spring, she wrote that for her it was 'still in the month of December'. Osborne remained for the rest of her life the favourite bolt-hole to escape from the pressure of Ministers, trying to drag her out of the sacred past into her public duty in the present. Gladstone wrote about her self-indulgent seclusion: 'There is no doubt that Osborne during the Session is the great enemy.'

At Osborne she surrounded herself with excessive protocol of mourning, and with ladies who were also widows, with a similar sorrowful duty to remember. Driving with her in the grounds, one of them [Lady Leila Errol] said: 'Oh, Your Majesty, think of when we shall see our dear ones again in Heaven.' 'Yes,' said Victoria.
Lady-in-waiting: 'We will all meet in Abraham's bosom.'
The Queen: 'I will not meet Abraham.'

In the winter of 1864 the Queen's 'particular gillie' John Brown was brought down to Osborne from Balmoral, partly in order to try to break the rigid royal melancholia and inertia. He brought with him the Queen's favourite pony, Lochnagar. The doctors wanted Victoria to keep up her riding, and for this a familiar groom was essential. Within a few months Brown was given the new status of 'The Queen's Highland Servant', and the Queen wrote in her Journal: 'Have decided that Brown should remain permanently & make himself useful in other ways besides leading my pony as he is so very dependable . . .'

This new and powerful influence helped the Queen to recover from her morbid isolation, though simultaneously it created much scurrilous scandal. According to the large corpus of anecdotes, Brown called her 'wumman', and said 'What's this ye've got on today?', if he didn't like her clothes. He was reported to have roared: 'Hoots, wumman, canna ye hold yer head still!', when he pricked her while pinning a plaid round her shoulders. The Queen described Brown's moral courage and discretion: '. . . in this House where there are so many people, & often so much indiscretion & no Male head now – such a person is invaluable.'

In a letter, revealingly, she wrote:

He comes to my room – after breakfast & luncheon to get his orders – & everything is always right. . . . It is an excellent arrangement, & I feel I have in the House a good devoted Soul . . . whose only object and interest is my service, & God knows how much I want to be taken care of.

*Punch* and pamphlets with names like *Mrs John Brown* made the most of their unconventional but innocent relationship. The Queen herself described her feelings for Brown, which were in a way an embodiment of her nostalgia for the Highlands, in a letter to his brother after his death. Victoria, in her sixties, wrote to Hugh Brown:

I was in great trouble about the Princess Royal who had lost her child in '66, and dear John said to me: 'I wish to take care of my dear good mistress till I die. You'll never have an honester servant.' I took and held his dear kind hand and I said I hoped he might long be spared to comfort me, and he answered, 'But we all <u>must</u> die.' Afterwards my beloved John would say, 'You haven't a more devoted <u>servant</u> than Brown' – and oh! <u>how</u> I felt <u>that</u>. Afterwards so often I told him no one loved him more than I did or had a better friend than me, and he answered, 'Nor you – than me. No one loves you more.'

Simultaneously with the Brown episode, the Queen found another therapeutic but bizarre influence in Disraeli, who called her 'The Faery', and laid on the flattery and gossip in his letters to her with a shovel. Lytton Strachey wrote that in Disraeli's expert hands, 'the trowel seemed to assume the qualities of some lofty masonic symbol and to be the ornate and glittering vehicle of verities unrealised by the profane'. Disraeli also kept his head sufficiently undazzled always to remember to inquire in his letters after the health and well-being of John Brown. The Queen sent Disraeli regular presents of primroses from Osborne. He thanked her for them in equally flowery terms: 'They seem an offering from the Fauns and Dryads of Osborne', and, 'They show that your Majesty's sceptre has touched the enchanted Isle'. And then, about snowdrops this time:

Yesterday eve there appeared, in Whitehall Gardens, a delicate-looking case, with a royal superscription, which when he opened, he thought, at first, that your Majesty had graciously bestowed upon him the stars of your Majesty's principal orders. And, indeed, he was so impressed with this graceful illusion, that, having a banquet, where there were many stars and ribbons, he could not resist the temptation, by placing some snowdrops on his heart, of showing that he, too, was decorated by a gracious Sovereign. Then, in the middle of the night, it occurred to him, that it might all be an enchantment, and that, perhaps, it was a Faery gift, and came from another monarch: Queen Titania, gathering Flowers, with her Court, in a soft and sea-girt isle, and sending magic blossoms, which, they say, turn the heads of those who receive them.

In fact, far from being turned, Disraeli's head was screwed on in exactly the right way to coax the susceptible Queen to do whatever he wanted. There was no room big enough at Osborne for great state receptions. A marquee was put up on the lawn as needed. This makeshift arrangement was replaced in 1890 by the Durbar Room, a large hall in the Indian style, encrusted with intricate, dazzling white Taj Mahal decorations, with plaster peacocks strutting, and obese Buddhas brooding. It was designed by Rudyard Kipling's father, the curator of the museum at Lahore, and its Oriental splendours reflected Victoria's pride and current preoccupation with her Indian empire.

Life at Osborne for a Maid of Honour during the second half of Victoria's reign seems to have been stiff and tedious, requiring the stamina of a horse. Marie Mallet left a vivid picture of it. In a letter to her mother from Osborne she wrote:

I had a very *mauvais moment* last night; Harriet and I dined with the Household and worn out with standing around the inevitable Christmas tree for hours after tea, we were toasting our toes after dinner and chaffing Mrs Moreton, thinking we were quite safe for the evening, when suddenly Prince Henry appeared and after announcing that the Ladies were to go to the Drawing Room the Prince came up to me and said: 'You are to sing.' I turned pea-green and stammered: 'I really can't, Sir', and with much confusion explained that I was prepared to play, but that my voice was feeble and that I never sang in public; it was alarming but I think I was right for without anyone to accompany and shaking with fright I should have broken down to a certainty; so he told the Queen and I was let off; however, I had to read a horrid duet with Princess Beatrice, the Queen sitting close by; I believe I got through it pretty well but I could hardly see the notes and simply prayed for the end. I suppose these horrible sensations will wear off in time and, of course, being ordered to do a thing is far better than being asked.

It was at Osborne, surrounded by the memories and relics of Albert, and by a large congregation of her children and grandchildren, including the Kaiser, that Queen Victoria died in 1901. Her last request was for her little Pomeranian dog, Turi, to be put on her bed. The melancholy, hushed, and long-drawn-out scene ended with a ludicrous bang as a Gadarene horde of reporters bicycled furiously from Osborne to Cowes to get to the telephone first, yelling as they pedalled: 'Queen dead! Queen dead!'

In odd contrast with her predilection for black mourning while alive, Victoria had a horror of black funerals. Hers, for which she had left minute instructions, was white and purple. The Kaiser started to lay her in her coffin, but the new King, Edward VII, and Prince Arthur insisted that this was the right of her sons. She lay in state at Osborne for ten days, dressed in white, with her lace wedding-veil over her face, and her white widow's cap covering her hair. Then her coffin, covered with a white and gold pall, was ferried by a royal yacht between miles of warships to the mainland on the first stage of the journey to Windsor, and to the mausoleum where she was to lie beside Albert again at last.

Edward VII already had a private home at Sandringham. He presented Osborne House to the nation. The household wing was turned into a convalescent home for officers. The house, almost obsessively unchanged since Albert's death, is open to the public, and is a perfect prototype of a Victorian interior, as well as a key-hole into the private life of the great Queen.

Victoria and Albert discovered the Highlands on a late summer holiday in 1842. It was the beginning of a life-long love affair for both of them. Looking out from the windows of Taymouth Castle upon herbaceous borders of kilts, parading pipers, tartan pageantry, the young Queen wrote: 'The coup d'oeil was indescribable.' Albert stalked deer assiduously, and in every mountain and loch found improbable geographical parallels with his native Thuringia, and with Switzerland. 'There were nine pipers at the castle,' wrote Victoria after their visit with the Marquis of Breadalbane;

Osborne House, the Isle of Wight

*Photo The Times*

Balmoral Castle

'sometimes one and sometimes three played. They always played about breakfast-time, again during the morning, at luncheon, and also whenever we went in and out; again before dinner, and during most of dinner-time. We have both become quite fond of the bag-pipes.'

Two years later they came back, this time to Blair Atholl, and the Queen's adjectives became so fond as to verge on the superlative: 'I can only say that the scenery is lovely, grand, romantic, & a great peace and wildness pervades all, which is sublime.'

The Queen was infected with her life-long and uncritical affection for the natives: they 'never make difficulties, but are cheerful, and happy, and merry, and ready to walk, and run, and do anything'. Albert 'highly appreciated the good-breeding, simplicity, and intelligence, which make it so pleasant and even instructive to talk to them'. And, 'We were always in the habit of conversing with the Highlanders – with whom one comes so much in contact in the Highlands.'

After an extremely damp, discouraging, and dismal cruise up the west coast of Scotland, the Queen decided to settle in the east. Her doctor, Sir James Clark, the fanatic for dry, bracing, fresh air, commmended the east with enthusiasm: '. . . the weather beautiful, and the place as regards healthiness of site and beauty of scenery, exceeding my expectations, great as they were.' So in 1848 the Queen took over the lease of Balmoral on the upper Dee in Aberdeenshire.

'It is a pretty little Castle in the old scotch style,' she wrote, '. . . one enters a nice little hall, & a billiard-room & Dining-room. A good broad staircase takes one upstairs & above the Dining-room is our sitting-room . . . a fine large room opening into our bedroom, etc.' Their first walk, inevitably 'reminding us very much of the Thuringerwald', established that the scenery was 'wild, but not desolate'. Albert wrote to one of his German relations:

We have withdrawn for a short time into a complete mountain solitude, where one rarely sees a human face, where the snow already covers the mountain tops, and the wild deer come creeping round the house. I, naughty man, have also been crawling after the harmless stags and to-day I shot two red deer – at least, I hope so, for they are not yet found, but I have brought home a fine roebuck with me. . . . The air is glorious and clear, but icy cold.

The new Highland home was a total success, even if one evening dinner was late 'owing to Albert's struggles to dress in his kilt'. Albert stalked, crawling through bogs on his hands and knees dressed in grey, looking like a 'little speck' in the distance to his admiring wife. She sketched,

fraternised informally with ghillies and the cottagers, and wrote: 'Oh!
What can equal the beauties of nature! What enjoyment there is in them!
Albert enjoys it so much; he is in ecstasies here.'

Albert told her that 'the chief beauty of mountain scenery consists in
its frequent changes', and she wrote it all down. Both developed their
rather idealised enthusiasm for the locals: 'They are marked by that
honesty and sympathy which always distinguish the inhabitants of
mountainous countries who live far away from towns.'

Next autumn they were back in Balmoral. Greville, summoned up from
London on official business, was for once impressed:

Much as I dislike Courts and all that appertains to them, I am glad to have made this
expedition, and to have seen the Queen and Prince in their Highland retreat, where
they certainly appear to great advantage. The place is very pretty, the house very
small. They live there without any state whatever; they live not merely like private
gentlefolks, but like very small gentlefolks, small house, small rooms, small establishment. There are no soldiers, and the whole guard of the Sovereign and the whole
Royal Family is a single policeman, who walks about the grounds to keep off impertinent intruders or improper characters. . . . They live with the greatest simplicity and ease. The Prince shoots every morning, returns to luncheon, and then they
walk and drive. The Queen is running in and out of the house all day long, and often
goes about alone, and walks into the cottages, and sits down and chats with the old
women.

After dinner the Queen, Prince, and their family were taught reels by
a Highland dancing master. Greville was not admitted to this interesting
and intimate exercise, and played billiards instead. The billiard-room which
served also as sitting-room and library, was so congested that the Queen
was always having to move her seat to give the players elbow-room, or
cue-room.

In 1852 an eccentric miser, John Camden Nield, died, leaving about a
quarter of a million pounds to Queen Victoria, because, Victoria deduced,
he knew she 'would not waste it'. 'It is astonishing,' wrote Victoria to her
Uncle Leopold, 'but it is satisfactory to see that people have so much
confidence that it will not be thrown away, and so it certainly will not be.
I am very curious to hear, however, what led this old gentleman to do it.'

She used £31,500 of the money to buy Balmoral and its 17,400 acres
from the Fife trustees. The cramped old house was at once pulled down,
and a new Balmoral in the Neo-Baronial style, multi-turreted, with
castellated gables, and a hundred-foot tower vaguely hinting at the presence of lurking archers and buckets of boiling oil, was erected in the
native granite.

Naturally Albert had a considerable hand in its architecture and interior decoration. The inside was infected with an epidemic of Tartanitis, which oozed gaudily over the chintzes, curtains, carpets, wallpapers, and extended to the linoleum in the servants' quarters. The Prince designed the Balmoral tartan of black, red, and lavender on a grey background. The Queen invented her own Victoria tartan, with a white stripe, and was also addicted to the Royal Stuart and the Hunting Stuart: she always claimed, illogically, to be an ardent Jacobite. Any area of the new Balmoral that was not profusely be-tartaned, was infested with ornamental thistles. A visiting Minister, Lord Clarendon, wrote: 'They would rejoice the heart of a donkey if they happened to *look like* his favourite repast, which they don't.'

The lamp-stands were models of kilted Highlanders. Innumerable antlers bristled on the walls. The Duchess of Cambridge summed it up convincingly as 'all highly characteristic and appropriate, but not all equally *flatteuse* to the eye'.

In spite of labour troubles (the Prince wrote to his guru, Baron Stockmar, 'the workmen . . . have already struck several times, which is now quite the fashion all over the country'), the new house was finished in 1855. Under September 7 in Queen Victoria's *Journal of Our Life in the Highlands* ('Silly books in bad English', sniffed jealous and discontented Ouida), she wrote:

At a quarter past seven o'clock we all arrived at dear Balmoral. Strange, very strange, it seemed to me to drive past, indeed through, the old house; the connecting part between it and the offices being broken through. The new house looks beautiful. . . . An old shoe was thrown after us into the house for good luck, when we entered the hall. The house is charming; the rooms delightful; the furniture, papers, everything perfection.

Three nights later news came that Sebastopol had fallen at last. Perhaps the Crimean War was at last coming to a triumphant conclusion. 'All the gentlemen, in every species of attire, sallied forth, followed by all the servants.' A great bonfire was lit, and around it dervished the inhabitants of Balmoral in what Albert described to his brother as 'a veritable Witch's dance supported by whiskey'. Ghillies discharged fusillades of ammunition into the night sky. The Queen, who in spite of her later reputation for stuffiness could always turn a blind and benevolent eye to the faults of her beloved Highlanders, noted in her journal: 'The people had been drinking healths and were in great ecstasy.'

Romance also arrived at Balmoral this year in the person of Prince

Frederick William of Prussia to court the fourteen-year-old Princess Royal, 'Vicky'. On a ride up Craig-na-Ban he jumped off his pony to pick the Princess a piece of white heather. On the way down the hill his proposal was accepted. Fritz wrote home:

Early tomorrow morning I must leave here; I am quite beside myself . . . the happiness I have found here is quite indescribable. These past sixteen days are like a beautiful dream and I shall count the months eagerly till I can return to this dear family.

They were married when the Princess was still under eighteen, and she disappeared to Germany, 'the English Empress', to produce in due course that unfortunate result of a Deeside romance, Kaiser Wilhelm II.

The next autumn, back in Balmoral in what had now become a regular royal routine, the Queen wrote:

Every year my heart becomes more fixed in this dear Paradise and so much more so now that all has become my dearest Albert's own creation, own work, own building, own laying-out, as at Osborne: and his great taste and the impress of his dear hand, have been stamped everywhere.

In spite of her fixation for Albert's Highland paradise, Victoria was still driven to look for more solitude, more privacy, more wilderness. Five miles beyond the castle, up Glen Muick, she turned two granite huts or 'shiels' into a favourite cottage for herself, called Allt-na-giubhsaich in one of the bewildering permutations of Highland spelling, 'the burn of the fir trees'. It was simpler to call it 'The Hut', an even more remote desert island on which to escape from public life. It had two sitting-rooms, bedroom and dressing-room for the Queen and the Prince, a small room for the lady-in-waiting, and one for her maid. The servants lived in the other bothie, 'the washing & cooking & everything going on in a line with one's own dwelling'. Here the Queen camped and enjoyed the 'real severe Highland scenery'. They rowed on loch Muick, hauling trout out of the dark water rather unsportingly by net. In the evenings in the hut there was whist and whisky and midges. One of the Queen's visitors there was moved to describe the origin of the Highland Fling as 'a kilt and midges'.

Every year the Queen became doggedly more Scottish. The royal family stalked; clambered up Cairngorms; littered the landscape with cairns. Albert, who never wasted a moment, even on holiday, studied Gaelic. Whenever something particularly exciting happened, when Vicky sat down on a wasp's nest, or the Minister preached a particularly fine sermon on Nicodemus, when they climbed Ben Macdhui, Victoria delightedly jotted it all down in her journal. Leaving for London at the end of the holiday was as melancholy as going back to school. The Queen watched the snow drifting down, disconsolate, and wished she could be snowed up.

Another speciality of Balmoral life was the curious affair of the 'Great Expeditions', which combined the Queen's passions for strenuous exploration, privacy, and charades. On the first of these, flimsily disguised as 'Lord & Lady Churchill & Party', the Queen, the Prince, Lady Churchill and General Grey made a formidable excursion around the Cairngorms to Glen Feshie, travelling seventy miles on the first day, sleeping in a public inn, and collapsing with laughter when John Brown forgot about the disguise, and called the Queen 'Your Majesty'. Grant and Brown, the ghillies, were supposed to wait at table at the inn, in order to keep the identity of the party secret. But they were too 'bashful', which is possibly a tactful euphemism for too drunk.

On another, less successful, expedition the party arrived unannounced, incognito, and damp at the inn at Dalwhinnie, where the supper was 'only tea, two miserable starved Highland chickens with no potatoes, no pudding and no fun'.

In 1859, while the Queen was climbing on her favourite peak of Loch-na-Gar, Prince Albert presided over the meeting of the British Association in Aberdeen. He spent days preparing for the ordeal: ' I read thick volumes, write, perspire, and tear what I have written to shreds in sheer vexation.' His speech began: 'To me Science in its most general and comprehensive acceptation means the knowledge of what I know, the consciousness of human knowledge. Hence, to know is the object of all science.'

It went on and on in much the same ponderous way, but was voted a triumph by his audience of 2,500, who knew on which side their bread was buttered. Victoria purred:

At ten minutes past seven arrived my beloved Albert. All had gone off most admirably; he had seen many learned people; all were delighted with his speech; the reception most gratifying.

As a reward the British Association was received at Balmoral a week later. Busloads of 'philosophers and savants' were delivered at the castle, and entertained with throwing-the-hammer, tossing-the-caber, putting-the-stone, and other hearty Highland mysteries, in a distinctly bracing wind. The Queen noted with something approaching awe that 'four weighty omnibuses filled with the scientific men' drove off.

In 1861, at the end of the Balmoral holiday Albert recorded in his journal his last day's stalking: 'Go out shooting for the last time and shoot nothing.' That December he died at Windsor. And the annual visits to the Highlands for the future became bitter-sweet with memory and regret, as well as protracted for as long as five months in the year. A stone was put up to mark the place where Albert had shot his last stag. There was a granite pyramid to 'Albert the Great and Good, raised by his broken-hearted widow', and in the hall of the castle stood a life-sized marble statue of the Prince in kilt, ready for the heather with his gun and dog.

Into the vacuum left by Albert's death inperceptibly stepped the former ghillie, now John Brown Esquire, the Queen's confidential attendant with a salary of £400. Part of the attraction was that he was a link with the Prince Consort and the past; partly Victoria had always enjoyed the simplicity and informality of the Highlanders. The increasingly dictatorial Queen also may have found some safety and psychological satisfaction in allowing a servant to order her around, while she almost hysterically resisted efforts by her family and politicians to persuade her to do anything. The Queen said that she liked to have him around her because he was so unlike a servant, being 'so cheerful and attentive'. Others, especially the Prince of Wales and the household, found him less cheerful company. He once halted Gladstone when in full flow of addressing the Queen like a public meeting with the unanswerable phrase, 'You've said enough'. There were frequent and furious rows over the Balmoral ponies which Brown rode while the courtiers walked, over the shooting and fishing off which he tended to skim the cream for himself, leaving inferior sport for the Prince of Wales, and over the general liberties above his station which he took with everyone.

'What a coarse animal that Brown is,' growled a visiting Lord Chancellor, watching him and the Queen on the ball-room floor at Balmoral.

The scandal inevitably leaked out. *Punch* printed an imaginary 'Court Circular':

Balmoral, Tuesday.

Mr John Brown walked on the Slopes. He subsequently partook of a haggis. In the evening, Mr John Brown was pleased to listen to a bag-pipe.

Mr John Brown retired early.

Even more lurid rumours spread. As well as domineering the Queen, and acting as a kind of uncouth court jester in a kilt, it was whispered by the excitable that he was the Queen's lover, or even that he had married her morganatically. This was not only sensational, but also silly. There was neither evidence nor probability for such a story. Had there been anything immoral in the Brown affair, presumably Victoria would have kept Brown discreetly in the background. She did the exact opposite. A great many of the Queen's private writings make it quite clear that her relationship with John Brown, though certainly unusual, was entirely proper and Platonic.

In her last will, for example, after Brown's death, Victoria wrote that she died in peace,

earnestly trusting to be reunited to my beloved Husband, my dearest Mother, my loved Children and 3 dear sons-in-law – And all who have been very near & dear to me on earth. Also I hope to meet those who have so faithfully & so devotedly served me especially good John Brown and good Annie Macdonald who I trusted would help to lay my remains in my coffin & to see me placed next to my dearly loved Husband in the mausoleum at Frogmore.

Brown certainly gets on to this exclusive catalogue, but it is still by the servants' entrance, no place for a lover or a second husband.

Another extravagant and recurrent rumour is that Brown acted as a medium through whom the Queen made contact behind the veil and through the mists of spiritualism with the Prince Consort. The psychical evidence for this remarkable proposition is all late, inaccurate in detail and spelling, and demonstrably bogus. It seems to be based on two undeniable but unremarkable facts: the Queen was morbidly obsessed with her bereavement and with mortality generally; and she found John Brown a comfort and a bridge back to the past. Lytton Strachey takes it one step further, and says that she believed that the spirit of Albert was nearer when Brown was around.

The most convincing analysis of the enigma of John Brown was written on his death by Sir Henry Ponsonby, the Queen's private secretary, who knew Brown better than most, and had no cause to extenuate or set down anything in malice:

Wreathes from Princesses, Empresses & Ladies in Waiting are lying on Brown's grave. He was the only person who could fight and make the Queen do what she did not wish. He did not always succeed nor was his advice always the best. But I believe he was honest and with all his want of education – his roughness – his prejudices and other faults he was undoubtedly a most excellent servant to her.

The Queen was crushed by Brown's death from erysipelas. She wrote that it was like 'one of those shocks in '61', the year of the deaths of her husband and mother. The Court Circular was congested with half a column of eulogy: 'The melancholy event has caused the deepest regret to the Queen and to all members of the Royal Household.'

The Queen wrote to a grandson: 'I have lost my dearest best friend who no-one in this World can ever replace . . . never forget your poor sorrowing old Grandmama's best & truest friend . . .'

The Prime Minister paid public tribute to 'Mr J Brown'. The Queen's wreath was 'a tribute of loving, grateful and everlasting friendship and affection from his honest, best, and most faithful friend'. A bronze statue of Brown was commissioned from the sculptor Edgar Boehm for the grounds of Balmoral. Tennyson, by royal command, produced a remarkably uninspiring inscription for it:

> Friend more than servant, loyal, truthful, brave:
> Self less than duty even to the grave.

A granite seat was dedicated to Brown at Osborne, with more lines from the Poet Laureate. Replicas of the Boehm statue and cairns were dotted liberally around the royal residences and grounds. All these memorials were ruthlessly removed by Edward VII, who in no way shared his mother's enthusiasm for her old ghillie.

The Queen caused considerable consternation among her advisers some years later by proposing to publish another instalment of 'Leaves' from her *Journal of Our Life in the Highlands* which would be a memoir of John Brown. The hair of her courtiers stood on end at the prospect of such inflammatory and emotional fuel being poured on the embers of the old scandal. Eventually the intrepid Dean of Windsor, Randall Davidson, the future Archbishop of Canterbury, advised the authoress against publication. He was punished with a long and awful silence of deep displeasure lasting several weeks, during which he offered to resign. But at the end of it nothing more was heard of Volume Three. Disappointingly, the 'Leaves' about John Brown appear to have been destroyed.

Like Osborne, Balmoral became one of the issues in the 1870's when, because of the Queen's seclusion and refusal to participate in public life, there was serious radical agitation that she should abdicate in favour of her son; or even that she should be deposed and replaced by a republic. During the 'royalty crisis' Gladstone fought furious and unsuccessful battles with her and her doctors to prevent her burying herself away in Balmoral.

But the saddest Highland phenomenon of the second half of Victoria's reign was the growth of what has been called 'Balmorality'. Balmoral had started life as a private retreat from the formality of court, a place where 'all seemed to breathe freedom and peace, and to make one forget the world and its sad turmoils', a place of midnight bonfires and impromptu expeditions. As the Queen grew older and lonelier and crustier, the regime at Balmoral atrophied and ossified into cold stiffness and stuffiness, a life of tedium, monotony, pointless protocol, and sheer boredom. All initiative was spent. Nobody could go outside until the Queen herself had ventured out. Fires were forbidden by Victoria, who always revelled in the cold. As the Queen herself had written years before, there was 'no pudding and no fun'. Communication was by frequent memoranda and fatuous in its trivialities. For instance, a Minister in attendance at Balmoral was exercised to know whether he should wear knee-breeches for dinner on a Sunday evening. Ponsonby sent a note back:

Dear Harcourt,
    As no ladies will be present trousers will be worn.
                                    H.F.P.

Relatives dreaded an invitation to Balmoral, and the ordeal of meal-time conversation with the formidable old matriarch.

In November of 1900 the Queen left her dear paradise for the last time. 'It was wretchedly gloomy & dark,' she wrote in her journal. In spite of the aberration of Balmorality in her closing years, Victoria's love for the Scottish Highlands, and for Balmoral, and for the Highlanders was essentially true and joyful, and appears to have been inherited by her descendants for ever.

# XVII

# THE NEW PALACE

IN the same way that a bookcase reveals an alarming amount about the man who collected the books, buildings reflect the life-style and functions of the people who live in them. A man does not need to be a professional sociologist (if that phrase is not a contradiction) to draw some elementary and superficial deductions about the lives of the people who live in a fifth-storey tenement in the Gorbals, or in a mock-Tudor, pseudo-baronial 'mansion' in the stockbroker belt of Surrey.

This obvious probability is confirmed in fact, as far as the royal palaces of Britain are concerned, by their history. The palace mirrors the powers, the functions, and the life-style of the monarch who builds it or who lives in it. When the king is a savage, sabre-toothed war-lord, his palace is a fortress stronghold. When he is a Renaissance prince, with supreme dominion over all matters spiritual and temporal in his kingdom, his palace is the political hub of England, opulent, trend-setting, with rooms for summit meetings of politics and church, and for great state pageants. When he becomes a limited monarch under licence to Parliament, his palace becomes more intimate and nostalgically old-fashioned, as the full tide of national affairs ceases to flow through its galleries and halls. It is less likely to set fashions; more likely wistfully to preserve the glories of the past.

What happens in the second half of the twentieth century, and in the twenty-first century, when the monarch has given up almost all the last shreds of political power? What will the next royal palace look like? How will it reflect the remaining constitutional functions of the sovereign, according to Walter Bagehot in *The English Constitution*, which is still the best authority on these matters, 'the right to be consulted, the right to encourage, the right to warn'? (In fact the sovereign, when Bagehot wrote, held a more optimistic opinion of the extent of her rights, which she exercised vehemently and perhaps unconstitutionally on occasions.)

Some idea of the remaining royal functions may give a clue to what the next palace will look like. One residual political power of the crown is the right in certain circumstances to choose the Prime Minister. According to Bagehot these circumstances were either when no single party held a clear majority, or when the majority party had no clearly recognised leader. The second of these two situations is now unlikely to arise, since the Conservative party in 1965, after the chaos, skulduggery, and acrimony of the selection of the then Lord Home to succeed Mr Macmillan, adopted a method of electing their leaders. The Socialists have always elected their leader. But the first situation is still a practical possibility. At a time when no party had a clear majority, or at a time of great national crisis and confusion, the monarch has the constitutional right to send for somebody to form a coalition government. This emergency constitutional safety-net is a considerable national asset.

The first question that needs to be ruminated is whether there will be a next royal palace; whether the monarchy will survive to build a new residence when the present ones finally and inevitably become uninhabitable. The prospects for its survival look reasonably healthy today. Overt republican sentiment is confined to a tiny, raucous caucus of Back Bench left-wing Members of Parliament, and is far less formidable than the republican movement of the 1860s, which was led by such political heavyweights as Charles Bradlaugh, Joseph Chamberlain, John Bright, Sir Charles Dilke, and John Morley.

And apart from practical prospects, the philosophical argument for keeping the hereditary monarchy is convincing. It is madness to destroy something which has lasted so long, and has become a symbol of stability in a disintegrating world, unless it is quite evident that the alternative will work better. Most countries find they need a head of state above the scrummage of day-to-day partisan politics. If he is an elected president, there is rivalry, jealousy, intrigue, resentment by the losing side, occasional assassination. And the state seems quite often to end up with a compromise head, a safe old political war-horse put out to grass, who has lost all his fire and most of his ability (which was often not spectacular in the first place). One of the minor arguments for monarchy is that it opens the door to youth. A presidency is, almost by definition, a senile gerontocracy.

Dr Johnson put the argument against electing people to the top job with his customary gruff bark and lucidity; he was talking about electing Lord Mayors of London.

Johnson: 'So the City of London will appoint its mayors again by seniority.'

Boswell: 'But is not that taking a mere chance for having a good or a bad mayor?'

Johnson: 'Yes, sir; but the evil of competition is greater than that of the worst mayor that can come; besides, there is no more reason to suppose that the choice of a rabble will be right, than that chance will be right.'

Bagehot took a distinctly dim view of the calibre of king that the hereditary system can be expected to throw up:

A constitutional sovereign must in the common course of government be a man of but common ability. I am afraid, looking to the early acquired feebleness of hereditary dynasties, that we must expect him to be a man of inferior ability. Theory and experience both teach that the education of a prince can be but a poor education and that a royal family will generally have less ability than other families. What right then have we to expect the perpetual entail on any family of an exquisite discretion, which if it be not a sort of genius, is at least as rare as genius?

The successful education of the present Prince of Wales shows that Bagehot took an unduly pessimistic view of royal education. Prince Charles is the first member of the royal family close to the throne who has ever taken a normal university degree. For that matter, he is the first since James I, or perhaps George IV, who has looked capable of taking one. But in spite of his unnecessarily gloomy prediction of the sort of kings the hereditary system was likely to produce, Bagehot concluded that this was preferable to the mad scramble if the highest post in the state were thrown open to public competition:

This low sort of ambition and envy would be fearfully increased. Politics would offer a prize too dazzling for mankind; clever base people would strive for it and stupid base people would envy it.

Elections for king conjure up the horrid prospect of party monarchical broadcasts on all channels, manifestoes full of incredible promises, and, on the model of American Presidential campaigns, only the richest and most ambitious millionaires being able to afford to run for monarch. England's eleven-year experiment with republicanism between 1649 and 1660 was not an encouraging advertisement for the system, and, interestingly enough, reintroduced the hereditary principle for selecting the head of state even before the kings were restored.

The invaluable Bagehot has another perceptive observation, which indicates that monarchy is likely to survive:

Royalty is a government in which the attention of the nation is concentrated on one person doing interesting actions. A Republic is a government in which that attention is divided between many, who are all doing uninteresting actions. Accordingly, so long as the human heart is strong and the human reason weak, Royalty will be strong because it appeals to diffused feeling, and Republics weak because they appeal to the understanding.

There seems a good chance then that the monarchy is going to survive, as well as good reason that it should survive. But it is going to be different. The Duke of Edinburgh himself has proclaimed the platitude: 'To survive the monarchy has to change.'

It can be argued that a significant change actually took place in the late 1960s, when the Palace plunged for the first time into modern public relations and promotion methods, with the Duke of Edinburgh as chief spokesman for the new image, and a new press officer organising the new product in the background. Television cameras were allowed to pry for the first time into the private life of the monarch. The Queen was shown to millions around the world cooking hamburgers for a picnic, buying ice-cream in a shop for her children, and twittering informally and indiscreetly to her family before a state reception. The Duke of Edinburgh and the Prince of Wales turned up persistently on radio and television to answer personal and probing questions of an intimacy which would have been unthinkable even ten years before.

The object of the campaign seems to be to demonstrate that the royal family are real people like everybody else, earning their keep, doing an important but not particularly abnormal job of public relations and high-level diplomacy for Britain. It is as if they have finally decided to clear their minds of the cant about the divine right and political power of kings, which was in fact killed in 1689, but lingered on, part myth, part remarkably active corpse, for some centuries.

As usual Dr Johnson recognised the death of monarchical power more clearly and sooner than most. General James Oglethorpe was grumbling about the corruption, credibility gap, and lack of public confidence in modern politicians.

Johnson: 'Sir, the want of inherent right in the King occasions all this disturbance. What we did at the Revolution was necessary: but it broke our constitution.'
Oglethorpe: 'My father did not think it necessary.'

In the nineteenth century when kings still clung to the myth and relics of political power, it was possible to argue that the modern king had become a vermiform appendix: useless when quiet; when obtrusive, in danger of removal. The new image of the monarch as the nation's chief symbol and public relations officer means that one of the functions of the royal family is to be obtrusive in a nice way, to bang the drum, and wave the flag, and boost exports for Britain. Appendectomy is no longer a fashionable operation, except in acute crisis. A modern king who is obtrusive in this way at British trade weeks and press receptions is in no serious danger of removal. He is in fact performing a more definite function than he has for years.

The question is, then, how will any palace of the future reflect these changing functions of the monarch. And any answer is a guess in the dark as black as the inside of a wolf. It might be expected to be more utilitarian and purposive than previous palaces, equipped with carefully planned office floors, broadcasting studios, a computer, closed circuit television, and the other *bric-à-brac* of modern technology. Time-and-motion study and management consultants may advise on its design. Presumably its exterior will be suitably stark and contemporary; ostentatious extravagance in building has ceased to be a royal function. If it follows the present pattern of building in overcrowded central London, it will be the first vertical palace, after two thousand years of horizontal palaces. There are no Nashes or Wrens or Inigo Joneses around these days to build it, so there is an ugly possibility that it may be designed and erected by modern 'developers', who were described with more truth than charity by a recent President of the Royal Academy: 'Men with insect minds on the pavement levels, and the ambitions of giants. They have strip-teased the buildings. Nothing is left – not even the ear-rings.' This may all sound fairly uninviting, but it seems a likely result of the decision to make the monarchy up-to-date, 'relevant', and practical.

One recurrent wild goose which is periodically hunted by newspapers, particularly in the dead dog days when there is an acute drought of news, is the story that the Queen is not happy in Buckingham Palace, and is spending more and more time at Windsor. A favourite explanation in Fleet Street for this myth is that Buckingham Palace is not liked because it has lost its privacy, since the Hilton Hotel and the other skyscrapers sprouting all round have impended over the Palace gardens. It is a story which the Palace is always brisk to deny. The memory of how 'the Widow at Windsor' became so unpopular that she almost lost her throne, because she retired from London and her state duties, lingers uncomfortably in court folk-memory. There is, in fact, no evidence for the story. The Queen's routine is regular, and the general pattern has not changed for years. She spends week-days at Buckingham Palace; week-ends at

Windsor; the Christmas holidays at Sandringham; a month at Windsor at Easter; and the long late summer holidays at Balmoral.

Windsor may be the first royal residence to need a major overhaul. But if and when a new palace has to be built, it looks as if it must be in London. And if in London, since space in the centre of the great wen is so scarce and so expensive, it must surely be either on the present site of or in the grounds of Buckingham Palace.

One thing that can safely be predicted about the next royal palace is that there will be noisy grumbles about its extravagance from the Left. There is nothing very new about that. Even under Henry VIII bolder spirits like Sir Thomas Cromwell complained about the expense of the royal building operations. And for the past 200 years no palace has been built or restored without hubbub of protest from devout republicans and professional protesters. A Prime Minister told the Prince Regent that his architectural adventures were endangering the existence of the government. Victoria's very necessary refurbishing at Buckingham Palace excited decidedly satirical comment. Any palace of the future can expect similar treatment. A sample of the hostility any royal building arouses was given when a dreadfully dilapidated wing of Kensington Palace was restored for Princess Margaret and her husband. Mr William Hamilton, Member of Parliament for West Fife, and one of the most dogged critics of royalty, said:

In view of the fact that thousands of families in London and elsewhere are homeless, such expenditure is socially squalid, wholly indefensible, and shows the most reprehensible insensitivity on the part of the royal recipients.

In fact £120,000 was spent on the restoration, of which £65,000 came from the Ministry of Public Building and Works. The Ministry's contribution was spent on repairing the decaying exterior and structure of a building that is a national ornament and asset.

A periodic day-dream of writers about royalty is that the next royal palace will be built somewhere in the Commonwealth outside Britain. With Commonwealth ties loosening annually, with Australia and New Zealand looking more and more towards the United States for defence and trade, with Canada torn with doubts about her identity, and with Britain committed by all main political parties to joining the European Common Market, this day-dream appears increasingly insubstantial. Learned Arundel Herald Extraordinary, Mr Dermot Morrah, recently put forward a slightly variant proposition, that the Queen and the Duke of Edinburgh should go and live for perhaps a year in one of the Dominions, while the Prince of Wales stayed at home and 'tried his hand' at reigning. Though highly original, in the present state of the Commonwealth this suggestion sounds like wishful thinking.

In any case history suggests that there is little point in predicting the building of future royal palaces. It is an incalculable business, that goes by fits and starts. The most far-sighted political expert at the end of the Wars of the Roses might well have wondered if a new royal palace would ever be built. He could not seriously have predicted the tremendous boom in palace-building under the Tudors. At irregular intervals a great palace-builder king, a Richard II, a Henry VIII, a William III, a George IV, emerges; sometimes because his present residences are obsolete; sometimes because he wants to leave a physical symbol of a new dynasty; sometimes just because he has a highly developed itch to build. There seems no strong reason why it should not happen again in the future.

# BIBLIOGRAPHY

## [GENERAL]

*The Oxford History of England.* Ed. Sir George Clark.
*The Dictionary of National Biography.*
L.C.C. *Survey of London.*
CHURCHILL, W. S. *A History of the English-Speaking Peoples.*
GREEN, J. R. *A Short History of the English People.* Everyman's Library, 1915.
MACAULAY, LORD. *The History of England,* 1863.

ANGLO-SAXON CHRONICLE. Everyman's Library, translated by James
    Ingram.
D'ARBLAY. *Diary and Letters of Madame D'Arblay.* Ed. Charlotte Barrett,
    1904.
BAGEHOT, WALTER. *The English Constitution,* 1963.
BOSWELL, JAMES. *The Journal of a Tour to the Hebrides with Samuel
    Johnson, LL.D.* Ed. J. Werner, 1956.
BOSWELL, JAMES. *The Life of Samuel Johnson, LL.D.* Everyman's Library,
    1920.
BRYANT, ARTHUR. *The Age of Elegance,* 1950.
BRYANT, ARTHUR. *Samuel Pepys: The Man in the Making,* 1933.
BRYANT, ARTHUR. *Samuel Pepys: The Years of Peril,* 1935.
BURNET, BISHOP GILBERT. *History of my own Time.* Ed. Osmond Airy,
    1897.
CAVENDISH, GEORGE. *The Life of Cardinal Wolsey,* 1905.
CLARENDON, EARL OF. *The History of the Rebellion and Civil Wars in
    England,* 1888.
COLLINGWOOD, R. G. *The Archaeology of Roman Britain,* 1930.
COULTON, G. G. *Medieval Panorama,* 1938.
COULTON, G. G. *Social Life in Britain from the Conquest to the Reformation,*
    1938.
CREEVEY, T. *Creevey.* Ed. John Gore, 1948.

CROKER, J. W. *The Croker Papers.* Ed. Louise J. Jennings, 1885.

DEFOE, DANIEL. *A Tour thro' the whole Island of Great Britain 1724-26.* Intro. by G. D. H. Cole, 1927.

EVELYN, JOHN. *The Diary of John Evelyn.* Everyman's Library, 1945.

FREEMAN, E. A. *The History of the Norman Conquest of England,* 1876.

FROISSART, JEAN. *Chroniques,* 1863.

GREVILLE, CHARLES. *The Greville Memoirs.* Ed. Lytton Strachey and Roger Fulford, 1938.

HALL, HUBERT. *Court Life under the Plantagenets,* 1890.

HENTZNER, PAUL. *A Journey into England in the Year 1598,* 1759.

HIBBERT, CHRISTOPHER. *The Court at Windsor,* 1964.

HOLINSHED, RAPHAEL. *The Chronicles of England, Scotland and Ireland,* 1577.

HOME, GORDON. *Roman London,* 1926.

JESSE, J. H. *Memoirs of the Court of England during the Reign of the Stuarts,* 1901.

JESSE, J. H. *Continuation of Memoirs of the Court of England from the Revolution in 1688 to the Death of George II,* 1901.

JESSE, J. H. *Literary and Historical Memorials of London,* 1901.

KLARWILL, V. VON. *Queen Elizabeth and Some Foreigners,* 1928.

LETHABY, W. R. *London Before the Conquest,* 1902.

MACHIAVELLI. *The Works of the Famous Nicholas Machiavel, Citizen and Secretary of Florence.* Published London, 1720.

MACKENZIE, COMPTON. *Prince Charlie,* 1932.

MALLET, MARIE. *Life with Queen Victoria: Marie Mallet's letters from Court.* Ed. Victor Mallet, 1968.

MALORY, SIR THOMAS. *Le Morte D'Arthur.* Everyman's Library, 1906.

MARIE LOUISE, PRINCESS. *My Memories of Six Reigns,* Penguin Books, 1959.

MEAD, W. E. *The English Medieval Feast,* 1967.

MITCHELL, R. J., and LEYS, M. D. R. *A History of London Life,* 1958.

MURRAY-BROWN, JEREMY [Ed.]. *The Monarchy and Its Future,* 1969.

NEWTON, DOUGLAS. *London West of the Bars,* 1951.

OMAN, CHARLES. *Castles,* 1926.

PEPYS, SAMUEL. *The Diary of Samuel Pepys.* Ed. H. B. Wheatley, 1893.

PETRIE, SIR CHARLES. *The Stuarts,* 1958.

PONSONBY, ARTHUR. *Henry Ponsonby: His Life from His Letters,* 1942.

POPE, ALEXANDER. *Collected Poems.* Everyman's Library, 1924.

POWELL, J. ENOCH, and WALLIS, KEITH. *The House of Lords in the Middle Ages,* 1968.

ROBSON-SCOTT, W. D. *German Travellers in England,* 1953.

RYE, W. B. *England as seen by Foreigners,* 1865.

STOW, JOHN. *Survey of London.* Ed. C. L. Kingsford, 1908.

TACITUS, C. *Agricola.* Ed. H. Furneaux and J. G. C. Anderson, 1922.

TACITUS, C. *The Annals of Tacitus.* Ed. H. Furneaux, 1896.

TACITUS, C. *Historiarum Libri.* Oxford University Press.

THACKERAY, W. M. *The Four Georges,* 1861.

TREVELYAN, G. M. *The English Revolution 1688–1689,* 1938.

WINDSOR, DUCHESS OF. *The Heart has its Reasons,* 1956.

WINDSOR, DUKE OF. *A King's Story: The Memoirs of H.R.H. The Duke of Windsor,* 1951.

# [THE PALACES]

DOUGLAS-IRVINE, HELEN. *Royal Palaces of Scotland,* 1911.

FLETCHER, B. *Royal Homes near London,* 1930.

RAIT, R. S. [Ed.]. *Royal Palaces of England,* 1911.

PYNE, W. H. *The History of the Royal Residences of Windsor Castle, St James's Palace, Carlton House, Kensington Palace, Hampton Court, Buckingham House and Frogmore,* 1829.

WILLIAMS, NEVILLE. *The Royal Residences of Great Britain,* 1960.

Many of the royal palaces have official guide-books produced for the Ministry of Public Building and Works.

Fishbourne:

CUNLIFFE, PROFESSOR B. *Fishbourne: The Roman Palace and its History,* 1968.

Camelot:

ASHE, GEOFFREY [Ed.]. *The Quest for Arthur's Britain,* 1969.

BRUCE, J. D. *The Evolution of Arthurian Romance,* 1923–4.

Winchester:

LLOYD WOODLEY, W. *Story of Winchester,* 1932.

VESEY-FITZGERALD, BRIAN. *Winchester,* 1953.

W.C.A.S. *Winchester: Its History, Buildings and People,* 1921.

Caernarvon:

H.M.S.O. *Caernarvon Castle,* 1969.

Tower of London:

BAYLEY, J. *The History and Antiquities of the Tower of London*, 1821–5.

BELL, W. G. *The Tower of London*, 1921.

BRITTON, J., and BRAYLEY, E. W. *Memoirs of the Tower of London*, 1830.

GOWER, LORD RONALD SUTHERLAND. *The Tower of London*, 1901–2.

Westminster Palace:

BESANT, SIR WALTER. *Westminster*, 1895.

BRAYLEY, E. W., and BRITTON, J. *The Ancient Palace of Westminster*, 1836.

FELL, SIR BRYAN. *The Houses of Parliament*, 1950.

SAUNDERS, HILARY ST G. *Westminster Hall*, 1951.

Woodstock:

BALLARD, A. *Chronicles of Woodstock*, 1896.

MARSHALL, EDWARD. *The Early History of Woodstock Manor and its Environs*, 1875.

MEADE FALKNER, J. *A History of Oxfordshire*, 1899.

HELTZEL, V. B. *Fair Rosamond*, 1947.

Windsor:

ASHMOLE, ELIAS. *The Institution, Laws and Ceremonies of the Most Noble Order of the Garter*, 1672.

BOLITHO, HECTOR. *The Romance of Windsor Castle*, 1947.

HEDLEY, OLWEN. *Windsor Castle*, 1967.

HOPE, W. H. ST J. *Windsor Castle, an Architectural History*, 1913.

MORSHEAD, SIR OWEN. *Windsor Castle*, 1957.

POTE, JOSEPH. *The History and Antiquities of Windsor Castle*, 1749.

TIGHE, R. R., and DAVIS, J. E. *Annals of Windsor*, 1858.

Richmond:

CHANCELLOR, E. BERESFORD. *Historical Richmond*, 1885.

Greenwich:

CHETTLE, G. H. *The Queen's House, Greenwich*, 1937.

Whitehall:

CHARLTON, JOHN. *The Banqueting House*, 1964.

DUGDALE, G. S. *Whitehall Through the Centuries*, 1950.

LOFTIE, W. J. *Whitehall*, 1895.

WHITAKER-WILSON, C. *Whitehall Palace*, 1934.

Nonsuch:
DENT, J. *The Quest for Nonsuch,* 1962.

Hampton Court:
CHETTLE, G. H. *Hampton Court Palace,* 1954.
LAW, ERNEST. *The History of Hampton Court Palace,* 1885–91.
LINDSAY, P. *Hampton Court: a History,* 1948.
YATES, EDWARD. *Hampton Court,* 1935.

St James's:
GRAEME, BRUCE. *The Story of St James's Palace,* 1929.
SHEPPARD, EDGAR. *Memorials of St James's Palace,* 1894.

Buckingham Palace:
GRAEME, BRUCE. *The Story of Buckingham Palace,* 1928.
GORING, O. G. *From Goring House to Buckingham Palace,* 1937.
MACKENZIE, COMPTON. *The Queen's House,* 1952.
SMITH, H. CLIFFORD. *Buckingham Palace,* 1931.

Kensington:
FAULKNER, THOMAS. *History and Antiquities of Kensington,* 1820.
HUDSON, DEREK. *Kensington Palace,* 1968.
LAW, ERNEST. *Kensington Palace: The Birthplace of the Queen,* 1899.

Brighton Pavilion:
BISHOP, J. G. *The Brighton Pavilion and Its Royal Associations,* 1903.
MUSGRAVE, CLIFFORD. *Royal Pavilion,* 1959.
ROBERTS, H. D. *The Royal Pavilion Brighton,* 1939.

Balmoral:
BROWN, IVOR. *Balmoral, the History of a Home,* 1955.

# [KINGS, QUEENS, AND THE LORD PROTECTOR]

Alfred:
ASSER. *Asser's Life of King Alfred.* Ed. W. H. Stevenson, 1904.
LEES, BEATRICE. *Alfred the Great.* 1919.

Henry II:
APPLEBY, J. T. *Henry II,* 1962.
EYTON, R. W. *Court, Household and Itinerary of Henry II,* 1878.
KELLY, AMY. *Eleanor of Aquitaine and the Four Kings,* 1952.

Richard II:

MATHEW, GERVASE. *The Court of Richard II*, 1968.

Henry IV:

DAVIES, J. D. GRIFFITH. *King Henry IV*, 1935.

Richard III:

LINDSAY, PHILIP. *King Richard III*, 1933.

Henry VIII:

POLLARD, A. F. *Henry VIII*, 1905.
SCARISBRICK, J. J. *Henry VIII*, 1968.

Mary Tudor:

PRESCOTT, H. F. M. *Mary Tudor*, 1953.

Elizabeth I:

ANTHONY, KATHARINE. *Queen Elizabeth*, 1929.
BIRCH, THOMAS. *Memoirs of the Reign of Queen Elizabeth*, 1754.
DUNLOP, IAN. *Palaces and Progresses of Elizabeth I*, 1962.
HANDOVER, P. M. *The Second Cecil*, 1959.
NICHOLS, J. *Progresses and Public Processions of Queen Elizabeth*, 1823.
NEALE, J. E. *Queen Elizabeth I*, 1934.
ROWSE, A. L. *The England of Elizabeth*, 1950.
STRACHEY, LYTTON. *Elizabeth and Essex*, 1928.
STRICKLAND, AGNES. *The Life of Queen Elizabeth*, 1848.

Mary Queen of Scots:

BOWEN, MARJORIE. *Mary Queen of Scots*. 1934.
LINKLATER, ERIC. *Mary Queen of Scots*, 1933.
MACCUNN, FLORENCE A. *Mary Stuart*, 1905.

James I:

ASHTON, ROBERT [Ed.]. *James I By His Contemporaries*, 1969.
MCELWEE, WILLIAM. *The Wisest Fool in Christendom*, 1958.
STEEHOLM, C. and H. *James I of England*, 1938.

Charles I:

BELLOC, HILAIRE. *Charles I*, 1933.
HIGHAM, F. M. G. *Charles I*, 1932.
PETRIE, SIR CHARLES [Ed.]. *The Letters of King Charles I*, 1935.

Oliver Cromwell:
BUCHAN, JOHN. *Oliver Cromwell*, 1934.
GARDINER, S. R. *Oliver Cromwell*, 1901.

Charles II:
AIRY, OSMOND. *Charles II*, 1904.
BRYANT, ARTHUR. *King Charles II*, 1931.
CRAWFORD, RAYMOND. *The Last Days of Charles II*, 1909.
LEE, MAURICE. *The Cabal*, 1965.

James II:
HIGHAM, F. M. G. *King James The Second*, 1934.

William and Mary:
OGG, DAVID. *William III*, 1956.

Anne:
CONNELL, NEVILLE. *Anne: The Last Stuart Monarch*, 1937.
HOPKINSON, M. R. *Anne of England*, 1934.
TREVELYAN, G. M. *England Under Queen Anne*, 1934.

George II:
HERVEY, LORD. *Some Materials for the Memoirs of the Reign of George II.*
    Ed. Romney Sedgwick, 1931.
WILKINS, W. H. *Caroline the Illustrious*, 1901.

George III:
DAVIES, J. D. GRIFFITH. *George the Third*, 1936.
HUISH, ROBERT. *Memoirs of George III*, 1821.
VULLIAMY, C. E. *Royal George*, 1937.
WALPOLE, HORACE. *Memoirs of the Reign of King George the Third*, 1894.
WITHERS, PHILIP. *History of the Royal Malady: Variety of Entertaining
    Anecdotes. By a Page of the Presence*, 1789.

George IV:
FULFORD, ROGER. *George the Fourth*, 1935.
LESLIE, SIR SHANE. *George IV*, 1926.
WILKINS, W. H. *Mrs Fitzherbert and George IV*, 1905.

William IV:
ALLEN, W. GORE. *King William IV*, 1960.
HOPKIRK, MARY. *Queen Adelaide*, 1950.

Victoria:

BOLITHO, HECTOR. *Albert the Good*, 1932.

CHANCELLOR, F. B. *Prince Consort*, 1931.

CORTI, E. C. C. *The English Empress*, 1957.

DUFF, DAVID [Ed.]. *Victoria in the Highlands*, 1969.

FULFORD, ROGER. *Queen Victoria*, 1951.

FULFORD, ROGER. *The Prince Consort*, 1949.

JAGOW, DR KURT [Ed.]. *Letters of the Prince Consort*. 1938.

LONGFORD, ELIZABETH. *Victoria R. I.*, 1964.

MARTIN, SIR THEODORE. *The Life of the Prince Consort*, 1875-80.

STRACHEY, LYTTON. *Queen Victoria*, 1921.

VICTORIA, QUEEN. *The Letters of Queen Victoria, A Selection from Her Majesty's Correspondence*. Published by John Murray, 1926, 1930.

# INDEX

Abraham, 241
Addison, Joseph, 196
Adelaide, Queen of William IV, 75, 235–6
Alais, Capet, Princess of France, 83
Albemarle, Van Keppel, Earl of, 195
Albert, of Saxe-Coburg, Prince Consort, 75;
  proposed to, 216; wedding, 162; honey-
  moon, 217; reorganises Buckingham
  Palace, 218–19; builds Osborne, 237–41;
  at Balmoral, 245–50; death, 77–8
Alençon, Duke of, 93, 111–12
Alexander, King of Scotland, 47
Alexander I, Tsar of Russia, 203
Alfred, King, 23, 29, 97
Allt-na-Giubhsaich (The Hut), 248
Alnoth, 44
Ambrose, 45
Anglesey, 25
Anglo-Saxon Chronicle, 5, 23, 24, 29, 42, 43,
  56–7
Anjou, 5
Anne, Queen, 86, 151, 209; at Windsor,
  69–70; touches for King's Evil, 125; at
  Hampton Court, 140–1; at St James's,
  151–4; at Kensington, 195–8
Anne, of Bohemia, Queen of Richard II, 90
Anne, of Cleves, Queen of Henry VIII, 92,
  100
Anne, of Denmark, Queen of James I, 102,
  113, 188
Arlington, Henry Bennet, Earl of, 209
Armada, 146
Arms, College of, 12
Arthur, King, 18–22, 60
Asser, 23
Astolat, Lady of, 21
Atrebates, tribe, 17
Aubrey, John, 15
Audley End, 13
Augusta, Princess of Cambridge, 217
Augustus, Emperor, 1, 17
Austen, Jane, 222
Avalon, Isle of, 19
Aylmer, Bishop of London, 185
Azioli, 225

Bacon, Sir Francis, 90, 145

Badon, battle of, 18
Bagehot, Walter, 195, 254–7
Bagshot, 55, 57, 62
Balmoral, 244–53; 4, 7, 10, 237, 239, 259
Bamburgh Castle, 13
Bassompierre, Marquis de, 136
Bayeux Tapestry, 42
Beatrice, Princess, 244
Becket, Thomas, 31, 44–5, 81
Bedchamber Plot, 77, 216
Bedingfield, Sir Henry, 85
Belgrade, Count of, 107
Belinus, King(?), 29
Bellin, Nicholas, 178
Benson, William, 198
Bentinck, William, Duke of Portland, 195
Bermondsey Palace, 44
Bessborough, Lady, 228–9
Bible, The Authorised Version, 136
Black Prince, Edward, son of Edward III,
  birth, 87; at Tower of London, 34; death,
  89
Blair Atholl, 245
Blenheim, battle of, 86
Blenheim Palace, 86, 154
Blois, Peter of, 3, 6, 57–8
Bloomfield, George IV's secretary, 225
Blore, Edward, 214
Boehm, Edgar, 252
Bohun, Edmund, 93
Boleyn, Anne, 105; at Greenwich, 99–100; at
  Whitehall, 108; at Hampton Court, 131;
  at St James's, 145
Boswell, James, 256
Bothwell, James Hepburn, Earl of, 171
Boudicca, Queen, 29
Bradlaugh, Charles, 255
Bradshawe, John, 118
Brantôme, Abbé de, 166
Braose, Maud de, 58
Breadalbane, Marquis of, 244
Bright, John, 255
Brighton Pavilion, 221–36; 8, 11, 213, 218,
  237
British Association, 249
Brown, Hugh, 242
Brown, John, 76, 241–3, 249, 250–2

Bruce, David, King of Scotland, 33
Brummell, Beau, 224
Buckingham, Edward, Duke of, 64
Buckingham, John Sheffield, Duke of, 209
Buckingham Palace, 208–20; 4, 9, 10, 11, 104, 161, 206–7, 236, 237, 239, 258–9
Burghley, Lord, see Cecil, William
Burnet, Bishop, 140
Burney, Fanny (Mme D'Arblay), at Windsor, 71–2, 211
Butler, Elizabeth, 199
Byron, Lord George, 175, 222, 231

Cadwallader, 90
Caerleon-upon-Usk, 21
Caernarvon Castle, 25–7
Cambridge, Duchess of, 247
Camden, William, 181
Camelford, 21
Camelot, 18–22
Campbell, Colin, 116
Campeggio, Cardinal, 99
Canongate, 164
Canute, King, 41
Carême, George IV's chef, 233–4
Carey, Sir Robert, 94
Carey, William, Lord Hunsdon, 136
Carlisle, 21
Carlton House, 11, 213, 223, 226–7, 229
Carisbrooke Castle, 137
*Carmarthen, Black Book of,* 22
Caroline, Queen of George II, at Hampton Court, 141–2; at St James's, 156–8; at Kensington, 200–2; death, 158
Caroline, Princess of Brunswick, wife of George IV, wedding, 73, 161; at Kensington, 202–3; separation, 226
Casket Letters, 171
Castlemaine, Countess of, see Villiers, Barbara
Catherine of Braganza, Queen of Charles II, 124, 126, 138
Cavendish, George, 105–6, 130
Caxton, William, 21
Cecil, Sir Robert, 86, 95, 186–8
Cecil, William, first Lord Burghley, 7
Chamberlain, Joseph, 255
Chambord, Château de, 177
Charing Cross, 107, 108, 117, 120
Charlemagne, 18, 22
Charles I, King, 96, 102, 201, 210; at Whitehall, 116–20; Banqueting House, 116; at Hampton Court, 138–9; at St James's, 147–50; Nonsuch, 188; trial in Westminster Hall, 52; execution, 118–20; burial at Windsor, 67–8
Charles II, King, 13, 24, 38, 40, 53, 103, 196, 209, 222; rebuilds Windsor, 68–9; at Whitehall, 122–7; at Hampton Court, 138–9; at St James's 150–1; rebuilds Holyroodhouse, 171–2; Nonsuch, 189; death, 126–7
Charles, Archduke, 101

Charles Edward, the Young Pretender, 125, 173–4
Charles, Prince of Wales, 256–7, 259–60
Charlotte, Princess, daughter of George IV, 204, 226
Charlotte Sophia of Mecklenburg-Strelitz, Queen of George III, 9, 55–6, 71–2; at St James's, 160–1; at Buckingham Palace, 210–11, 220
Chastelard, Pierre de, 169
Chaucer, Geoffrey, 3, 62–3; *Book of the Duchesse,* 50; *Legend of Good Women,* 89
Chiffinch, William, 124, 126
Chrétien de Troyes, 21
Cibber, Colley, 141
Civil War, 67, 86, 96, 103, 117–20, 136–7, 149–50, 172, 188
Clarence, George, Duke of, 37
Clarence House, 162
Clark, Sir James, 238, 245
Clarendon, hunting-lodge, 8, 44
Clarendon, Lord, 247
Clifford, Rosamond, legend of Fair Rosamond, 79–84, 87
Clifford, Walter de, 81
Cliveden, 7
Clovis, King of the Franks, 125
Cobbett, William, 231
Cockpit, The, 107, 110
Codington, Richard, 178
Cogidubnus, King, 17
Colchester, 21, 30
Connaught, Prince Arthur, Duke of, 241, 244
Conroy, Sir John, 77, 204–6, 237
Constantine, Emperor, 26
*Constitutio Domus Regis,* 2–3
Conyngham, Lady, 107, 110
Coronations, 14, 28, 34, 36, 40, 47, 53, 97, 99, 160
Corregio, 194
Cranmer, Thomas, Archbishop of Canterbury, 109, 131
Crécy, battle of, 60
Creevey, Thomas, 215
Crimea, 219, 247
Croker, J. W., 230, 232–3
Cromwell, Elizabeth, 120
Cromwell, Frances, 121
Cromwell, Oliver, 32, 52–3, 125, 150, 172; at Whitehall, 120–2; at Hampton Court, 137–8; death, 121
Cromwell, Thomas, 100, 131, 259
Crusaders, 31, 59
Cubbie Roo, 25
Cubitt, Thomas, 238
Culpeper, Thomas, 131
Cumberland, Duchess of, 225–6
Cumberland, Duke of, 174, 201, 222
Curtis, Sir William, 174

Darnley, Henry, husband of Mary Stuart, 169–71

Dash, Victoria's spaniel, 215
David, King of Scotland, 57, 164
Davidson, Randall, Archbishop of Canterbury, 252
Death-beds, Richard II, 36; Edward the Confessor, 42; John, 59; Albert, Prince Consort, 77; Edward III, 89; Henry VII, 91; Elizabeth I, 94–6; Henry VIII, 108–9; Charles I, 118–20; Cromwell, 121–2; Charles II, 126–7; Mary Tudor, 146; Mary II, 194; William III, 194–5; Prince George of Denmark, 197; Queen Anne, 198; Queen Victoria, 244
Dee, John 85
Defoe, Daniel, 140, 156
Deloraine, Lady, 201
Denny, Sir Anthony, 109
Dettingen, battle of, 202
Devereux, Robert, Earl of Essex, 95, 185–8
Dickens, Charles, 219
Dighton, John, 38
Dilke, Sir Charles, 255
Disraeli, Benjamin, 242
Domesday Book, 24, 56, 80
Dogs, 17, 46, 66, 123, 125–6, 129, 215, 244
Douglas-Home, Sir Alec, 255
Dover, 9, 21
Druids, 14
Dryden, John, 209
Dudley, Robert, Earl of Leicester, 7, 101, 109, 133–4
Dunbar, William, 3

Edgehill, battle of, 67
Edinburgh, 164–75, 21
Edinburgh, Prince Philip, Duke of, 220, 257, 259–60
Edward, the Confessor, at Westminster, 42, 49; 125
Edward I, King, 11; builds Caernarvon, 25–6; at Tower, 33; at Westminster, 44, 47–8; at Windsor, 59–60; at Richmond, 89
Edward II, King at Caernarvon, 26; at Westminster, 48
Edward III, King, 22; at Tower, 33; at Westminster, 48; at Windsor, 60–2; at Woodstock, 84; death at Richmond, 89
Edward IV, King, 36, 63
Edward V, King, 38
Edward VI, King, birth at Hampton Court, 131; at Windsor, 55
Edward VII, King, 4, 77, 208, 241, 244, 250, 252
Edward VIII, Duke of Windsor, 162–3; abdication, 78
Egbert, King, 22
Eleanor of Aquitaine, Queen of Henry II, 26, 45; and Rosamond, 81–4
Elizabeth I, Queen, 5, 7, 10, 11, 52, 108, 137; birth, 99; at Tower, 39; at Windsor, 65–6; at Woodstock, 84–5; at Richmond, 93–6; at Greenwich, 100–2; at Whitehall,
109–13; at Hampton Court, 133–6; at St James's, 146; at Nonsuch, 180–8
Elizabeth II, Queen, 7, 257–60
Elizabeth Woodville, Queen of Edward IV, 37
Elizabeth of York, Queen of Henry Tudor, 97, 108
Elizabeth, Princess, daughter of Charles I, 118
Eltham Ordinances, 64–5, 145, 153
Eltham Palace, 11
Engelard, de Cygony, 58–9
Enriquez, Pedro, 93
Ernest, King of Hanover, 217
Errol, Lady Leila, 241
Esher Palace, 106
Ethandune, battle of, 23
Eton College, 63, 144
Eugene, Prince of Savoy, 152
Evelyn, John, 68–9, 121, 122, 128, 191; scrofula, 125; Charles II's death, 126–7; at Hampton Court, 138; at St James's, 151; at Nonsuch, 189; at Kensington, 192, 194; at Mulberry Garden, 208
Examiner, The, 221
Excalibur, 20

Fabyan, Robert, 37–8
Fergus, King of Scotland, 172
Fermor, Arabella, 141
Field of Cloth of Gold, 177
Fiennes, Celia, 70
Fishbourne, Roman palace, 15–18
Fitzalan, Henry Earl of Arundel, 179–81
Fitzherbert, Maria, 73, 161, 235; at Brighton, 223–6; discarded, 229
Fitz-Stephen, William, 30, 44
Flagellum, 137–8
Fleet Street, 78, 258
Flodden, battle of, 165
Fontainebleau, 138, 177
Food in palaces, 6, 46, 47, 52, 53, 58, 60, 64, 68, 116–17, 233–4
Fontenoy, M. de, 147
Fordun, John, 48
Forest, Miles, 38
Foulques the Black, Count of Anjou, 81
Fox, Charles James, 224
Fox, George, 138
Frampton, Mary, 235
Francis I, King of France, 99, 177
Francis, Philip, 225
Frederick, Emperor, 32
Frederick, 'Fitz', Prince of Wales, 142, 157–8, 159
Frederick William, Prince of Prussia, 248
Freeman, Mrs, see Sarah Churchill
Frogmore, 251
Froissart, Jean, 3, 21, 33, 34–6, 48, 60–1

Garter, Order of the, 55, 68, 118, 199, 239; foundation of, 60–4
Gawaine, 19, 21

Geddington, hunting-lodge, 44
Geoffrey of Monmouth, 18–19, 29
George I, King, at Windsor, 70; at Hampton Court, 141–2; at St James's, 154–7; at Kensington, 198–200
George II, King, 210; at Windsor, 70; at Hampton Court, 141–2; at St James's, 155–60; at Kensington, 200–2
George III, King, 9, 203, 218, 220, 223, 226; at Windsor, 70–3; builds Queen's Lodge, 71; insanity, 72; at Hampton Court, 143; at St James's 160–1; at Buckingham Palace, 210–13
George IV, King, 11, 53, 205, 256, 259–60; at Windsor, 73–4; wedding, 161, 162; honeymoon, 73; rebuilds Windsor, 74; Edinburgh visit, 174; at Victoria's christening, 203–4; at Buckingham Palace, 213–14; at Brighton, 221, 235; marriage, 226; relations with Mrs Fitzherbert, 223–6; death, 74.
George VI, 162
George of Denmark, husband of Queen Anne, 152, 153, 196–7
Gerard, Sir Thomas, 187
Gering, Giles, 179
Gibbon, Edward, 19
Gibbons, Grinling, 68–9, 139
Gildas, 18
Giraldus Cambrensis, 3, 81
Giustiniani, Sebastian, 129, 131
Gladstone, W. E., 250, 252
Glastonbury, 19
Gloucester, 5
Gloucester, Duke of, son of Queen Anne, 193–4
Gloucester, Henry, Duke of, son of Charles I, 118
Gloucester, Humphrey, Duke of, 96–7
Godolphin, Lord, 87
Godstow nunnery, 82–3
Goethe, J. W. von, 222
Goldsworthy, Colonel, 71
Goodman, Godfrey, Bishop of Gloucester, 113
Goring, George, 209
Gordon, Lord George, 212–13
Grail, Holy, 19–20
Grant, John, Balmoral ghillie, 249
Greenwich Palace, 96–103; 11, 88
Greville, Charles, 13, 75–6, 162; at Kensington, 204–6; at Buckingham Palace, 216–18; at Brighton Pavilion, 233, 235; at Osborne, 238–9; at Balmoral, 246
Grey of Wilton, Lord, 187
Guinevere, 19
Gundulf, 29
Gunn, Martha, 224
Guthrum, 23
Guizot, F. P. G., 76
Gwynn, Nell, 123–4, 126

Hall's chronicle, 38

Hamilton, Duchess of, 160
Hamilton, William, 259
Hampton Court, 129–43; 8, 11–12, 92, 104, 157, 181
Handkerchief, invention of, 89
Hanger, George, 225
Hardyng, John, 51
Harington, Sir John, 93–4, 114, 185
Hartington, Spencer, Lord, 76
Hastings, Lady Flora, 77, 216
Hatfield House, 11
Hatton, Sir Christopher, 101
Hawksmoor, Nicholas, 196
Haydon, B. R., 222
Heath, James, 137
Henrietta Maria, Queen of Charles I, Queen's House, Greenwich, 102–3; at Hampton Court, 136–7; at St James's, 148–9; Nonsuch, 188–9
Henry I, King, 2, 83; at Westminster, 43; at Windsor, 57; at Woodstock, 80–1
Henry II, King, 3, 5–6, 10–11; at Winchester, 24; at Westminster, 44–5; at Windsor, 57–8; at Woodstock, 81–4
Henry III, King, at Tower, 31; at Westminster, 46–7; at Windsor, 59; at Woodstock, 84
Henry IV, King (Bolingbroke), at Tower, 35–6; at Westminster, 50
Henry V, King, 96; at Sheen, 90
Henry VI, King, 10; at Tower, 36–7; founds Eton, 63; at Placentia, 144
Henry VII, King (Tudor), 88, 108, 113, 121; at Tower, 38; at Richmond, 90–2; at Greenwich, 97–8
Henry VIII, King, 4, 8–9, 10–11, 12–13, 20, 52, 88, 123, 165–6, 190, 259–60; at Tower, 39; at Westminster, 41; at Windsor, 63–5; at Richmond, 92; at Greenwich, 98–100; at Whitehall, 105–9; the masque, 113; at Hampton Court, 130–2; builds St James's, 144–5; builds Nonsuch, 176–9; death, 108–9
Henry Grâce à Dieu, 98
Henry, Prince (son of Henry II), 45
Henry, Prince of Wales (son of James I), 96, 147
Hentzner, Paul, at Tower, 33, 39; at Westminster, 51; at Windsor, 65; at Greenwich, 102; at Whitehall, 108; at Hampton Court, 135
Herland, Hugh, 49
Herrenhausen, 198
Hertford, Lady, 228–9, 234
Hertford, Lord, 101
Hervey, John, Lord, at St James's, 157–9; at Kensington, 200–1
Hilton hotel, 258
Hobbes, Thomas, 1
Hoefnagel, 178
Holbein, Hans, 100, 117, 150, 194; at Whitehall, 107–8
Holinshed, Raphael, 34, 37–8, 62, 85

Holland, Henry, 224
Holland House, 191
Holland, Philemon, 181
Holyroodhouse, 164–75; 3–4
Howard, Mrs, later Countess of Suffolk, 142
Howard, Charles, Earl of Nottingham, Lord High Admiral, 95, 101
Howard, Katherine, Queen of Henry VIII, at Hampton Court, 131–32
Howard, Thomas, Duke of Norfolk, 133
Hugh, Bishop of Lincoln, 83
Huddleston, John, 126
Huish, Robert, 223
Hunt, Leigh, 221
Hutchinson, Lucy, 121
Hyde, Edward, Earl of Clarendon, 139

Isabel of France, Queen of Richard II, 63

James IV, King of Scotland, 3, 165
James V, King of Scotland, 3, 165–6
James I, King, 33, 40, 95, 208, 256; at Windsor, 66–7; at Woodstock, 86; at Greenwich, 102; at Whitehall, 112–16; builds Banqueting House, 115; at Hampton Court, 136; at St James's, 146–7; description, 147; at Holyroodhouse, 172; at Nonsuch, 188;
James II, King, 40, 103, 125, 150, 172, 191, 209–10; at Windsor 69; succeeds, 126; retires, 127; at St James's, 149
James Edward, the Old Pretender, 125, 151
Jersey, Frances, Countess of, 73, 161, 226
Joan, Fair Maid of Kent, 60–1
John, King, 24, 31, 58–9; birth, 82; death, 59
John, King of France, 33, 45–6
Johnson, Samuel, on Druids, 14; at Caernarvon, 26–7; touched for King's Evil, 125; meets George III, 211–12; on elections, 255–6; on kings, 257
Jones, Inigo, 258; builds Queen's House, Greenwich, 102–3; masque, 113; builds Banqueting House, 115
Jonson, Ben, 113, 115
Jousting, 60, 98, 107, 109, 131
Juxon, Bishop, 118–20

Katherine of Aragon, Queen of Henry VIII, 92, 99, 105
Kensington Gardens, 193, 196, 199–201
Kensington Palace, 191–207; 5, 9, 11, 74
Kensington, system, 204–6
Kent, Edward, Duke of, 203–4
Kent, Victoria of Saxe-Coburg, Duchess of, Victoria's mother, 74–5, 77, 203–6, 215
Kent, William, 198–9
Kérouaille, Louis de, Duchess of Portsmouth, 123, 126
Kew, 228
Kingston, 41, 50
Kinver hunting-lodge, 8
Kipling, Rudyard, 243
Knight, Charles, 70–1

Knox, John, 166–71

La Hogue, battle of, 103
Lamb, Charles, 221
Lambert, John, Major-General, 189
Lancelot, 19
Le Neyt, 89–90
Lavatories, 8, 45, 70, 77, 89, 91, 93, 193, 202, 215, 219, 239–40
Lear, King, 21
Leaves from the Journal of Our Life in the Highlands, 219, 247, 252
Lehzen, Louise, 204, 206, 215
Leicester, Earl of, see Robert Dudley
Leland, John, 20–1
Le Mans, 5
Le Nôtre, 150
Leopold, King of the Belgians, 238, 246
Lepell, Molly, 141–2
Lieven, Princess, 232, 234
Lilly, William, 149
Lindsay, Sir David, 3, 165
Llywelyn, Prince of Wales, 25
Lochnagar, Victoria's pony, 242
Louis VII, King of France, 84
Louis IX, King of France, 32
Louis XIV, King of France, 11, 103, 201
Louis Frederick, Prince of Württemburg, 181
Louvre, 139
Lumley, John, Lord, 181, 190
Luxemburgh Palace, 139
Lyttelton, Lady, 240–1
Lyttelton, Lord 211

Mabinogion, 26
Macaulay, Lord, 95, 103, 127–8, 139, 140
Macdonald, Annie, 251
Machiavelli, Nicholas, 129
Machyn, Henry, 109
Macmillan, Harold, 255
Magna Carta, 31, 58
Mallet, Marie, 243–4
Malmesbury, William of, 80–1
Malmsey, 37
Malory, Sir Thomas, 20–1
Map, Walter, 3, 6, 44
Marble Arch, 214, 218
Margaret of Anjou, Queen of Henry VI, 97
Margaret Tudor, daughter of Henry VII, 165
Margaret, Princess, Countess of Snowdon, 259
Marie de Médicis, 148–9
Marignano, battle of, 177
Marnock, 168
Marvell, Andrew, 120
Mary I, Queen (Tudor), 84–5; at Richmond, 93; at Hampton Court, 132–3; at St James's, 145–6; at Nonsuch, 179
Mary II, Queen of William III, 40, 103, 127; at Whitehall, 127–8; at Hampton Court,

139–40; at St James's, 151; at Kensington, 191–4
Mary of Modena, Queen of James II, 127, 151
Mary Stuart, Queen of Scots, 134–5, 166–72, 175
Masham, Abigail (née Hill), 153, 197
Masque, 113–16, 135
Matilda (or Maud), Queen, 43, 57
Maundy, 101
May Fair, 144
May, Hugh, 68
Melbourne, William Lamb, Viscount, 206, 216, 237–8
Melville, Sir James, 134
Mercia, 2
Merlin, 19
Merton Priory, 178
Miles, 'Smoaker', 224
Milton, John, 67
Monk, General George, 122
Montfort, Simon de, 31, 47
Montmorency, Duke of, 110
Mordaunt, John, Baron, 68
More, Sir Thomas, 8, 38
Morley, Mrs, see Queen Anne
Morley, John, 255
Morton, John, Bishop of Ely, 38–9
Morrah, Dermot, 259
Motte-and-bailey castles, 2, 5, 29, 56
Murimuth, Adam de, 60
Murray, Dr Margaret, 61

Nash, John, 11, 218, 258; Buckingham Palace, 213; Brighton Pavilion, 229–30
National Maritime Museum, 103
Nennius, 18
New Brighton Chronicle, The, 225
New College, Oxford, 62
New Forest, 24
Newmarket, 226
Nield, John Camden, 246
Nonsuch Palace, 176–90, 8, 11
Norfolk, Duke of, see Thomas Howard
Norden, John, 52, 67
Normans, 5, 11, 19, 23–4, 25, 29, 44, 56
Northumbria, 2
Nottingham, Sir Daniel Finch, Earl of, 191

Oates, Titus, 122
Odiham Castle, 13
Oglethorpe, General James, 257
O'Neill, Hugh, Earl of Tyrone, 186
Orangery, The, 196
Orkney, 15, 25
Osborne House, 237–44; 10, 236, 252
Ouida (Louise Ramée), 247
Oxford, 62, 82, 85, 96–7

Palatine Hill, 1
Pall Mall, 123, 159
Palmerstone, Henry Temple, 3rd Viscount, 75
Paris, Matthew, 31, 43, 46

Paris, Paulin, 21
Parliament, 41–2, 47, 259
'Pasquin', Antony, 225
Parr, Katherine, Queen of Henry VIII, 8, 132, 179
Pearson, Anthony, 65
Peasant Revolt, 35, 49
Peel, Sir Robert, 77, 216, 218, 235, 237–8
Pepys, Samuel, 13, 40, 53, 68, 124–5; at Greenwich, 103; at Whitehall, 122; at St James's, 160–1; at Nonsuch, 189; at Mulberry Garden, 209
Perrers, Alice, 89
Persia, Shah of, 219–20
Peter the Great, Tsar of Russia, 194
Philip II, King of Spain, husband of Mary Tudor, 93, 132–3, 146
Philip I, King of France, 125
Philip VI, King of France, 22
Pilgrimage of Grace, 65
Platter, Thomas, 110; at Woodstock, 85; at Richmond, 93–4; at Hampton Court, 135; at Nonsuch, 184–5
Poitiers, battle of, 33
Ponsonby, Sir Henry, 251, 253
Pontefract Castle, 36
Pope, Alexander, 141, 142, 200
Portchester Castle, 9
Pulteney, William, 158
Punch, 242, 250

Queen's Camel, 21
Queen's House, see Greenwich, or Buckingham Palace, 102–3

Raleigh, Sir Walter, 100–1, 102, 147, 157
Rape of the Lock, 141
Raphael, 103, 138, 150, 194
Rathgeb, Jacob, 7
Redwald, King 25
Reith, Sir John, 78
Rendlesham, 25
Reresby, Sir John, 69
Reynolds, Dr, 136
Rhuddlan Castle, 26
Ribblesdale, Lord, 76
Rich, Robert, 121
Richard I, King, 5, 83; at Tower, 31; at Westminster, 45
Richard II, King, 10, 260; at Tower, 34–6; Westminster Hall, 49–51; at Windsor, 62–3; at Sheen, 89–90; deposition and death, 35–6
Richard III, King, 90; at Tower, 38–9
Richbell, Jeffry and Richard, 66
Richmond Palace, 88–96; 181, 199
Richmond, Duke of, 137
Rizzio, David, 169–72, 175
Roger of Hoveden, 83
Romans, 15–18, 25–6, 28–9, 41
Ronsard, Pierre de, 3, 169
Rosamunda, Queen of Lombards, 83
Rose, Charles II's gardener, 139

Rosebery, Lord, 239
Rosenau, The, 240
Rotten Row, 192
Round Pond, 201
Rubens, Peter Paul, 103, 116
Rupert, Prince, Count Palatine, 67-8
Ruthven, Lord Patrick, 170

St Eustache, 164
St George, 60-2
St Germain's, 139
St Hubert, 164
St James's Palace 144-63; 4, 8-9, 11, 52, 118, 195
St James's Park, 104, 107, 122, 150-1, 214
St Laurent, Mme Julie de, 203
Salisbury, 82
Sandringham House, 4, 7, 10, 259
Savoy Palace, 33
Saxons, 1, 18-19, 22, 24, 29, 44, 56, 80
Scaramelli, Giovanni, 94
Schliemann, Heinrich, 20
Schulenberg, Ermengarda von, Duchess of Kendal, 141, 154-5
Schwellenberg, Mme, 71
Scott, Sir Walter, 173-4, 222
Scrofula, the King's Evil, 4, 124-5, 173
Sebastopol, 247
Sedley, Catherine, 209-10
Segontium, 25
Serpentine, 202
Serre, Sieur de la, 148-9
Seymour, Jane, Queen of Henry VIII, description, 108; at Hampton Court, 131
Seymour, Mary, 'Minnie', 228
Sezincote, 228
Shakespeare, William, on Camelot, 21; on Richard III, 38; Merry Wives of Windsor, 66; 67, 105; Henry VIII, 106, 109; Comedy of Errors, 135, 141, 211
Tristram Shandy, 241
Sheen, see Richmond
Sheridan, Richard, 224-5
Sidney, Sir Robert, 187
Siege Perilous, 20
Silbury Hill, 15
Simier, M. de, 111
Simpson, Mrs Wallis, Duchess of Windsor, 78, 162-3
Skarabrae, 15
Skelton, John, 129
Slaughter (or Slater), Will, 38
Smith, Sydney, 231
Smythe, Henry le, 62
Somerset, Duke of, Lord Protector, 166
Sophia Dorothea, Queen of George I, 154
Sorrel, William III's horse, 194
Southampton, 23-4, 41
South Cadbury, 20
Spectator, The, 196
Steine, The, 223-4
Stephen, King, 22, 24; at Tower, 30; at Westminster, 43-4

Stewart, Frances, 123
Stockmar, Baron, 247
Stonehenge, 14
Stow, John, 29, 38-9, 65
Strachey, Lytton, 242-3, 251
Stuart, James, Duke of Richmond, 137
Stubbs, John, 111
Sudbury, Simon, 35
Sussex, Augustus, Duke of, 206
Swift, Jonathan, 69-70, 141
Switzer, Stephen, 193

Tacitus, Cornelius, 29
Tayleur, William, 68
Taymouth Castle, 244
Tennis, 107, 123, 131
Tennyson, Alfred, Lord, 252
Testwood, Robert, 65
Thackeray, W. M., 221
Thames, 8-9, 31-2, 41, 46, 49, 51, 55-6, 88, 96, 127
Thompson, Isaac, 193
Thrale, Mrs Henry (afterwards Piozzi), 26
Tickell, Thomas, 199-200
Tintagel, 21
Tintoretto, 194
Titian, 103, 150, 194
Tower of London, 28-40; 5, 11-12, 165
Trafalgar, battle of, 214
Tristram, 19
Turi, Victoria's dog, 244
Tyler, Wat, 35
Tynemouth, 9
Tyrrel, Sir James, 38

Usher, Archbishop, 119

Vanbrugh, Sir John, 86, 196
Van Dyck, Sir Anthony, 103, 148, 150, 194, 200-1
Vane, Anne, 158-9
Vane, Sir Harry, 137
Vatican, 104
Venn, Colonel John, 67
Vergil, Polydore, 38
Verrio, Antonio, 68, 139
Versailles, 104, 140
Vespasian, Emperor, 17
Victoria, Princess Royal, 248
Victoria, Queen, 4, 7, 9, 13, 208, 214, 259; born, 203; succeeds, 206-7; declaration of marriage, 216; wedding, 162; swims for first time, 240; widowed, 241; relationship with John Brown, 241-3, 250-2; dies, 244; at Windsor, 74-8; Hampton Court, 143; at St James's, 162; at Holyroodhouse, 175; at Kensington, 203-7; at Buckingham Palace, 215-20; at Brighton, 236; at Osborne, 237-44; at Balmoral, 245-53
Vikings, 23-4, 41
Villiers, Barbara, Countess of Castlemaine, Duchess of Cleveland, 123, 126, 138-9; pulls down Nonsuch, 189-90

Villiers, George, Duke of Buckingham, 136, 209

Wallace, William, 48
Waller, Edmund, 123
Wallop, Sir John, 177–8
Walpole, Horace, 155, 157, 160, 200, 201
Walpole, Sir Robert, 142, 155, 156
Walter of Hereford, 26
Warming-pans, 127, 151
Wars of the Roses, 36–8, 51–2, 97, 260
Warwick, Earl of (Kingmaker), 37
Warwick, Lady, wife of Ambrose Dudley, 134
Waterloo, battle of, 214
Watson, Dr Anthony, 179, 182–3
*Waverley*, 173
Webb, John, 103
Wedel, Lupold von, at Westminster, 7; at Greenwich, 101–2; at Hampton Court, 135
Weldon, Sir Anthony, 147
Wellington, Duke of, 204, 213, 221, 235
Weltje, George IV's cook, 222
Wessex, 2, 22
Westminster Abbey, 29, 38, 146
Westminster Hall, 9–10, 43, 47, 49–50, 51–3, 118
Westminster Palace, 41–54; 4, 5, 22, 39, 106; Painted Chamber, 42, 46, 48, 51, 53; St Stephen's, 22, 44, 48, 51, 53
Wet, Jacob de, 172
Whitehall Palace, 104–8; 9, 11, 52, 147
Whitgift, John, Archbishop of Canterbury, 95
Whyte, Rowland, 187–8
Wilberforce, William, 231, 233
Wilhelm II, Kaiser, 244, 248
Wilkes, John, 212
William I, King, 5, 23–4, 29, 42, 56

William II, King (Rufus), 9–10, 24, 29; at Westminster, 43, 49
William III (of Orange), 11, 40; offered Crown, 127; builds Greenwich Hospital, 103; at Windsor, 69–70; at Whitehall, 125, 127–8; at Hampton Court, 139–40; at St James's, 151; at Kensington, 191–5; accident, 140; death, 195; 260
William IV, King, 205, 237; at Windsor, 74–5; at Hampton Court, 143; at Buckingham Palace, 214–15; at Brighton Pavilion, 235–6; death, 206
Winchester, 20, 21, 23, 62
Winchester Palace, 22–5; 5, 41, 82
Windsor Castle, 55–78; 4, 8, 11–13, 22, 210, 213, 237, 239, 258–9
Withers, Philip, 72
Wolsey, Thomas, 92, 99, 145; rebuilds York Place, 104; builds Hampton Court, 129–30; his fall, 106
Wolvesey, 23
Woodstock Palace, 79–87; 8, 44
Wren, Sir Christopher, 8, 127, 198–9, 258; at Winchester, 24; at Tower, 30; at Windsor, 70; at Hampton Court, 139; rebuilds Kensington, 191–2; dismissed, 141
Wyatt, James, 72
Wyatt, Thomas, 84–5, 146
Wyattville, Jeffry, 73–4
Wykeham, William of, 62

Yevele, Henry, 49
Young, Francis Brett, 22
York Castle, 9
York Place, 104, 106; *see* Whitehall
York, Richard, Duke of (Prince in Tower), 38

Zel, King, 15

L. Knyff Delin.

*The Tower of London, Commanded in Chief*

*la Tour*